WHAT IS THE NATURE OF ANTI-SEMITISM?

WHAT IS THE ROLE OF THE ARTIST IN SOCIETY?

WHEN IS THE TIME RIPE FOR REVOLUTION?

WHAT IS THE FUNCTION OF THE STATE?

CAN PRESS CENSORSHIP EVER BE JUSTIFIED?

CAN CHRISTIANITY AND SOCIALISM BE RECONCILED?

WHAT IS THE ESSENTIAL CHARACTER OF THE BOURGEOIS FAMILY?

These are among the multitude of fascinating questions that Karl Marx confronted with an honesty and a brilliance that make his writings of enduring significance.

Saul K. Padover is Distinguished Service Professor Emeritus of Political Science at The New School for Social Research. He is the author of *Jefferson*, *The Living U.S. Constitution*, and *Thomas Jefferson on Democracy*, all available in Mentor editions. Volumes VI and VII of his "Karl Marx Library" series appeared in 1977, and his *Karl Marx: An Intimate Biography* appeared in 1978.

THE ESSENTIAL MARX

The Non-Economic Writings—A Selection

Edited, with new translations, by
Saul K. Padover

A MENTOR BOOK
NEW AMERICAN LIBRARY
TIMES MIRROR
NEW YORK AND SCARBOROUGH, ONTARIO
THE NEW ENGLISH LIBRARY LIMITED, LONDON

NAL BOOKS ARE ALSO AVAILABLE AT DISCOUNTS IN BULK
QUANTITY FOR INDUSTRIAL OR SALES-PROMOTIONAL USE.
FOR DETAILS, WRITE TO PREMIUM MARKETING DIVISION,
NEW AMERICAN LIBRARY, INC., 1301 AVENUE OF THE
AMERICAS, NEW YORK, NEW YORK 10019.

Copyright © 1978 by Saul K. Padover

All rights reserved.

Library of Congress Catalog Card Number: 78-61907

MENTOR TRADEMARK REG. U.S. PAT. OFF. AND FOREIGN COUNTRIES
REGISTERED TRADEMARK—MARCA REGISTRADA
HECHO EN CHICAGO, U.S.A.

SIGNET, SIGNET CLASSICS, MENTOR, PLUME AND MERIDIAN BOOKS
are published *in the United States* by
The New American Library, Inc.,
1301 Avenue of the Americas, New York, New York 10019,
in Canada by The New American Library of Canada Limited,
81 Mack Avenue, Scarborough, Ontario M1L 1M8,
in the United Kingdom by The New English Library Limited,
Barnard's Inn, Holborn, London, E.C. 1, England.

First Mentor Printing, January, 1979

1 2 3 4 5 6 7 8 9

PRINTED IN THE UNITED STATES OF AMERICA

CONTENTS

Karl Marx—A Biographical Sketch 2

Chronology: Essential Dates in Marx's Life ... 14

I. ART and AUTHORS 21

Note 21

A. *Art*
Material Development and Art 22
Productive Labor and Art 24

B. *Authors*
Honoré de Balzac 28
Jeremy Bentham 28
Thomas Carlyle 29
François René de Chateaubriand 31
Henry George 33
Karl Marx 34
Adolphe Thiers 35
François Marie Arouet de Voltaire 37

II. CLASSES 39

Note 39
Ruling Class and Ruling Ideas 39
Social Classes in England 42
"The Chartists" 48
The Rise of Classes and Cities 57
Monarchy, Aristocracy and Bourgeoisie
  in Prussia 59

v

CONTENTS

III. CLASS STRUGGLE and REVOLUTION   63

Note 63
A Radical German Revolution 66
The Role of the Proletariat 70
The Class Necessity of Revolution 71
Origins and Meaning of the Class
    Struggle 73
International Class Conflict 75
The English and French Revolutions 76
Revolution in India 77
The Labour Parliament 79
Workers' Poverty Amidst Prosperity 81
Emancipation of the Working Classes ... 89
Class Conflict and the Historic Revolt
    Against Machines 90
Class Conflicts in Ancient Rome 92
The Coming Revolutions in England,
    Russia and United States 93
The Proletarian Conquest of Power 95
The Prospects of Violent Revolution 96
Strategy and Tactics of the Class Struggle 97
The Time Is Not Yet Ripe for Revolution 100

IV. COMMUNISM and SOCIALISM 102

Note 102
"Communism and the Augsburg
    Allgemeine Zeitung" 103
"Communism Is a Dogmatic Abstraction" 107
A Critique of Proudhon 111
A Further Re-evaluation of Proudhon ... 123
Lamartine's View of Communism 131
Manifesto of the Communist Party:
    Selections 133
The Communist Party Program 152
The Permanent Revolution 154

	Contents	vii
	Statutes of the Communist League	165
	Marginal Notes to the Program of the German Workers' Party (Critique of the Gotha Program)	168
	Socialist Program for Germany	185
V.	EDUCATION	188
	Note	188
	Reflections of a Young Man on Choosing an Occupation	189
	Marx's Intellectual Travail	193
	Education and Environment	203
	Education for the Worker	205
	Elementary Education and Children in Factories	206
	Compulsory Education	224
	Universal Free Education	225
VI.	HISTORY	227
	Note	227
	What History Is	229
	The Role of the Past	234
	Spanish History	237
	The Role of the Army in History	238
	Materialist Interpretation of History	239
	Agriculture in History	242
VII.	PHILOSOPHY	246
	Note	246
	Socrates and Christ	247
	Philosophy Above Religion	247
	Epicurus' Natural Philosophy	249
	Epicurus, "The Radical Enlightener" ...	252
	Philosophy, Religion and the Press	252
	Hegel's Dialectic	259

CONTENTS

VIII. PRESS and CENSORSHIP 261

Note 261
Who Should Censor? 262
Human Imperfection and Press Freedom 273
Censorship and Press Law 275
The Voice of the People 277
The Harsh Censorship 278
The Duty of a Revolutionary Press 279

IX. RELIGION 281

Note 281

A. *Religion in General*

Proof of the Existence of God 283
Religion and Animals 285
Criticism of Religion Is the Presupposition of All Criticism 286
Hegel and "Religion as Alienated Human Self-Consciousness" 288
Men Are the Producers of Their Own Conceptions 293
Materialism 297
Theses on Feuerbach 304

B. *Christianity* 307

The Union of the Faithful with Christ ... 307
The Social Principles of Christianity 311
Christian Socialism 313
Changing Religious Ideas 313
The Anti-Church Movement 314
The Medieval Church and Money 320
Christianity and the Material Conditions of Society 322
Protestant Parsons and the Population Theory 323
Religion and the Monetary System 326

Contents

C. Jews and Judaism
"On the Jewish Question" 326

X. SCIENCE and TECHNOLOGY 354

Note 354
Science: The Real Nineteenth-Century Revolution 355
Electricity and Agriculture 356
Electricity 359
Darwin's Natural Selection 359
The Meaning of Machinery 361
Roman Arithmetic 364
Theory of Light 365
Astronomy 366
Differential Calculus 368
Technology 369
Technology and Industry 370

XI. THE STATE 372

Note 372
The Christian State 372
The Political State 374
The Reliance of the State on Administration 375
The French Bourgeois State 378
What Is the "Free State"? 381

XII. WOMEN and CHILDREN 384

Note 384
The Divorce Law Draft 385
The Community of Women 388
Family 390
The Bourgeois Family 391
Child Psychology 393
Juvenile and Child Labor 394

CONTENTS

Women and Children in Industry 396
The Influence of Machinery on Child and
  Woman Labor 401
Child Labor 402
Female and Child Labor 402

SELECTED BIBLIOGRAPHY 403

BIOGRAPHIC INDEX 406

SUBJECT INDEX 425

Note

Except for selections from *Capital* and *The Communist Manifesto*, or where otherwise noted, translations are by Saul K. Padover.

KARL MARX—
A BIOGRAPHICAL SKETCH

Karl Marx, who died in comparative obscurity in London in 1883, has become the personification of revolution in our time. The very words "Marxism" and "Marxist" have become the equivalent of radicalism. His physical appearance, too, conveys this idea. Marx's leonine head, the thick, bushy beard and flashing eyes form the very picture of a radical.

A superbly educated middle-class intellectual, a *Herr Doktor* with a Ph.D. in philosophy, he differed from the norm of similarly trained "bourgeois" (one of his favorite words) contemporaries in the whole pattern of his life and thought.

In his youth Marx wanted to be a poet, dramatist, and literary critic but found that he was not especially gifted in those fields. After he was awarded his doctorate by Jena University in 1841,[1] at the age of twenty-three, he hoped to become a professor, but there was no opening in the German academic world for radicals like him. One of the few fields open to nonconformists was journalism. His first newspaper position was that of editor of the *Rheinische Zeitung*, a Cologne daily, which, at the age of twenty-five, he transformed into a fighting organ for liberal ideas. Within less than a year, the Prussian censorship[2] closed the newspaper, and Marx, in disgust, left the country and moved to Paris, where he published a journal, *Deutsch-Französische Jahrbücher*. After one

[1] His doctoral dissertation was on classic Greek thought: *Difference Between the Democritean and Epicurean Philosophy of Nature*. Marx was fluent in Greek and Latin and did his research in the original sources.

[2] For Marx's ideas on censorship, see Chapter VIII of this volume.

issue, which contained some radical as well as scholarly articles (among them Marx's lengthy polemic against Judaism, "On the Jewish Question"), the magazine suspended publication for lack of readers. He then associated with *Vorwärts!*, a German-language semiweekly published by radical émigrés, who were under surveillance of the Paris police.

Marx's residence in Paris was a turning point in his life. In the French capital he met famous people, notably the self-exiled German poet Heinrich Heine and Pierre Joseph Proudhon, the radical social theorist whose ideas he was soon to demolish in his book, *The Poverty of Philosophy* (1847). But more important than meeting famous individuals was contact with real working men. Paris, in addition to being the center of European culture, was the center of revolutionary ferment. The great French Revolution of 1789 continued to be a living tradition, both for the bourgeoisie, then triumphantly entrenched in power under King Louis Philippe, and the discontented workers, seething with radical idealism. In Paris, class divisions and hatreds were palpable and uncompromising. Marx did not have to imagine or invent the idea of the class struggle; he only had to look around him.

Paris provided Marx with the opportunity of getting to know proletarians, both foreign and indigenous. There were then about 10,000 German artisans in the city under the influence of the Bund der Kommunisten (Communist League). Marx met a number of them and attended their meetings. He also visited French communist groups and was impressed by their intelligence, which, he noted, "shines from the labor-hardened faces." He wrote to the philosopher Ludwig Feuerbach (August 11, 1844): "You have to attend one of the meetings of the French *ouvriers* to realize the virginal freshness and nobility among these workingmen." Marx, indeed, had a lifelong love affair with France.

It was in Paris, and soon thereafter in Brussels, that Marx became a communist, shifting intellectually from Hegelian idealism to economic materialism. In this period he also began the serious study of economics, or political economy as it was then known, which he was to continue, even if intermittently, for the rest of his life. He became convinced that in the field of economics lay the master key to an understanding of all social phenomena and the processes of history.[3]

---

[3] See especially Chapters IV and VI of this volume.

Another fateful event for Marx in Paris was his meeting with Friedrich (Frederick) Engels in the summer of 1844. The two men had once met briefly in Cologne, but this time they struck up a permanent friendship that was radically to affect their lives and, indeed, the course of modern history. Engels, on his way back to Germany from Manchester, where he had spent nearly two years in the English branch of his father's textile business and had, among other things, collected materials for his notable book, *The Condition of the Working Class in England in 1844*,[4] stopped over in Paris and saw Marx.

Engels, then twenty-four years old, was already a communist, with a knowledge of economics, a subject of which Marx was still ignorant. The two young Germans found that they were in accord about virtually everything, and they decided then and there to collaborate in their future writings. They had so much to say to each other that their enthusiastic conversations lasted ten days and probably as many nights. It is likely that Engels provided Marx with the final stimulus toward communism.

From that time on, the lives and destinies of the two men were so intertwined as to be practically inseparable. After their exile from Europe in 1849, both were to spend the rest of their lives in England, Marx as a penniless refugee and Engels as a businessman in Manchester for at least twenty years. They were to be in uninterrupted contact, Engels providing Marx with continuous financial assistance and encouragement. On the night when Marx finished correcting the last page proofs of Volume I of *Capital* (August 16, 1867), he dashed off a moving note to Engels:

> Only YOU alone I have to thank for making this possible! Without your self-sacrifice for me I could never possibly have done the enormous work for the three volumes. I embrace you full of thanks! Greetings, my beloved, dear friend!

Marx was expelled from Paris in January 1845 and moved to Brussels, where he was soon followed by Engels. For

---

[4]The book, *Die Lage der arbeitenden Klasse in England*, was published in Leipzig, 1845. The English translation, by Florence Kelley-Wischnewetzky, came out in London, 1892.

Marx, his three-year residence in the Belgian capital, where two more of his children were born,[5] was marked by important literary work and clandestine political activities.

In Brussels, Marx wrote the terse "Theses on Feuerbach," which Engels later described as the "first document in which the brilliant germ of the new philosophy is laid down."[6] He also collaborated with Engels in writing *The Holy Family*, a criticism of the Young Hegelians with whom the two friends were then making a break, and *The German Ideology*, a satirical critique of German Idealism.[7] It was in Brussels, too, that Marx wrote, and published in 1847, his first book, *La Misère de la Philosophie* ("The Poverty of Philosophy"), without Engels' collaboration. This work, a critical reply to Pierre Joseph Proudhon's *La Philosophie de la Misère* ("The Philosophy of Poverty"), was written by the linguistically gifted Marx in French. Its polemical tone against the prominent French social theorist, whose ideas on property Marx detested, was set in a brief, sarcastic preface:

> M. Proudhon enjoys the misfortune of being singularly misunderstood. In France he has the right to be a bad economist, because he passes for a competent German philosopher. In Germany, on the other hand, he has the right to be a bad philosopher, because he passes for one of the greatest French economists. We, in our dual capacity as German and economist, feel it necessary to protest against this double error.[8]

Marx's writings were reinforced by political activism in Brussels. He worked with foreign radicals, whom he attempted to win over to communism. He organized a Communist Correspondence Committee and became a member of the secret Communist League, which had for its objective the "destruction ... and overthrow of the bourgeoisie."[9]

---

[5] Laura on September 6, 1845, and Edgar on December 17, 1847; the first Marx child, Jenny (Jennychen), was born in Paris on May 1, 1844.

[6] For text, see Chapter VI of this volume.

[7] Selections from *The Holy Family* and *The German Ideology* are to be found in Chapters II and VI of this volume.

[8] For other criticisms of Proudhon, with whom Marx felt himself in intellectual rivalry, see Chapter IV of this volume.

[9] Text in Chapter IV.

A sympathetic foreign observer, the liberal Russian landowner-writer Pavel Annenkov, who attended a small communist meeting in Marx's home, thus described his impression of Marx, then twenty-eight years old:

> Marx was the type of man who is made up of energy, will power and unshakable conviction. . . . A mane of thick black hair, hairy hands, his coat buttoned awry, he nevertheless looked like a man who had the right and the power to command respect. . . . His movements were clumsy, but bold and self-assured; his manners defied all the usual social conventions. But they were proud, with a tinge of contempt, and his sharp, metallic voice was remarkably suited to the radical judgments he delivered on men and things. He spoke in nothing but imperatives.

Annenkov, who recorded this in 1880, nearly four decades before Marx's disciple Lenin seized power in Russia, concluded with keen insight: "Before my eyes stood the personification of a democratic dictator, such as might float before one's mind in a moment of fantasy."

At the end of November 1847, the second congress of the Communist League, which met in London and which Marx and Engels attended, commissioned them to write the *Manifesto of the Communist Party*. The brochure was completed two months later and was published anonymously in London in February of the revolutionary year 1848.[10] It had, however, no immediate effect on the revolutions that were then breaking out in Europe. But the long-run influence of this widely translated masterpiece of Marxian propaganda, which came to be known as the *Communist Manifesto*, has been incalculable. In 1888, five years after Marx's death, Engels wrote in the preface of the "Authorized English Translation" of the *Manifesto* that it was "presently beyond doubt the most widespread, most international work in the entire socialist literature, a common program which is acknowledged by millions from Siberia to California."

The month in which the *Manifesto* was published saw the opening of Europe's revolutions, which began as usual in Paris and soon spread. When the news reached Brussels,

[10] Selections from text in Chapter IV.

Marx urged German refugees to join the Belgians in revolt. He had just received 6,000 francs in partial settlement of his father's estate, and he contributed about 5,000 francs to buy weapons. This was naturally reported to the Belgian police. The government of King Leopold I reacted swiftly. It declared martial law, smashed workers' meetings, beat up and imprisoned German radicals. Marx and his wife were arrested in the middle of the night. On the following day they were released from jail and expelled from Brussels. They went to Paris, then in the throes of revolution.

Soon insurrections broke out in Germany, and Marx, although he found revolutionary Paris exciting, decided to return to his homeland to help stoke the flames there. On April 11, he arrived in Cologne and, with Engels' help, set out to raise money to found a radical newspaper there. By June 1, they had collected enough funds to bring out the first issue of the *Neue Rheinische Zeitung*, the title being a revival of his old Cologne newspaper with the word *neue* ("new") added to it. The subtitle of the paper was *Organ der Demokratie*—"Organ of Democracy." It was, however, a communist journal, all the editors, including Engels, being members of the Communist League. The *Neue Rheinische Zeitung* was under "Marx's dictatorship," gladly accepted, according to Engels.

The paper opened with 6,000 subscribers, a number that began to dwindle as it became increasingly strident and hostile to any moderate elements. Its communist shrillness antagonized those who might otherwise have been sympathetic to its battle against royal autocracy. Soon the *Neue Rheinische Zeitung* fell foul of the Prussian censorship. Marx was tried in court for incitement to rebellion, and, although he was acquitted by a jury of Rhinelanders hostile to Berlin rule, the government, having defeated the revolutionary uprisings everywhere, felt itself strong enough to close Marx's newspaper, which was then dying of financial malnutrition anyhow. On May 16, 1849, Marx was expelled from Prussia and once again made his way to Paris.

In the French capital, where the revolution was already suppressed by the time Marx arrived, the police caught up with him. In July, he was informed by the police that he would be banished to Morbihan, in Brittany. Since Morbihan was considered to be a most unhealthful region, Marx was convinced that the French government was making a "cloaked attempt" to murder him. On the Continent there was nowhere for him to go. Even neutral Switzerland was impossible, since he had no passport.

On August 24, Marx left Paris for London. Engels joined him there two and a half months later, both of them hoping to publish a German-language journal in the British capital, then swarming with European refugees. Marx, who could not speak English, thought that his stay in London would be of short duration. He was sure that the defeat of the European uprisings was merely a temporary interruption in the inexorable march of revolution. He was to be disillusioned. What followed the uprisings of 1848–1849 was not economic ruin but prosperity, not revolution but stability. Europe, in fact, grew richer and mightier than ever, dominating the world until World War I. There was to be no real revolution in Europe (except for the short-lived Paris Commune in 1871) for the rest of the nineteenth century.

Marx spent the remaining thirty-four years of his life in London, the biggest city in the Western world, with a population of over 3,000,000 and constantly growing and expanding. It was a roaring metropolis with an international flavor, containing more Irish than Dublin, more Greeks than Athens, more Catholics than Rome. Termed "Babylon the Great," it was described in the *City Press* (1870) as having 20,000 public houses and beer shops frequented by 500,000 customers—or 20 percent of the population.

In the end Marx and his family came to love the robust metropolis, where an air of political freedom prevailed palpably, and wanted to live nowhere else. His three surviving daughters considered themselves English. Eleanor, the youngest, who was born in London in 1855, became a part-time Shakespearean actress and labor organizer. Laura, the middle daughter, after she moved to Paris with her French husband Paul Lafargue, expressed her loneliness for Britain in a two-line stanza:

My heart is in England (my heart is not here)
With her brown kippered herrings and blond Pilsner beer![11]

Above all, London provided Marx with the priceless opportunity for the continuing study of political economy. The British Museum was then probably the world's biggest library.

[11]Laura Lafargue to Engels, December 15, 1886.

It possessed, as Marx noted in the preface to his first book on economics, *Critique of Political Economy* (1859), an "enormous amount" of material in the form of rare books, newspapers, brochures, and government reports. Until chronic illnesses (bronchitis, pleurisy, liver distention, carbuncles, among others) felled him in the 1870s, he would spend his working days in the spacious reading room of the British Museum—cool in the summer and warm in the winter, as he was happy to discover—doing research in preparation for his journalistic articles as well as for his masterpiece, *Capital*. He usually did his writing late at night when the family was asleep.

The newspapers and reports in the British Museum were the main source of Marx's journalism, by which he made his precarious living. For about a decade, until 1862, he was the London correspondent of the *New-York Daily Tribune*, which he proudly described as "the foremost English-language American newspaper." Despite its large circulation of 200,000, the *Tribune* paid pitifully little—five dollars per article—and rarely bought more than two a week, often less. The few German-language newspapers for which Marx wrote occasionally such as the *Neue Oder-Zeitung* of Breslau and *Die Presse* of Vienna, paid even less. Marx would have starved without constant financial help from Engels; in the first twenty years of exile in England, this assistance averaged about 200 pounds sterling annually. In 1868, Engels, having become a full partner in his family's Manchester business, finally saved Marx from the indignity of perpetual indigence by settling upon him a most generous lifelong annuity of 350 pounds sterling. This was more money than Marx had ever earned by himself in any one year as a journalist. In 1870, Engels sold his share in the Manchester firm to his partner and happily retired to London to be near Marx. Thenceforth, so long as they were in London, the two friends were in nearly daily contact.

There were long periods of time when Marx did little research or writing on *Capital—das Buch* ("the book"), as the family referred to it, on which he staked his reputation. The intermittence was due partly to wretched personal circumstances and debilitating illnesses, and partly to his preoccupation with the First International, which he helped to organize in 1864 and which came to absorb his energies as its leader and animating force. In the International, a loose organization of the world's working men. Marx hoped to find a lever of personal power. "In the next revolution, which is perhaps nearer than it seems," he wrote to Engels on September 11, 1867, "we (that is, you and I) will have this mighty engine in our hands." But this was another illusion on his part. By 1872, the International fell apart through bitter internal dissensions, and Marx found it necessary to dissolve it.

Capital. Volume I, came out in Hamburg on September 14, 1867, in an edition of 1,000 copies. It was not an immediate success, and this may have been a reason why Marx did not complete the other two volumes, as planned, in his lifetime.[12] Having put so much of himself into *Capital*, which was years in the making, Marx was hurt and dismayed that it found almost no response among his countrymen for whom the work was designed. *Capital* had few sales and was all but ignored by German scholars and economists. The book was also neglected in the English-speaking world, where a translation did not appear until 1887, two decades after the original German and four years after Marx's death.

The work did better elsewhere. In France, where a translation (under Marx's personal supervision) came out in 1875, an edition of 10,000 copies was quickly sold out. But to Marx's pleasure and amazement, *Capital* met its most striking success in Russia, a country he dreaded as "barbaric." A Russian translation appeared in St. Petersburg in 1872, and of an edition of 3,000 copies, about 900 were sold within the first month, constituting something of a record in a land with relatively few educated people. The work was reviewed and discussed and had a widening effect in circles that mattered most, that is, students and intellectuals in rebellion against czarist tyranny. Marx was pleased with the attention paid to him in the land of the czars. After reading V. P.

---

[12]Engels brought out Volume II in 1885 and Volume III in 1894, from the hardly legible manuscripts and inaccurate tables that Marx had left behind. It was a hard task for a man in his sixties and seventies, particularly as it required a complete revision of Marx's statistics, which, as the ailing Engels (who died of cancer on August 5, 1895) wrote to Laura Lafargue (April 11, 1894), were "almost without exception miscalculated." *Theories of Surplus Value*, which Marx had intended to be Volume IV of *Capital*, was published in English by Progress Publishers, Moscow, in three parts: I (1963), II (1968), III (1971).

Vorontzov's *Sudby Kapitalismu v Rossiyi* ("The Fate of Capitalism in Russia"), a book that discussed "the influence of the socialists of the Marxist school," Marx wrote to his daughter Laura Lafargue in his own brand of English (December 14, 1882):

> Some recent Russian publications, printed in Holy Russia . . . show the great run of my theories in that country. Nowhere my success is to be more delightful; it gives me the satisfaction that I damage a power, which, besides England, is the true bulwark of the old society.

There seems to have been a symbiotic relationship between Marx and Russia, in whose affairs he took a keen interest. At home in Europe's major languages, Marx also began to learn Russian at the age of fifty-two, as he wrote to a German-born communist friend in the United States:

> . . . since the beginning of 1870 I had to teach myself Russian, which I now read quite fluently. The thing came about when they sent me Flerovsky's *Condition of the Working Class* (especially the peasants) *in Russia* [1869] and I also wanted to become acquainted with the (splendid) economic works of Tshernyshevsky. . . .[13] The intellectual movement that is now taking place in Russia shows that it is in a deep ferment.[14]

Marx was prescient about Russia, always convinced that an uprising there was inevitable. In an interview in the *New York Herald* (August 3, 1871), he stated: "There is a revolution coming in Russia, slowly, but surely." Half a dozen years later, he wrote to a friend in America:

> Russia—and I have studied conditions there in the original *Russian* sources—. . . has long been on the threshold of an upheaval. . . . The upheaval will begin . . . with some playing at constitutionalism. . . . If Mother

[13] Nicolai Gavrilovich Tshernyshevsky, *Sotshinenya* [*Works*] (Vol. IV, Geneva and Basel, 1970).
[14] Marx to Sigfrid Meyer, January 21, 1871.

Nature is not particularly unfavorable to us, we shall yet live to see the fun.[15]

In the last decade or so of his life, Marx did little scholarly writing, but retained an unflagging interest in radical politics. The Paris Commune of 1871 stirred him to deep passion, and its brutal end came as a shock of horror. In the defense of the Commune he wrote *The Civil War in France,* a polemical brochure that communists consider "a most important work of scientific communism."[16] In May 1875, when the two main German labor parties met in Gotha for the purpose of amalgamating, Marx sent their leaders an incisive critique of socialist policy. Known historically as the Gotha Program,[17] it became a major guideline for the united German Social-Democratic Party, the most powerful in Europe.

His health continued to deteriorate. His coughing was so severe that he was unable to sleep without drugs. He sought relief in resort after resort, including the Jersey Islands and Karlsbad, the fashionable Austro-Bohemian spa which he loved and visited three times (1874, 1875, 1876). In the year before his death, Marx journeyed as far as Algiers, then a French colony, in desperate search of sun and dry air, but found mostly rain and humidity.

Marx's intellectual interests remained unabated, his wide-ranging mind continuing his lifelong attempt to absorb the totality of human experience. A correspondent for the *Chicago Tribune,* who interviewed the sixty-year-old Marx on December 18, 1878, was particularly impressed by his "vast range of knowledge of men and things throughout the world."[18] Always an avid reader, Marx, despite tormenting illnesses, kept up his studies and annotations in many areas, including natural science, mathematics, and history. He read and excerpted from the writings of geologists and agricultural chemists, and made systematic studies of pioneer mathematicians such as Euler, Leibnitz, and Colin MacLaurin, in preparation for a work on mathematics. In his sixty-first year he began to read and annotate the nineteen volumes of

[15] Marx to Friedrich Adolph Sorge, September 27, 1877.
[16] Text in Saul K. Padover, ed., *Karl Marx on Revolution* (New York, 1971), pp. 332–72.
[17] Text in *ibid.,* pp. 488–506.
[18] The interview was published in the *Chicago Tribune,* January 5, 1879; text in Saul K. Padover, ed., *Karl Marx on the First International* (New York, 1973), pp. 351–361.

Friedrich Christoph Schlosser's *Weltgeschichte fur das deutsche Volk*.[19]

On May 14, 1883, two months short of his sixty-fifth birthday, Marx died in an easy chair in his home in London. His death was caused by complications from a bleeding lung, laryngitis, and bronchitis. He was buried in the family grave in London's Highgate Cemetery, in the presence of about twenty people, only three of whom were English. In his speech at the graveside, Engels said:

"His name and his works will live on through the centuries."

This volume, the first of its kind in English, contains the essence of Marx's writings on culture and society, mostly translated by me. The Note preceding each chapter provides brief introductory explanations of the various facets of his thought.

SAUL K. PADOVER

---

[19] Schlosser, *World History for the German People* (Frankfurt, 1844–1857). A selection of Marx's annotations that dealt with the German Reformation and the Thirty Years War ran into 229 pages when published posthumously in 1961.

CHRONOLOGY:

Essential Dates in Marx's Life

1818

May 5   Birth of Karl Marx, son of lawyer Heinrich Marx and Dutch-born Henriette Marx (née Presburg or Presborck), in Trier, Rhenish Prussia, No. 664 Brückengasse (now N. 10 Brückenstrasse). The birth house is now a museum.

1824

August 26   Baptized, together with seven siblings, in Lutheran church, Trier. The Marx family had been Jewish.

1830

October   Entered Friedrich Wilhelm Gymnasium, Trier.

1835

September 24   Graduated from Gymnasium.
October 15   Matriculated at Bonn University.

1836

August 22   Left Bonn University.
October 22   Matriculated at Berlin University, Faculty of Law.

1841

March 30	Completed studies at Berlin University.
April 15	Received Ph.D. degree from Jena University (*in absentia*) for his dissertation, *Differenz der demokritischen und epikureischen Naturphilosophie* ("The Difference Between the Democritean and Epicurean Philosophy of Nature").

1842

May 5	Began to contribute articles to the *Rheinische Zeitung* in Cologne.
Mid-October	Became editor in chief of *Rheinische Zeitung*.
November	Met Frederick Engels in the office of the *Rheinische Zeitung*.

1843

March 17	Resigned from the *Rheinische Zeitung* (closed by the censorship on April 1).
June 19	Married childhood sweetheart, Jenny von Westphalen, in Kreuznach.
October	Moved to Paris, to be co-publisher (with Arnold Ruge) of *Deutsch-Französische Jahrbücher*.

1844

February	Published first and last double issue of *Deutsch-Französische Jahrbücher*.
May 1	Birth of daughter Jenny in Paris.
July	Met Pierre Joseph Proudhon.
August 28	Met Engels for the second time, and struck up a permanent friendship.

1845

February 3	After expulsion from Paris, settled in Brussels.
February 24	Published, in collaboration with Engels, *Die Heilige Familie* ("The Holy Family").

Spring	Wrote "Theses on Feuerbach" (first published in 1888).
September 6	Birth of daughter Laura.
December 1	Gave up Prussian citizenship.

1846

Early in year	Founded, with Engels, Communist Correspondence Committee in Brussels.
Summer	Completed, with Engels, *Die deutsche Ideologie* ("The German Ideology," first published in 1932).

1847

Early July	Published, in French, *La Misère de la Philosophie* ("The Poverty of Philosophy").
December 17	Birth of son Edgar.

1848

February 24	Publication, in German, of *Manifesto of the Communist Party*, in London (with Engels).
March 5	After expulsion from Brussels, arrived in Paris.
April 11	Arrived, with Engels, in Cologne, to publish a newspaper there.
June 1	Published first issue of *Neue Rheinische Zeitung*, of which Marx was editor in chief.
September 25	Outbreak of revolution in Cologne.
December 6	Indicted for incitement to rebellion against Prussian state.

1849

February 7–8	Acquitted by jury in Cologne.
May 19	Publication of last issue of *Neue Rheinische Zeitung*.
June 3	After expulsion from Prussia, arrived in Paris.

August 24	After expulsion from Paris, moved to London, where he spent the rest of his life.
November 10	Arrival of Engels in London.

1850

March 6	Published, with Engels, first issue of *Neue Rheinische Zeitung. Politisch-Oekonomische Revue*.
Late March	Second issue of *Revue*.
April 17	Third issue of *Revue*.
May 19	Fourth issue of *Revue*.
November 29	Fifth, sixth, and last, issue of *Revue*.
Late November	Engels moved to Manchester, to enter his father's business and help support Marx financially, which he did for the rest of the latter's life.
November 30	First English translation (by Helen MacFarlane) of *Manifesto of the Communist Party*, in Chartist journal, *The Red Republican*.

1851

March 28	Birth of daughter Franziska.

1852

January–May	Publication, in two installments, of *Der achtzehnte Brumaire des Louis Bonaparte* ("The Eighteenth Brumaire of Louis Bonaparte") in the New York German-language weekly *Die Revolution*. A revised edition, in book form, under the title *The Eighteenth Brumaire of Louis Napoleon*, came out in Hamburg, 1869.
August 21	Publication of "The Elections in England: Tories and Whigs," in *New-York Daily Tribune*.

1855

January 16	Birth of daughter Eleanor ("Tussy").
April 6	Death of eight-year old Edgar ("Musch").

1859

June 11 — Publication of *Zur Kritik der Politischen Oekonomie* ("Critique of Political Economy"), by Franz Duncker in Berlin, in an edition of 1,000 copies; this was Marx's first book on economics.

1860

December 1 — Publication of *Herr Vogt*, a bitter polemic against Karl Vogt, by a "German Bookseller" in London.

1864

September 28 — Attended meeting which founded International Working Men's Association (First International), at St. Martin's Hall, London.

October 21–27 — Drafted Provisional Rules and Inaugural Address of the International, published in December.

1867

Late March — Completed *Capital*, Vol. I, which he took to his publisher, Otto Karl Meissner, in Hamburg on April 10.

September 14 — Publication of *Capital*.

1868

April 2 — Marriage of Laura to French socialist Paul Lafargue.

November 29 — Engels endowed Marx with an annuity of £350; henceforth, for the last fifteen years of his life, the constantly ailing Marx was permanently relieved of financial distress.

1871

April 18–May 29   Wrote *The Civil War in France*, a pamphlet defending the Paris Commune, published in English and in German (July).

1872

March 27   Publication of first foreign translation—in Russian—of *Capital*, in an edition of 3,000 copies, of which 900 were sold in the first six weeks.

September 2–7   Participated actively in the last congress of the First International in The Hague; the expulsion of the Bakuninists led to the dissolution of that organization in Europe.

October   Marriage of Jenny Marx to the French socialist Charles Longuet.

1873

Early June   Publication of the second German edition of *Capital*.

1875

March   Moved to 41 Maitland Park Road (or Crescent), London, N.W., where he lived for eight years, until his death.

May 5   Sent to Wilhelm Bracke, a German Social-Democratic leader, "Marginal Notes to the Program of the German Workers' Party." Known as the "Gotha Program," these "Notes," used in the unifying meeting of the German socialists at Gotha, constitute a major document of Marxism.

Late November   Publication of French edition of *Capital*.

1881

December 2   Death of Jenny Marx (wife), of cancer, after thirty-eight years of marriage; Marx was too ill to attend the funeral.

1883

January 11	Death of Jenny Longuet, in Argenteuil, France, of cancer.
March 14, 2:45 P.M.	Marx died in his London home, sitting in an easy chair, of a complication of laryngitis, bronchitis, lung tumor.
March 17	Buried in Highgate Cemetery, London.

CHAPTER I

ART AND AUTHORS

Note

Marx, preoccupied primarily with social and economic problems, did not develop any elaborate aesthetic or literary theories. He had, however, certain definite opinions in those fields, consonant with his general philosophy. He saw art as a reflection of the general level of social development. Classic Greek art, for example, was intimately connected with the mythology of the period, which was unique and not to be compared with more developed social systems. In modern times, as Marx pointed out in his *Theories of Surplus Value,* selections from which are to be found in this chapter, art is an integral part of industrial production. In an economic system based on profit, the artist, including the theater actor, is to be looked upon as performing a dual role. In relation to the public, Marx wrote, he is an artist, "but in relation to his employer he is a productive laborer."

As for writers, Marx read widely and was familiar with the world's best literature. He read for both enjoyment and edification. Some of the foremost novelists provided him with insights which he used in his own critical writings. He was, for example, greatly impressed by Honoré de Balzac as a social critic. In *Capital* (Vol. III, Sec. 1, Ch. 1) he quoted Balzac as "remarkable for his profound grasp" of the French peasant mentality. He was similarly impressed with the "splendid" contemporary English novelists and their realistic analyses of middle-class behavior, as he wrote in the *New-York Daily Tribune* (August 1, 1854):

> The present splendid brotherhood of fiction-writers in England, whose graphic and eloquent pages have issued to the world more political and social truths than have

been uttered by all the professional politicians, publicists and moralists put together, have described every section of the middle-class from the "highly genteel" annuitant and Fund-holder who looks upon all sorts of business as vulgar, to the little shopkeeper and lawyer's clerk. And how have Dickens and Thackeray, Miss Brontë and Mrs. Gaskell painted them? As full of presumption, affection, petty tyranny and ignorance.

A. ART

MATERIAL DEVELOPMENT AND ART

From introduction to *Critique of Political Economy* (written in 1857, but not published when the book came out in 1859), Part 4, Sec. 8. This introduction was found among Marx's papers in 1902 and was published in the socialist journal, *Die Neue Zeit*, in March 1903.

In art it is well known that certain flourishing periods in no way correspond to the general development of society; hence also not to the material foundation, the skeleton of its organization. For example, the Greeks compared with moderns, or also Shakespeare. It is even acknowledged that certain forms of art, for example the epic, can never be produced in their epoch-making classical form after artistic production as such has begun; hence within the scope of art itself certain important forms are possible only in an undeveloped stage of artistic development. If this is the case in regard to the various branches of art within the realm of art itself, it is the less remarkable that this should also be the case in regard to the relation of the entire realm of art to the general development of society. The difficulty lies only in the general conception of these contradictions. As soon as they are made specific they are already explained.

Let us take, for example, the relation of Greek art, and

then that of Shakespeare, to the present time. It is known that Greek mythology is not only the arsenal of Greek art, but also its foundation. Is the contemplation of nature and of social relations, which is at the basis of the Greek imagination and hence of Greek [mythology], possible when there are mechanical mules, railroads, and electric telegraphs? What is a Vulcan compared to Roberts & Co., Jupiter compared to a lightning conductor, and Hermes compared to the Crédit Mobilier?[1] All mythology subdues, dominates and shapes the forces of nature in the imagination and through the imagination; mythology therefore disappears with the establishment of real domination over those forces. What becomes of Fama alongside Printing House Square?[2] Greek art presupposes Greek mythology, that is, that nature and social forms are already assimilated in an unconscious artistic manner through the people's imagination. This is its material. Not just any kind of mythology, that is, not every unconsciously artistic assimilation of nature (here are included all objects, including society). Egyptian mythology could never become the basis or womb of Greek art. But in any case [it presupposes] a mythology. But in no way a societal development that excludes all mythological relation to nature, all mythologizing relation to it, demanding from the artist an imagination independent of mythology.

Viewed from another side: Is Achilles possible in a time of gunpowder and shot? Or is the *Iliad* possible in a time of the printing press or printing machine? Do not the necessary conditions of epic poetry, songs and legends and the muse, disappear with the coming of the printing-press handle?

But the difficulty does not lie in understanding how Greek art and epic poetry are linked to certain forms of social development. The difficulty is that they will still provide us with aesthetic pleasure and in certain respects serve as a standard and unattainable ideal.

A man cannot become a child again, or he becomes childish. But does not the naiveté of the child give him enjoyment, and must he not himself strive for a higher level to

---

[1] Crédit Mobilier was a French bank, founded in 1852, with speculative investments throughout Europe; it went bankrupt in 1867 and was liquidated four years later.

[2] Printing House Square was the location of the influential *Times* of London.

reproduce the child's truth? Does not the nature of the child in every epoch represent the epoch in its natural truth? Why should the historical childhood of humanity, where it had unfolded most beautifully in a stage that will never recur again, not exert an eternal charm? There are ill-bred children and precocious children. Many of the ancient peoples belong in this category. The Greeks were normal children. The charm their art has for us is not in conflict with the undeveloped stage of society on which it grew. Its charm is, rather, the result of the fact, with which it is rather inseparably linked, that the immature social conditions, under which it arose, and could only arise, can never recur again.

PRODUCTIVE LABOR AND ART

From *Theories of Surplus Value* (Vol. IV of *Capital*), Part I (Progress Publishers, Moscow, 1963; trans. by Emile Burns), p. 185

Theories of Surplus Value consists of voluminous research which Marx left undeveloped at the time of his death in 1883.

Thirdly. Here Garnier[1] falls into "moralizing." Why should the "manufacturer of perfumery, who flatters my sense of smell," be productive and not the musician, who "enchants my ear"? Smith would reply: because the former supplies a material product and the latter does not. Morals and the "merits" of the two lads have nothing to do with the distinction.

Fourthly. Is it not a contradiction that the "violin maker, the organ builder, the music dealer, the mechanic, etc.," are productive, and the professions for which these labors are only "preparations" are unproductive?

"All of them have as the final aim of *their labor* a *consumption of the same kind*. If the result which some of them have in view does not deserve to be counted among *the products* of the labor of society, why should one treat more fa-

---

[1]Germain Garnier, *"Notes du traducteur,"* in Adam Smith, *Recherches sur la nature et les causes de la richesse des nations,* Vol. V (Paris, 1802).

vorably what is nothing but a *means for attaining this result?*" (p. 173).

On this reasoning, a man who eats corn is just as productive as the man who produces it. For with what aim is corn produced? In order to eat it. So if the labor of eating is not productive, why should the labor of cultivating corn be productive, since it is only a means for attaining this aim? Besides, the man who eats produces brain, muscles, etc., and are these not just as worthy products as barley or wheat?—an indignant friend of humanity might ask Adam Smith.

In the first place, Adam Smith does not deny that the unproductive laborer produces a product of some sort. Otherwise he would not be a laborer at all. Secondly, it may seem strange that the doctor who prescribes pills is not a productive laborer, but the apothecary who makes them up is. Similarly the craftsman that makes the fiddle, but not the musician who plays it. But that would only show that "productive laborers" produce products which have no purpose except to serve as means of production for unproductive laborers. Which however is no more surprising than that all productive laborers, when all is said and done, produce firstly the means for the payment of unproductive laborers, and secondly, products which are consumed by those who *do not perform any labor.*

From *Theories of Surplus Value* (Vol. IV of *Capital*), Part I (Progress Publishers, Moscow, 1963; trans. by Emile Burns), p. 298

Here once again we meet the nonsense that every kind of service produces something—the courtesan sensual pleasure, the murderer homicide, etc. Moreover, Smith said that every form of this trash[1] has its *value*. All that is missing is that these services are rendered gratis. That is not the point in question. But even if they are rendered gratis, they will not increase (material) wealth by a single farthing.

Then the belletristic piffle:

"The singer (they claim), when he has finished singing, leaves us nothing. He leaves us a memory!" (Very fine!) "When you have drunk champagne, what remains? . . .

[1] Marx used the word *"Scheisse"*: "shit."

Whether the consumption does or does not follow closely on the act of production, whether it takes place more or less rapidly, will bring about different economic results, but the fact of consumption, of whatever kind it may be, cannot deprive the product of its character as wealth. There are immaterial products which are of greater durability than certain material products. A palace lasts a long time, but the *Iliad* is a source of even more durable pleasures" (pp. 277–78).[2]

What rubbish!

In the sense in which he is here speaking of wealth, as use-value, it is precisely *consumption,* whether slow or rapid (its length depends on its own nature and on the nature of the object). Use-value has only value for use, and its existence for use is only existence as an object for consumption; its existence is in consumption. Drinking champagne, although this may produce a "hangover," is as little productive consumption as listening to music, although this may leave behind "a memory." If the music is good and if the listener understands music, the consumption of music is more sublime than the consumption of champagne, although the production of the latter is a "productive labor" and the production of the former is not.

From *Theories of Surplus Value* (Vol. IV of *Capital*), Part I (Progress Publishers, Moscow, 1963; trans. by Emile Burns), p. 401

For example, Milton, who wrote *Paradise Lost* for £5, was an unproductive laborer. On the other hand, the writer who turns out material for his publisher in factory style is a productive laborer. Milton produced *Paradise Lost* for the same reason that a silkworm produces silk. It was an activity of his nature. Later he sold the product for £5. But the literary proletarian of Leipzig, who fabricates books (for example, Compendia of Economics) under the direction of his publisher, is a productive laborer, for his product is from the outset subsumed under capital and comes into being only for the purpose of increasing that capital. A singer who sells her song for her own account is an unproductive laborer. But the same singer commissioned by an entrepreneur to sing in order to

[2] Pellegrino Luigi Edoardo Rossi, *Cours d'Économie Politique* (Brussels, 1842).

make money for him is a productive laborer, for she produces capital.

From *Theories of Surplus Value* (Vol. IV of *Capital*), Pt. I (Progress Publishers, Moscow, 1963; trans. by Emile Burns), pp. 410–11

Nonmaterial production, even when it is carried on purely for exchange, that is, when it produces commodities, may be of two kinds:

1. It results in commodities, use-values, which have a form different from and independent of producers and consumers; these commodities may therefore exist during an interval between production and consumption and may in this interval circulate as vendible commodities, such as books, paintings, in a word, all artistic products which are distinct from the artistic performance of the artist performing them. Here capitalist production is applicable only to a very restricted extent: as for example when a writer of a joint work—say an encyclopedia—exploits a number of others as hacks. In this sphere for the most part, a transitional form to capitalist production remains in existence, in which the various scientific or artistic producers, handicraftsmen or experts, work for the collective trading capital of the book trade—a relation that has nothing to do with the capitalist mode of production proper and even formally has not yet been brought under its sway. The fact that the exploitation of labor is at its highest precisely in these transitional forms in no way alters the case.

2. The production cannot be separated from the act of production as is the case with all performing artists, orators, actors, teachers, physicians, priests, etc. Here too the capitalist mode of production is met with only to a small extent, and from the nature of the case can only be applied in a few spheres. For example, teachers in educational establishments may be mere wage-laborers for the entrepreneur of the establishment; many such educational factories exist in England. Although in relation to the pupils these teachers are not productive laborers, they are productive laborers in relation to their employer. He exchanges this capital for their labor-power and enriches himself through this process. It is the same with enterprises such as theaters, places of entertainment, etc. In such cases the actor's relation to the public is

that of an artist, but in relation to his employer he is a productive laborer. All these manifestations of capitalist production in this sphere are so insignificant compared with the totality of production that they can be left entirely out of account.

B. AUTHORS

HONORÉ de BALZAC

From *Capital*, Vol. I, Sec. 7, Ch. 22, fn.

Thus, for instance, Balzac, who had so thoroughly studied all the shadings of avarice, represents the old usurer Gobsec as in his second childhood when he begins to heap up a storehouse of commodities.

From *Capital*, Vol. III, Book 3, Sec. 1, Ch. 1

In a society ruled by capitalist production, even the non-capitalist producer is dominated by capitalist conceptions. In his last novel, *Les Paysans* ["The Peasants"], Balzac, who is generally remarkable for his profound grasp of actual conditions, aptly describes how the little peasant, in order to retain the goodwill of his usurer, performs many small tasks gratuitously for him and believes that he does not give him anything for nothing, because his own labor does not cost him any cash outlay. The usurer, for his part, thereby kills two flies at one stroke. He saves cash outlay for wages and gets the peasant more and more entangled in the net of the usurer-spider, by gradually ruining him through withdrawing him from work in his own fields.

JEREMY BENTHAM

From *Capital*, Vol. I, Pt. VII, Ch. 24, Sec. 5

Classical economy always loved to conceive social capital as a fixed magnitude of a fixed degree of efficiency. But this prejudice was first established as a dogma by the arch-Philistine, Jeremy Bentham, that insipid, pedantic, leather-tongued oracle of the ordinary bourgeois intelligence of the nineteenth century. Bentham is among philosophers what Martin Tupper is among poets. Both could have been manufactured only in England.

[Footnote]: Bentham is a purely English phenomenon. Not even excepting our philosopher Christian Wolff, in no time and in no country has the most homespun commonplace ever strutted about in so self-satisfied a way. The principle of utility was no discovery of Bentham. He simply reproduced in his dull way what Helvétius and other Frenchmen had said with esprit in the eighteenth century. To know what is useful for a dog, one must study dog nature. This nature itself is not to be deduced from the principle of utility. Applying this to man, he that would criticize all human acts, movements, relations, etc., by the principle of utility, must first deal with human nature in general, and then with human nature as modified in each historical epoch. Bentham makes short work of it. With the dryest naïveté, he takes the modern shopkeeper, especially the English shopkeeper, as the normal man. Whatever is useful to this queer normal man, and to his world, is absolutely useful. This yard measure, then, he applies to past, present and future. The Christian religion, e.g., is "useful" because it forbids in the name of religion the same faults that penal code condemns in the name of the law. Artistic criticism is "harmful" because it disturbs worthy people in their enjoyment of Martin Tupper, etc. With such rubbish has the brave fellow, with his motto, *"nulla dies sine linea,"*[1] piled up mountains of books. Had I the courage of my friend, Heinrich Heine, I should call Mr. Jeremy a genius in the way of bourgeois stupidity.

THOMAS CARLYLE

From Marx and Engels, review of Thomas Carlyle's *Latter-day Pamphlets: No. 1, "The Present Time,"* in *Neue Rheinische Zeitung. Politisch-Oekonomische Revue,* Heft 4, April 1850

Thomas Carlyle is the only English writer on whom German literature has had a direct and very important influence.

[1] "No day without a stroke of [painting]," words attributed to the Greek painter Apelles.

Even if only out of courtesy, a German should not let his writings pass without notice.

In the latest work by Guizot,[1] we have seen the capacities of the bourgeoisie in their decline. In the two brochures by Carlyle before us, we experience the decline of the literary genius in the historical struggles, which had become acute, against which he seeks to assert his mistaken, direct, prophetical inspiration.

Thomas Carlyle has the merit of having come out against the bourgeoisie at a time when its opinions, tastes and ideas had thoroughly shackled the whole official English literature, and he did it in a way that is even downright revolutionary. So it is in his history of the French Revolution,[2] in his Apology to Cromwell,[3] in his pamphlet on Chartism,[4] in *Past and Present*.[5] But in all these writings, criticism of the present is closely linked to an unusually unhistorical apotheosis of the Middle Ages, frequently also found among revolutionaries, for example, Cobbett and some of the Chartists. While he admires at least the Classical epochs of a certain phase of Society in the past, he is moved to despair by the present and dreads the future. Even where he recognizes the revolution or apotheosizes it, he concentrates on single individuals, on a Cromwell or a Danton. To them he devotes the same hero worship that he preached in his Lectures on Heroes and Hero-Worship,[6] as a refuge from a despair-filled present, as a new religion.

Like the ideas, so is the style of Carlyle. It is a direct, powerful reaction to the modern-bourgeois English Pecksniff style, whose bombastic flabbiness, cautious long-windedness, and moral-sentimental, scatterbrained tediousness have spilled over from its original inventors, the cockneys, into all English literature. In contrast to them, Carlyle treats the English lan-

---

[1] François Pierre Guillaume Guizot, author of *Pourquoi la Révolution d'Angleterre a-t-elle Réussi?* ("Why Did the Revolution in England Succeed?" Paris, 1850).

[2] *The French Revolution: A History* (3 vols., London, 1837).

[3] *Oliver Cromwell's Letters and Speeches, with Elucidations* (2 vols. London, 1845).

[4] *Chartism* (London, 1840).

[5] *Past and Present* (London, 1843).

[6] *On Heroes, Hero-Worship, and the Heroic in History* (London, 1841).

guage as completely raw material, which he had to recast from its foundations. Obsolete turns of phrase and words were sought out and new ones discovered, following the German, especially the Jean Paul, model. The new style has often been heaven-storming and tasteless, but frequently brilliant and always original. Here too the *Latter-Day Pamphlets* show a remarkable retrogression.

Moreover, it is characteristic that of all German literature, the mind that exercised influence on Carlyle was not Hegel, but the literary apothecary Jean Paul.

FRANÇOIS RENÉ de CHATEAUBRIAND

From letter to Frederick Engels (in Manchester), October 26, 1854

Dear Frederick!

In studying the Spanish shit,[1] I again came across the worthy Chateaubriand, that literary calligraphist who combines in the most offensive way the elegant scepticism and Voltaireanism of the eighteenth century with the elegant sentimentalism and romanticism of the nineteenth. *Stylistically*, of course, this combination was bound to be the rage in France, even though in his style, despite some artistic pieces, the false often leaps to the eye. In regard to the *political* Chateaubriand, he revealed himself completely in his *Congrès de Vérone*,[2] and the only question is whether he got "cash" from Alexander Pavlovich [Czar Alexander I] or was simply bribed by flatteries, to which the conceited fop is as susceptible as nobody else. In any case, he received the Order of Saint Andrew from Petersburg. Vanity peeps from every pore of the Herr "Vicomte" (?), despite his now Mephistophelian, now Christian flirting with the *vanitatum vanitas* [vanity of vanities]. You know that in the time of the Congress,[3] Villèle was Prime Minister of Louis XVIII and Chateaubriand was French Ambassador in Verona. In his *Congrès de Vérone*—which perhaps you may have read once—he re-

[1] Between September and December 1854, Marx published in the *New-York Daily Tribune* a series of eight articles on Spain.

[2] Published in Brussels, 1838.

[3] The Congress of Verona, assembled by the Holy Alliance, took place in 1822.

ports on the documents, negotiations, etc. He begins with a short history of the Spanish revolution of 1820–23. As far as this "history" is concerned, it suffices to cite that he places Madrid on the Tajo (simply in order to introduce the Spanish proverb that his river *cria oro* [produces gold]); and he says that Riego at the head of *10,000 men* (in reality, there were 5,000) attacked General Freire at the head of 13,000; that Riego was defeated and then retreated with 15,000 men. Instead of retiring to the Sierra de Ronda, he has him retire to the Sierra Morena, in order to compare him with the hero of Mancha [Don Quixote]. I mention this in passing, in order to characterize his method. Almost not a single fact is correct. . . .

When you read the book again, your contempt for the "*crapauds*" [toads] and their "*grands hommes*" [great men] will hardly decrease.

Adieu.

Yours,
K.M.

From letter to Frederick Engels (in London); Harrogate, November 30, 1873

Dear Fred:

. . . Last night, Tussy and I took refuge in chess. For the rest, I read St. Beuve's book on *Chateaubriand*,[1] a writer whom I have always found distasteful. If he has become so famous in France, it is because in every respect he is the classic incarnation of French vanity, and he embodies this vanity not in a light and frivolous eighteenth century sense, but in romantic garb, flaunting new-baked expressions, false depth, Byzantine exaggeration, toying with emotions, motley sheen, word painting, theatrical, sublime in a word, a mishmash of lies, as never before rendered in such form and content. . . .

Yours,
K.M.

---

[1] Charles Augustin Sainte-Beuve, *Chateaubriand et son groupe littéraire sous l'Empire* ("Chateaubriand and His Literary Group Under the Empire," 2 vols., Paris, 1861).

HENRY GEORGE

From letter to John Swinton, June 2, 1881 (in New York)

As to the book of Mr. Henry George,[1] I consider it as a last attempt—to save the capitalistic regime. Of course, this is not the meaning of the author, but the older disciples of Ricardo—the radical ones—fancied already that by the public appropriation of the rent of the land everything would be righted.

From letter to Friedrich Adolph Sorge (in Hoboken, N.J.), June 20, 1881[2]

Before I received your copy of Henry George I had received two others.... Today I must confine myself to a very brief formulation of my opinion of the book. In theory, the man is totally *arrière* [backward]. He understands nothing about the nature of surplus value, and so he wanders about in speculations that follow the English pattern, but are even behind the English.... His fundamental dogma is that everything would be all right if land rent were paid to the state. (You will also find payment of this kind among the transitional measures included in the *Communist Manifesto*.) This idea originally belonged to the bourgeois economists; it was first put forward ... by the earliest radical disciples of Ricardo, just after his death....

The whole thing is thus merely a socialistically embellished attempt to save the capitalist rule, and, indeed, to establish it anew on an even wider basis than the present one.

This cloven hoof which is at the same time an ass's hoof also unmistakably peeps out of the declarations of Henry George. It is the more unforgivable in him, since he, on the contrary, should have asked the question: How did it happen that in the United States, where relatively—that is, compared to civilized Europe—land was accessible to the great masses

---

[1] George, *Progress and Poverty* (New York, 1880).
[2] The original is in the New York Public Library, Manuscript Division.

of the people and to a certain degree (again relatively) still is, the capitalist economy and the corresponding enslavement of the working class have developed more rapidly and more shamelessly than in any other country?

On the other hand, George's book, like the sensation it has made among you, has importance in that it is a first, even though disappointing, attempt at emancipation from orthodox political economy.

Moreover, H. George does not seem to know about the earlier *American* Anti-Renters,[3] who were more practical than theoretical. He is otherwise a writer of talent (with a Yankee talent for advertising too), as, for example, is shown by his article on California in the *Atlantic*.[4] He also has the repulsive presumption and arrogance that invariably characterize all such panacea-hatchers.

KARL MARX

Bekenntnisse ("Confessions"), written (in English) in an album of Marx's relatives, the Lion Philips family, in Zalt-Bommel, Holland, April 1, 1865. A slightly different version of this self-portrait is found in the album of Marx's daughter Jenny. Marx was then forty-seven years old.

Questions	Answers by Marx
The quality you like best	Simplicity
In man	Strength
In woman	Weakness
Your chief characteristic	Singleness of purpose
Your favorite occupation	Glancing at Netjen[5]
The vice you hate most	Servility

[3] A tenant-farmer movement of the 1840s.
[4] The reference is probably to George's article, "The Kearney Agitation in California," in *Popular Science Monthly*, August 1880.
[5] Antoinette (Nannette) Philips, Marx's cousin, with whom he carried on a flirtation.

The vice you excuse most	Gullibility
Your idea of happiness	To fight
Your idea of misery	To submit
Your aversion	Martin Tupper
Your hero	Spartacus, Kepler
Your heroine	Gretchen
The poet you like best	Aeschylus, Shakespeare, Goethe
The prose writer you like best	Diderot
Your favorite flower	Daphne
Your favorite dish	Fish
Your maxim	*Nihil humani a me alienum puto*[1]
Your motto	*De omnibus dubitandum*[2]

ADOLPHE THIERS

From *The Civil War in France* (1871)

... Thiers, that monstrous gnome, has charmed the French bourgeoisie for almost half a century, because he is the most consummate intellectual expression of their own class corruption. Before he became a statesman he had already proved his lying powers as a historian. The chronicle of his public life is the record of the misfortunes of France. Banded, before 1830, with the republicans, he slipped into office under Louis Philippe by betraying his protector Laffitte, ingratiating himself with the king by exciting mob riots against the clergy, during which the church of St. Germain l'Auxerrois and the Archbishop's palace were plundered, and by acting the minister-spy upon, and the jail *accoucheur* of, the Duchess de Berry. The massacre of the republicans in the rue Transnonain and the subsequent infamous laws of September against the press and the right of association were his work....

A few days before the Revolution of February [1848], fretting at the long exile from place and pelf to which Guizot had condemned him, and sniffing in the air the scent of an approaching popular commotion, Thiers, in that pseudo-heroic style which won him the nickname of Mirabeau *mouche* [Mirabeau the fly,] declared to the Chamber of

---

[1] "Nothing human is alien to me."
[2] "Doubt everything."

Deputies: "I am of the party of revolution, not only in France but in Europe...."

The Revolution of February came. Instead of displacing the Guizot cabinet by the Thiers cabinet, as the little man had dreamed, it superseded Louis Philippe by the republic. On the first day of the popular victory he carefully hid himself, forgetting that the contempt of the workingmen screened him from their hatred. Still, with his legendary courage, he continued to shy the public stage, until the June massacres had cleared it for his sort of action. Then he became the leading mind of the "party of Order" and its parliamentary republic, that anonymous interregnum in which all the rival factions of the ruling class conspired together to crush the people, and conspired against each other to restore each of them its own monarchy. Then, as now, Thiers denounced the republicans as the only obstacle to the consolidation of the republic; then, as now, he spoke to the republic as the hangman spoke to Don Carlos: "I shall assassinate thee, but for thy own good." Now, as then, he will have to exclaim on the day after victory: *"L'Empire est fait"*—the Empire is consummated. Despite his hypocritical homilies about necessary liberties and his personal grudge against Louis Bonaparte, who had made a dupe of him, and kicked out parliamentarianism—and outside of its factitious atmosphere the little man is conscious of withering into nothingness—he had a hand in all the infamies of the Second Empire, from the occupation of Rome by French troops to the war with Prussia, which he incited by his fierce invective against German unity, not as a cloak of Prussian despotism but as an encroachment upon the vested right of France in German disunion. Fond as he was of brandishing, with his dwarfish arms, in the face of Europe the sword of the first Napoleon, whose historical shoeblack he had become, his foreign policy always culminated in the utter humiliation of France, from the London convention of 1840 to the Paris capitulation of 1871, and the present civil war, where he hounds on the prisoners of Sedan and Metz against Paris by special permission of Bismarck. Despite his versatility of talent and shiftiness of purpose, this man has his whole lifetime been wedded to the most fossil routine. It is self-evident that to him the deeper undercurrents of modern society remained forever hidden, but even the most palpable changes on its surface were abhorrent to a brain all of whose vitality had fled to the tongue. Thus he never tired of denouncing as a sacrilege any deviation from the old French protective system. When a minister of Louis Philippe, he railed at railways as a wild chimera; and when in opposition under Louis Bonaparte, he branded as a profanation every attempt to reform the rotten French army system. Never in his long political career has he been guilty of a single—even the smallest—measure of any practical use. Thiers was consistent only in his greed for wealth and his hatred for the men that produce it. Having entered his first ministry under Louis Philippe poor as Job, he left it a millionaire. His last ministry under the same king (of March 1, 1840) exposed him to public taunts of peculation in the Chamber of Deputies, to which he was content to reply with tears—a commodity he deals in as freely as Jules Favre, or any other crocodile. At Bordeaux, his first measure for saving France from impending financial ruin was to endow himself with three millions a year....

A master in small state roguery, a virtuoso in perjury and treason, a craftsman in all the petty stratagems, cunning devices and base perfidies of parliamentary party warfare; never scrupling, when out of office, to fan a revolution, and to stifle it in blood when at the helm of the state; with class prejudices standing him in the place of ideas, and vanity in the place of a heart; his private life as infamous as his public life is odious—even now, when playing the part of a French Sulla, he cannot help setting off the abomination of his deeds by the ridicule of his ostentation.

FRANÇOIS MARIE AROUET DE VOLTAIRE

From "Spree und Mincio," in *Das Volk* (London German-language weekly), June 25, 1859

As is well known, Voltaire kept at Ferney four apes whom he gave the names of his four literary opponents, Fréron, Beaumelle, Nonnotte, and de Pompignan. No day passed but that the poet fed them with his own hand, regaled them with kicks, tweaked their ears, stuck needles in their noses, stepped on their tails, stuck them into monk's cowls and maltreated them in every conceivable way. These apes, an outlet for his bile, a satisfaction of his hate and an appeasement of his fears of the polemical weapons of the critics, were as necessary for the Old Man of Ferney as the apes of revolution are for Louis Bonaparte. . . .

CHAPTER II

CLASSES

Note

Marx viewed society as made up of different classes but dominated by a particular class at any given time. The dominant class, which represents special interests, imposes its own ideas on the whole. These ideas become the "ruling intellectual force," but they are not fixed or permanent. Despite the dominance of a particular class, and within its framework, there are other groupings and ideas that struggle for supremacy. When the challengers have universal appeal, they succeed in replacing the previously dominant class—as was the case when the French bourgeoisie overthrew the aristocracy in 1789. The process continues until there is no longer any need for "class rule."

In this chapter, the reader will find essays in which Marx describes and analyzes the class structures of Britain and Prussia, two countries with which he was intimately familiar.

RULING CLASS AND RULING IDEAS

From *The German Ideology*, written by Marx and Engels in 1845–46, but not published until 1932. The main targets of this book were Max Stirner, Karl Gruen, and the so-called "true socialists." The English-language edition on which this text is based is by Progress Publishers, translated from the German by S. Ryazanskaya (Moscow, 1964), pp. 61–63.

The ideas of the ruling class are in every epoch the ruling ideas: i.e., the class, which is the ruling *material* force of society, is at the same time its ruling *intellectual* force. The class which has the means of material production at its disposal, has control at the same time over the means of mental production, so that thereby, generally speaking, the ideas of those who lack the means of mental production are subject to it. The ruling ideas are nothing more than the ideal expression of the dominant material relationships, the dominant material relationships grasped as ideas; hence of the relationships which make the one class the ruling one, therefore, the ideas of its dominance. The individuals composing the ruling class possess among other things consciousness, and therefore think. Insofar, therefore, as they rule as a class and determine the extent and compass of an epoch, it is self-evident that they do this in its whole range, hence among other things rule also as thinkers, as producers of ideas, and regulate the production and distribution of the ideas of their age: thus their ideas are the ruling ideas of the epoch. For instance, in an age and in a country where royal power, aristocracy and bourgeoisie are contending for mastery and where, therefore, mastery is shared, the doctrine of the separation of powers proves to be the dominant idea and is expressed as an "eternal law."

The division of labour, which we already saw above as one of the chief forces of history up till now, manifests itself also in the ruling class as the division of mental and material labour, so that inside this class one part appears as the thinkers of the class (its active, conceptive ideologists, who make the perfecting of the illusion of the class about itself their chief source of livelihood), while the others' attitude to these ideas and illusions is more passive and receptive, because they are in reality the active members of this class and have less time to make up illusions and ideas about themselves. Within this class this cleavage can even develop into a certain opposition and hostility between the two parts, which, however, in the case of a practical collision, in which the class itself is endangered, automatically comes to nothing, in which case there also vanishes the semblance that the ruling ideas were not the ideas of the ruling class and had a power distinct from the power of this class. The existence of revolutionary ideas in a particular period presupposes the existence of a revolutionary class; about the premises for the latter sufficient has already been said above.

If now in considering the course of history we detach the ideas of the ruling class from the ruling class itself and attribute to them an independent existence, if we confine ourselves to saying that these or those ideas were dominant at a given time, without bothering ourselves about the conditions of production and the producers of these ideas, if we thus ignore the individuals and world conditions which are the source of the ideas, we can say, for instance, that during the time that the aristocracy was dominant, the concepts honour, loyalty, etc., were dominant, during the dominance of the bourgeoisie the concepts freedom, equality, etc. The ruling class itself on the whole imagines this to be so. This conception of history, which is common to all historians, particularly since the eighteenth century, will necessarily come up against the phenomenon that increasingly abstract ideas hold sway, i.e., ideas which increasingly take on the form of universality. For each new class which puts itself in the place of one ruling before it, is compelled, merely in order to carry through its aim, to represent its interest as the common interest of all the members of society, that is, expressed in ideal form: it has to give its ideas the form of universality, and represent them as the only rational, universally valid ones. The class making a revolution appears from the very start, if only because it is opposed to a *class*, not as a class but as the representative of the whole of society; it appears as the whole mass of society confronting the one ruling class.[1] It can do this because, to start with, its interest really is more connected with the common interest of all other non-ruling classes, because under the pressure of hitherto existing conditions its interest has not yet been able to develop as the particular interest of a particular class. Its victory, therefore, benefits also many individuals of the other classes which are not winning a dominant position, but only insofar as it now puts these individuals in a position to raise themselves into the ruling class. When the French bourgeoisie overthrew the power of the aristocracy, it thereby

[1] Marginal note by Marx: "Universality corresponds to (1) the class versus the estate, (2) the competition, world-wide intercourse, etc., (3) the great numerical strength of the ruling class, (4) the illusion of the *common* interests (in the beginning this illusion is true), (5) the delusion of the ideologists and the division of labour."

made it possible for many proletarians to raise themselves above the proletariat, but only insofar as they became bourgeois. Every new class, therefore, achieves its hegemony only on a broader basis than that of the class ruling previously, whereas the opposition of the non-ruling class against the new ruling class later develops all the more sharply and profoundly. Both these things determine the fact that the struggle to be waged against this new ruling class, in its turn, aims at a more decided and radical negation of the previous conditions of society than could all previous classes which sought to rule.

This whole semblance, that the rule of a certain class is only the rule of certain ideas, comes to a natural end, of course, as soon as class rule in general ceases to be the form in which society is organised, that is to say, as soon as it is no longer necessary to represent a particular interest as general or the "general interest" as ruling.

SOCIAL CLASSES IN ENGLAND

"The Elections in England—Tories and Whigs," *New-York Daily Tribune,* August 21, 1852. This was Marx's first article for the *Tribune,* whose London correspondent he continued to be for another ten years. Engels translated the article from German into English.

The results of the General Election for the British Parliament are now known. This result I shall analyze more fully in my next letter.

What were the parties which during this electioneering agitation opposed or supported each other?

Tories, Whigs, Liberal Conservatives (Peelites),[1] Free Traders *par excellence* (the men of the Manchester School, Parliamentary Financial Reformers), and lastly, the Chartists.[2]

[1] Followers of Sir Robert Peel.
[2] See the next selection.

Whigs, Free Traders and Peelites coalesced to oppose the Tories. It was between this coalition on one side, and the Tories on the other, that the real electoral battle was fought. Opposed to Whigs, Peelites, Free Traders and Tories, and thus opposed to entire official England, were the Chartists.

The political parties of Great Britain are sufficiently known in the United States. It will be sufficient to bring to mind, in a few strokes of the pen, the distinctive characteristics of each of them.

Up to 1846 the Tories passed as the guardians of the traditions of Old England. They were suspected of admiring in the British Constitution the eighth wonder of the world; to be *laudatores temporis acti*,[1] enthusiasts for the throne, the High Church, the privileges and liberties of the British subject. The fatal year, 1846, with its repeal of the Corn Laws, and the shout of distress which this repeal forced from the Tories, proved that they were enthusiasts for nothing but the rent of land, and at the same time disclosed the secret of their attachment to the political and religious institutions of Old England. These institutions are the very best institutions, with the help of which the *large landed property*—the landed interest—has hitherto ruled England, and even now seeks to maintain its rule. The year 1846 brought to light in its nakedness the *substantial class interest* which forms the *real base* of the Tory party. The year 1846 tore down the traditionally venerable lion's hide, under which Tory class interest had hitherto hidden itself. The year 1846 transformed the Tories into *Protectionists*. Tory was the sacred name, Protectionist is the profane one; Tory was the political battle-cry, Protectionist is the economical shout of distress; Tory seemed an idea, a principle; Protectionist is an interest. Protectionist of what? Of their own revenues, of the rent of their own land. Then the Tories, in the end, are Bourgeois as much as the remainder, for where is the Bourgeois who is not a protectionist of his own purse? They are distinguished from the other Bourgeois, in the same way as the rent of land is distinguished from commercial and industrial profit. Rent of land is conservative, profit is progressive; rent of land is national, profit is cosmo*political;* rent of land believes in the State Church, profit is a dissenter by birth. The repeal of the Corn Laws of 1846 merely recognized an already accomplished fact, a

---

[1] People who laud the past.

change long since enacted in the elements of British civil society, *viz.*, the subordination of the landed interest under the moneyed interest, of property under commerce, of agriculture under manufacturing industry, of the country under the city. Could this fact be doubted since the country population stands, in England, to the towns' population in the proportion of one to three? The substantial foundation of the power of the Tories was the rent of land. The rent of land is regulated by the price of food. The price of food, then, was artificially maintained at a high rate by the Corn Laws. The repeal of the Corn Laws brought down the price of food, which in its turn brought down the rent of land, and with sinking rent broke down the real strength upon which the political power of the Tories reposed.

What, then, are they trying to do now? To maintain a political power, the social foundation of which has ceased to exist. And how can this be attained? By nothing short of a *Counter-Revolution*, that is to say, by a reaction of the State against Society. They strive to retain forcibly institutions and a political power which are condemned from the very moment at which the rural population found itself outnumbered three times by the population of the towns. And such an attempt must necessarily end with their destruction; it must accelerate and make more acute the social development of England; it must bring on a crisis.

The Tories recruit their army from the farmers, who have either not yet lost the habit of following their landlords as their natural superiors, or who are economically dependent upon them, or who do not yet see that the interest of the farmer and the interest of the landlord are no more identical than the respective interests of the borrower and of the usurer. They are followed and supported by the Colonial Interest, the Shipping Interest, the State Church Party, in short, by all those elements which consider it necessary to safeguard their interests against the necessary results of modern manufacturing industry, and against the social revolution prepared by it.

Opposed to the Tories, as their hereditary enemies, stand the *Whigs*, a party with whom the American Whigs have nothing in common but the name.

The British Whig, in the natural history of politics, forms a species which, like all those of the amphibious class, exists very easily, but is difficult to describe. Shall we call them, with their opponents, Tories out of office? or, as continental writers love it, take them for the representatives of certain *popular* principles? In the latter case we should get embarrassed in the same difficulty as the historian of the Whigs, Mr. Cooke, who, with great *naïveté* confesses in his "History of Parties" that it is indeed a certain number of "liberal, moral and enlightened principles" which constitutes the Whig party, but that it was greatly to be regretted that during the more than a century and a half that the Whigs have existed, they have been, when in office, always prevented from carrying out these principles. So that in reality, according to the confession of their own historian, the Whigs represent something quite different from their professed "liberal and enlightened principles." Thus they are in the same position as the drunkard brought up before the Lord Mayor who declared that he represented the Temperance principle but from some accident or other always got drunk on Sundays.

But never mind their principles; we can better make out what they are in historical fact; what they carry out, not what they once believed, and what they now want other people to believe with respect to their character.

The Whigs as well as the Tories, form a fraction of the large landed property of Great Britain. Nay, the oldest, richest and most arrogant portion of English landed property is the very nucleus of the Whig party.

What, then, distinguishes them from the Tories? The Whigs are the *aristocratic representatives* of the bourgeoisie, of the industrial and commercial middle class. Under the condition that the Bourgeoisie should abandon to them, to an oligarchy of aristocratic families, the monopoly of government and the exclusive possession of office, they make to the middle class, and assist it in conquering, all those concessions, which in the course of social and political development have shown themselves to have become *unavoidable* and *undelayable*. Neither more nor less. And as often as such an unavoidable measure has been passed, they declare loudly that herewith the end of historical progress has been obtained; that the whole social movement has carried its ultimate purpose, and then they "cling to finality." They can support more easily than the Tories, a decrease of their rental revenues, because they consider themselves as the heavenborn farmers of the revenues of the British Empire. They can renounce the monopoly of the Corn Laws, as long as they maintain the monopoly of government as their family property. Ever since the "glorious revolution" of 1688 the Whigs, with short intervals, caused principally by the first French Revolution and the consequent reaction, have found themselves in the enjoyment of the public offices. Whoever recalls to his mind this period of English history, will find no other distinctive mark of Whigdom but the maintenance of their family oligarchy. The interests and principles which they represent besides, from time to time, do not belong to the Whigs; they are forced upon them by the development of the industrial and commercial class, the Bourgeoisie. After 1688 we find them united with the Bankocracy, just then rising into importance, as we find them in 1846, united with the Millocracy. The Whigs as little carried the Reform Bill of 1831, as they carried the Free Trade Bill of 1846. Both Reform movements, the political as well as the commercial, were movements of the Bourgeoisie. As soon as either of these movements had ripened into irresistibility; as soon as, at the same time, it had become the safest means of turning the Tories out of office, the Whigs stepped forward, took up the direction of the Government, and secured to themselves the governmental part of the victory. In 1831 they extended the political portion of reform as far as was necessary in order not to leave the middle class entirely dissatisfied; after 1846 they confined their Free Trade measures so far as was necessary, in order to save to the landed aristocracy the greatest possible amount of privileges. Each time they had taken the movement in hand in order to prevent its forward march, and to recover their own posts at the same time.

It is clear that from the moment when the landed aristocracy is no longer able to maintain its position as an independent power, to fight, as an independent party, for the government position, in short, that from the moment when the Tories are definitively overthrown, British history has no longer any room for the Whigs. The aristocracy once destroyed, what is the use of an aristocratic representation of the Bourgeoisie against this aristocracy?

It is well known that in the middle ages the German Emperors put the just then arising towns under Imperial Governors, "*advocati*," to protect these towns against the surrounding nobility. As soon as growing population and wealth gave them sufficient strength and independence to resist, and even to attack the nobility, the towns also drove out the noble Governors, the *advocati*.

The Whigs have been these *advocati* of the British Middle Class, and their governmental monopoly must break down as soon as the landed monopoly of the Tories is broken down. In the same measure as the Middle Class has developed its independent strength, they have shrunk down from a party to a coterie.

It is evident what a distastefully heterogeneous mixture the character of the British Whigs must turn out to be: Feudalists, who are at the same time Malthusians, money-mongers with feudal prejudices, aristocrats without point of honor, Bourgeois without industrial activity, finality-men with progressive phrases, progressists with fanatical Conservatism, traffickers in homeopathical fractions of reforms, fosterers of family-nepotism, Grand Masters of corruption, hypocrites of religion, Tartuffes of politics. The mass of the English people have a sound aesthetical common sense. They have an instinctive hatred against everything motley and ambiguous, against bats and Russellites. And then, with the Tories, the mass of the English people, the urban and rural proletariat, has in common the hatred against the "money-monger." With the Bourgeoisie it has in common the hatred against aristocrats. In the Whigs it hates the one and the other, aristocrats and Bourgeois, the landlord who oppresses, and the money lord who exploits it. In the Whig it hates the oligarchy which has ruled over England for more than a century, and by which the People is excluded from the direction of its own affairs.

The Peelites (Liberals and Conservatives) are no party; they are merely the *souvenir* of a partyman, of the late Sir Robert Peel. But Englishmen are too prosaical, for a *souvenir* to form, with them, the foundation for anything but elegies. And now that the people have erected brass and marble monuments to the late Sir R. Peel in all parts of the country, they believe they are able so much the more to do without those perambulant Peel monuments, the Grahams, the Gladstones, the Cardwells, etc. The so-called Peelites are nothing but this staff of bureaucrats which Robert Peel had schooled for himself. And because they form a pretty complete staff, they forget for a moment that there is no army behind them. The Peelites, then, are old supporters of Sir R. Peel, who have not yet come to a conclusion as to what party to attach themselves to. It is evident that a similar scruple is not a sufficient means for them to constitute an independent power.

Remain the Free Traders and the Chartists, the brief delineation of whose character will form the subject of my next.

"THE CHARTISTS"

In the *New-York Daily Tribune*, August 25, 1852; and also, in abridged form, in *The People's Paper*, October 9, 1852. This was Marx's second article in the *Tribune*.

While the Tories, the Whigs, the Peelites—in fact, all the parties we have hitherto commented upon—belong more or less to the past, the Free Traders (the men of the Manchester School, the Parliamentary and Financial Reformers) are the *official representatives of modern English society*, the representatives of that England which rules the market of the world. They represent the party of the self-conscious Bourgeoisie, of industrial capital striving to make available its social power as a political power as well, and to eradicate the last arrogant remnants of feudal society. This party is led on by the most active and most energetic portion of the English Bourgeoisie—the *manufacturers*. What they demand is the complete and undisguised ascendancy of the Bourgeoisie, the open, official subjection of society at large under the laws of modern, bourgeois production, and under the rule of those men who are the directors of that production. By Free Trade they mean the unfettered movement of capital, freed from all political, national and religious shackles. The soil is to be a marketable commodity, and the exploitation of the soil is to be carried on according to the common commercial laws. There are to be manufacturers of food as well as manufacturers of twist and cottons, but no longer any lords of the land. There are, in short, not to be tolerated any political or social restrictions, regulations or monopolies, unless they proceed from "the eternal laws of political economy," that is, from the conditions under which Capital produces and distributes. The struggle of this party against the old English institutions, products of a superannuated, an evanescent stage of social development, is resumed in the watchword: *Produce as cheap as you can, and do away with all the faux frais of production* (with all superfluous, unnecessary expenses in production). And this watchword is addressed not only to the private individual, but to the *nation at large* principally.

Royalty, with its "barbarous splendors," its court, its civil list and its flunkeys—what else does it belong to but to the *faux frais* of production? The nation can produce and exchange without royalty; away with the crown. The sinecures of the nobility, the House of Lords? *faux frais* of production. The large standing army? *faux frais* of production. The Colonies? *faux frais* of production. The State Church, with its riches, the spoils of plunder or of mendicity? *faux frais* of production. Let parsons compete freely with each other, and every one pay them according to his own wants. The whole circumstantial routine of English Law, with its Court of Chancery? *faux frais* of production. National wars? *faux frais* of production. England can exploit foreign nations more cheaply while at peace with them.

You see, to these champions of the British Bourgeoisie, to the men of the Manchester School, every institution of Old England appears in the light of a piece of machinery as costly as it is useless, and which fulfills no other purpose but to prevent the nation from producing the greatest possible quantity at the least possible expense, and to exchange its products in freedom. Necessarily, their last word is the Bourgeois Republic, in which free competition rules supreme in all spheres of life; in which there remains altogether that *minimum* only of government which is indispensable for the administration, internally and externally, of the common class, interest and business of the Bourgeoisie; and where this minimum of government is as soberly, as economically organized as possible. Such a party, in other countries, would be called *democratic*. But it is necessarily revolutionary, and the complete annihilation of Old England as an aristocratic country is the end which it follows up with more or less consciousness. Its nearest object, however, is the attainment of a Parliamentary reform which should transfer to its hands the legislative power necessary for such a revolution.

But the British Bourgeois are not excitable Frenchmen. When they intend to carry a Parliamentary reform they will not make a Revolution of February. On the contrary. Having obtained, in 1846, a grand victory over the landed aristocracy by the repeal of the Corn Laws, they were satisfied with following up the material advantages of this victory, while they neglected to draw the necessary political and economical conclusions from it, and thus enabled the Whigs to reinstate themselves into their hereditary monopoly of government. During all the time, from 1846 to 1852, they exposed themselves to ridicule by their battle-cry: Broad principles and practical (read *small*) measures. And why all this? Because in every violent movement they are obliged to appeal to the *working class*. And if the aristocracy is their vanishing opponent the working class is their arising enemy. They prefer to compromise with the vanishing opponent rather than to strengthen the arising enemy, to whom the future belongs, by concessions of a more than apparent importance. Therefore, they strive to avoid every forcible collision with the aristocracy; but historical necessity and the Tories press them onwards. They cannot avoid fulfilling their mission, battering to pieces Old England, the England of the Past; and the very moment when they will have conquered exclusive political dominion, when political dominion and economical supremacy will be united in the same hands, when, therefore, the struggle against capital will no longer be distinct from the struggle against the existing Government—from that very moment will date the *social revolution of England*.

We now come to the *Chartists*, the politically active portion of the British *working class*. The six points of the Charter which they contend for contain nothing but the demand of *Universal Suffrage*, and of the conditions without which Universal Suffrage would be illusory for the working class; such as the ballot, payment of members, annual general elections. But Universal Suffrage is the equivalent *for* political power for the working class of England, where the proletariat forms the large majority of the population, where, in a long, though underground civil war, it has gained a clear consciousness of its position as a class, and where even the rural districts know no longer any peasants, but only landlords, industrial capitalists (farmers) and hired laborers. The carrying of Universal Suffrage in England would, therefore, be a far more socialistic measure than anything which has been honored with that name on the Continent.

Its inevitable result, here, is *the political supremacy of the working class*.

I shall report, on another occasion, on the revival and the reorganization of the Chartist Party. For the present I have only to treat of the recent election.

To be a voter for the British Parliament, a man must occupy, in the Boroughs, a house rated at £10 to the poor's-rate, and, in the counties, he must be a freeholder to the annual amount of 40 shillings, or a leaseholder to the amount of £50. From this statement alone it follows, that the Chartists could take, officially, but little part in the electoral battle just concluded. In order to explain the actual part they took in it, I must recall to mind a peculiarity of the British electoral system:

Nomination day and Declaration day! Show of hands and Poll!

When the candidates have made their appearance on the day of election, and have publicly harangued the people, they are elected, in the first instance, by the show of hands, and every hand has the right to be raised, the hand of the non-elector as well as that of the electors. For whomsoever the majority of the hands are raised, that person is declared, by the returning officer, to be (provisionally) elected by show of hands. But now the medal shows its reverse. The election by show of hands was a mere ceremony, an act of formal politeness toward the "sovereign people," and the politeness ceases as soon as privilege is menaced. For if the show of hands does not return the candidates of the privileged electors, these candidates demand a poll; only the privileged electors can take part in the poll, and whosoever has there the majority of votes is declared duly elected. The first election, by show of hands, is a show satisfaction allowed, for a moment, to public opinion, in order to convince it, the next moment, the more strikingly of its impotency.

It might appear that this election by show of hands, this dangerous formality, had been invented in order to ridicule universal suffrage, and to enjoy some little aristocratic fun at the expense of the "rabble," (expression of Major Beresford, Secretary of War). But this would be a delusion, and the old usage, common originally to all Teutonic nations, could drag itself traditionally down to the nineteenth century, because it gave to the British class-parliament, cheaply and without danger, an appearance of popularity. The ruling classes drew from this usage the satisfaction that the mass of the people took part, with more or less passion, in their sectional interests as its national interests. And it was only since the Bourgeoisie took an independent station at the side of the two official parties, the Whigs and Tories, that the working masses stood up, on the nomination days in their own name. But in no former year the contrast of show of hands and poll, of Nomination day and Declaration day, has been so serious, so well defined by opposed principles, so threatening, so general, upon the whole surface of the country, as in this last election of 1852.

And what a contrast! It was sufficient to be named by show of hands in order to be beaten at the poll. It was sufficient to have had the majority at a poll, in order to be saluted, by the people, with rotten apples and brickbats. The duly elected members of Parliament, before all, had a great deal to do, in order to keep their own parliamentary bodily selves in safety. On one side the majority of the people, on the other the twelfth part of the whole population, and the fifth part of the sum total of the male adult inhabitants of the country. On one side enthusiasm, on the other bribery. On one side parties disowning their own distinctive signs. Liberals pleading the conservatism, Conservatives proclaiming the liberalism of the views; on the other, the people, proclaiming their presence and pleading their own cause. On one side a worn-out engine which, turning incessantly in its vicious circle, is never able to move a single step forward, and the impotent process of friction by which all the official parties gradually grind each other into dust; on the other, the advancing mass of the nation, threatening to blow up the vicious circle and to destroy the official engine.

I shall not follow up, over all the surface of the country, this contrast between nomination and poll, of the threatening electoral demonstration of the working class, and the timid electioneering manoeuvres of the ruling classes. I take one borough from the mass, where the contrast is concentrated in a focus: the Halifax election. Here the opposing candidates were: Edwards (Tory); Sir Charles Wood (late Whig Chancellor of the Exchequer, brother-in-law to Earl Grey); Frank Crossley (Manchester man); and finally Ernest Jones, the most talented, consistent and energetic representative of Chartism. Halifax being a manufacturing town, the Tory had little chance. The Manchester man Crossley, was leagued with the Whigs. The serious struggle, then, lay only between Wood and Jones, between the Whig and the Chartist.

Sir Charles Wood made a speech of about half an hour, perfectly inaudible at the commencement, and during its latter half for the disapprobation of the immense multitude. His speech, as reported by the reporter, who sat close to him, was merely a recapitulation of the Free Trade measures passed, and an attack on Lord Derby's Government, and a laudation of *"the unexampled prosperity of the country and the people!"*—(Hear, hear.) He did not propound one single new measure of reform; and but faintly, in very few words, hinted at Lord John Russell's bill for the franchise.

I give a more extensive abstract of E. Jones's speech, as you will not find it in any of the great London ruling class papers.

Ernest Jones, who was received with immense enthusiasm, then spoke as follows: Electors and Non-electors, you have met upon a great and solemn festival. To-day, the Constitution recognizes Universal Suffrage in theory that it may, perhaps, deny it in practice on the morrow. To-day the representatives of two systems stand before you, and you have to decide beneath which you shall be ruled for seven years. Seven years—a little life! I summon you to pause upon the threshold of those seven years: to-day they shall pass slowly and calmly in review before you: to-day decide, you 20,000 men, that perhaps five hundred may undo your will tomorrow. (Hear, hear.) I say the representatives of two systems stand before you. Whig, Tory, and moneymongers are on my left, it is true, but they are all as one. The moneymonger says, buy cheap and sell dear. The Tory says, buy dear, sell dearer. Both are the same for labour. But the former system is in the ascendant, and pauperism rankles at its root. That system is based on foreign competition. Now, I assert, that under the buy cheap and sell dear principle, brought to bear on foreign competition, the ruin of the working and small trading classes must go on. Why? Labor is the creator of all wealth. A man must work before a grain is grown, or a yard is woven. But there is no self-employment for the working-man in this country. Labor is a hired commodity—labor is a thing in the market that is bought and sold; consequently, as labor creates all wealth, labor is the first thing bought—"Buy cheap! buy cheap!" Labor is bought in the cheapest market. But now comes the next: "Sell dear! sell dear!" Sell what? *Labor's produce.* To whom? To the foreigner—aye! and to *the laborer himself*—for labor, not being self-employed, the laborer is *not* the partaker of the first fruits of his toil. "Buy cheap, sell dear." How do you like it? "Buy cheap, sell dear." Buy the workingman's labor cheaply, and sell back to that very workingman the produce of his own labor dear! The principle of inherent loss is in the bargain. The employer buys the labor cheap—he sells, and on the sale he must make a profit; he sells to the working-man himself—and thus every bargain between employer and employed is a deliberate cheat on the part of the employer. Thus labor has to sink through eternal loss, that capital may rise through lasting fraud. But the system stops not here. *This is brought to bear on foreign competition—which means, we must ruin the trade of other countries, as we have ruined the labor of our own.* How does it work? The high-taxed country has to undersell the low-taxed. Competition abroad is constantly increasing—consequently cheapness must increase constantly also. Therefore, wages in England must keep constantly falling. And how do they effect the fall? By *surplus labor.* How do they obtain the surplus labor? By monopoly of the land, which drives more hands than are wanted into the factory. By monopoly of machinery, which drives those hands into the street—by woman labor which drives the man from the shuttle—by child labor which drives the woman from the loom. Then planting their foot upon that living base of surplus, they press its aching heart beneath their heel, and cry "Starvation! Who'll work? A half loaf is better than no bread at all"—and the writhing mass grasps greedily at their terms. (Loud cries of "Hear, hear.") Such is the system for the working-man. But Electors! How does it operate on you? How does it affect home trade, the shopkeeper, poor's-rate and taxation? For every increase of competition abroad, there must be an increase of cheapness at home. Every increase of cheapness in labor is based on increase of labor surplus, and this surplus is obtained by an increase of machinery. I repeat, how does this operate on you! The Manchester Liberal on my left establishes a new patent, and throws three hundred men as a surplus in the streets. Shopkeepers! Three hundred customers less. Rate payers! Three hundred paupers more. (Loud cheers.) But, mark me! The evil stops not there. These three hundred men operate first to bring down the wages of those who remain at work in their own trade. The employer says, "Now I reduce your wages." The men demur. Then he adds: "Do you see those three hundred men who have *just* walked out—*you may change places if you like*, they're sighing to come in on any terms, for they're starving." The men feel it, and are crushed. Ah! you Manchester Liberal! Pharisee of was a scene that will long be unforgotten. On the show of hands being taken, very few, and those chiefly of the hired or intimidated, were held up for Sir C. Wood; but almost every one present raised both hands for Ernest Jones, amidst cheering and enthusiasm it would be impossible to describe.)

The Mayor declared Mr. Ernest Jones and Mr. Henry Edwards to be elected by show of hands. Sir C. Wood and Mr. Crossley then demanded a poll.

What Jones had predicted took place; he was nominated by 20,000 votes, but the Whig Sir Charles Wood and the Manchester Man Crossley were elected by 500 votes.

THE RISE OF CLASSES AND CITIES

From letter to Frederick Engels (in Manchester), London, July 27, 1854

Dear Engels:

... A book that has interested me very much is Thierry's *History of the Formation and Progress of the Third Estate*, 1853. It is remarkable how, in his Preface, this gentleman, *le père* [the father] of the "class struggle" in French historiography, waxes indignant at the "new people" who now see an antagonism between the bourgeoisie and the proletariat, and who claim to detect traces of this antagonism even in the history of the Third Estate before 1789. He takes great pains to prove that the Third Estate includes all social ranks that are not *noblesse* and clergy, and that bourgeoisie plays its part as the representative of all these other elements. He quotes, for example, from the reports of the Venetian Embassy: *"Questi che si chiamano li stati del regno sono di tre ordini di persone, cioè del clero, della nobiltà, e del restante di quelle persone che, per voce commune, si può chiamare populo"* ["Those who are called the Estates of the realm consist of three orders of persons, namely, the clergy, the nobility, and the rest of those persons who by common consent may be called the *people*"]. Had Mr. Thierry read our things, he would know that the decisive opposition of the bourgeoisie to the people naturally begins only when the bourgeoisie as the Third Estate ceases to be opposed to the clergy and nobility. In regard to the "roots of history," of "an antagonism born only yesterday," his book provides the best proof that these "roots" came into existence with the Third Estate. From the *"Senatus populusque Romanus*" ["The Senate and the Roman People"], the critic, otherwise clever in his own way, ought to have concluded that in Rome there was never any other antagonism except that between the Senate and the people. What has interested me was to see from the documents he quotes that the word *"catalla," "capitalia"*—capital—arises with the appearance of the communes. Moreover, he has proved despite himself that nothing did more to retard the French bourgeoisie in its victory than the fact that it did not decide until 1789 to make common cause with the peasants. He describes well, if not coherently:

(1) How from the first, or at least since the rise of the towns, the French bourgeoisie gains very much influence by constituting itself the Parliament, the bureaucracy, etc., and not as in England merely through commerce and industry.

(2) From his account, it can well be demonstrated how the class arises—when the various forms which lie at the center of gravity at different times, and the various factions which gain influence through these forms, are breaking down. In my opinion, this series of metamorphoses, leading up to the domination of the class, has never—at least so far as the material is concerned—been presented in this way. Unfortunately, in dealing with the *maitrises, jurandes* [guilds, officials], etc.—in short, with the forms in which the industrial bourgeoisie developed itself—he has confined himself almost entirely to general and generally known phrases, although here, too, he alone knows the material. What he develops and emphasizes well is the conspiratorial and revolutionary character of the municipal movement in the Twelfth Century. The German Emperors, Frederick I and II, for example, issued edicts against these *communiones, conspirationes, conjurationes* [communes, conspiracies, sworn confederacies], quite in the spirit of the German Federal Diet.[1] For instance, in 1226, Frederick II takes it upon himself to declare all "consulates"[2] and other free municipal bodies in the cities of Provence null and void:

> *Pervenit nuper ad notitiam nostram quod quarumdam civitatum, villarum et aliorum locorum universitates ex*

[1] The diet of the German Confederation, established in 1815, and continuing until 1866; it had its seat in Frankfurt.
[2] In the Middle Ages, members of the municipal councils in Provence were called *consuls*.

proprio motu constituerunt juridictiones, potestates (Potestad), consulatus, regimina et alia quaedam statuta . . . et cum jam apud quasdam . . . in abusum et pravam consuetudinem inoleverunt . . . nos ex imperiali auctoritate tam juridictiones etc. atque concessiones super his, per comites Provinciae et Forcalquerii ab eis obtentas, ex certa scientia revocamus, et inania esse censemus.[3]

MONARCHY, ARISTOCRACY AND BOURGEOISIE IN PRUSSIA

From "Affairs in Prussia," *New-York Daily Tribune*, February 1, 1859 (in English)

The history of the past ten years in this country [Prussia] has been so one-sidedly (to use a pet word of the Germans, who, like Buridan's animal, are so many-sided that they stick every moment in a dead lock) judged, that some general considerations may not appear out of place. When the King [Frederick William IV] with the brainless head ascended the throne, he was full of the visions of the romantic school. He wanted to be a king by divine right, and to be at the same time a popular king; to be surrounded by an independent aristocracy in the midst of an omnipotent bureaucratic administration; to be a man of peace at the head of barracks; to promote popular franchises in the medieval sense while opposing all longings of modern liberalism; to be a restorer of ecclesiastic faith while boasting of the intellectual preeminence of his subjects; to play in one word, the medieval king while acting as the King of Prussia—that abortion of the Eighteenth Century. But from 1840 to 1848, everything went the wrong way. The *Landjunkers*, who had hoped that the crowned collaborator of the *Politische Wochenblatt*, which

---

[3] "It has recently come to our attention that the citizenry of certain cities, market towns, and other places, have, of their own accord, constituted tribunals, authorities, consulates, administrations, and certain other institutions of this kind . . ., and that since in some of them . . . this has already led to abuse and malpractices . . ., we hereby, by virtue of our imperial authority, revoke these tribunals, etc., and also the concessions obtained, of our sure knowledge, by the Counts of Provence and of Forcalquier, and declare them null and void."

day by day had preached the necessity of engrafting the poetical rule of aristocracy upon the Prussian prosaic rule by the schoolmaster, the drill-sergeant, the policeman, the taxgatherer and the learned mandarin, were forced to accept the King's secret sympathies in lieu of real concessions. The middle class, still too weak to venture upon active movements, felt themselves compelled to march in the rear of the theoretical army led by Hegel's disciples against the religion, the ideas and the politics of the old world. In no former period was philosophical criticism so bold, so powerful and so popular as in the first eight years of the rule of Frederick William IV, who desired to supplant the "shallow" rationalism, introduced into Prussia by Frederic II, by medieval mysticism. The power of philosophy during that period was entirely owing to the practical weakness of the bourgeoisie; as they could not assault the antiquated institutions in fact, they must yield precedence to the bold idealists who assaulted them in the region of thought. Finally, the romantic King himself, was, after all, like all his predecessors, but the visible hand of a commonplace bureaucratic Government which he tried in vain to embellish with the fine sentiments of by-gone ages.

The revolution, or rather the counter revolution to which it gave birth, altogether changed the face of things. The *Landjunkers* turned the private crochets of the King to practical account, and succeeded in driving the Government back, not behind 1848, not behind 1815, but even behind 1807. There was an end of coy, romantic aspirations; but in their place there sprang up a Prussian House of Lords; mortmain was restored, the private jurisdiction of the manor flourished more than ever, exemption from taxation became again a sign of nobility, the policemen and the Government men had to stoop to the noblemen, all places of power were surrendered to the scions of the landed aristocracy and gentry, the enlightened bureaucrats of the old school were swept away, to be supplanted by the servile sycophants of rent-rolls and landlords, and all the liberties won by the revolution—liberty of the press, liberty of meeting, liberty of speech, constitutional representation—all these liberties were not broken up, but maintained as the privileges of the aristocratic class. On the other hand, if the bourgeoisie, in the by-gone period, had fostered the philosophical movement, the aristocracy now rooted it out and put pietism in its place. Every enlightened professor was driven away from the University and the *viri obscuri* [obscure men], the Hengstenbergs, the Stahls and *tutti-quanti* [all of them] seized upon all the educational institutions of Prussia, from the village school to the great seminary in Berlin. The police and administrative machinery were not destroyed, but converted into the mere tools of the ruling class. Even industrial liberty was struck at, and as the license system was turned into a mighty engine of patronage, intimidation and corruption, so the artisans in the great towns were again pressed into corporations, guilds, and all the other extinct forms of a departed epoch. Thus, then the dreams of the King, which had remained dreams during the eight years of his absolute regime, had all become fulfilled by the Revolution, and shone as palpable realities in the light of day during the eight years from 1850 to 1857.

But there is another side to the medal. The revolution had dispelled the ideological delusions of the bourgeoisie, and the counter revolution had done away with their political pretensions. Thus they were thrown back upon their real resources—trade and industry—and I do not think that any other people have relatively made so immense a start in this direction during the last decennial epoch as the Germans, and especially the Prussians. If you saw Berlin ten years ago, you would not recognize it now. From a stiff place of parade it has been transformed into the bustling center of German machine-building. If you travel through Rhenish Prussia and the Duchy of Westphalia, Lancashire and Yorkshire will be recalled to your memory. If Prussia cannot boast one Isaac Péreire, she possesses hundreds of Mevissens, at the head of more Crédits Mobiliers than the German Diet numbers princes.

The rage of getting rich, of going ahead, of opening new mines, of building new factories, of constructing new railways, and above all of investing in and gambling with jointstock company shares, became the passions of the day, and infected all classes from the peasant even to the coronated prince, who had once been a *Reichsunmittelbarer Fürst* [Direct Imperial Prince]. So you see the days when the bourgeoisie wept in Babylonian captivity and drooped their diminished heads, were the very days when they became the effective power of the land, while even the inner man of the overbearing aristocrat became converted into a profit-loving, money-mongering stock-jobber. If you want an example of speculative philosophy converted into commercial speculation, look at Hamburg in 1857. Did not these speculative Germans then prove masters in the swindling line? Still this upward movement of the Prussian middle class, strengthened by the general rise in the prices of commodities, and, consequently, the general fall of the fixed incomes of their bureaucratic rulers, was, of course, accompanied by the ruin of the small middle class and the concentration of the working class. The ruin of the small middle class during the last eight years is a general fact to be observed all over Europe, but nowhere so strikingly as in Germany. Does this phenomenon need any explanation? I answer in one word: Look at the millionaires of today who were the poor devils of yesterday. For one man of nothing to become a millionaire overnight, a thousand $1,000-men must have been turned into beggars during the day. The magic of the Stock Exchange will do this sort of thing in the twinkling of an eye, quite apart from the slower methods by which modern industry centralizes fortunes. A discontented small middle class and a concentrated working class have, therefore, during the last ten years, grown up in Prussia simultaneously with the bourgeoisie.

CHAPTER III

CLASS STRUGGLE AND REVOLUTION

Note

The idea of the class struggle, which Marx popularized and introduced into modern political thought, is rooted in the concept of the existence of distinct classes (see the preceding chapter) in constant antagonism to one another. Class hostility originates in material inequality, which is the result of human exploitation by the dominant class. This leads to unending conflict, as is stated in the opening sentence of the *Communist Manifesto*: "The history of all hitherto existing society is the history of class struggles."

The constant struggles of classes leads to revolution which ultimately ends in the victory of the proletariat, the class with the most numerous members. The aim of the proletariat is the establishment of a communist society wherein all classes would finally be abolished. But after the previously dominant capitalist class has been defeated by the working class, there is a transition period which Marx characterized as the "dictatorship of the proletariat."

Marx claimed that he did not invent the concept of the class struggle, which had already been recognized previously by middle-class scholars, but that he added a new slant to the whole idea. As he wrote to Joseph Weydemeyer, a German-born communist friend in New York (March 5, 1852):

> As far as I am concerned, the credit for having discovered the existence and the conflict of classes in modern society does not belong to me. Bourgeois historians presented the historical development of this class struggle, and economists showed its economic anatomy, long before I did. What I did that was new was to prove (1) that the existence of classes is linked to predeter-

mined historical phases of the development of production; (2) that the class struggle necessarily leads to the dictatorship of the proletariat; and (3) that this dictatorship itself is only the transition leading to the abolition of all classes and the establishment of a classless society.

Marx's sweeping assertion of the universality of the class struggle is hardly tenable historically. While the idea may be applicable to certain times, places and cultures, particularly in Western civilization, it is not universally true. There have been societies marked by occasional conflict; but there have also been others marked by long periods, often centuries, of quiescence and harmony. This may also be said of primitive societies, some of which have been bellicose and many others peaceful and stable.

It is also not clear how conflict and violence necessarily lead to victory by one class and the abolition of all classes. Profound social and economic changes often come about through the power of ideas, which in themselves may not be the products of violence. Marx's formulation of the universality of conflict-induced change has had a strong appeal politically, but the idea is not susceptible to objective proof.

As to Marx's position on revolution, it underwent some changes over the years. His economic studies and observations during his London period led to modifications in his theory of revolution. Greater economic knowledge and deeper political insight modified his conception of the real nature of modern revolution. The experience of living in a well-functioning parliamentary democracy, which England was, suggested to him the possibilities of social-economic reform through legislation, rather than through class violence. He did not give up his belief in ultimate revolution, but he now took a longer view, which in fact amounted to a significant shift in position. His English-influenced attitude attenuated and qualified the sweeping revolutionary assertions found in the *Communist Manifesto*.

In a little speech which he delivered (in English) on April 16, 1856, at a banquet celebrating the anniversary of the Chartist weekly, *The People's Paper,* Marx revealed the shift in his thinking. "The so-called revolutions of 1848," he said, were but pathetic episodes that merely exposed the fissures and fractures of the hard crust of European society. Those uprisings proclaimed the emancipation of the proletariat "noisily and confusedly." The real revolution, he stated, lay elsewhere. It was to be found in the products of science and technology, which were causing fundamental transformations, first in the economic structure and then unavoidably in the social superstructure. Steam, electricity, powered machinery, Marx said sardonically, with an eye to his former Paris colleagues-in-revolution, were "revolutions of a more dangerous character than even Citizens Barbès, Raspail, and Blanqui." These men were leading revolutionary politicians.

Marx now observed that the revolutionary force of science was creating new conditions and a new world in which industrialization must spread and workers must inevitably increase in numbers. At some—undefined—point in history the working class would be numerous and strong enough to make a successful bid for power. In the interim period the proletariat must be made aware that it needed to buy time and acquire training for the historic role that Marx assigned to it. With this in mind, in September, 1864, he helped to organize the International Working Men's Association—the so-called First International—of which he became the leading spirit until its dissolution in 1872. The objective of the International was not to foment revolution or conspiracy but to unite workers on an international scale and to provide them with an educational program for the future.

The International was destroyed by internal dissensions and clashing political opinions. It was discredited by the follies of the Paris Commune of 1871 and the brutal French military excesses against it. Marx read the lesson of the Commune, in which he had invested passionate hopes, namely, that no successful revolution can be made without the support of a majority. In September, 1872, at a conference in The Hague which met to dissolve the First International, Marx gave a press interview in which he came close to expressing an evolutionary idea of revolution. While revolutionary transformation was still inevitably the world-wide goal, he remarked, the method of achieving it could vary in different countries. Where democracy really existed, and the workers had political rights and knew how to use them legally, violence might not be necessary. He said: "You know that the institutions, mores, and traditions of various countries must be taken into consideration, and we do not deny that there are countries—such as America, England, and . . . perhaps also . . . Holland—where the workers can attain their goal by peaceful means."

Marx repeated this relatively evolutionary idea of revolution, with emphasis on the ripeness of social-economic conditions as a necessary prerequisite, in subsequent press interviews and statements.

A RADICAL GERMAN REVOLUTION*

From "Toward the Critique of Hegel's Philosophy of Law: Introduction," written at the end of 1843 and early 1844; published in *Deutsch-Französische Jahrbücher*, 1844

A *radical* German revolution, however, is confronted with a major difficulty.

For revolutions require a *passive* element, a *material* basis. Theory is actualized in a people only insofar as it actualizes their needs. But will the enormous discrepancy between the demands of German thought and the answers of German reality correspond to a similar discrepancy between civil society and the state and within civil society itself? Will theoretical needs be directly practical needs? It does not suffice that thought should press for actualization; reality must itself press toward thought.

But Germany has not risen to the intermediate states of political emancipation at the same time as modern nations. It has not yet reached in practice even the stages it has surmounted in theory. How could it clear with a *salto mortale* [mortal leap] not only its own limitations but at the same time those of modern nations—limitations which it must actually attain and experience as an emancipation from its own actual limitations? A radical revolution can only be a revolution of radical needs, whose preconditions and birthplaces seem to be lacking.

But though Germany followed the development of modern nations only through the abstract activity of thought, without

*From *Karl Marx on Revolution* by Saul K. Padover, pp. 422–26. Copyright © 1971 by Saul K. Padover. Used with permission of McGraw-Hill Book Co.

taking an active part in the real struggles of that development, it did, nevertheless, share the *sufferings* of that development even without sharing its enjoyment or partial satisfaction. Abstract activity on one side corresponds to abstract suffering on the other. One fine day Germany will find itself at the level of European decay before ever having reached the level of European emancipation. One will then be able to compare it to a fetishist wasting away from the diseases of Christianity.

If next we consider *German governments*, we find that, owing to the conditions of the time, the position of Germany, the standpoint of German education, and finally, driven by their own fortunate instinct, these governments combine the civilized deficiencies of the modern political order, whose advantages we [Germans] do not possess, with the barbaric deficiencies of the *ancien régime*, which we enjoy in full measure; consequently Germany must participate more and more, if not in the sense at least in the non-sense, in the political forms transcending its own status quo.

Is there, for example, another country in the world which shares so naïvely all the illusions of a constitutional system without sharing its realities, as does so-called constitutional Germany? And was it not, necessarily, a German government's brainstorm to combine the tortures of censorship with the tortures of the French September laws [1835] which presuppose freedom of the press? Just as the gods of all nations were found in the Roman pantheon, so one can find the sins of all forms of state in the Holy Roman Empire of the German nation. That this eclecticism will reach an unprecedented height is especially guaranteed by the politico-aesthetic gourmanderie of a German king [Frederick William IV], who plans to play all the roles of kingship—feudal as well as bureaucratic, absolute as well as constitutional, autocratic as well as democratic—if not in the person of the people at least in his own person, if not for the people, at least for himself. Germany, as a political system lacking the political reality of the present, will not be able to shed the specific German limitations without shedding the general limitations of the political present.

It is not radical revolution, or universal human emancipation, that is a utopian dream for Germany, but rather the partial, the *merely* political revolution that would leave the pillars of the house standing. What is the basis of a partial, a merely political revolution? It is part of civil society emancipating itself and attaining universal supremacy; it is a particular class undertaking a general emancipation of society by virtue of its special situation. This class emancipates the whole of society, but only on condition that the whole of society finds itself in the same situation as this class; for example, that it has or can easily acquire money and education.

No class of civil society can play this role without arousing an impulse of enthusiasm in itself and in the masses, an impulse in which it fraternizes and merges with society in general, identifies itself with it, and is felt and recognized as its general representative—an impulse in which its claims and rights are truly the rights and claims of society itself, in which it is actually the social head and the social heart. Only in the name of general rights of society can a particular class claim general authority. Revolutionary energy and intellectual self-confidence are not by themselves sufficient for the seizure of this emancipatory position and thereby of the political control of all spheres of society in the interests of its own sphere. For a *popular revolution* and the *emancipation of a particular class* of civil society to coincide, for *one* class to stand for the whole society, all the defects of society must conversely be concentrated in another class; a particular class must be the class of general compulsion and must incorporate the general limitation. In addition, a particular social sphere must stand for the notorious crime of the whole society, so that the emancipation of this sphere appears as general self-emancipation. For one class to be the class of emancipation par excellence, conversely another one must be the obvious class of oppression. The negative-general significance of the French nobility and the French clergy determined the positive-general significance of the adjoining and opposing bourgeois class.

But in Germany every class lacks not only the consistency, penetration, courage, and ruthlessness which could stamp it as the negative representation of society, but also that breadth of soul which identifies itself, if only momentarily, with the soul of the people—lacks that genius for inspiring material force toward political power, that revolutionary audacity which hurls at its opponent the defiant words: *I am nothing, and I should be everything*. The main feature of German morality and honor, in classes as well as individuals, is rather that modest egoism which asserts its narrowness and lets others do the same against it. The relationship of different spheres of German society is therefore not dramatic but epic. Each of them begins to be aware of itself and place itself beside the others, not as soon as it is oppressed but as soon as circumstances, without its initiative, create a social underpinning on which it can exert pressure in turn. Even the moral self-esteem of the German middle class rests only on its awareness of being the general representative of the philistine mediocrity of all the other classes. Hence not only do German kings ascend their throne *mal à propos,* but every section of civil society goes through a defeat before it celebrates victory, develops its own obstacles before it overcomes those facing it, asserts its narrow-minded nature before it can assert its generous one, so that even the opportunity of playing a great role is always gone before it has actually existed and each class is involved in a struggle with the class beneath it as soon as it begins a struggle with the class above it. Thus the princely domain struggles against the monarchy, the bureaucrat against the aristocracy, and the bourgeoisie against them all, while the proletariat is already beginning to find itself in a struggle against the bourgeois. The middle class hardly dares to conceive, from its own standpoint, the idea of emancipation, and the development of social conditions, as well as the progress of political theory, show that standpoint to be already antiquated or at least problematical.

In France it is enough that one be something in order to be everything. In Germany no one can be anything unless he renounces everything. In France partial emancipation is the basis of universal emancipation. In Germany universal emancipation is the *sine qua non* of any partial emancipation. In France it is the reality, in Germany the impossibility, of gradual emancipation which must give birth to complete freedom. In France every class in the nation is politically idealistic and experiences itself first of all not as a particular class but as a representative of the social needs of society in general. Hence the role of emancipator passes successively and dramatically to different classes of people until it finally reaches the class which actualizes social freedom, no longer assuming certain conditions which are external to man and yet are created by human society, but rather organizing all the conditions of human existence on the hypothesis of social freedom. By contrast, in Germany, where practical life is as mindless as intellectual life is impractical, no class of civil society has any need or capacity for general emancipation until it is forced to it by its immediate condition, by the material necessity, by its *very chains*.

THE ROLE OF THE PROLETARIAT

Concluding remarks of "Toward the Critique of Hegel's Philosophy of Law: Introduction," written at the end of 1843 and early 1844; published in *Deutsch-Französische Jahrbücher*, 1844. In this essay Marx first introduced his concept of the proletariat.

Where, then, is the *positive* possibility of German emancipation?

Answer: In the formation of a class with *radical chains*, a class in civil society that is not a class of civil society, a class which is the dissolution of all classes, a sphere of society which has a universal character of its universal suffering and which claims no particular right because no particular wrong but simply general wrong is perpetrated on it, which can no longer invoke a *historical* but only a *human* title, which does not one-sidedly oppose the consequences but totally opposes the premises of the German political system—a sphere, finally, which cannot emancipate itself without emancipating itself from all the other spheres of society and thereby emancipating all the other spheres of society; a sphere, in short, that is the *complete loss* of humanity and can redeem itself only through the *complete redemption of society*. This dissolution of society as a particular class is the *proletariat*.

The proletariat began to appear in Germany only as a result of the emerging industrial movement; for it is not naturally induced poverty but only artificially produced poverty, not the masses mechanically oppressed by the weight of society but the masses arising from the acute disintegration of society—preferably of the middle class—which produces the proletariat, although, needless to say, naturally induced poverty and Christian-Germanic serfdom gradually also enter its ranks.

When it heralds the *dissolution of the existing world order*, the proletariat merely expresses the secret of its own existence, because it *is* the factual dissolution of this world order. When the proletariat demands the *negation of private property*, it merely raises to the principle of society that which society has raised to its principle, what the proletariat already embodies in *itself* as the negative result of society without any assistance from it. The proletarian then finds himself in the same relation to the emerging world as the German king finds himself in relation to the existing world when the king calls the people *his* people or a horse *his* horse. In declaring the people to be his private property, he merely proclaims that the private property owner is king.

As philosophy finds its material weapons in the proletariat, so the proletariat finds in philosophy its intellectual weapons, and once the lightning of thought has struck deeply in this unsophisticated soil of the people, the emancipation of the Germans to become men will be realized.

Let us summarize the result:

The only possible practical emancipation of Germany is emancipation based on the theory proclaiming man as the highest essence of humanity. In Germany, emancipation from the Middle Ages is possible only with emancipation at the same time from the partial victories over the Middle Ages. In Germany *no* sort of bondage can be broken without *every* sort of bondage being broken. Thorough-minded Germany cannot make a revolution without making a fundamental revolution. The *emancipation of the German is the emancipation of mankind*. The *head* of this emancipation is philosophy, its *heart* is the *proletariat*. Philosophy cannot actualize itself without the elevation of the proletariat; the proletariat cannot raise itself without the actualization of philosophy.

When all the inner conditions are fulfilled, the day of German resurrection will be heralded by the crowing of the Gallic rooster.

THE CLASS NECESSITY OF REVOLUTION

From *The German Ideology*, Ch. I

Finally, from the conception of history we have sketched we obtain these further conclusions: (1) In the development of productive forces there comes a stage when productive forces and means of intercourse are brought into being, which, under the existing relationships, only cause mischief, and are no longer productive but destructive forces (machinery and money); and connected with this a class is called forth, which has to bear all the burdens of society without enjoying its advantages, which, ousted from society, is forced into the most decided antagonism to all other classes; a class which forms the majority of all members of society, and from which emanates the consciousness of the necessity of a fundamental revolution, the communist consciousness, which may, of course, arise among the other classes too through the contemplation of the situation of this class. (2) The conditions under which definite productive forces can be applied, are the conditions of the rule of a definite class of society, whose social power, deriving from its property, has its *practical*-idealistic expression in each case in the form of the State; and, therefore, every revolutionary struggle is directed against a class, which till then has been in power.[1] (3) In all revolutions up till now the mode of activity always remained unscathed and it was only a question of a different distribution of this activity, a new distribution of labour to other persons, whilst the communist revolution is directed against the preceding *mode* of activity, does away with the *labour*,[2] and abolishes the rule of all classes with the classes themselves, because it is carried through by the class which no longer counts as a class in society, is not recognised as a class, and is in itself the expression of the dissolution of all classes, nationalities, etc., within present society; and (4) Both for the production on a mass scale of this communist consciousness, and for the success of the cause itself, the alteration of men on a mass scale is necessary, an alteration which can only take place in a practical movement, a *revolution*; this revolution is necessary, therefore, not only because the *ruling* class cannot be overthrown in any other way, but also because the class *overthrowing* it can only in a revolution succeed in ridding itself of all the muck of ages and become fitted to found society anew.

---

[1] Marginal note by Marx: "The people are interested in maintaining the present state of production."

[2] The following words are crossed out in the manuscript: "... the modern form of activity under the rule of ..."

ORIGINS AND MEANING OF THE CLASS STRUGGLE

Concluding paragraphs of *The Poverty of Philosophy* (1847), which Marx wrote in French (*La Misère de la Philosophie*), a reply to Pierre Joseph Proudhon's *La Philosophie de la Misère* (1846). Translated by Progress Publishers, Moscow, 1955.

Economic conditions have in the first place transformed the masses of the people into wage-workers. The domination of capital has created for this mass of people a common situation with common interests. Thus this mass is already a class in the face of capital, but not yet for itself. In the struggle, of which we have characterized only some phases, this mass unites, constitutes itself as a class. The interests which it defends become class interests. But the struggle between class and class is a political struggle.

In the case of the bourgeoisie, we have to distinguish two phases: that during which it is constituted as a class under the regime of feudalism and absolute monarchy, and that wherein, already constituted as a class, it overthrew feudalism and monarchy in order to form society into a bourgeois society. The first of these phases was the longest and necessitated the greatest effort. The bourgeois too began with partial coalitions against the feudal lords.

Many researches have been made to trace the different historical phases through which the bourgeoisie has passed from the early city commune to its constitution as a class.

But when it becomes a question of rendering an account of the strikes, coalitions and other forms in which before our eyes proletarians effect their organization as a class, some are seized with real fear while others express a *transcendental* disdain.

An oppressed class is the vital condition of every society based on the antagonism of classes. The emancipation of the oppressed class therefore necessarily implies the creation of a new society. In order for the oppressed class to emancipate itself it must have reached a stage where the acquired productive powers and the existing social relations can no longer exist side by side. Of all the instruments of production, the greatest productive power is the revolutionary class itself. The organization of the revolutionary elements as a class supposes the existence of all the productive forces which could have been engendered in the bosom of the old society.

Does this mean that after the fall of the old society there will be a new class domination culminating in a new political power? No.

The condition of the emancipation of the working class is the abolition of all classes, just as the condition of the emancipation of the Third Estate, the bourgeois order, had been the abolition of all estates, all orders.

The working class will substitute, in the course of its development, for the old order of civil society an association which will exclude classes and their antagonism, and there will no longer be any actual political power, because political power is simply the official expression of class antagonism in civil society.

In the meantime, the antagonism between the proletariat and the bourgeoisie is a struggle between class and class, a struggle that, carried to its highest expression, signifies a total revolution. Would it, moreover, be a matter of surprise if a society, based on *antagonism* of classes, should lead ultimately to a brutal *conflict*, to a hand-to-hand struggle as its final solution?

One does not say that the social movement excludes the political one. There has never been a political movement which was not at the same time also a social one.

It is only in an order of things where there will be no classes and no class antagonism that *social evolutions* will cease to be *political revolutions*. Until then, on the eve of each general reconstruction of society, the last word of social science will always be:

"Le combat ou la mort; la lutte sanguinaire ou le néant. C'est ainsi que la question est invinciblement posée."[1]

George Sand

---

[1]"Combat or death; bloody struggle or extinction. It is thus that the question is irresistibly posed."

INTERNATIONAL CLASS CONFLICT*

A speech on Poland at the international meeting organized by the Fraternal Democrats in London, November 29, 1847, on the occasion of the seventeenth anniversary of the Polish Revolution of 1830. Published in *Deutsche-Brüsseler-Zeitung*, December 9, 1847.

The unification and fraternization of nations is a phrase used today by all parties, particularly the bourgeois free-trade men. Of course there does exist a certain kind of fraternization among the bourgeois classes of all nations. It is the fraternization of the oppressors against the oppressed, the exploiters against the exploited. Just as the bourgeois press of any one country unites and fraternizes against the proletarians of that country, despite competition and conflict among the members of the bourgeoisie themselves, so also the bourgeoisie of all countries fraternize and unite against the proletarians of all countries, despite their mutual conflict and competition in the world market. For nations really to unite, they must have a mutual interest. For their interest to become mutual, the present property relationships must be abolished, for they condition the exploitation of nations among themselves. To abolish the present property relationships is the interest of the working class. It alone, moreover, possesses the means to do it. The victory of the proletariat over the bourgeoisie is at the same time a victory over the national and industrial conflicts with which the various nations nowadays confront each other inimically. The victory of the proletariat over the bourgeoisie is therefore at the same time the liberation signal of all oppressed nations.

The old Poland is indeed lost, and we would be the last to wish its restoration. But not only is the old Poland lost. The old Germany, the old France, the old England, the whole old social system is lost. The loss of the old social system, how-

*From *Karl Marx on Revolution* by Saul K. Padover, pp. 35–36. Copyright ©1971 by Saul K. Padover. Used with permission of McGraw-Hill Book Co.

ever, is not a loss for those who have nothing to lose by it, and in all contemporary countries this is the case with the great majority. They have, rather, everything to gain through the ruin of the old system, which will lead to the creation of a new one that is no longer based on class conflicts.

Of all countries, England is the one where the conflict between proletariat and bourgeoisie is most developed. Hence the victory of the English proletarians over the English bourgeoisie is decisive for the victory of all the oppressed over their oppressors. Hence Poland is not to be freed in Poland, but in England. You Chartists therefore do not have to express pious wishes for the liberation of nations. Defeat your own internal enemies and you will have the proud awareness of having defeated the entire old social system.

THE ENGLISH AND FRENCH REVOLUTIONS

"The Bourgeoisie and the Counter-Revolution," in *Neue Rheinische Zeitung*, December 15, 1848

The *Prussian March* [1848] *revolution* must not be confused with the English Revolution of 1648 or the French of 1789.

In 1648, the bourgeoisie was allied with the modern aristocracy against the monarchy, the feudal nobility and the dominant church.

In 1789, the bourgeoisie was allied with the people against the monarchy, nobility and the dominant church.

The Revolution of 1789 had for its model (at least in Europe) only the Revolution of 1648, the Revolution of 1648 had only the revolt of the Dutch against Spain. Both revolutions were a century apart not only in time but also in content.

In both revolutions, the bourgeoisie was the class which *really* led the movement. The proletariat and the *fragments* of citizens not connected with the bourgeoisie had as yet no interests separate from those of the bourgeoisie or had not yet developed independent classes of class divisions. Hence wherever it confronted the bourgeoisie, as for example in France from 1793 to 1794, it fought for the realization of the interests of the bourgeoisie, if not quite in the same manner. The whole French Reign of Terror was nothing but a plebeian way of getting rid of the enemies of the bourgeoisie—absolutism, feudalism, philistinism.

The revolutions of 1648 and 1789 were not English or French revolutions, but revolutions in the European style. They were not the triumph of a particular class of society over the old political order; they were the proclamation of the political order of the European society. The bourgeoisie won that victory, but its victory was then that of a new social order—the victory of bourgeois over feudal property, of nationalism over provincialism, of competition over guilds, of equal inheritance over primogeniture, of the domination of the owners of land over the rule by landowners, of enlightenment over superstition, of family over family name, of industry over heroic idleness, of civic rights over medieval privileges. The Revolution of 1648 was the triumph of the seventeenth century over the sixteenth, the Revolution of 1789 was the victory of the eighteenth century over the seventeenth. These revolutions were more the expressions of the needs of the then existing world than of the mere geographic sectors of that world—England and France—in which they occurred.

In the Prussian March revolution there was nothing of all this.

REVOLUTION IN INDIA

From "The British Rule in India," *New-York Daily Tribune*, June 25, 1853

Hindostan is an Italy of Asiatic dimensions, the Himalayas for the Alps, the Plains of Bengal for the Plains of Lombardy, the Deccan for the Appenines, and the Isle of Ceylon for the Island of Sicily. The same rich variety in the products of the soil, and the same dismemberment[1] in the political configuration. Just as Italy has, from time to time, been compressed by the conqueror's sword into different national masses, so do we find Hindostan, when not under the pressure of the Mohammedan, or the Mogul, or the Briton, dissolved into as many independent and conflicting States as

[1] The Italian kingdom was proclaimed by the first Italian parliament on March 17, 1861.

it numbered towns, or even villages. Yet, in a social point of view, Hindostan is not the Italy, but the Ireland of the East. And this strange combination of Italy and of Ireland, of a world of voluptuousness and of a world of woes, is anticipated in the ancient traditions of the religion of Hindostan. That religion is at once a religion of sensualist exuberance, and a religion of self-torturing asceticism; a religion of the Lingam [the cult of Siva] and of the Juggernaut [the cult of Vishna]. . . .

These small stereotype forms of social organism have been to the greater part dissolved, and are disappearing, not so much through the brutal interference of the British tax-gatherer and the British soldier, as to the working of English steam and English Free Trade. Those family-communities were based on domestic industry, in that peculiar combination of hand-weaving, hand-spinning, and hand-tilling agriculture which gave them self-supporting power. English interference having placed the spinner in Lancashire and the weaver in Bengal, or sweeping away both Hindoo spinner and weaver, dissolved these small semi-barbarian, semi-civilized communities, by blowing up their economical basis, and thus produced the greatest, and to speak the truth, the only *social* revolution ever heard of in Asia.

Now, sickening as it must be to human feeling to witness those myriads of industrious patriarchal and inoffensive social organizations disorganized and dissolved into their units, thrown into a sea of woes, and their individual members losing at the same time their ancient form of civilization, and their hereditary means of subsistence, we must not forget that these idyllic village communities, inoffensive though they may appear, had always been the solid foundation of Oriental despotism, that they restrained the human mind within the smallest possible compass, making it the unresisting tool of superstition, enslaving it beneath traditional rules, depriving it of all grandeur and historical energies. We must not forget the barbarian egotism which, concentrating on some miserable patch of land, had quietly witnessed the ruin of empires, the perpetration of unspeakable cruelties, the massacre of the population of large towns, with no other consideration bestowed upon them than on natural events, itself the helpless prey of any aggressor who deigned to notice it at all. We must not forget that this undignified, stagnatory, and vegetative life, that this passive sort of existence evoked on the other part, in contradistinction, wild, aimless, unbounded forces of destruction and rendered murder itself a religious rite in Hindostan. We must not forget that these little communities were contaminated by distinctions of caste and by slavery, that they subjugated man to external circumstances instead of elevating man to be the sovereign of circumstances, that they transformed a self-developing social state into never changing natural destiny, and thus brought about a brutalizing worship of nature, exhibiting its degradation in the fact that man, the sovereign of nature, fell down on his knees in adoration of *Kanuman*, the monkey, and *Sabbala*, the cow.

England, it is true, in causing a social revolution in Hindostan, was actuated only by the vilest interests, and was stupid in her manner of enforcing them. But that is not the question. The question is, can mankind fulfil its destiny without a fundamental revolution in the social state of Asia? If not, whatever may have been the crimes of England she was the unconscious tool of history in bringing about that revolution.

Then, whatever bitterness the spectacle of the crumbling of an ancient world may have for our personal feelings, we have the right, in point of history, to exclaim with Goethe:

> *Sollte diese Qual uns quaelen,*
> *Da sie unsre Lust vermehrt,*
> *Hat nicht myriaden Seelen*
> *Timur's Herrschaft aufgezehrt?*[22]

THE LABOUR PARLIAMENT

"Letter to the Labour Parliament," written March 9, 1854; published in *The People's Paper*, March 18. Marx also wrote an article, "The Labor Parliament," on March 10, published in the *New-York Daily Tribune*, March 29, 1854.

[2]"Should this torture torment us,
  Since it brings us greater pleasure?
  Were not myriads of souls
   Devoured by Timur's rule?" —From Goethe's *Westostlicher Diwan: An Suleika*.

I regret deeply to be unable, for the moment at least, to leave London, and thus to be prevented from expressing verbally my feelings of pride and gratitude on receiving the invitation to sit as Honorary Delegate at the Labour Parliament.[1] The mere assembling of such a Parliament marks a new epoch in the history of the world. The news of this great fact will arouse the hopes of the working-classes throughout Europe and America.

Great Britain, of all other countries, has been developed on the greatest scale, the despotism of Capital and the slavery of Labour. In no other country have the intermediate stations between the millionaire commanding whole industrial armies and the wage-slave living only from hand to mouth so gradually been swept away from the soil. There exist here no longer, as in continental countries, large classes of peasants and artisans almost equally dependent on their own property and their own labour. A complete divorce of property from labour has been effected in Great Britain. In no other country, therefore, the war between the two classes that constitute modern society has assumed so colossal dimensions and features so distinct and palpable.

But it is precisely from these facts that the working-classes of Great Britain, before all others, are competent and called to act as leaders in the great moment that must finally result in the absolute emancipation of Labour. Such they are from the conscious clearness of their position, the vast superiority of their numbers, the disastrous struggles of their past, and the moral strength of their present.

It is the working millions of Great Britain who first have laid down—the real basis of a new society—modern industry, which transformed the destructive agencies of nature into the productive power of man. The English working-classes, with invincible energies, by the sweat of their brows and brains, have called into life the material means of ennobling labour itself, and of multiplying its fruits to such a degree as to make general abundance possible.

By creating the inexhaustible productive powers of modern industry they have fulfilled the first condition of the emancipation of Labour. They have now to realize its other condition. They have to free those wealth-producing powers from

[1] The "Labour Parliament" was a Chartist congress held in Manchester in March 1854.

the infamous shackles of monopoly, and subject them to the joint control of the producers, who, till now, allowed the very products of their hands to turn against them and be transformed into as many instruments of their own subjugation.

The labouring classes have conquered nature; they have now to conquer man. To succeed in this attempt they do not want strength, but the organization of their common strength, organization of the labouring classes on a national scale—such, I suppose, is the great and glorious end aimed at by the Labour Parliament.

If the Labour Parliament proves true to the idea that called it into life, some future historian will have to record that there existed in the year 1854 two Parliaments in England, a Parliament in London, and a Parliament at Manchester—a Parliament of the rich, and a Parliament of the poor—but that men sat only in the Parliament of the men and not in the Parliament of the masters.

Yours truly,

Karl Marx.

WORKERS' POVERTY AMIDST PROSPERITY

From "Inaugural Address of the International Working Men's Association," written in English, October 21–27, 1864, adopted November 1, and published together with the "Provisional Rules . . ." as a brochure on November 24. The International ("First International"), of which Marx was a founder, was established in London on September 28, 1864. The "Address" was Marx's first political effort since the *Communist Manifesto*, which he wrote sixteen years earlier.

Workingmen:

It is a great fact that the misery of the working masses has not diminished from 1848 to 1864, and yet this period is unrivaled for the development of industry and the growth of its commerce. In 1850 a moderate organ of the British middle class, of more than average information, predicted that if the exports and imports of England were to rise 50 percent, English pauperism would sink to zero. Alas! On April 7, 1864, the Chancellor of the Exchequer delighted his parliamentary audience by the statement that the total import and export of England had grown in 1863 "to £443,955,000! That astonishing sum is about three times the trade of the comparatively recent epoch of 1843!" With all that, he was eloquent upon "poverty." "Think," he exclaimed, "of those who are on the border of that region," upon "wages . . . not increased;" upon "human life . . . in nine cases out of ten but a struggle of existence!" He did not speak of the people of Ireland, gradually replaced by machinery in the north and by sheepwalks in the south, though even the sheep in that unhappy country are decreasing, it is true, not at so rapid a rate as the men. He did not repeat what then had been just betrayed by the highest representatives of the upper ten thousand in a sudden fit of terror. When garrote panic had reached a certain height the House of Lords caused an inquiry to be made into, and a report to be published upon, transportation and penal servitude. Out came the murder in the bulky Blue Book of 1863[1] and proved it was, by official facts and figures, that the worst of the convicted criminals, the penal serfs of England and Scotland, toiled much less and fared far better then the agricultural laborers of England and Scotland. But this was not at all. When, consequent upon the Civil War in America, the operatives of Lancashire and Cheshire were thrown upon the streets, the same House of Lords sent to the manufacturing districts a physician commissioned to investigate into the smallest possible amount of carbon and nitrogen, to be administered in the cheapest and plainest form, which on average might just suffice to "avert starvation diseases." Dr. Smith, the medical deputy, ascertained that 28,000 grains of carbon and 1,330 grains of nitrogen were the weekly allowance that would keep an average adult . . . just over the level of starvation diseases, and he found furthermore that quantity pretty nearly to agree with the scanty nourishment to which the pressure of extreme distress had ac-

[1] Report of the Commissioners Appointed to Inquire into the Operation of the Acts Relating to Transportation and Penal Servitude (Vol. I, London, 1863). The Blue Books were official government publications.

tually reduced the cotton operatives.[2] But now mark! The same learned doctor was later on again deputed by the medical officer of the Privy Council to enquire into the nourishment of the poorer laboring classes. The results of his research are embodied in the *Sixth Report on Public Health*, published by order of Parliament in the course of the present year. What did the doctor discover? That the silk weavers, the needlewomen, the kid glovers, the stocking weavers, and so forth received on an average, not even the distress pittance of the cotton operatives, not even the amount of carbon and nitrogen "just sufficient to avert starvation diseases."

"Moreover"—we quote from the report—"as regards the examined families of the agricultural population, it appeared that more than a fifth were with less than the estimated sufficiency of carbonaceous food, that more then one-third were with less than the estimated sufficiency of nitrogenous food, and that in three counties (Berkshire, Oxfordshire, and Somersetshire) insufficiency of nitrogenous food was the average diet. "It must be remembered," adds the official report, "that privation of food is very reluctantly borne, and that, as a rule, great poorness of diet will only come when other privations have preceded it. . . . Even cleanliness will have been found costly or difficult, and if there still be self-respectful endeavors to maintain it, every such endeavor will represent additional pangs of hunger." "There are painful reflections, especially when it is remembered that the poverty to which they advert is not the deserved poverty of idleness; in all cases it is the poverty of working populations. Indeed the work which obtains the scanty pittance of food is for the most part excessively prolonged." The report brings out the strange and rather unexpected fact: "That of the divisions of the United Kingdom," England, Wales, Scotland, and Ireland, "the agricultural population of England," the richest division, "is considerably the worst fed;" but that even the agricultural laborers of Berkshire, Oxfordshire, and Somersetshire fare

[2]Footnote by Marx: "We need hardly remind the reader that, apart from the elements of water and certain inorganic substances, carbon and nitrogen form the raw materials of human food. However, to nourish the human system, these simple chemical constituents must be supplied in the form of vegetable or animal substances. Potatoes, for instance, contain mainly carbon, while wheaten bread contains carbonaceous and nitrogenous substances in a due proportion."

better than great numbers of skilled indoor operatives of the East of London.

Such are the official statements published by order of Parliament in 1864, during the millennium of free trade, at a time when the Chancellor of the Exchequer told the House of Commons that "the average condition of the British laborer has improved in a degree we know to be extraordinary and unexampled in the history of any country or any age." Upon these official congratulations jars the dry remark of the official Public Health Report: "The public health of a country means the health of its masses, and the masses will scarcely be healthy unless, to their very base, they be at least moderately prosperous."

Dazzled by the "Progress of the Nation" statistics dancing before his eyes, the Chancellor of the Exchequer exclaims in wild ecstasy: "From 1842 to 1852 the taxable income of the country increased from the basis taken in 1853, 20 percent! The fact is so astonishing to be almost incredible! . . . This intoxicating augmentation of wealth and power," adds Mr. Gladstone, "is entirely confined to classes of property."

If you want to know under what conditions of broken health, tainted morals, and mental ruin that "intoxicating augmentation of wealth and power . . . entirely confined to classes of property" was, and is, being produced by the classes of labor, look to the picture hung up in the last Public Health Report of the workshops of tailors, printers and dressmakers! Compare the "Report of the Children's Employment Commission" of 1863, where it is stated, for instance, that "the potters as a class, both men and women, represent a much degenerated population, both physically and mentally," that "the unhealthy child is an unhealthy parent in his turn," that "a progressive deterioration of the race must go on," and that "the degenerescence of the population of Staffordshire would be even greater were it not for the constant recruiting from the adjacent country, and the intermarriages with more healthy races." Glance at Mr. Tremenheere's Blue Book on the "Grievances Complained by the Journeyman Bakers"! And who has not shuddered at the paradoxical statement made by the inspectors of factories, and illustrated by the Registrar General, that the Lancashire operatives, while put upon the distress pittance of food, were actually improving in health, because of their temporary exclusion by the cotton famine from the cotton factory, and that the mortality of the children was decreasing, because their mothers were now at last allowed to give them, instead of Godfrey's cordial, their own breasts.

Again reverse the medal. The income and property tax returns laid before the House of Commons on July 20, 1864, teach us that the persons with yearly incomes valued by the tax gatherer at £50,000 and upwards, had, from April 5, 1862, to April 5, 1863, been joined by a dozen and one, their number having increased in that single year from 67 to 80. The same returns disclose the fact that about 3,000 persons divide among themselves as yearly income of about £25,000-000 sterling, rather more than the total revenue doled out annually to the whole mass of agricultural laborers of England and Wales. Open the census of 1861 and you will find that the number of the male landed proprietors of England and Wales had decreased from 16,934 in 1851, to 15,066 in 1861, so that the concentration of land had grown in 10 years 11 percent. If the concentration of the soil of the country in a few hands proceeds at the same rate, the land question will become singularly simplified, as it had become in the Roman Empire when Nero grinned at the discovery that half of the province of Africa was owned by six gentlemen.

We have dwelt so long upon these facts "so astonishing to be almost incredible" because England heads the Europe of commerce and industry. It will be remembered that some months ago one of the refugee sons of Louis Philippe publicly congratulated the English agricultural laborer on the superiority of his lot over that of his less florid comrade on the other side of the Channel. Indeed, with local colors changed, and on a scale somewhat contracted, the English facts reproduce themselves in all the industrious and progressive countries of the Continent. In all of them there has taken place, since 1848, an unheard-of expansion of imports and exports. In all of them the "augmentation of wealth and power . . . entirely confined to classes of property" was truly "intoxicating." In all of them, as in England, a minority of the working classes got their real wages somewhat advanced; while in most cases the monetary rise of wages denoted no more a real access of comforts than the inmate of the metropolitan poorhouse or orphan asylum, for instance, was in the least benefited by his first necessaries costing £9 15s. 8d. In 1861 against £7 7s. 4d. in 1852. Everywhere the great mass of the working classes were sinking down to a lower depth, at the same rate at least that those above them were rising in the social scale. In all countries of Europe it has now become a truth demonstrable to every unprejudiced mind, and only denied by those whose interest it is to hedge other people in a fool's paradise, that no improvement of machinery, no appliance of science to production, no contrivances of communication, no new colonies, no emigration, no opening of markets, no free trade, nor all these things put together, will do away with the miseries of the industrious masses; but that, on the resent false base, every fresh development of the productive powers of labor must tend to deepen social contrasts and point social antagonisms. Death of starvation rose almost to the rank of an institution, during this intoxicating epoch of economical progress, in the metropolis of the British Empire. That epoch is marked in the annals of the world by the quickened return, the widening compass, and the deadlier effects of the social pest called a commercial and industrial crisis.

After the failure of the Revolution of 1848 all party organizations and party journals of the working classes were, on the Continent, crushed by the iron hand of force, the most advanced sons of labor fled in despair to the transatlantic republic, and the short-lived dreams of emancipation vanished before an epoch of industrial fever, moral marasm, and political reaction. The defeat of the Continental working classes, partly owed to the diplomacy of the English government, acting then as now in fraternal solidarity with the Cabinet of St. Petersburg, soon spread its contagious effects to this side of the Channel. While the rout of their Continental brethren unmanned the English working classes, and broke their faith in their own cause, it restored to the landlord and the money lord their somewhat shaken confidence. They insolently withdrew concessions already advertised. The discoveries of new gold lands led to an immense exodus, leaving an irreparable void in the ranks of the British proletariat. Others of its formerly active members were caught by the temporary bribe of greater work and wages, and turned into "political blacks." All the efforts made at keeping up, of remodeling, the Chartist movement failed signally; the press organs of the working class died one by one of the apathy of the masses, and in point of fact never before seemed the English working class so thoroughly reconciled to a state of political nullity. If, then, there had been no solidarity of action between the British and the Continental working classes, there was, at all events, a solidarity of defeat.

And yet the period passed since the Revolution of 1848 has not been without its compensating features. We shall here only point to two great facts.

After a thirty years' struggle, fought with most admirable perseverance, the English working classes, improving a momentaneous split between the landlords and money lords, succeeding in carrying the Ten Hours' Bill.[3] The immense physical, moral, and intellectual benefits hence accruing to the factory operatives, half-yearly chronicled in the reports of the inspectors of factories, are now acknowledged on all sides. Most of the Continental governments had to accept the English Factory Act in more or less modified forms, and the English Parliament itself is every year compelled to enlarge its sphere of action. But besides its practical import, there was something else to exalt the marvelous success of this workingmen's measure. Through their most notorious organs of science, such as Dr. Ure, Professor Senior, and other sages of that stamp, the middle class had predicted, and to their heart's content proved, that any legal restriction of the hours of labor must sound the death knell of British industry, which, vampirelike, could but live by sucking blood, and children's blood, too. In olden times, child murder was a mysterious rite of the religion of Moloch, but it was practiced on some very solemn occasions only, once a year perhaps, and then Moloch had no exclusive bias for the children of the poor. This struggle about the legal restriction of the hours of labor raged the more fiercely since, apart from frightened avarice, it told indeed upon the great contest between the blind rule of the supply and demand laws which form the political economy of the middle class, and social production controlled by social foresight, which forms the political economy of the working class. Hence the Ten Hours' Bill was not only a great practical success; it was the victory of a principle; it was the first time that in broad daylight the political economy of the middle class succumbed to the political economy of the working class.

But there was in store a still greater victory of the political

[8]The bill, limiting the work of children to ten hours a day, was passed by Parliament on June 8, 1847.

economy of labor over the political economy of property. We speak of the cooperative movement, especially the cooperative factories raised by the unassissted efforts of a few bold "hands." The value of these great social experiments cannot be overrated. By deed instead of by argument, they have shown that production on a large scale, and in accord with the behests of modern science, may be carried on without the existence of a class of masters employing a class of hands; that to bear fruit, the means of labor need not be monopolized as a means of dominion over, and of extortion against, the laboring man himself; and that, like slave labor, hired labor is but a transitory and inferior form, destined to disappear before associated labor plying its toil with a willing hand, a ready mind, and a joyous heart. In England, the seeds of the cooperative system were sown by Robert Owen; the workingmen's experiments tried on the Continent were, in fact, the practical upshot of the theories, not invented, but loudly proclaimed, in 1848.

At the same time the experience of the period from 1848 to 1864 has proved beyond doubt that, however excellent in principle and however useful in practice, cooperative labor, if kept within the narrow circle of the casual efforts of private workmen, will never be able to arrest the growth in geometrical progression of monopoly, to free the masses, nor even to perceptibly lighten the burden of their miseries. It is perhaps for this very reason that plausible noblemen, philanthropic middle-class spouters, and even keen political economists have all at once turned nauseously complimentary to the very cooperative labor system they had vainly tried to nip in the bud by deriding it as the utopia of the dreamer, or stigmatizing it as the sacrilege of the socialist. To save the industrious masses, cooperative labor ought to be developed to national dimensions, and, consequently, to be fostered by national means. Yet the lords of the land and the lords of capital will always use their political privileges for the defense and perpetuation of their economical monopolies. So far from promoting, they will continue to lay every possible impediment in the way of the emancipation of labor. Remember the sneer with which, last session, Lord Palmerston put down the advocates of the Irish Tenants' Rights Bill. The House of Commons, cried he, is a house of landed proprietors.[4] To conquer

[4] Lord Palmerston, the British prime minister, used this expression in a parliamentary debate on June 23, 1863.

political power has therefore become the great duty of the working classes. They seem to have comprehended this, for in England, Germany, Italy, and France there have taken place simultaneous revivals, and simultaneous efforts are being made at the political organization of the workingmen's party.

One element of success they possess—numbers; but numbers weigh in the balance only if united by combination and led by knowledge. Past experience has shown how disregard of that bond of brotherhood incites them to stand firmly by each other in all their struggles for emancipation, will be chastised by the common discomfiture of their incoherent efforts. This thought prompted the workingmen of different countries assembled on September 28, 1864, in public meeting at St. Martin's Hall, to found the International Association.

EMANCIPATION OF THE WORKING CLASSES

From "General Rules and Administrative Regulations of the International Working Men's Association," written (in English) in October 1864; approved by the General Council of the International on November 1, 1864

Considering,

That the emancipation of the working classes must be conquered by the working classes themselves; that the struggle for the emancipation of the working classes means not a struggle for class privileges and monopolies, but for equal rights and duties, and the abolition of all class rule;

That the economical subjection of the man of labor to the monopolizer of the means of labor—that is, the sources of life—lies at the bottom of servitude in all its forms, of all social misery, mental degradation, and political dependence;

That the economical emancipation of the working classes is therefore the great end to which every political movement ought to be subordinate as a means;

That all efforts aiming at the great end have hitherto failed labor in each country, and from the absence of a fraternal bond of union between the working classes of different countries;

That the emancipation of labor is neither a local nor a national, but a social problem, embracing all countries in which modern society exists, and depending for its solution on the concurrence, practical and theoretical, of the most advanced countries;

That the present revival of the working classes in the most industrious countries of Europe, while it raises a new hope, gives solemn warning against a relapse into the old errors, and calls for the immediate combination of the still disconnected movements;

For these reasons—

The International Working Men's Association has been founded.

It declares:

That all societies and individuals adhering to it will acknowledge truth, justice, and morality as the basis of their conduct toward each other and toward all men, without regard to color, creed, or nationality;

That it acknowledges *no rights without duties, no duties without rights*.

CLASS CONFLICT AND THE HISTORIC REVOLT AGAINST MACHINES

From *Capital*, Vol. I, Ch. 3, Sec. 3b

The class struggles of the ancient world, for example, took the form primarily of a contest between debtors and creditors, and in Rome it ended in the ruin of the plebeian debtors, who were replaced by slaves. In the Middle Ages the struggle ended with the ruin of the feudal debtors, who lost their political power with its economic basis. Nevertheless, the money form—and the relation between debtor and creditor possesses the form of a money relationship—reflects only the antagonism of deeper-lying economic conditions of existence.

From *Capital*, Vol. I, Ch. 13, Sec. 5

The struggle between capitalist and wage laborer dates back to the origins of capital itself. It raged throughout the whole period of manufacturing. But only since the introduction of machinery has the workman fought the instrument of labor itself, the material existence of capital. He revolts against this particular form of the means of production as being the material basis of the capitalist mode of production.

In the seventeenth century virtually all Europe experienced labor revolts against the so-called *Bandmühle* (also called *Schnurrmühle* or *Mühlenstuhl*), machines for weaving ribbons and trimmings.[1]

At the end of the first third of the seventeenth century, a wind sawmill, erected by a Dutchman near London, succumbed to mob excesses. Even as late as the beginning of the eighteenth century, waterdriven sawmills in England overcame the opposition of the people, supported by Parliament,

[1] Footnote by Marx: "The *Bandmühle* was invented in Germany. The Italian Abbé Lancellotti, in a work published in Venice in 1636 (L. wrote in 1629), says: 'Anton Mueller of Danzig saw there about 50 years ago a very ingenious machine which weaves 4 to 6 pieces at once; but the city council being apprehensive that this invention would turn a large number of workers into beggars, it caused the inventor to be secretly strangled or drowned.' In Leyden, this machine was not used until 1629; there the riots of the ribbon weavers compelled the magistrature to prohibit it; its use was restricted by various decrees of the States General in 1623, 1639, etc.; finally it was permitted to be used, under certain conditions, by the decree of December 15, 1661. 'In this city,' says Boxhorn (Inst. Pol., 1663) about the introduction of the *Bandmühle* in Leyden, 'about twenty years ago some people invented for weaving with which a single person could weave more and more easily than a number of persons in the same time. Hence it resulted in revolts and complaints by the weavers until the magistrature forbade the use of this machine.' The same machine was forbidden in Cologne in 1676, while its introduction in England was causing disturbances among workers. By an Imperial Edict of February 19, 1685, its use was forbidden in all Germany. In Hamburg it was burned in public by order of the magistrature. On February 9, 1719, Emperor Charles VI renewed the Edict of 1685, and not till 1765 was its use openly allowed in the Electorate of Saxony. This machine, which caused such an uproar in the world, was in fact the precursor of the spinning and weaving machines, thus of the industrial revolution of the eighteenth century. It enabled a boy entirely inexperienced in weaving to set the whole loom with all its shuttles in motion by simply moving a rod back and forth, and in its improved form produced from 40 to 50 pieces at once."

only with difficulty. No sooner had Everet in 1758 erected the first water-power-driven wool-shearing machine than it was set on fire by a mob 100,000 people who had been thrown out of work. Fifty thousand workers, who had previously lived by carding wool, petitioned Parliament against Arkwright's scribbling mills and carding machines. The enormous destruction of machinery that occurred in the English manufacturing districts during the first fifteen years of the nineteenth century, specifically caused by the employment of the steam-powered loom, and known as the Luddite movement, gave the anti-Jacobin government of a Sidmouth, Castlereagh, etc., the pretext for the most reactionary forcible measures. Both time and experience were needed for the workers to learn to distinguish between machinery and its employment by capital, and to direct their attacks from the material instruments of production to their social form of exploitation.[2]

CLASS CONFLICTS IN ANCIENT ROME

From the preface to the second German edition (1869) of *The Eighteenth Brumaire of Louis Bonaparte*. Published in New York, in German, in 1852 under the title *Der 18te Brumaire des Louis Napoleon* ("The 18th Brumaire of Louis Napoleon").

Finally, I hope that my work will contribute toward the elimination of the school phrase now current, particularly in Germany, of so-called *Caesarism*. In this superficial historical analogy one forgets the main point, namely, that in ancient Rome the class struggle took place only within a privileged minority, between the free rich and the free poor, while the great productive mass of the population, the slaves, formed the merely passive pedestal for these combatants. One forgets

---

[2] Footnote by Marx: "In old-fashioned manufactures the revolts of the workers against machinery assumes occasionally a savage character, even to this day, as witness, for example, the file cutters in Sheffield, in 1865."

Sismondi's significant pronouncement: The Roman proletariat lived at the expense of society, while modern society lives at the expense of the proletariat. With so complete a difference between the material, economic conditions of the ancient and the modern class struggles, the political figures produced by them can likewise have no more in common with each other than the Archbishop of Canterbury has with the High Priest Samuel.

THE COMING REVOLUTIONS IN ENGLAND, RUSSIA AND THE UNITED STATES

From interview in the *New York Herald*, August 3, 1871[1]

Correspondent: What is the principal object of your attack now, monarchy or capital—that is, as you understand it, monopoly.

Dr. Marx: Both. One is the natural result of the other, or, rather, both belong to an age and a civilization that are fast passing away. The feudal system, slavery, monarchy, capital, monopoly—all are bound to follow each other in rapid succession and pass from this earth. The feudal system went first, then slavery; monarchy is going fast, so fast that we scarcely considered it worthy of our steel, and monopoly, or capital, must and will follow. The struggle will be a bitter one, it will bring to the surface all the scum of humanity; it will bring in its train all the miseries that the evil passions of men let loose invariably bring, but it is necessary and inevitable. Capital will never be warned in time, and it will have to take the consequences. What better is the condition of the man who works for a dollar a day—that is, sells himself for a day at a time for just enough to support life—than that of the Negro slave who is clothed and fed by his master? Capital is, after all, only another form of slavery. . . .

---

[1] The interview, which contained many uncomplimentary comments on radical personalities, caused so much criticism that Marx felt compelled to repudiate it, at least in part. He wrote to the editor of the *Herald,* August 17, 1871: "Of what I am supposed to have said, partly I said it differently and partly I did not say it at all." But the opinions expressed sounded essentially Marxian.

Correspondent: Do you look for a civil war soon in England?

Dr. Marx: We do not intend to make war. We hope to be able to gain our rights in a legal and lawful way by act of Parliament, and it is the aristocracy and the moneyed men who will rebel. It is they who will attempt a revolution. But we have the force of numbers. We shall have the strength of intelligence and discipline. Let them put us down if they can.

Correspondent: Do you expect to succeed soon in England?

Dr. Marx: Sooner than in any other country, for the reason that labor and capital are already organized upon the co-operative system where the work is done by many skilled hands, each doing a part, and where all sorts of labor-saving machines are used on the farm and in the factory. Labor is already cooperative. It is only necessary to make the profits mutual by dividing them equally among those engaged in it, indeed of giving them all to our own. In this respect the labor system in England is much better adopted to our needs, and to the changes which must inevitably take place, than that existing in France, where land as well as manufactures are parceled out in small quantities. . . .

Correspondent: What would be your first step if you should come into power in Parliament?

Dr. Marx: Evidently to set aside the Queen, the House of Lords, and declare the republic. . . . And then we would proceed to the transformation of all great properties, such as manufactures and all the land, in favor of the state, which should work them for the benefit of every person engaged in producing. The drones, or those who would not work, should have nothing. . . .

Correspondent: Have you a strong organization in Russia?

Dr. Marx: No; it is impossible as yet. The government permits nothing of the sort. There is a revolution coming in Russia, however, slowly, but surely. There are two classes there that are greatly discontented with the recent abolition of serfdom[2]—the laborer, whose position has not been in the least improved by it, and the smaller nobility, who have been ruined by it—and these two elements, once they can be induced to work together, will overthrow that tyrannical form of gov-

---

[2] On March 3, 1861, Czar Alexander II issued an edict liberating the Russian serfs.

ernment easily when the first weak czar succeeds to the throne.

Correspondent: Have you a strong organization in the United States?

Dr. Marx: Yes, but we apprehend no violence or trouble there, unless, indeed, some of your great iron or other monopolists should take it into their hands to employ force to put down strikes, as they had done in one or two instances, in which case they will be swept away like chaff before the wind.

Correspondent: What are the principal aims of the society [First International] in the United States?

Dr. Marx: To emancipate the workingman from the rule of the politicians, and to combat monopoly in all the great many forms it is assuming there, especially that of the public lands. We want no more monstrous land grabs, no more grants to swindling railroad concerns, no more schemes for robbing the people of their birthright for the benefit of a few purse-proud monopolists. More than that, let these men be warned in time; their ill-gotten goods shall be taken from them, and their wealth shall vanish like the baseless fabric of a vision. We oppose also all protectionist measures, which make all the necessaries of life dear to the poor man merely to put money into the pockets of a few aristocrats, who know how to buy over your corrupt politicians.

THE PROLETARIAN CONQUEST OF POWER

Postscript of a letter to Friedrich Bolte (in New York), November 23, 1871*

Nota bene as to *Political Movement*.

The political movement of the working class has, naturally, as its final object the conquest of political power for itself, and this of course necessitates a previous organization of the working class developed up to a certain point, being itself an outgrowth of its economic struggles.

But on the other hand, every movement in which the working class as a *class* confronts the ruling classes and tries to

*From Saul K. Padover, ed., *Karl Marx on Revolution*, pp. 61-62. Copyright © 1971 by Saul K. Padover. Used with permission of McGraw-Hill Book Co.

vanquish them by pressure from without is a political movement. For example, an attempt in a particular factory or in a particular trade to force shorter working hours on individual capitalists through strikes, etc., is a purely economic movement; but a movement to compel the enactment of an eight-hour law, etc., is a political movement. And in this way, out of separate economic movements of the workers there grows everywhere a political movement, that is, a movement of the class, aiming to effect its interests in a general form which possesses general, socially coercive force. Although these movements presuppose a certain degree of previous organization, they are in turn equally a means for its further development.

Where the working class is not yet far enough advanced in its organization to undertake a decisive campaign against the collective power, that is, the political power, of the ruling classes, it must in any case be trained for this by constant agitation against (and a hostile attitude to) the policies of the ruling classes. Otherwise it remains a plaything in their hands, as the September [1870] revolution in France has shown and as is also proved to a certain degree by the game that Messrs. Gladstone & Co. still succeed in playing in England up to this hour.

THE PROSPECTS OF VIOLENT REVOLUTION

From interview in the *Chicago Tribune*, January 5, 1879

In a lecture lately upon the subject, he [the Reverend Joseph Cook, of Boston] said "Karl Marx is credited now with saying that, in the United States, and in Great Britain, and perhaps in France, a reform of labor will occur without bloody revolution, but that blood must be shed in Germany, and in Russia, and in Italy, and in Austria."

"No socialist," remarked the Doctor [Marx], smiling, "need predict that there will be a bloody revolution in Russia, Germany, Austria, and possibly in Italy if the Italians keep on in the policy they are now pursuing. The deeds of the French Revolution may be enacted again in those countries. That is apparent to any political student. But those revolutions will be made by the majority. No revolution can be made by a party, but by a nation. . . ."

"But you have written in sympathy with the Paris Communists."

"Certainly I have, in consideration of what was written of them in leading articles. . . . The Commune killed only about sixty people; Marshal MacMahon and his slaughtering army killed over 60,000. There has never been a movement as slandered as that of the Commune."

"Well, then, to carry out the principles of socialism do its believers advocate assassination and bloodshed?"

"No great movement," Karl answered, "has ever been inaugurated without bloodshed. The independence of America was won by bloodshed, Napoleon captured France through a bloody process, and he was overthrown by the same means. Italy, England, Germany, and every other country gives proof of this, and as for assassination it is not a new thing, I need scarcely say. Orsini tried to kill Napoleon; kings have killed more than anybody else; the Jesuits have killed; the Puritans killed at the time of Cromwell. These deeds were all done or attempted before socialism was born."

STRATEGY AND TACTICS OF THE CLASS STRUGGLE*

Marx and Engels, Circular Letter to August Bebel, Wilhelm Liebknecht, Friedrich Wilhelm Fritzsche, Bruno Geiser, Wilhelm Hasenclever, and Wilhelm Bracke, September 17–18, 1879. First drafted by Engles, it was designed for "private circulation," as Marx wrote, among the social-democratic leadership in Germany.

It is an unavoidable phenomenon, well established in the course of development, that people from the ruling class also join the proletariat and supply it with educated elements. This

*From Saul K. Padover, ed., *Karl Marx on Revolution*, pp. 507-09. Copyright © 1971 by Saul K. Padover. Used with permission of McGraw-Hill Book Co.

we have already clearly stated in the *Manifesto*. Here, however, two remarks are to be made:

First, such people, in order to be useful to the proletarian movement, must bring with them really educated elements. This, however, is not the case with the great majority of German bourgeois converts. Neither the *Zukunft*[1] nor the *Neue Gesellschaft*[2] has provided anything to advance the movement one step. They are completely deficient in real, factual, or theoretical material. Instead, there are efforts to bring superficial socialist ideas into harmony with the various theoretical viewpoints which the gentlemen from the universities, or from wherever, bring with them, and among whom one is more confused than the other, thanks to the process of decomposition in which German philosophy finds itself today. Instead of first studying the new science [Marxist socialism] thoroughly, everyone relies rather on the viewpoint he brought with him, makes a short cut toward it with his own private science, and immediately steps forth with pretensions of wanting to teach it. Hence there are among those gentlemen as many viewpoints as there are heads; instead of clarifying anything, they only produce arrant confusion—fortunately, almost always only among themselves. Such educated elements, whose guiding principle is to teach what they have not learned, the party can well dispense with.

Second, when such people from other classes join the proletarian movement, the first demand upon them must be that they do not bring with them any remnants of bourgeois, petty-bourgeois, etc., prejudices, but that they irreversibly assimilate the proletarian viewpoint. But those gentlemen, as has been shown, adhere overwhelmingly to petty-bourgeois conceptions. In so petty-bourgeois a country as Germany, such conceptions certainly have their justification, but only *outside* the Social-Democratic Labor party. If the gentlemen want to build a social-democratic petty-bourgeois party, they have a full right to do so; one could then negotiate with them, conclude agreements, etc., according to circumstances. But in a labor party they are a falsifying element. If there are grounds which necessitate tolerating them, it is a duty *only* to tolerate them, to allow them no influence in party leadership, and to keep in mind that a break with them is only a matter

---

[1] *Zukunft*, a Berlin fortnightly.
[2] *Neue Gesellschaft*, a Zurich monthly.

of time. In any case, the time seems to have come. It is inconceivable to us how the party can any longer tolerate in its midst the authors of that article.[3] If the party leadership more or less falls into the hands of such people, the party will simply be emasculated and, with it, an end to the proletarian order.

So far as we are concerned, after our whole past only one way is open to us. For nearly forty years we have raised to prominence the idea of the class struggle as the immediate driving force of history, and particularly the class struggle between the bourgeoisie and the proletariat as the great lever of the modern social revolution; hence we can hardly go along with people who want to strike this class struggle from the movement. At the founding of the International, we expressly formulated the battle cry: The emancipation of the working class must be the work of the working class itself. We cannot, therefore, go along with people who openly claim that the workers are too ignorant to emancipate themselves but must first be emancipated from the top down, by the philanthropic big and petty bourgeois. Should the new party [socialist] organ take a position that corresponds with the ideas of those gentlemen, become bourgeois and not proletarian, then there is nothing left for us, sorry as we should be to do so, than to speak out against it and publicly dissolve the solidarity within which we have hitherto represented the German party abroad. But we hope it will not come to that.

This letter is to be communicated to all the five members of the Committee in Germany, as well as Bracke. . . .

On our part, we have no objection to this being communicated to the gentlemen in Zurich.

---

[3] "Retrospects on the Socialist Movement in Germany," in *Jahrbuch für Sozialwissenschaft und Sozialpolitik*, August, 1879, published in Zurich. The article, written by Karl Hoechberg, Eduard Bernstein, and Carl August Schramm, advocated a transformation of the Social-Democratic party from a revolutionary to a reformist one.

THE TIME IS NOT YET RIPE FOR REVOLUTION

Letter to Ferdinand Domela Nieuwenhuis, February 22, 1881.* In a letter of January 6, 1881, the Dutch socialist (later anarchist) leader Nieuwenhuis had asked Marx what political and social action socialists should take if they should seize power.

Honored Party Comrade:

The "question" before the forthcoming Zurich Congress, which you report to me, seems to me to be a blunder. What is to be done *immediately* at a given, exact moment in the future depends entirely on the historical circumstances. The question you posed exists in the land of mist; it is actually a phantom problem to which the only answer must be a critique of the question itself. We cannot solve an equation which does not include the elements of its solution in its data. For the rest, the dilemmas of a government that suddenly emerges as a result of a popular victory are in no way specifically "socialistic." Quite the contrary. The victorious bourgeois politicians feel immediately embarrassed by their "victory," while the socialist can at least proceed without embarrassment. Of one thing you can be sure—a socialist government does not come to the helm of a country without such developed conditions that it can take the necessary measures without frightening the bulk of the bourgeoisie, which is the first desideratum—time for lasting action—to be gained.

You may perhaps point out to me the example of the Paris Commune; but apart from the fact that this was merely a revolt of a city under exceptional conditions, the majority of the Commune was in no way socialist, and could not be. Nevertheless, with a minimum quantity of common sense, it could have achieved a compromise with the Versailles government useful for the whole mass of the people—which was then attainable. The appropriation of the Bank of France

---

*From Saul K. Padover, ed., *Karl Marx on Revolution*, pp. 66-67. Copyright © 1971 by Saul K. Padover. Used with permission of McGraw-Hill Book Co.

alone would have put a fearful end to the Versailles machinations, etc., etc.

The general demands of the French bourgeoisie before 1789 were, *mutatis mutandis,* approximately as well established as the present-day demands of the proletariat in all countries with a capitalist form of production. But the way the demands of the French bourgeoisie were carried out—did any Frenchman of the eighteenth century have, *a priori,* the slightest idea about it? The doctrinal and necessarily fantastic anticipation of the action program of a revolution of the future emerges only from contemporary struggle. The dream of the imminent destruction of the world inspired the early Christians in their struggle with the Roman world empire and gave them a certainty of victory. Scientific insight into the unavoidable and continuing disintegration of the dominant order of society, constantly visible before our eyes, and the increasingly passionate whipping of the masses by the old government specters, as well as the gigantically advancing positive development of the means of production—all this serves as a guarantee that at the moment of outbreak of a real proletarian revolution its very conditions (even if surely not idyllic ones) will directly bring forth the next *modus operandi.*

According to my conviction, the critical conjunction of a new international workers' association does not yet exist; I therefore consider all labor congresses, particularly socialist congresses, insofar as they are not related directly to specific conditions in this or that nation, as useless, even harmful. They will always be dissipated in a lot of banal, chewed-over generalities.

Your most devoted,

KARL MARX

CHAPTER IV

COMMUNISM AND SOCIALISM

Note

In Marx's youth, the term "communism" was used loosely and ambiguously by many utopian idealists. The word was often used in the same context as "socialism," the two terms expressing more or less the same hopes, aspirations, and programs.

Marx began to read the writings of such popular utopians as Charles Fourier, Pierre Joseph Proudhon, Claude Henri de Saint-Simon, and their followers at the age of about twenty-three or twenty-four. He found their writings interesting but not persuasive. As he wrote to Arnold Ruge in September 1843 (see the letter in this chapter), he thought their ideas too dogmatic and too anti-humanist. But he soon changed his position, and by the end of 1844 or early 1845 he adopted communism as he, with the help of Engels, shaped and formulated it. In the course of developing his communist ideas, which found their most eloquent early expression in the *Communist Manifesto*, Marx rejected the French utopians, particularly Proudhon, his most famous rival. The lengthy critique of Proudhon is included in this volume.

Marx's own idea of communism can be seen from the program he outlined for Germany. About one month after the publication of the *Manifesto*, in March 1848, Marx and Engels published a Communist Party program for Germany. It included "demands" for: a working-class army; abolition of feudal dues; confiscation of landed estates and peasant farms; nationalization of banks and means of transportation; equalization of all salaries; separation of church and state; limitation of the rights of inheritance; introduction of "heavy progressive taxation"; establishment of national workshops, guaranteeing work for all; and universal, free education.

Nearly three decades later, Marx developed some of the above ideas in the Gotha Program for the German Social Democratic Party. At the end of 1878, in an interview he gave to the correspondent of the *Chicago Tribune* (published on January 5, 1879), Marx dictated a "socialist" program for Germany: universal, secret male suffrage; direct legislation by the people; universal militia duty, but no standing army; abolition of press laws; free legal remedies; obligatory free education; freedom of science and religion; abolition of indirect taxes; reduction of working hours for men and women; and abolition of child labor.

This final view of "socialism" does contain elements found in democracies.

"COMMUNISM AND THE AUGSBURG *ALLGEMEINE ZEITUNG*"*

In *Rheinische Zeitung,* October 16, 1842. This article was written on the day Marx was appointed editor of the paper. It was his first published essay on communism.

Cologne, October 15

Issue No. 284 of the Augsburg paper is so inept as to find the *Rheinische Zeitung* to be a Prussian *communist*—not a real communist, to be sure, but still one that fantastically flirts with and platonically ogles communism.

Whether this ill-mannered fantasy of the Augsburger is unselfish or whether this idle trick of its excited imagination is connected with speculation and diplomatic affairs, the reader may decide—after we have presented the alleged corpus delicti.

The *Rheinische Zeitung,* they say, has printed a communistic essay on Berlin family dwellings,[1] accompanied by the following comment: This report "might not be without interest for the history of this important issue." From this it fol-

*From *Karl Marx on Revolution* by Saul K. Padover, pp. 3-6. Copyright © 1971 by Saul K. Padover. Used with permission of McGraw-Hill Book Co.

lows, according to the Augsburger's logic, that the *Rheinische Zeitung* "served up such dirty linen with approval." Thus, for example, if I say: "The following report from *Mefistofeles*[2] about the household affairs of the Augsburg paper might *not be without interest* for the history of this pretentious lady," do I thereby recommend dirty "material" from which the Augsburg lady could tailor a colorful wardrobe? Or should we not consider communism an important current issue because it's not a current issue privileged to appear at court, since it wears dirty linen and does not smell of rosewater?

But the Augsburg paper has reason to be angry at our misunderstanding. The importance of communism does not lie in its being a current issue of highest moment for France and England. Communism has "European significance," to repeat the phrase used by the Augsburg paper. One of its Paris correspondents, a convert who treats history the way a pastry cook treats botany, has recently had the notion that monarchy, in its own fashion, must seek to appropriate socialist-communist ideas. Now you understand the displeasure of the Augsburg paper, which will never forgive us for revealing communism to the public in its *unwashed* nakedness; now you understand the sullen irony that tells us: So you recommend communism, which once had the fortunate elegance of being a phrase in the Augsburg paper!

The second reproach to the *Rheinische Zeitung* deals with the conclusion of a report on the communist speeches given at the congress in Strasbourg, because the two stepsister papers had so divided the booty that the Rhineland sister took the proceedings and the Bavarian one the fruits of the Strasbourg scholars. The exact wording of the incriminating passage is: "It is with the middle class today as it was with the nobility in 1789. At that time the middle class claimed the privileges of the nobility and got them; *today the class which possesses nothing demands to share in the wealth of the middle classes that are now in control.* Today, however, the middle class is better prepared for a surprise attack than the nobility

[1] On September 30, 1842, the *Rheinische Zeitung* reprinted an article from *Die Junge Generation* ("The Young Generation"), a weekly edited by the communist Wilhelm Weitling.

[2] *Mefistofeles*, a journal published in Leipzig between 1842 and 1844.

was in 1789, and it is to be expected that the problem will be solved peacefully."

That Sieyès' prophecy has come true and that the *tiers état* [Third Estate] has become everything and wants to be everything—all this is recognized with the most sorrowful indignation by Buelow-Cummerow, by the former *Berliner Politische Wochenblatt* [*Berlin Political Weekly*], by Dr. Kosegarten, and by all the feudalistic writers. That the class that today possesses nothing demands to share in the wealth of the middle classes is a fact that, without the Strasbourg speeches and the silence of the Augsburg paper, is clearly recognized in the streets of Manchester, Paris, and Lyon. Does the Augsburger really believe that indignation and silence refute the facts of the time? The Augsburger is impertinent in fleeing. The Augsburg paper runs away from captious issues and believes that the dust it stirs up, and the nervous invectives it mutters in its flight, will blind and confuse the uncomfortable issue as well as the comfortable reader.

Or is the Augsburger angry at our correspondent's expectation that the undeniable collision will be solved in a "peaceful way"? Or does the Augsburger reproach us for not having given immediately a good prescription and not having put into the surprised reader's pocket a report as clear as daylight on the solution of the enormous problem? We do not possess the art of mastering problems which two nations are working on with one phrase.

But my dear, best Augsburger! In connection with communism, you give us to understand that Germany is now poor in independent people, that nine-tenths of the better educated youth are begging the state for their future bread, that our rivers are neglected, that shipping has declined, that our once-flourishing commercial cities have faded, that in Prussia very slow progress is made toward free institutions, that the surplus of our population helplessly wanders away and ceases to be German among foreign nations—and for all these problems there is not a single prescription, no attempt to become "clearer about the means of achieving" the great act that is to redeem us from all these sins! Or don't you expect a peaceful solution? It almost seems that another article in the same issue, date-lined from Karlsruhe, points in that direction when you pose for Prussia the insidious question of the Customs Union: "Does anyone believe that such a crisis would pass like a brawl over smoking in the Tiergarten?" The reason you offer for your disbelief is *communistic:* "Let a crisis break out in industry; let millions in capital be lost; let thousands of workers go hungry." How inopportune our "peaceful expectation," after you had decided to let a bloody revolution break out! Perhaps for this reason, your article on Great Britain by your own logic points approvingly to the demagogic physician, Dr. M'Douall, who emigrated to America because "nothing can be done with this royal family after all."

Before we part from you, we would, in passing, like to call your attention to your own wisdom—your method which, with no shortage of phrases but without even a harmless idea here and there, makes you nevertheless *speak up.* You find that the polemic of Mr. Hennequin in Paris against parceling out the land puts him in surprising harmony with the *Autonomes* [aristocratic landowners]! Surprise, says Aristotle, is the beginning of philosophizing. You have ended at the beginning. Otherwise, would the surprising fact have escaped you that in Germany communistic principles are spread, not by the liberals, but by your reactionary friends?

Who speaks of handicraft corporations? The reactionaries. The artisan class is to form a state within a state. Do you find it extraordinary that such ideas, couched in modern terms, thus read: "The state should transform itself into an artisan class"? If the state is to be a state for the artisan, but if the modern artisan, like any modern man, understands and can understand the state only as a sphere shared by all his fellow citizens—how can you synthesize both of these ideas in any other way except in an *artisan state?*

Who polemicizes about parceling out the land? The reactionaries. A recently published feudalistic writing (Kosegarten on land parceling) went so far as to call private property a privilege. This is Fourier's principle. Once there is agreement on principles, may not there then be disagreement over consequences and implications?

The *Rheinische Zeitung,* which cannot concede the theoretical reality of communist ideas even in their present form, and can even less wish or consider possible their practical realization, will submit these ideas to a thorough criticism. If the Augsburg paper demanded and wanted more than slick phrases, it would see that writings such as those of Leroux, Considérant, and above all Proudhon's penetrating work can be criticized, not through superficial notions of the moment, but only after long and deep study. We consider such "theoretical" works the more seriously as we do not agree with the Augsburg paper, which finds the "reality" of communist ideas not in Plato but in some obscure acquaintance who, not without some merit in some branches of scientific research, gave up the entire fortune that was at his disposal at the time and polished his confederates' dishes and boots, according to the will of Father Enfantin. We are firmly convinced that it is not the *practical attempt*, but rather the *theoretical application* of communist ideas, that constitutes the real *danger*; for practical attempts, even those on a large scale, can be answered with cannon as soon as they become dangerous, but ideas, which conquer our intelligence, which overcome the outlook that reason has riveted to our conscience, are chains from which we cannot tear ourselves away without tearing our hearts; they are demons that man can overcome only by submitting to them. But the Augsburg paper has never come to know the troubled conscience that is evoked by a rebellion of man's subjective wishes against the objective insights of his own reason, *because it possesses neither reason nor insight nor conscience.*

"COMMUNISM IS A DOGMATIC ABSTRACTION"

From letter to Arnold Ruge (in Dresden), September 1843*

I am pleased that you have decided to turn your thoughts from the past to undertake a new venture.[1] So be it in Paris, the ancient university of philosophy, *absit omen* [may there be no ill omen], and the new capital of the new world. Necessity finds a way. Hence I do not doubt that all obstacles, whose gravity I do not ignore, will be overcome.

Whether the venture comes to fruition or not, I will be in Paris at the end of this month, since the atmosphere here enslaves and I see absolutely no room in Germany for any free activity.

*From *Karl Marx on Revolution* by Saul K. Padover, pp. 515-18. Copyright © 1971 by Saul K. Padover. Used with permission of McGraw-Hill Book Co.

[1] The publication of *Deutsch-Französische Jahrbücher*, of which only one issue appeared.

In Germany everything is suppressed violently; a true anarchy of spirit, a regime of stupidity itself, has broken out, and Zurich obeys Berlin's orders. It is therefore increasingly evident that one has to look for a new rallying point for truly thoughtful and independent minds. I am convinced that our plan will correspond to the real needs, and the real needs must end in their fulfillment. Hence I have no doubt about the venture, if it is undertaken seriously.

The internal difficulties seem to be almost greater than the external obstacles. If there is no doubt about the "whence," there is the more confusion about the "whither." It is not only that a general anarchy has broken out among the reformers, but also that, as everybody would admit, none of them has an exact view of what the future should be. Still, this is the advantage of the new direction, that we do not anticipate the world dogmatically but we first try to discover the new world from a critique of the old one. Until now the philosophers have had the solution of all riddles lying on their lecterns, and the stupid exoteric world only had to open its mouth for the ready-roasted pigeons of absolute knowledge to fly in. Philosophy has become secularized, and the striking proof thereof is that the philosophical consciousness itself has been pulled into the torment of struggle not only externally but also internally. If the construction and preparation of the future is not our business, then it is the more certain what we do have to achieve—I mean the *ruthless criticism of all that exists,* ruthless also in the sense that criticism does not fear its results and even less so a struggle with the existing powers.

I am therefore not in favor of raising a dogmatic flag; quite the contrary. We should try to help the dogmatists clarify their ideas. Thus communism, in particular, is a dogmatic abstraction, and by this I do not mean some fanciful or possible communism, but the real, existing communism, as Cabet, Dézamy, Weitling, etc., teach and conceive it. This communism is itself separate from the humanist principle, merely a phenomenon affected by its opposite, private existence. Hence abolition of private property and communism are by no means identical, and communism has different doctrines from those of Fourier, Proudhon, etc., not accidentally, but necessarily in contradiction to them, because it is itself only a special, one-sided consummation of the socialist principle.

And the whole socialist principle is again only one aspect

of *reality* as it affects the genuine human being. We must likewise concern ourselves with the other aspect, the theoretical existence of man—that is, religion, science, etc.—and make it the object of our criticism. In addition, we want to have an effect on our contemporaries, and especially our German contemporaries. One asks: How is one to achieve that? Two facts cannot be denied. First religion and then politics are the subjects that form the main interest of present-day Germany. We have to connect with these, but not to confront them with some ready-made system like the *Voyage en Icarie*.[2]

Reason has always existed, but not always in reasonable form. Hence the critic can choose any form of theoretical and practical consciousness and develop the true reality in its "ought" and final goal out of its own forms of existing reality. In regard to real life, the political state, even where it is not yet permeated with socialist demands, contains the demands of reason in all its *modern* forms. And it does not stop with that. Everywhere it subordinates reason to reality. But everywhere also it falls into the contradiction between its ideal destiny and its presuppositions.

Out of this conflict of the political state within itself, therefore, social truth can develop everywhere. Just as *religion* is the index to the theoretical struggles of mankind, so the *political state* is the index to its practical ones. Hence the political state expresses within its form *sub specie rei publicae* [as a special political form] all social conflicts, needs, truths, etc. It is therefore definitely not beneath the *hauteur des principes* [level of principles] to make the most specialized political questions—say, the difference between a *ständisch* [estate] system and a representative system—the object of criticism. For this question expresses only in a *political* way the difference between government by the people and the rule of private property. Hence the critic not only can but must enter into these political questions (which in the view of the crude socialists is beneath all dignity). In demonstrating the advantage of the representative system over the estate one, the critic interests a large part of the people in a *practical* subject. In raising the representative system out of its own political form to a general form and validating the true

[2] By Étienne Cabet, published in 1842.

significance that lies at its foundation, he forces that part to rise above itself, for its victory is at the same time its loss.

Hence nothing prevents us from tying our criticism in with a criticism of and participation in politics, that is, in *real* conflicts, and in identifying with them. Thus we do not confront the world dogmatically with a new principle, proclaiming: Here is the truth, kneel before it! We develop for the world new principles out of the principles of the world. We do not say to the world: Give up your struggles, they are stupid stuff; we will provide you with the true watchword of the struggle. We merely demonstrate to the world why it really struggles, and consciousness is something that it *must* adopt, even if it does not want to do so.

The reform of the world's consciousness consists only in making it aware of its perception, in waking it up from its own dream, in explaining to it its own actions. Our whole purpose can consist of nothing else than in bringing out religious and political questions in self-aware human form, as Feuerbach did in his critique of religion.

Our slogan must therefore be reform of consciousness, not through dogmas but through analysis of the mystic consciousness which is unclear to itself, regardless of whether it is religious or political. It will then be shown that the world has long possessed the dream of a thing, of which it only needs to have awareness in order to possess it in reality. It will be shown that what is involved is not a great stroke of thought between past and future, but a *consummation* of the ideas of the past. It will finally be shown that humanity begins no *new* task, but with consciousness consummates its old task.

Hence we can summarize the tendency of our paper in one word: Self-understanding (critical philosophy) of our epoch's struggles and desires. This is a task for the world and for us. It can only be the labor of combined forces. What is involved is a *confession*, and nothing else. In order to have its sins pardoned, mankind only needs to interpret them for what they are.

A CRITIQUE OF PROUDHON*

Letter to Pavel V. Annenkov (in Paris), Brussels, December 28, 1846 (in French). Pierre Joseph Proudhon was a leading French social theorist whose work, especially *What Is Property?* (1840), Marx at first admired and later criticized. In this and the following letter, Marx brings out his sharp points of disagreement with Proudhon, a thinker popular with contemporary radicals, particularly in France.

Dear Mr. Annenkov:

You would have received my answer to your letter of November 1st long ago but for the fact that my bookseller sent me M. Proudhon's book, *The Philosophy of Poverty*, only last week. I have gone through it in two days in order to be able to give you my opinion of it at once. Since I have read the book very hurriedly, I cannot go into details but can only convey to you the general impression it has made on me. If you wish, I could go into details in a second letter.

I must confess to you frankly that I find the book on the whole bad, very bad. You yourself in your letter make fun over the "morsel of German philosophy"[1] which M. Proudhon parades in his formless and pretentious work, but you assume that the economic statement has not been infect-

---

*From *Karl Marx on History and People* by Saul K. Padover, pp. 32-42. Copyright © 1977 by Saul K. Padover. Used with permission of McGraw-Hill Book Co.

[1] In his letter to Marx, November 1, 1846, Annenkov wrote about Proudhon's book: *"Je vous avoue que le plan même de l'ouvrage me parait plutôt un jeu d'esprit, auquel on a montré un coin de la philosophie allemande, qu-une chose produite naturellement par le sujet et les nécessités de son développement logique."*

("I admit to you that even the plan of the work appeared to me to be a witticism showing a morsel of German philosophy, rather than something naturally produced by the subject and the necessities of its logical development.")

ed by the philosophic poison. I, too, am far from imputing the faults in the economic argument to M. Proudhon's philosophy. M. Proudhon does not give us a false criticism of political economy because he possesses a ridiculous philosophy, but he gives us a ridiculous philosophy because he fails to understand the contemporary social conditions in their concatenation [*engrènement*]—to use a word which, like much else, M. Proudhon has borrowed from Fourier.

Why does M. Proudhon talk about God, about universal reason, about the impersonal reason of humanity which never errs, which remains ever the same and of which one needs to have only a proper awareness in order to know the truth? Why does he spin feeble Hegelianism to give himself the air of a strong thinker?

He himself provides the clue to the enigma. M. Proudhon sees in history a definite series of social developments; he finds progress realized in history; he finds, finally, that men, as individuals, did not know what they were doing and were mistaken about their own movement, that is, that their social development seems at first glance to be distinct, separate, and independent from their individual development. He cannot explain these facts, and the hypothesis of the universal reason revealing itself is the purest invention. Nothing is easier than to invent mystical causes, that is, phrases, which lack common sense.

But when M. Proudhon confesses that he understands nothing about the historical development of humanity—and he admits this by using such high-sounding terms as universal reason, God, etc.—is he not thereby implicitly and necessarily admitting that he is incapable of understanding *economic development*?

What is society, whatever its form may be? It is the product of men's reciprocal activity. Are men free to choose this or that form of society? Not at all. Postulate a particular state of development of man's productive forces, and you will get a particular form of commerce and consumption. Postulate particular stages of development of production, commerce, and consumption, and you will get a corresponding social order, a corresponding organization of family, ranks, and classes—in short, a corresponding civil society [*société civile*]. Presuppose such a society, and you will get a corresponding political state [*état politique*] which is but the official expression of civil society. This is something M.

Proudhon will never understand, because he thinks he is doing something great when he appeals from the State to society—that is, from the official résumé of society to official society.

It is superfluous to add that men are not free to choose their *productive forces*—which are the basis of their whole history—for every productive force is an acquired force, the product of former activity. The productive forces are, therefore, the result of applied human energy, but this energy is itself limited by the circumstances in which men find themselves, by the productive forces already acquired, by the societal form which antecedes them, which they do not create, and which is the product of the previous generation. Thanks to the simple fact that every new generation finds itself in possession of the productive forces acquired by the preceding one which serve it as the raw material for new production, a connection arises in human history, a history of humanity begins, which is all the more a history of humanity in that the productive forces of men and, consequently, their social relations are extended. The necessary consequence is: The social history of men is never anything but the history of their individual development, whether they are conscious of it or not. Their material relations are the basis of all their relations. These material relations are nothing but the necessary forms in which their material and individual activity is realized.

M. Proudhon confuses ideas with things. Men never relinquish what they have won, but this does not mean that they never give up the societal form in which they had acquired certain definite productive forces. On the contrary. In order not to lose results already attained and not to forfeit the fruits of civilization, men are obliged, the moment when the means of their intercourse [French: *commerce*] no longer correspond to the acquired productive forces, to change all their traditional social forms. I am using the word "commerce" in the widest sense, as one uses *"Verkehr"* in German. For example: Privilege, the institution of guilds and corporations, the regulatory system of the Middle Ages, all these were societal relations corresponding solely to the acquired productive forces and to the social conditions which had preceded them, and from which those institutions had arisen. Under the protection of this associative and regulatory regime, capital was accumulated, overseas trade was developed, colonies were founded. But men would have forfeited these fruits if they had attempted to retain the forms under whose shelter these fruits had ripened. Thus came two thunderclaps—the revolutions of 1640 and of 1688 [in England]. All old economic forms, the social relations corresponding to them, the political system [*état politiqu.*] which was the official expression of the old society, were destroyed in England. The economic forms in which men produce, consume, and exchange are thus *transitional and historical*. With the acquisition of new productive forces, men change their method of production, and with the method of production they change all the economic relations, which are merely the necessary conditions of this particular method of production.

This is precisely what M. Proudhon has not understood and still less demonstrated. Incapable of following the real movement of history, M. Proudhon produces a phantasmagoria which claims to be dialectical. He does not feel the need to speak of the seventeenth, eighteenth, or nineteenth centuries, for his history takes place in the misty realm of imagination and is above time and place. In short, this is old Hegelian junk [*vieillerie*]; it is not history, not profane history—the history of man—but sacred history, the history of ideas. From this point of view, man is only the instrument which the Idea or the eternal reason uses for its unfolding. The *evolutions* of which M. Proudhon speaks are the sort of evolutions which are consummated in the mystical womb of the absolute Idea. If you tear the veil from this mystical language, you see that what M. Proudhon offers us is the order in which economic categories arrange themselves inside his own mind. It will not require any great exertion on my part to prove to you that it is the order of a very disorderly mind.

M. Proudhon opens his book with a dissertation on *value*, which is his pet subject. I will not examine this topic this time.

The series of economic evolutions of eternal reason begins with the *division of labor*. For M. Proudhon the division of labor is a perfectly simple thing. But was not the caste regime a particular division of labor? And was not the guild system also another division of labor? And is not the division of labor in the period of manufactures, which in England began in the middle of the seventeenth century and ended toward the end of the eighteenth, totally different from the division of labor in large-scale modern industry?

M. Proudhon is so far removed from the truth that he neglects what even the profane economists do. When he talks about the division of labor, he does not think it necessary to mention the world *market*. Good! Yet must not the division of labor in the fourteenth and fifteenth centuries—when there were as yet no colonies, when America did not yet exist for Europe, when East Asia existed only through the medium of Constantinople—have been fundamentally different from what it was in the seventeenth century when colonies were already developed?

And that is not all. What else is the whole internal organization of nations, all their international relations, than the expression of a particular division of labor? And must these not change when the division of labor changes?

M. Proudhon has so little understood the problem of the division of labor that he does not even mention the separation of city and country, which, in Germany for example, took place between the ninth and twelfth centuries. For M. Proudhon this separation would be an eternal law, since he knows neither its origin nor its development. Hence throughout his book he speaks as if this creation of a particular mode of production would endure until the end of time. Everything that M. Proudhon says about the division of labor is only a résumé, and a very superficial, very incomplete résumé at that, of what Adam Smith and a thousand others have said before him.

The second evolution is *machinery*. To M. Proudhon, the connection between the division of labor and machinery is completely mystical. Every kind of division of labor has its specific instruments of production. For example, from the middle of the seventeenth to the middle of the eighteenth century everything was made by hand. Men had instruments, even very complicated ones—work-benches, ships, levers, etc.

Thus there is nothing more ridiculous than to derive machinery from the division of labor in general.

I may also remark in passing that while M. Proudhon has not understood the historical origins of machinery, he has understood its development even less. One can say that up to 1825—the period of the first worldwide crisis—the demands of consumption in general increased more rapidly than production, and the development of machinery was a necessary consequence of the needs of the market. Since 1825 the invention and application of machinery has been simply the result of the war between entrepreneurs and workers. And this is true only of England. As for European nations, they were compelled to adopt machinery by the competition of the English in their domestic as well as in the world's market. In North America, finally, the introduction of machinery was due both to competition with other countries and to the lack of workers, that is, to the disproportion between the population of North America and its industrial needs. From these facts you can see what sharpness of mind M. Proudhon develops when he conjures up the specter of competition as the third evolution, as the antithesis of machinery!

Finally, it is altogether truly absurd to treat *machinery* as an economic category, on a level with division of labor, competition, credit, etc.

Machinery is no more an economic category than the ox that draws the plow. The current *application* of machinery belongs to the relationship of our present economic system, but the way in which the machinery is utilized is totally distinct from the machinery itself. Powder remains powder, whether one uses it to wound a man or to dress his wounds.

M. Proudhon surpasses himself when he allows competition, monopoly, taxes, or police, the balance of trade, credit, and property to develop inside his head in the order I have quoted them. Virtually the whole credit system was developed in England in the eighteenth century, before the discovery of machinery. Public credit was only a new method of increasing taxes and of satisfying the new demands created by the rise to power of the bourgeois class.

The last category in M. Proudhon's system, finally, is constituted by *property*. In the real world, on the other hand, the division of labor and all M. Proudhon's other categories are societal relations, constituting, in their totality, what is today called *property;* outside these relations, bourgeois property is nothing but a metaphysical or juridical illusion. The property of a different epoch, feudal property, develops under entirely different social relations. When M. Proudhon presents property as an independent relationship, he commits more than a mistake in method; he clearly shows that he has not grasped the bond which holds together all forms of *bourgeois* production, that he has not understood the *historic and transient* character of the forms of production in a particular epoch. M. Proudhon, who does not see our social institutions as a historical product, who understands neither their origin

Communism and Socialism

nor their development, can only apply to them a dogmatic criticism.

Thus M. Proudhon is also obliged to take refuge in a *fiction* in order to explain development. He imagines that the division of labor, credit, machinery, etc., were all invented to serve his fixed idea, the idea of equality. His explanation is exquisitely naïve. These things were invented for the purpose of equality, but alas they turned against equality. This constitutes his entire argument. In other words, he makes a gratuitous assumption, and then, as the actual development contradicts his fiction at every step, he concludes that there is a contradiction. By this, he conceals that the contradiction exists only between his fixed ideas and the real movement.

Hence M. Proudhon, mainly because of a lack of historical knowledge, has not perceived that as men develop their productive forces—that is, as they live and develop particular relations with one another—the nature of these relations necessarily changes with the growth of the productive forces. He has not perceived that the *economic categories* are only the *abstractions* of these actual relations, which remain true only so long as these relations exist. He therefore falls into the error of the bourgeois economists who see in these economic categories eternal laws rather than historical ones, which are valid only for a particular historical development that is determined by productive forces. Instead, therefore, of viewing the political-economic categories as abstractions of the actual, transitory, historical social relations, M. Proudhon sees only, thanks to a mystical transposition, the real relations as embodiments of these abstractions. These abstractions themselves are formulae which have been slumbering in the bosom of God since the beginning of the world.

But here our good M. Proudhon falls into severe intellectual convulsions. If all these economic categories are emanations from the heart of God, if they are the hidden and eternal life of man, how is that, first, there is such a thing as development, and, second, that M. Proudhon is not a conservative? He explains these obvious contradictions by a whole system of antagonism.

Let us, in order to illuminate this system of antagonism, take an example.

Monopoly is a good thing because it is an economic category, that is, an emanation of God. Competition is a good thing, because it, too, is an economic category. What is not good, however, is the reality of monopoly and of competition. What is even worse is that monopoly and competition devour each other. What to do? Since these two eternal ideas of God contradict each other, it seems obvious to [M. Proudhon] that there is also a synthesis of both in the bosom of God, in which the evils of monopoly are balanced by competition, and vice versa. The result of the struggle between the two ideas is the victory of the good side. One must snatch from God this secret idea, then apply it, and everything will turn out for the best. All one has to do is to reveal the formula of the synthesis which is hidden in the darkness of the impersonal reason of man. M. Proudhon does not hesitate for a moment to come forward as the revealer.

But look for a moment at real life. In the economic life of our time you find not only competition and monopoly but also their synthesis, which is not a *formula* but a *movement*. Monopoly produces competition; competition produces monopoly. But this equation, far from removing the difficulties of the present situation, as the bourgeois economists think that it does, results in a situation still more difficult and confused. If, therefore, you change the basis on which present-day economic relations rest, if you destroy the present-day *method* of production, you do not destroy only competition, monopoly, and their antagonism, but also their unity, their synthesis, the movement which represents the real equilibrium between competition and monopoly.

Now I will give you an example of M. Proudhon's dialectic.

Freedom and *slavery* form an antagonism. I need not speak of the good and the bad side of freedom. As for slavery, I need not speak of its bad side. The only thing that has to be explained is the good side of slavery. We are not dealing with indirect slavery, the slavery of the proletariat, but with direct slavery, the slavery of the blacks in Surinam, in Brazil, in the southern states of North America.

Direct slavery is as much the pivot of today's industry as machinery, credit, etc. Without slavery, no cotton; without cotton, no modern industry. Only slavery has given colonies their value; only the colonies have created world trade; and world trade is the necessary condition of mechanized large-scale industry. Before the slave trade, the colonies of the Old World supplied few products and made no visible change in the face of the earth. Slavery is thus an economic category of the highest importance. Without slavery, North America, the most advanced country, would be transformed into a patriarchal land. Strike North America off the map, and you get anarchy, the total collapse of trade and of modern civilization. But to let slavery disappear is to wipe North America off the world's map. Thus, because slavery is an economic category, we find it among all nations since the world began. Modern nations have merely known how to mask the slavery in their own countries while they openly imported it into the New World. After these reflections, what then is M. Proudhon to do with slavery? He will seek the golden mean in the synthesis between freedom and slavery; in other words, the equilibrium between slavery and freedom.

M. Proudhon has very well grasped the fact that it is men who produce cloth, linen, silks—undoubtedly a great achievement on his part to have grasped such a trifle. But what he has not grasped was that men, according to their productive forces, also produce the *societal relations* amid which they fabricate cloth and linen. Still less has M. Proudhon understood that men, who fashion their societal relations in accordance with their material productiveness [*productivité matérielle*], also fashion *ideas* and *categories*, that is to say, the abstract, ideal expression of these same societal relations. Thus the categories are no more eternal than the relations they express. They are historical and transitory products. For M. Proudhon, on the contrary, abstractions and categories are the primordial cause. According to him, they, and not men, make history. The *abstraction*, the *category, as such*, that is, apart from men and their material activities, is of course immortal, unchangeable, immovable; it is merely a being of pure reason, which is only another way of saying that abstraction as such is abstract—a splendid *tautology!*

Thus economic relations, viewed as categories, are for M. Proudhon eternal formulae that have neither origin nor progress.

Let us put it in another way: M. Proudhon does not directly maintain that he considers *bourgeois life* an *eternal* verity. He states it indirectly by deifying the categories which express bourgeois relations in the form of thought. He considers the products of bourgeois society as having arisen spontaneously, as having an independent, eternal existence, since to him they appear in the form of categories, in the form of thought. Thus he does not rise above the bourgeois horizon.

Since he is operating with bourgeois ideas as if they were eternal verities, he seeks a synthesis of these ideas, their equilibrium, and does not see that the method by which they achieve equilibrium is the only possible one.

In truth, he does what all good bourgeois do. They all say that, in principle, competition, monopoly, etc., are abstract ideas and the only basis of life, but that in practice they leave much to be desired. They all want the impossible, namely, the conditions of bourgeois existence without their necessary consequences. None of them understands that the bourgeois form of production is historical and transitory, exactly as the feudal form was. This mistake arises from the fact that the bourgeois-man is to them the only possible basis of every society, that they cannot conceive a social order in which men have ceased to be bourgeois.

M. Proudhon is thus necessarily a *doctrinaire*. The historic movement which is transforming the world today reduces itself for him to the problem of discovering the correct equilibrium, the synthesis of two bourgeois ideas. And so the clever fellow is able by his ingenuity to discover the hidden thought of God, the unity of two isolated ideas, which are only two isolated ideas because M. Proudhon has isolated them from practical life, from present-day production, that is, from the combination of realities which they express. In place of the great historic movement, which arises from the conflict between men's already acquired productive forces and the societal relations which no longer correspond to them; in place of the dreadful wars which are in preparation between different classes within each nation and between different nations; in place of the practical and violent action of the masses, which alone can resolve these conflicts—in place of all this comprehensive, continuing, and complicated movement, M. Proudhon gives us an evacuating movement [*le mouvement cacadauphin*] out of his own head. It is thus that learned persons, men who know how to snatch from God his secret thoughts, make history. The common people have only to make use of their revelations.

You will now understand why M. Proudhon is the declared enemy of every political movement. The solution of present problems do not lie for him in public action but in the dialectical contortions inside his own head. Since to him categories are the moving force, it is not necessary to change practical life in order to change the categories. Quite the contrary:

Change the categories, and the result will be a transformation of the actual social order.

In his eagerness to reconcile the contradictions, M. Proudhon does not even ask himself whether the very basis of these contradictions must not itself be overthrown. He is like all those doctrinaire politicians who see in the king, the Chamber of Deputies, and the Chamber of Peers integral parts of social life, eternal categories. All he is looking for is a new formula by which to establish an equilibrium between those forces—whose equilibrium actually depends on the present-day movement, wherein one force is now the conqueror and now the slave of the other. Thus in the eighteenth century a number of mediocrities occupied themselves with finding the one and only true formula that would bring the social orders, the nobility, the king, the parliaments, etc., into equilibrium; and overnight everything—king, parliament, nobility—disappeared. The true equilibrium in this antagonism was the overthrow of all social relationships which had served as a basis for those feudal existences and their antagonisms.

Since M. Proudhon places eternal ideas, the categories of pure reason, on one side, and human beings and their practical life, which according to him is the application of these categories, on the other, you find in him from the beginning a *dualism* between life and ideas, between soul and body—a dualism which recurs in many forms. You can see now that this antagonism is nothing but the incapacity of M. Proudhon to comprehend the earthly origin and profane history of the categories which he deifies.

My letter is already too long for me to go on to discuss the ridiculous case which M. Proudhon makes against communism. For the moment you will grant me that a man who had not understood the present social order is even less capable of understanding both the movement which is tending to overthrow it and the literary expression of this revolutionary movement.

The *only point* on which I am in complete agreement with M. Proudhon is his aversion to sentimental Socialistic giddiness. Long before him, I had already made myself very unpopular with my ridicule of this mutton-headed, sentimental, utopian socialism. But is not M. Proudhon strangely deluding himself when he himself sets up his petty-bourgeois sentimentality—I am referring to his twaddle about home, conjugal love, and all such banalities—in opposition to socialist sentimentality, which, in Fourier for example, is much deeper than the pretentious platitudes of our worthy Proudhon? He himself is so conscious of the emptiness of his arguments, his total incapacity to speak of such things, that he hurls himself head over heels into screams of rage, the *irae hominis probi* [wrath of the righteous man], foams at the mouth, curses, denounces, cries shame and murder, beats his breast and boasts before God and man that he has nothing to do with the socialist vilenesses. He does not criticize socialist sentimentalities, or what he regards as such. Like a holy man, a pope, he excommunicates poor sinners and sings hymns of glory to the petty bourgeoisie and to the miserable patriarchal and amorous illusions of the domestic hearth. And this is in no way accidental. M. Proudhon is from head to foot the philosopher and economist of the petty bourgeoisie. In an advanced society the petty bourgeois is of necessity partly a socialist and partly an economist; that is to say, he is blinded by the magnificence of the big bourgeoisie and at the same time has sympathy for the sufferings of the people. He is at once bourgeois and common man. In his innermost conscience he flatters himself that he has found the right equilibrium, which pretends to be something different from mediocrity. Such a petty bourgeois deifies contradiction because contradiction is the pith of his existence. He himself is nothing but a social contradiction in action. He must justify in theory what he is in practice, and M. Proudhon has the merit of being the scientific interpreter of the French petty bourgeoisie—a genuine merit, since the petty bourgeoisie will be an integral part of all the impending social revolutions.

I would gladly have sent you my book on political economy with this letter, but so far it has been impossible for me to get this work printed, as well as the criticism of the German philosophers and socialists about which I spoke to you in Brussels. You cannot imagine the difficulties which a publication of this kind encounters in Germany, on the one side from the police and on the other from the publishers, who are themselves the interested representatives of all the tendencies I am attacking. And as for our own party, it is not only poor, but also large numbers inside the German communist party are angry with me for opposing their utopianism and declamations.

Devotedly yours,

KARL MARX

P.S. You will ask why I am writing you in bad French[2] instead of good German? Because I am addressing this to a French author.

I would be grateful to you if you would not delay your reply too long, so that I would know whether I have made myself comprehensible through this husk of a barbarous French.

A FURTHER RE-EVALUATION OF PROUDHON

Letter to Johann Baptist von Schweitzer (in Berlin), London, January 24, 1865.* This letter was published in the Berlin socialist newspaper, *Der Social-Demokrat*, of which von Schweitzer was the editor, February 1, 3 and 5, 1865.

Dear Sir:

Yesterday I received a letter in which you ask me for a detailed judgment of Proudhon. Time does not allow me to satisfy your wish. In addition, I have none of his writings at hand. But to assure you of my good will, I am hastily jotting down a short sketch. You can complete it, add to it, cut it—in short, do what you like with it.

Proudhon's earliest efforts I no longer remember. His school lesson work on the *Langue Universelle*[1] shows how unembarrassedly he tackled problems for the solution of which he lacked the first principles of knowledge.

His first work, *What Is Property?*,[2] is undoubtedly his best.

---

[2] Marx was too modest; his French was nearly perfect, although he spoke it with a heavy German accent.

*From *Karl Marx on History and People* by Saul K. Padover, pp. 277-84. Copyright © 1977 by Saul K. Padover. Used with permission of McGraw-Hill Book Co.

[1] Proudhon, *"Essai de grammaire générale,"* in N. S. Bergier's *Les Éléments Primitifs des Langues* ("Primitive Elements of Language," Besançon, 1837).

[2] Proudhon, *Qu'est-ce que la propriété. Ou recherches sur le principe du droit et du gouvernement* ("What Is Property? Or Inquiry into the Principle of Law and Government," Paris, 1840).

It is epoch-making, if not from new content, at least from the new and audacious way of stating the old. In the works of French socialists and communists that were known to him, "property," of course, was not only variously criticized but also "repealed" in a utopian fashion. In that book, Proudhon's relation to Saint-Simon and Fourier was about the same as that of Feuerbach to Hegel. Compared to Hegel, Feuerbach is positively poor. Nevertheless, he was epoch-making *after* Hegel because he laid *stress* on certain points that were disagreeable to the Christian consciousness but important for the progress of criticism, which Hegel had left in mystical semi-obscurity.

In Proudhon's book, there prevails, if I may say so, a strong musculature of style. And I consider the style its chief merit. Even when he is reproducing old stuff, one can see that Proudhon has found it out for himself, that what he is saying is new to him and considered so by him. Provocative defiance, the questioning of the economic "holy of holies," the brilliant paradox that mocked the ordinary bourgeois mind, the withering criticism, the bitter irony, and here and there a deep and genuine feeling of indignation at the infamy of the existing order, a revolutionary earnestness—all these electrified the readers of *What Is Property?* and produced a great sensation at its first appearance. In any strictly scientific history of political economy, the book would hardly be worth mentioning. But sensational works of this kind play the same role in the sciences as much as they do in the history of the novel. Take, for example, Malthus' book on *Population*.[3] In its first edition it was nothing but a "sensational pamphlet" and a plagiarism from beginning to end, to boot. And yet, what a stimulus was produced by this libel on the human race!

If I had Proudhon's book before me, I could easily give a few examples to illustrate his early style. In the passages which he himself regarded as the most important, he imitates Kant's treatment of the antinomies—Kant, whose works he had read in translations, was at that time the only German philosopher he knew—and he leaves one with a strong im-

---

[3] Thomas Robert Malthus, *An Essay on the Principle of Population, as It Affects the Future Improvement of Society, with Remarks on the Speculations of Mr. Godwin, Mr. Condorcet, and Other Writers* (London, 1798).

pression that to him, as to Kant, the resolution of the antinomies is something "beyond" the human understanding, that is, something about which his own understanding remains in the dark.

But despite all his apparent iconoclasm, one already finds in *What Is Property?* the contradiction that Proudhon is criticizing society from the standpoint of a French small peasant (later petty bourgeois), on the one hand, and, on the other, with the yardstick he derived from the socialists.

The deficiency of the book is indicated by its very title. The question was put so falsely that it could not be answered correctly. "Property relationships" of antiquity were swallowed up by feudal ones and the latter by bourgeois ones. Thus history itself had practiced its criticism on past property relationships. What Proudhon was actually dealing with was the existing modern bourgeois property. The question of what this is could have been answered only by a critical analysis of "political economy," embracing the totality of those property relationships, not in their juridical expression as relations of volition but in their real form, that is, as relations of production. But as he entangled the totality of these economic relationships in the general juristic conception of "property," Proudhon could not get beyond the answer that Brissot,[4] in a similar work, had already given before 1789: "Property is theft."

The most that can be got out of this is that bourgeois-juristic conceptions of "theft" apply equally well to the bourgeois "honest" earning itself. On the other hand, since "theft" as a forcible violation of property presupposes the existence of property, Proudhon entangled himself in all sorts of fantasies, obscure even to himself, about true bourgeois property.

During my stay in Paris in 1844, I came into personal contact with Proudhon. I mention this here because to a certain extent I am to blame for his "sophistication," as the English call the adulteration of commercial goods. In the course of lengthy debates often lasting all night, I infected him to his great injury with Hegelianism, which, owing to his ignorance

---

[4]Jean-Pierre Brissot de Warville, *Recherches philosophiques sur le droit de propriété et sur le vol, considérés dans la nature et dans la société* ("Philosophic Inquiries into the Right of Property and of Theft, Considered in Nature and in Society," Berlin, Paris, Lyons, 1782).

of the German language, he could not study properly. After my expulsion from Paris, Herr Karl Grün continued what I had begun. As a teacher of German philosophy, Grün had an advantage over me in that he understood nothing about it himself.

Shortly before the appearance of his second important work, *The Philosophy of Poverty*,[5] Proudhon himself announced it to me in a very detailed letter in which he said, among other things: *"J'attends votre férule critique"* ["I await the lash of your criticism"]. This soon fell upon him (in my book *The Poverty of Philosophy*, Paris, 1847), which ended our friendship forever.

From what I have already said, you can see that Proudhon's *Philosophy of Poverty or System of Economic Contradictions* first actually contained his answer to the question: *What Is Property?* In fact, it was only after the publication of the latter work that he had begun his economic studies; he had discovered that the question he had raised could not be answered by invective, but only by an analysis of modern "political economy." At the same time he attempted to present the system of economic categories dialectically. In place of Kant's insoluble "antinomies," the Hegelian "contradiction" was to be introduced as the means of development.

For an estimate of his work, which is in two fat volumes, I must refer you to the book I wrote against it. There I showed, among other things, how little he had penetrated into the secret of scientific dialectics and how, on the contrary, he shared the illusions of speculative philosophy in his treatment of economic categories; how, instead of conceiving them as the theoretical expressions of historical relations of production corresponding to a particular stage of development of material production, he drivels them into pre-existing, eternal ideas, and in this roundabout way arrives once more at the standpoint of bourgeois economy.

I also show, furthermore, how very deficient and sometimes even schoolboyish is his knowledge of the "political economy" that he undertook to criticize, and how he and the utopians are hunting for a so-called science by which a formula for the "solution of the social question" is to be excogi-

---

[5] Proudhon, *Système des contradictions économiques, ou philosophie de la misère* (Paris, 1846).

tated *a priori*, instead of deriving their science from a critical knowledge of the historical movement, a movement that itself produces the material conditions of emancipation. But I show especially how confused, wrong and superficial Proudhon remains with regard to exchange value, the foundation of the whole thing, and how he even views the utopian interpretation of Ricardo's theory of value as the basis of a new science. In regard to his general viewpoint, I made the following comprehensive judgment:

"Every economic relationship has a good and a bad side; this is the only point on which Mr. Proudhon does not give himself the lie. He sees the good side expounded by the economists; the bad one, denounced by the socialists. He borrows from the economists the necessity of eternal relationships; he borrows from the socialists the illusion of seeing in misery nothing but misery (instead of seeing in it the revolutionary, subversive aspect which will overthrow the old society). He agrees with both in wanting to rely on the authority of science. For him, science reduces itself to the tiny proportions of a scientific formula; he is the man hunting for formulas. Hence Mr. Proudhon flatters himself on having given a critique of both political economy and communism—he is way beneath them both. Beneath the economists, because as a philosopher who has a magical formula at hand, he believed he could dispense with going into purely economic details; beneath the socialists, because he has neither courage nor sufficient insight to rise above the bourgeois horizon, even if only speculatively. . . . He wants to soar as a man of science above the bourgeois and the proletarians; he is merely the petty bourgeois who is constantly tossed back and forth between capital and labor, between political economy and communism."

Severe though the above judgment sounds, I must still endorse every word of it today. At the same time, however, it must be remembered that at the time when I declared Proudhon's book to be the petty-bourgeois code of socialism and proved it theoretically, Proudhon was still being branded by the political economists and socialists as an *ultra* archrevolutionist. That is why later on I never joined in the outcry about his "treachery" to the revolution. It was not his fault that, originally misunderstood by others as well as by himself, he did not fulfill unjustified hopes.

In the *Philosophy of Poverty*, all the defects of Proudhon's method of presentation stand out very unfavorably in contrast to *What Is Property?* The style is often what the French call *ampoulé* [bombastic]. High-sounding, speculative gibberish, supposed to be German-philosophical, appears regularly when his Gallic acuteness fails him. A quacking, self-glorifying, boastful tone, especially the pompous drivel about "science," always so stale, continually screams in one's ears. Instead of the genuine warmth that glowed in his first book, here certain passages are systematically worked up by rhetoric into transient heat. Added to this, the clumsy, distasteful erudition of the self-taught, whose natural pride in his original thought has already been broken and who now, as a parvenu of science, feels it necessary to bolster himself up with what he is not and what he has not. Then the mentality of the petty bourgeois, who with indecent brutality—and neither acutely nor profoundly nor even correctly—attacks a man like Cabet, who is respected for his practical attitude toward the proletariat, while he [Proudhon] flatters, for example, a man like Dunoyer (a "State Councillor," to be sure), even though the whole significance of the latter lay in the comic zeal with which he preached, in three thick, unbearably boring tomes, the rigorism [*Rigorismus*] that Helvétius had characterized thus: *"On veut que les malheureux soient parfaits"* ["One expects the unfortunate to be perfect"].

The February Revolution certainly came at a very inopportune moment for Proudhon, since only a few weeks previously he had irrefutably demonstrated that "the era of revolutions" was past forever. His appearance in the National Assembly, however little insight it showed into existing conditions, deserves every praise.[6] *After* the June insurrection, that was an act of great courage. In addition, it had the fortunate consequence that M. Thiers, in his speech opposing Proudhon's proposals which was later issued in a special publication, proved to the whole of Europe on what a small children's-catechism pedestal that intellectual pillar of the French bourgeoisie stood. Indeed, compared to M. Thiers, Proudhon expanded to the size of an antediluvian colossus.

Proudhon's discoveries of *"crédit gratuit"* [free credit] and

[6] In the National Assembly session of July 31, 1848, Proudhon attacked the violence used against the insurrectionists of June 1848.

the *banque du peuple* [people's bank] based upon it, were his last economic "deeds." In my book *A Contribution to the Critique of Political Economy*, Part I (Berlin, 1859, pp. 59–64), will be found the proof that the theoretical basis of his idea arises from a misunderstanding of the first elements of bourgeois "political economy," namely, the relationship between commodities and money, while the practical superstructure is simply a reproduction of much older and far better developed schemes. That the credit system can serve to hasten the emancipation of the working class under certain economic and political conditions—as, for example, at the beginning of the eighteenth and later again in the nineteenth century in England it served toward transferring the wealth of one class to another—is quite unquestionable and self-evident. But to regard interest-bearing capital as the main form of capital, while trying to use a special form of credit—the alleged abolition of interest—as the basis for a transformation of society, is a thoroughly petty-bourgeois fantasy. One already finds this fantasy, padded out further, among the economic spokesmen of the English petty bourgeoisie in the seventeenth century. Proudhon's polemic with Bastiat (1850) about interest-bearing capital[7] is on a far lower level than the *Philosophy of Poverty*. He manages to get himself beaten even by Bastiat and breaks into burlesque rumbling when his opponent drives his blows home.

A few years ago, Proudhon—induced I believe by the Lausanne government—wrote a prize essay on *Taxation*.[8] Here the last vestige of genius is extinguished. Nothing remains but the *petit bourgeois tout pur* [petty bourgeois pure and simple].

In regard to Proudhon's political and philosophical writings, they all show the same contradictory, dual character as his economic works. In addition, they have only a local-French value. Nevertheless, his attacks on religion, the church, etc., were of great merit locally at a time when the French socialists thought it desirable to show by their religiosity how superior they were to the bourgeois Votaireanism of

[7]*Gratuité du crédit. Discussion entre M. Fr. Bastiat et M. Proudhon* ("Free Credit. A Discussion Between Mr. Fr. Bastiat and M. Proudhon," Paris, 1850).

[8]Proudhon, *Théorie de l'impot* ("Theory of Taxation," Paris, 1861).

the eighteenth century and the German atheism of the nineteenth. Just as Peter the Great defeated Russian barbarism with barbarism, so also Proudhon did his best to defeat French phrase-mongering with phrases.

His work on the coup d'etat,[9] in which he flirts with Louis Bonaparte and, in fact, strives to make him palatable to the French workers, and his last work, written against Poland,[10] in which to the greater glory of the Czar he expresses cretinous cynicism, must be characterized as not only bad but also base productions, the baseness of which, however, corresponds to the petty bourgeois point of view.

Proudhon has often been compared with Rousseau. Nothing could be more false. He is, rather, like Nicolas Linguet,[11] whose *Theory of Civil Law*, by the way, is a very brilliant book.

Proudhon had a natural inclination for dialectics. But as he never grasped the really scientific dialectics, he never got further than sophistry. In fact, this hung together with his petty-bourgeois viewpoint. The petty bourgeois is, like the historian Raumer, composed of On the One Hand and On the Other Hand. This is so in his economic interests and hence also in his politics, in his religious, scientific and artistic views. It is so in his morals, so in everything. He is a living contradiction. If, like Proudhon, the bourgeois is in addition a gifted man, he will soon learn to play with his own contradictions and develop them according to circumstances into striking, ostentatious, occasionally scandalous and occasionally brilliant paradoxes. Charlatanism in science and accommodation in politics are inseparable from such a point of view. There remains only one governing motive, the vanity of the subject, and the only question for him, as for all vain people, is the success of the moment, the attention of the day. Thus the simple moral sense, which always kept a Rousseau, for example, far from even the semblance of compromise with the powers that be, is necessarily extinguished.

[9] Proudhon, *La révolution sociale démontrée par le coup d'état du 2 décembre* ("The Social Revolution as Demonstrated by the Coup d'État of December 2d," Paris, 1852).

[10] Proudhon, *Si les traités de 1815 ont cessé d'exister?* ("Did the Treaties of 1815 Cease to Exist?" Paris, 1863).

[11] Simon-Nicolas-Henri Linguet, *Théories des loix civiles, ou principes fondamentaux de la société* ("Theory of Civil Law, or Fundamental Principles of Society," 2 vols., London, 1767).

Perhaps future generations will characterize the latest phase of Frenchism by saying that Louis Bonaparte was its Napoleon and Proudhon its Rousseau-Voltaire.

And now you must take upon yourself the responsibility of having imposed upon me the role of this man's judge so soon after his death.[12]

Yours very respectfully,
KARL MARX

LAMARTINE'S VIEW OF COMMUNISM

"Lamartine and Communism," in *Deutsche-Brüsseler-Zeitung*, December 26, 1847

Brussels, December 24.

The French newspapers are once more publishing a letter from Mr. de Lamartine. This time it is communism on which the poetical socialist expresses himself frankly, after having been challenged by Cabet to do so. At the same time, Lamartine promises to examine this "important subject" *thoroughly* next time. For the moment, he contents himself with a few brief oracular dicta:

"My opinion of communism," he writes, "can be summed up (!) in a *feeling*, as follows: If God entrusted me with a society of savages in order to civilize them and make them moral people, the first institution that I would give them would be property.

"That man," Lamartine continues, "appropriates elements, is a law of nature and a condition of life. He appropriates air when he breathes, space when he traverses it, earth when he builds upon it, even time itself when he perpetuates himself through children; property is the organization of the life principle throughout the world; communism would be the death of work and of all humanity."

"Your dream," Mr. Lamartine consoles Mr. Cabet, "is too beautiful for this earth."

Thus Mr. Lamartine opposes communism, and not merely the communist system, but he also enters the ranks in favor of the "perpetuation of property." For his "feeling" tells him three things: (1) that property civilizes man; (2) that it is

---

[12] Proudhon died in Passy on January 16, 1865.

the organization of the life principle in the world; and (3) that, in contrast, communism is too beautiful a dream for this wicked world.

Mr. Lamartine undoubtedly "feels" a better world in which the "life principle" is "organized" differently. But in this wicked world, "adoption" is, after all, a life condition.

It is not necessary to analyze Mr. Lamartine's confused feeling to dissolve his contradictions. We want to make only one remark. Mr. Lamartine believes to have proved the perpetuity of bourgeois property when he indicates that property in general forms a transition between a primitive and a civilized condition, and when he lets it be understood that the process of breathing and the making of children presuppose a right to property as much as does social private property.

Mr. Lamartine sees no difference between the epoch of transition from primitiveness to civilization and our own epoch, any more than he sees the difference between the "appropriation" of air and the "appropriation" of social products; for both are, after all, "appropriations," just as both epochs are "transition epochs"!

In his "thorough" polemic against communism, Mr. Lamartine will undoubtedly find an opportunity of having this general rhetoric, which springs from his "feeling," be followed "logically" by a whole series of even more general rhetorical statements. Perhaps he will then also find an opportunity to illuminate his rhetoric "more thoroughly." For the time being, we content ourselves with reporting to our readers the "feelings" of a monarcho-Catholic newspaper which opposes those of Mr. Lamartine. The *Union Monarchique*, in yesterday's issue, expresses itself as follows against the Lamartine feeling:

"Here we see how these enlighteners of humanity leave it without a leader. The unfortunate ones! They robbed the poor of their God who consoled them; they took Heaven away from them; they left man alone in his privation, in his misery. And then they come and say: You want to possess the earth; it is not thine. You want to enjoy the good things of life; they belong to others. You want to share in the wealth; that is not acceptable. Remain poor, remain naked, remain abandoned—die!"

The *Union Monarchique* consoles the proletarians with

God. The *Bien Publique*,[1] Mr. Lamartine's journal, consoles them with the "life principle."

MANIFESTO OF THE COMMUNIST PARTY: SELECTIONS[1]

The *Manifesto* was written in German by Marx and Engels between December, 1847, and January, 1848. It was published anonymously in February, 1848, under the title *Manifest der Kommunistischen Partei*. (The twenty-three-page brochure was printed in the office of the Bildungs-Gesellschaft für Arbeiter, 46 Liverpool Street, Bishopsgate, London.) Between March and July of 1848 it was reprinted in the *Deutsche Londoner Zeitung*, an organ of German émigrés in London. In the same year it appeared in the Danish, Flemish, French, Italian, Polish, and Swedish languages —again anonymously. In 1850 George Julian Harney published the first English translation (by Helen MacFarlane) of the *Manifesto* in his Chartist publication, *Red Republican*, and for the first time Marx and Engels were mentioned as its authors. Since then there have been numerous editions of the *Manifesto* in every conceivable language.

Marx's sketch for the *Manifesto*, written in December 1847, or January 1848, is reproduced below. This is the only original sketch of the document that has been preserved.

---

[1] *Le Bien Publique*, a daily journal that appeared in Macon and Paris.

[1] Complete text in Saul K. Padover, ed., *Karl Marx on Revolution* (New York, 1971), pp. 80-107.

(The words in brackets were crossed out by Marx.)

For the rest we have seen:

The communists do not propose a new theory of private property. They only express the historic fact that [productions and] bourgeois production—and with it bourgeois property relationships [and] [or] [definite] of [social] the development of social forces of production are no longer [appropriate] and hence [in the development of industry itself] and in d.

But do not quarrel with us when you measure the elimination of bourgeois property [against] from the point of view of your bourgeois ideas of freedom, education, etc. Your ideas themselves [are] [engender] [are] [corresponding to] are the products of the [existing] bourgeois production and property relationships, just as is your right, which is only the will of your class raised to the status of law. [A] A will whose content is determined by the material life conditions of your class.

[Your] The interesting conception of transforming [the] your production and property relationships from a historical [and only], transitory, definite [mature] state of development of the forces of production [forces corresponding to] corresponding to the relationships into eternal and rational natural laws, you share with all extinct ruling classes.

What you understand in the matter of feudal property, you no longer understand when it comes to bourgeois property.

And yet you cannot deny the fact that [in the course of the bourgeois] with the process of industrial development the one-sided, on—

The communists posit no new theory of property. They express a fact. You deny the most striking facts. You have to deny it. You are utopians in reverse.

[The text of the *Manifesto* used here is based on the English translation by Samuel Moore, published, with a preface by Engels, in 1888.]

A specter is haunting Europe—the specter of communism. All the powers of old Europe have entered into a holy alliance[1] to exorcise this specter: Pope and Czar, Metternich and Guizot, French radicals and German police spies.

Where is the party in opposition that has not been decried as communistic by its opponents in power? Where the opposition that has not hurled back the branding reproach of communism, against the more advanced opposition parties, as well as against its reactionary adversaries?

Two things result from this fact.

1. Communism is already acknowledged by all European powers to be itself a power.

2. It is high time that Communists should openly, in the face of the whole world, publish their views, their aims, their tendencies, and meet this nursery tale of the specter of communism with a manifesto of the party itself.

To this end, Communists of various nationalities have assembled in London and sketched the following manifesto, to be published in the English, French, German, Italian, Flemish, and Danish languages.

I

BOURGEOIS AND PROLETARIANS

The history of all hitherto existing society is the history of class struggles.

Freeman and slave, patrician and plebeian, lord and serf, guild master and journeyman—in a word, oppressor and oppressed—stood in constant opposition to one another, carried on an uninterrupted, now hidden, now open fight, a fight that each time ended either in a revolutionary reconstitution of society at large, or in the common ruin of the contending classes.

In the early epochs of history, we find almost everywhere a complicated arrangement of society into various orders, a manifold graduation of social rank. In ancient Rome we have patricians, knights, plebeians, slaves; in the Middle Ages, feudal lords, vassals, guild masters, journeymen, apprentices, serfs; in almost all of these classes, again, subordinate gradations.

---

[1] The Holy Alliance was formed in 1815 by the Czar of Russia and the monarchs of Austria and Prussia; it survived until the revolution of 1848.

The modern bourgeois society that has sprouted from the ruins of feudal society has not done away with class antagonisms. It has but established new classes, new conditions of oppression, new forms of struggle in place of the old ones.

Our epoch, the epoch of the bourgeoisie, possesses, however, this distinctive feature: it has simplified the class antagonisms. Society as a whole is more and more splitting up into two great hostile camps, into two great classes directly facing each other: Bourgeoisie and Proletariat.

From the serfs of the Middle Ages sprang the chartered burghers of the earliest towns. From these burgesses the first elements of the bourgeoisie were developed.

The discovery of America, the rounding of the Cape, opened up fresh ground for the rising bourgeoisie. The East Indian and Chinese markets, the colonization of America, trade with the colonies, the increase in the means of exchange and in commodities generally, gave to commerce, to navigation, to industry, an impulse never before known, and thereby, to the revolutionary element in the tottering feudal society, a rapid development.

The feudal system of industry, under which industrial production was monopolized by closed guilds, now no longer sufficed for the growing wants of the new markets. The manufacturing system took its place. The guild masters were pushed to one side by the manufacturing middle class; division of labor between the different corporate guilds vanished in the face of division of labor in each single workshop.

Meantime the markets kept ever growing, the demand ever rising. Even manufacturing no longer sufficed. Thereupon steam and machinery revolutionized industrial production. The place of manufacture was taken by the giant, Modern Industry, the place of the industrial middle class by industrial millionaires, the leaders of whole industrial armies, the modern bourgeoisie.

Modern industry has established the world market for which the discovery of America paved the way. This market has given an immense development to commerce, to navigation, to communication by land. This development has, in its turn, reacted on the extension of industry; and in proportion as industry, commerce, navigation, railways extended, in the same proportion the bourgeoisie developed, increased its capital, and pushed into the background every class handed down from the Middle Ages.

We see, therefore, how the modern bourgeoisie is itself the product of a long course of development, of a series of revolutions in the modes of production and of exchange.

Each step in the development of the bourgeoisie was accompanied by a corresponding political advance of that class. An oppressed class under the sway of the feudal nobility, an armed and self-governing association in the medieval commune, here independent urban republic (as in Italy and Germany), there taxable "third estate" of the monarchy (as in France), afterwards, in the period of manufacturing proper, serving either the semifeudal or the absolute monarchy as a counterpoise against the nobility, and in fact a cornerstone of the great monarchies in general, the bourgeoisie has at last, since the establishment of Modern Industry and of the world market, conquered for itself, in the modern representative state, exclusive political sway. The executive of the modern state is but a committee for managing the common affairs of the whole bourgeoisie.

The bourgeoisie, historically, has played a most revolutionary part.

The bourgeoisie, wherever it has got the upper hand, has put an end to all feudal, patriarchal, idyllic relations. It has pitilessly torn asunder the motley feudal ties that bound man to his "natural superiors," and has left remaining no other nexus between man and man than naked self-interest, than callous "cash payment." It has drowned the most heavenly ecstasies of religious fervor, of chivalrous enthusiasm, of philistine sentimentalism, in the icy water of egotistical calculation. It has resolved personal worth into exchange value, and in place of the numberless indefeasible chartered freedoms has set up that single, unconscionable freedom—free trade. In a word, for exploitation veiled by religious and political illusions, it has substituted naked, shameless, direct, brutal exploitation.

The bourgeoisie has stripped of its halo every occupation hitherto honored and looked up to with reverent awe. It has converted the physician, the lawyer, the priest, the poet, the man of science, into its paid wage laborers.

The bourgeoisie has torn away from the family its sentimental veil, and has reduced the family relation to a mere money relation.

The bourgeoisie has disclosed how it came to pass that the

brutal display of vigor in the Middle Ages, which reactionists so much admire, found its fitting complement in the most slothful indolence. It has been the first to show what man's activity can bring about. It has accomplished wonders far surpassing Egyptian pyramids, Roman aqueducts, and Gothic cathedrals; it has conducted expeditions that put in the shade all former exoduses of nations and crusades.

The bourgeoisie cannot exist without constantly revolutionizing the instruments of production, and thereby the relations of production, and with them the whole relations of society. Conservation of the old modes of production in unaltered form was, on the contrary, the first condition of existence for all earlier industrial classes. Constant revolutionizing of production, uninterrupted disturbance of all social conditions, everlasting uncertainty and agitation distinguish the bourgeois epoch from all earlier ones. All fixed, fast-frozen relations, with their train of ancient and venerable prejudices and opinions, are swept away, all newly formed ones become antiquated before they can ossify. All that is solid melts into air, all that is holy is profaned, and man is at last compelled to face with sober senses his real conditions of life, and his relations with his kind.

The need of a constantly expanding market for its products chases the bourgeoisie over the whole surface of the globe. It must nestle everywhere, settle everywhere, establish connections everywhere.

The bourgeoisie has through its exploitation of the world market given a cosmopolitan character to production and consumption in every country. To the great chagrin of reactionists, it has drawn from under the feet of industry the national ground on which it stood. All old-established national industries have been destroyed or are daily being destroyed. They are dislodged by new industries, whose introduction becomes a life-and-death question for all civilized nations, by industries that no longer work up indigenous raw material but raw material drawn from the remotest zones; industries whose products are consumed, not only at home, but in every quarter of the globe. In place of the old wants, satisfied by the productions of the country, we find new wants, requiring for their satisfaction the products of distant lands and climes. In place of the old local and national seclusion and self-sufficiency, we have intercourse in every direction, universal interdependence of nations. And as in material, so also in intellectual production. The intellectual creations of individual nations become common property. National one-sidedness and narrow-mindedness become more and more impossible, and from the numerous national and local literatures there arises a world literature.

The bourgeoisie, by the rapid improvement of all instruments of production, by the immensely facilitated means of communication, draws all, even the most barbarian, nations into civilization. The cheap prices of its commodities are the heavy artillery with which it batters down all Chinese walls, with which it forces the barbarians' intensely obstinate hatred of foreigners to capitulate. It compels all nations, on pain of extinction, to adopt the bourgeois mode of production; it compels them to introduce what it calls civilization into their midst, i.e., to become bourgeois themselves. In a word, it creates a world after its own image.

The bourgeoisie has subjected the country to the rule of the towns. It has created enormous cities, has greatly increased the urban population as compared with the rural, and has thus rescued a considerable part of the population from the idiocy of rural life. Just as it has made the country dependent on the towns, so it has made barbarian and semibarbarian countries dependent on the civilized ones, nations of peasants on nations of bourgeois, the East on the West.

The bourgeoisie keeps more and more doing away with the scattered state of the population, of the means of production, and of property. It has agglomerated population, centralized means of production, and concentrated property in a few hands. The necessary consequence of this was political centralization. Independent or but loosely connected provinces, with separate interests, laws, governments, and systems of taxation, became lumped together in one nation, with one government, one code of laws, one national class interest, one frontier, and one customs tariff.

The bourgeoisie, during its rule of scarcely one hundred years, has created more massive and more colossal productive forces than have all preceding generations together. Subjection of Nature's forces to man, machinery, application of chemistry to industry and agriculture, steam navigation, railways, electric telegraphs, clearing of whole continents for cultivation, canalization of rivers, whole populations conjured out of the ground—what earlier century had even a presentiment that such productive forces slumbered in the lap of social labor?

We see then: The means of production and of exchange on whose foundations the bourgeoisie built itself up were generated in feudal society. At a certain stage in the development of these means of production and of exchange, the conditions under which feudal society produced and exchanged, the feudal organization of agriculture and manufacturing industry—in a word, the feudal relations of property—became no longer compatible with the already developed productive forces; they became so many fetters. They had to be burst asunder; they were burst asunder.

Into their places stepped free competition, accompanied by a social and political constitution adapted to it, and by the economic and political sway of the bourgeois class.

A similar movement is going on before our own eyes. Modern bourgeois society with its relations of production, of exchange, and of property, a society that has conjured up such gigantic means of production and of exchange, is like the sorcerer who is no longer able to control the powers of the nether world whom he has called up by his spells. For many a decade past, the history of industry and commerce is but the history of the revolt of modern productive forces against modern conditions of production, against the property relations that are the condition for the existence of the bourgeoisie and of its rule. It is enough to mention the commercial crises that by their periodic return put on trial, each time more threateningly, the existence of the entire bourgeois society. In these crises a great part not only of the existing products, but also of the previously created productive forces, are periodically destroyed. In these crises there breaks out an epidemic that, in all earlier epochs, would have seemed an absurdity—the epidemic of overproduction. Society suddenly finds itself put back into a state of momentary barbarism; it appears as if a famine, a universal war of devastation, had cut off the supply of every means of subsistence; industry and commerce seem to be destroyed; and why? Because there is too much civilization, too much means of subsistence, too much industry, too much commerce. The productive forces at the disposal of society no longer tend to further the development of the conditions of bourgeois property; on the contrary, they have become too powerful for these conditions, by which they are fettered, and so soon as they overcome these fetters, they bring disorder into the whole of bourgeois society, endangering the existence of bourgeois property. The conditions of bourgeois society are too narrow to comprise the wealth created by them. And how does the bourgeoisie get over these crises? On the one hand by enforced destruction of a mass of productive forces; on the other by the conquest of new markets, and by the more thorough exploitation of the old ones. That is to say, by paving the way for more extensive and more destructive crises, and by diminishing the means whereby crises are prevented.

The weapons with which the bourgeoisie felled feudalism to the ground are now turned against the bourgeoisie itself.

But not only has the bourgeoisie forged the weapons that bring death to itself; it has also called into existence the men who are to wield those weapons—the modern working class—the proletarians.

In proportion as the bourgeoisie, i.e., capital, is developed, in the same proportion is the proletariat, the modern working class, developed, a class of laborers who live only so long as they find work, and who find work only so long as their labor increases capital. These laborers, who must sell themselves piecemeal, are a commodity, like every other article of commerce, and are consequently exposed to all the vicissitudes of competition, to all the fluctuations of the market.

Owing to the extensive use of machinery and to division of labor, the work of the proletarians has lost all individual character, and consequently all charm for the workman. He becomes an appendage of the machine, and it is only the most simple, most monotonous, and most easily acquired knack that is required of him. Hence the cost of production of a workman is restricted almost entirely to the means of subsistence that he requires for his maintenance, and for the propagation of his race. But the price of a commodity, and also of labor, is equal to its cost of production. In proportion, therefore, as the repulsiveness of the work increases, the wage decreases. Nay, more—in proportion as the use of machinery and division of labor increases, in the same proportion the burden of toil also increases, whether by prolongation of the working hours, by increase of the work done in a given time, or by increased speed of the machinery, etc.

Modern industry has converted the little workshop of the patriarchal master into the great factory of the industrial capitalist. Masses of laborers, crowded into the factory, are organized like soldiers. As privates of the industrial army they are placed under the command of a perfect hierarchy of officers and sergeants. Not only are they the slaves of the bourgeois class, and of the bourgeois state, they are daily and hourly enslaved by the machine, by the overlooker, and above all by the individual bourgeois manufacturer himself. The more openly this despotism proclaims gain to be its end and aim, the more petty, the more hateful, and the more embittering it is.

The less the skill and exertion or strength implied in manual labor—in other words, the more modern industry becomes developed—the more is the labor of men superseded by that of women. Differences of age and sex have no longer any distinctive social validity for the working class. All are instruments of labor, more or less expensive to use according to their age and sex.

No sooner is the exploitation of the laborer by the manufacturer so far at an end that he receives his wages in cash, than he is set upon by the other portions of the bourgeoisie, the landlord, the shopkeeper, the pawnbroker, etc.

The low strata of the middle class—the small tradespeople, shopkeepers, and retired tradesmen generally, the handicraftsmen and peasants—all these sink gradually into the proletariat, partly because their diminutive capital does not suffice for the scale on which Modern Industry is carried on and is swamped in the competition with the large capitalists, partly because their specialized skill is rendered worthless by new methods of production. Thus the proletariat is recruited from all classes of the population.

The proletariat goes through various stages of development. With its birth begins its struggle with the bourgeoisie. At first the contest is carried on by individual laborers, then by the workpeople of a factory, then by the operatives of one trade, in one locality, against the individual bourgeois who directly exploits them. They direct their attacks not against the bourgeois conditions of production, but against the instruments of production themselves; they destroy imported wares that compete with their labor, they smash machinery to pieces, they set factories ablaze, they seek to restore by force the vanished status of the workman of the Middle Ages.

Communism and Socialism

At this stage the laborers still form an incoherent mass scattered over the whole country and broken up by their mutual competition. If anywhere they unite to form more compact bodies, this is not yet the consequence of their own active union, but of the union of the bourgeoisie, which class, in order to attain its own political ends, is compelled to set the whole proletariat in motion, and is moreover yet, for a time, able to do so. At this stage, therefore, the proletarians do not fight their enemies, but the enemies of their enemies, the remnants of absolute monarchy, the landowners, the non-industrial bourgeoisie, the petty bourgeoisie. Thus the whole historical movement is concentrated in the hands of the bourgeoisie; every victory so obtained is a victory for the bourgeoisie.

But with the development of industry the proletariat not only increases in number, it becomes concentrated in great masses, its strength grows, and it feels that strength more. The various interests and conditions of life within the ranks of the proletariat are more and more equalized, in proportion as machinery obliterates all distinction of labor and nearly everywhere reduces wages to the same low level. The growing competition among the bourgeoisie, and the resulting commercial crises, make the wages of the worker ever more fluctuating. The unceasing improvement of machinery, ever more rapidly developing, makes their livelihood more and more precarious, the collisions between individual workmen and individual bourgeois take more and more the character of collision between two classes. Thereupon the workers begin to form combinations (trade unions) against the bourgeoisie; they club together in order to keep up the rate of wages; they found permanent associations in order to make provision beforehand for these occasional revolts. Here and there the contest breaks out into riots.

Now and then the workers are victorious, but only for a time. The real fruits of their battles lie, not in the immediate result, but in the ever expanding union of the workers. This union is helped on by the improved means of communication that are created by modern industry and that place the workers of different localities in contact with one another. It was just this contact that was needed to centralize the numerous local struggles, all of the same character, into one national struggle between classes. But every class struggle is a political struggle. And that union, to attain which the burghers of the Middle Ages, with their miserable highways, required centuries, the modern proletarians, thanks to railways, achieve in a few years.

This organization of the proletarians into a class, and consequently into a political party, is continually being upset again by the competition between the workers themselves. But it ever rises up again, stronger, firmer, mightier. It compels legislative recognition of particular interests of the workers by taking advantage of the divisions among the bourgeoisie itself. Thus the ten-hour bill in England was carried.

Altogether, collisions between the classes of the old society further in many ways the course of development of the proletariat. The bourgeoisie finds itself involved in a constant battle. At first with the aristocracy, later on with those portions of the bourgeoisie itself whose interests have become antagonistic to the progress of industry, at all times with the bourgeoisie of foreign countries. In all these battles it sees itself compelled to appeal to the proletariat, to ask for its help, and thus to drag it into the political arena. The bourgeoisie itself, therefore, supplies the proletariat with its own elements of political and general education; in other words, it furnishes the proletariat with weapons for fighting the bourgeoisie.

Further, as we have already seen, entire sections of the ruling classes are, by the advance of industry, precipitated into the proletariat, or are at least threatened in their conditions of existence. These also supply the proletariat with fresh elements of enlightenment and progress.

Finally, in times when the class struggle nears the decisive hour, the process of dissolution going on within the ruling class—in fact, within the whole range of old society—assumes such a violent, glaring character that a small section of the ruling class cuts itself adrift and joins the revolutionary class, the class that holds the future in its hands. Just as, therefore, at an earlier period, a section of the nobility went over to the bourgeoisie, so now a portion of the bourgeoisie goes over to the proletariat, and in particular, a portion of the bourgeois ideologists, who have raised themselves to the level of comprehending theoretically the historical movements as a whole.

Of all the classes that stand face to face with the bour-

Communism and Socialism

geoisie today, the proletariat alone is a really revolutionary class. The other classes decay and finally disappear in the face of modern industry; the proletariat is its special and essential product.

The lower middle class, the small manufacturer, the shopkeeper, the artisan, the peasant, all these fight against the bourgeoisie, to save from extinction their existence as fractions of the middle class. They are therefore not revolutionary, but conservative. Nay, more—they are reactionary, for they try to roll back the wheel of history. If by chance they are revolutionary, they are so only in view of their impending transfer into the proletariat; they thus defend not their present, but their future interests, they desert their own standpoint to place themselves at that of the proletariat.

The "dangerous class," the social scum, that passively rotting mass thrown off by the lowest layers of old society, may, here and there, be swept into the movement by a proletarian revolution; its conditions of life, however, prepare it far more for the part of a bribed tool of reactionary intrigue.

In the conditions of the proletariat, those of old society at large are already virtually swamped. The proletarian is without property; his relation to his wife and children has no longer anything in common with the bourgeois family relations; modern industrial labor, modern subjugation to capital, the same in England as in France, in America as in Germany, has stripped him of every trace of national character. Law, morality, religion are to him so many bourgeois prejudices, behind which lurk in ambush just as many bourgeois interests.

All the preceding classes that got the upper hand sought to fortify their already acquired status by subjecting society at large to their conditions of appropriation. The proletarians cannot become masters of the productive forces of society except by abolishing their own previous mode of appropriation, and thereby also every other previous mode of appropriation. They have nothing of their own to secure and to fortify; their mission is to destroy all previous securities for, and insurances of, individual property.

All previous historical movements were movements of minorities, or in the interests of minorities. The proletarian movement is the self-conscious, independent movement of the immense majority, in the interest of the immense majority. The proletariat, the lowest stratum of our present society, cannot stir, cannot raise itself up, without the whole superincumbent strata of official society being sprung into the air.

Though not in substance, yet in form, the struggle of the proletariat with the bourgeoisie is at first a national struggle. The proletariat of each country must, of course, first of all settle matters with its own bourgeoisie.

In depicting the most general phases of the development of the proletariat, we traced the more or less veiled civil war raging within existing society up to the point where that war breaks out into open revolution, and where the violent overthrow of the bourgeoisie lays the foundation for the sway of the proletariat.

Hitherto every form of society has been based, as we have already seen, on the antagonism of oppressing and oppressed classes. But in order to oppress a class, certain conditions must be assured to it under which it can at least continue its slavish existence. The serf, in the period of serfdom, raised himself to membership in the commune, just as the petty bourgeois, under the yoke of feudal absolutism, managed to develop into a bourgeois.

The modern laborer, on the contrary, instead of rising with the progress of industry, sinks deeper and deeper below the conditions of existence of his own class. He becomes a pauper, and pauperism develops more rapidly than population and wealth. And here it becomes evident that the bourgeoisie is unfit any longer to be the ruling class in society, and to impose its conditions of existence upon society as an overriding law. It is unfit to rule because it is incompetent to assure an existence to its slave within his slavery, because it cannot help letting him sink into such a state that it has to feed him, instead of being fed by him. Society can no longer live under this bourgeoisie; in other words, its existence is no longer compatible with society.

The essential condition for the existence and for the sway of the bourgeois class is the formation and augmentation of capital; the condition for capital is wage labor. Wage labor rests exclusively on competition between the laborers. The advance of industry, whose involuntary promoter is the bourgeoisie, replaces the isolation of the laborers, due to competition, by their revolutionary combination, due to association. The development of Modern Industry, therefore, cuts from under its feet the very foundation on which the bourgeoisie produces and appropriates products. What the bourgeoisie therefore produces, above all, is its own gravediggers. Its fall and the victory of the proletariat are equally inevitable.

Conservative or Bourgeois Socialism

A part of the bourgeoisie is desirous of redressing social grievances, in order to secure the continued existence of bourgeois society.

To this section belong economists, philanthropists, humanitarians, improvers of the condition of the working class, organizers of charity, members of societies for the prevention of cruelty to animals, temperance fanatics, hole-and-corner reformers of every imaginable kind. This form of socialism has, moreover, been worked out into complete systems.

We may cite Proudhon's *Philosophie de la Misère* as an example of this form.

The socialistic bourgeois want all the advantages of modern social conditions without the struggles and dangers necessarily resulting therefrom. They desire the existing state of society minus its revolutionary and disintegrating elements. They wish for a bourgeoisie without a proletariat. The bourgeoisie naturally conceives the world in which it is supreme to be the best; and bourgeois socialism develops this comfortable conception into various more or less complete systems. In requiring the proletariat to carry out such a system, and thereby to march straightway into the social New Jerusalem, it but requires, in reality, that the proletariat should remain within the bounds of existing society, but should cast away all its hateful ideas concerning the bourgeoisie.

A second and more practical, but less systematic, form of this socialism sought to depreciate every revolutionary movement in the eyes of the working class by showing that no mere political reform, but only a change in the material conditions of existence, in economical relations, could be of any advantage to them. By changes in the material conditions of existence, this form of socialism, however, by no means understands abolition of the bourgeois relations of production, an abolition that can be effected only by a revolution, but administrative reforms, based on the continued existence of these relations; reforms, therefore, that in no respect affect the relations between capital and labor, but, at the best, lessen the cost, and simplify the administrative work, of bourgeois government.

Bourgeois socialism attains adequate expression when, and only when, it becomes a mere figure of speech.

Free trade: for the benefit of the working class. Protective duties: for the benefit of the working class. Prison reform: for the benefit of the working class. This is the last word and the only seriously meant word of bourgeois socialism.

It is summed up in the phrase: the bourgeois is a bourgeois—for the benefit of the working class.

Critical-Utopian Socialism and Communism

We do not here refer to that literature which, in every great modern revolution, has always given voice to the demands of the proletariat: such as the writings of Babeuf and others.

The first direct attempts of the proletariat to attain its own ends were made in times of universal excitement, when feudal society was being overthrown. These attempts necessarily failed, owing to the then undeveloped state of the proletariat, as well as to the absence of the economic conditions for its emancipation, conditions that had yet to be produced, and could be produced by the impending bourgeois epoch alone. The revolutionary literature that accompanied these first movements of the proletariat had necessarily a reactionary character. It inculcated universal asceticism and social leveling in its crudest form.

The socialist and communist systems properly so called, those of St. Simon, Fourier, Owen, and others, spring into existence in the early undeveloped period, described above, of the struggle between proletariat and bourgeoisie (see Section I, Bourgeois and Proletarians).

The founders of these systems see, indeed, the class antagonisms, as well as the action of the decomposing elements in the prevailing form of society. But the proletariat, as yet in its infancy, offers to them the spectacle of a class without any historical initiative or any independent political movement.

Since the development of class antagonism keeps even pace with the development of industry, the economic situation, as they find it, does not as yet offer to them the material conditions for the emancipation of the proletariat. They therefore search after a new social science, after new social laws that are to create these conditions.

Historical action is to yield to their personal inventive action, historically created conditions of emancipation to fantastic ones, and the gradual, spontaneous class organization of the proletariat to an organization of society specially contrived by these inventors. Future history resolves itself, in their eyes, into the propaganda and the practical carrying out of their social plans.

In the formation of their plans they are conscious of caring chiefly for the interests of the working class, as being the most suffering class. Only from the point of view of being the most suffering class does the proletariat exist for them.

The undeveloped state of the class struggle, as well as their own surroundings, causes socialists of this kind to consider themselves far superior to all class antagonisms. They want to improve the condition of every member of society, even that of the most favored. Hence they habitually appeal to society at large, without distinction of class; nay, by preference to the ruling class. For how can people, when once they understand their system, fail to see in it the best possible plan of the best possible state of society?

Hence they reject all political, and especially all revolutionary action; they wish to attain their ends by peaceful means, and endeavor, by small experiments, necessarily doomed to failure, and by the force of example, to pave the way for the new social Gospel.

Such fantastic pictures of future society, painted at a time when the proletariat is still in a very undeveloped state, and has but a fantastic conception of its own position, correspond with the first instinctive yearnings of that class for a general reconstruction of society.

But these socialist and communist publications contain a critical element. They attack every principle of existing society. Hence they are full of the most valuable materials for the enlightenment of the working class. The practical measures proposed in them, such as the abolition of the distinction between town and country, of the family, of the carrying on of industries for the account of private individuals, and of the wage system, the proclamation of social harmony, the conversion of the functions of the state into a mere superintendence of production, all these proposals point solely to the disappearance of class antagonisms which were at that time only just cropping up, and which in these publications are recognized under their earliest, indistinct and undefined forms only. These proposals, therefore, are of a purely utopian character.

The significance of critical-utopian socialism and communism bears an inverse relation to historical development. In proportion as the modern class struggle develops and takes definite shape, this fantastic standing apart from the contest, these fantastic attacks on it, lose all practical value and all theoretical justification. Therefore, although the originators of these systems were in many respects revolutionary, their disciples have in every case formed mere reactionary sects. They hold fast to the original views of their masters, in opposition to the progressive historical development of the proletariat. They therefore endeavor, and that consistently, to deaden the class struggle and to reconcile the class antagonisms. They still dream of experimental relations of their social Utopias, of founding isolated "phalansteries," of establishing "Home Colonies," of setting up a "Little Icaria"—duodecimo editions of the New Jerusalem—and to realize all these castles in the air, they are compelled to appeal to the feelings and purses of the bourgeois. By degrees they sink into the category of the reactionary conservative socialists depicted above, differing from these only by more systematic pedantry, and by their fanatical and superstitious belief in the miraculous effects of their social science.

They therefore violently oppose all political action on the part of the working class; such action, according to them, can only result from blind unbelief in the new Gospel.

The Owenites in England and the Fourierists in France, respectively, oppose the Chartists and the "Reformists."

IV

POSITION OF THE COMMUNISTS IN RELATION TO THE VARIOUS EXISTING OPPOSITION PARTIES

Section II has made clear the relations of the Communists to the existing working-class parties, such as the Chartists in England and the Agrarian Reformers in America.

The Communists fight for the attainment of the immediate aims, for the enforcement of the momentary interests of the working class; but in the movement of the present, they also represent and take care of the future of that movement. In France the Communists ally themselves with the Social Democrats against the conservatives and radical bourgeoisie, reserving, however, the right to take up a critical position in regard to phrases and illusions traditionally handed down from the great Revolution.

In Switzerland they support the Radicals, without losing sight of the fact that this party consists of antagonistic elements, partly of democratic socialists in the French sense, partly of radical bourgeois.

In Poland they support the party that insists on an agrarian revolution as the prime condition for national emancipation, that party which fomented the insurrection of Cracow in 1846.

In Germany they fight with the bourgeoisie whenever it acts in a revolutionary way, against the absolute monarchy, the feudal squirearchy, and the petty bourgeoisie.

But they never cease, for a single instant, to instill into the working class the clearest possible recognition of the hostile antagonism between bourgeoisie and proletariat, in order that the German workers may straightway use, as so many weapons against the bourgeoisie, the social and political conditions that the bourgeoisie must necessarily introduce along with its supremacy, and in order that, after the fall of the reactionary classes in Germany, the fight against the bourgeoisie itself may immediately begin.

The Communists turn their attention chiefly to Germany because that country is on the eve of a bourgeois revolution that is bound to be carried out under more advanced conditions of European civilization, and with a more developed proletariat, than that of England was in the seventeenth, and of France in the eighteenth century, and because the bourgeois revolution in Germany will be but the prelude to an immediately following proletarian revolution.

In short, the Communists everywhere support every revolutionary movement against the existing social and political order of things.

In all these movements they bring to the front, as the leading question in each, the property question, no matter what its degree of development at the time.

Finally, they labor everywhere for the union and agreement of the democratic parties of all countries.

The Communists disdain to conceal their views and aims.

They openly declare that their ends can be attained only by the forcible overthrow of all existing social conditions. Let the ruling classes tremble at a Communist revolution. The proletarians have nothing to lose but their chains. They have a world to win.

Workingmen of all countries, unite!

THE COMMUNIST PARTY PROGRAM

From Marx and Engels, "Demands of the Communist Party in Germany," a brochure written March 21-29, 1848; printed in Paris, March 30, and in Cologne, September 10, 1848

"Proletarians of all countries, unite!"

1. All of Germany is to be declared a united, indivisible republic.
2. Every German aged twenty-one is eligible to vote, provided he has no criminal record.
3. The representatives of the people are to be paid, so that workers shall also be able to sit in the parliament of the German people.
4. General arming of the people. In the future, the armies are to be at the same time working armies, so that troops are no longer as hitherto, consumers but, rather, producers of more than the maintenance cost.

    This is, moreover, a means for the organization of labor.
5. The performance of justice is to be free of charge.
6. All feudal burdens, dues, socages, tithes, etc., which hitherto burdened the country people, are abolished without any compensation.
7. Princely and other feudal landed estates, all mines, pits, etc. are transformed into state property. On those landed estates agricultural land will be cultivated on a large scale and with the most modern

scientific methods for the benefit of the whole people.

8. Mortgages on peasant farms are declared to be state property. Interest on them is to be paid by the peasants to the state.

9. In the areas where tenant farming is developed, ground rents or tenant dues are to be paid to the state as taxes.

All the measures under Nos. 6, 7, 8 and 9 are conceived with a view toward diminishing the official and other burdens of the peasants and small tenant farmers, without decreasing the necessary means for the defrayal of state costs and without endangering production itself.

The landowner who is neither a peasant nor a tenant has no share in production at all. His consumption is therefore merely a misuse.

10. Private banks are to be replaced by state banks, whose paper currency is to have a legal rate of exchange.

This measure makes it possible to regulate the credit system in the interest of *all* the people and thereby undermines the domination of the big money men. As paper money by and by replaces gold and silver, it reduces the latter's value as an indispensable medium of exchange of bourgeois business and allows gold and silver to operate in foreign trade. This measure, finally, is necessary in order to tie conservative bourgeois interests to the revolution.

11. All means of transportation—railroads, canals, steamers, roads, posts, etc.—are taken over by the state. They are to be transformed into state property and put at the disposal of the impecunious class free of charge.

12. In the salary scale of all government officials there is to be no differential except that those with a family, that is, those who have greater needs, are to receive a higher salary than the others.

13. Complete separation of church and state. The

clergy of all confessions are to be paid solely by their voluntary communities.

14. Limitation of the right of inheritance.
15. Introduction of heavy progressive taxes and abolition of consumer taxes.
16. Establishment of national workshops. The state guarantees all workers their existence and provides for those unable to work.
17. Universal, free education.

It is in the interest of the German proletariat, the small bourgeoisie, and the peasantry to work with all their energies for the realization of the above measures. For only through their realization will the millions of people in Germany who have hitherto been exploited by a small number, and who are in danger of further oppression, be able to attain the rights and power which belong to them as producers of all wealth.

The Committee:
KARL MARX   KARL SCHAPPER   H. BAUER   F. ENGELS
J. MOLL   W. WOLFF

THE PERMANENT REVOLUTION

"Address of the Central Committee to the Communist League," written by Marx and Engels, March 1850. This address, an analysis of the prospects of revolution in Germany based on the experiences of 1848-49, has been described by Moscow's Marx-Engels-Lenin Institute as "one of the most important historical documents of Marxism."[1] It expounded the theory of permanent revolution.

---

[1] In V. Adoratsky, ed., *Karl Marx: Selected Works* (Co-Operative Publishing Society of Foreign Workers in the U.S.S.R., Moscow and Leningrad, 1936), II, 154. The following text is from that edition.

Communism and Socialism 155

Brothers! In the two revolutionary years 1848–49 the League proved itself in double fashion: first, in that its members energetically took part in the movement in all places, that in the press, on the barricades and on the battlefields, they stood in the front ranks of the only decidedly revolutionary class, the proletariat. The League further proved itself in that its conception of the movement as laid down in the circulars of the congresses and of the Central Committee of 1847 as well as in the *Communist Manifesto* turned out to be the only correct one, that the expectations expressed in those documents were completely fulfilled and the conception of present-day social conditions, previously propagated only in secret by the League, is now on everyone's lips and is openly preached in the market places. At the same time the former firm organization of the League was considerably slackened. A large part of the members who directly participated in the revolutionary movement believed the time for secret societies to have gone by and public activities alone sufficient. The individual circles and communities allowed their connections with the Central Committee to become loose and gradually dormant. Consequently, while the democratic party, the party of the petty bourgeoisie, organized itself more and more in Germany, the workers' party lost its only firm foothold, remained organized at the most in separate localities for local purposes and in the general movement thus came completely under the domination and leadership of the petty-bourgeois democrats. An end must be put to this state of affairs, the independence of the workers must be restored. The Central Committee realized this necessity and therefore already in the winter of 1848–49 it sent an emissary, Josef Moll, to Germany for the reorganization of the League. Moll's mission, however, was without lasting effect, partly because the German workers at that time had not acquired sufficient experience and partly because it was interrupted by the insurrection of the previous May. Moll himself took up the musket, entered the Baden-Palatinate army and fell on July 19 in the encounter at the Murg. The League lost in him one of its oldest, most active and most trustworthy members, one who had been active in all the congresses and Central Committees, and even prior to this had carried out a series of missions with great success. After the defeat of the revolutionary parties of Germany and France in July 1849, almost all the members of the Central Committee came together again in

London, replenished their numbers with new revolutionary forces and set about the reorganization of the League with renewed zeal.

Reorganization can only be carried out by an emissary, and the Central Committee considers it extremely important that the emissary should leave precisely at this moment when a new revolution is impending, when the workers' party, therefore, must act in the most organized, most unanimous and most independent fashion possible if it is not to be exploited and taken in tow again by the bourgeoisie as in 1848.

Brothers! We told you as early as 1848 that the German liberal bourgeois would soon come to power and would immediately turn their newly acquired power against the workers. You have seen how this has been fulfilled. In fact it was the bourgeois who, immediately after the March movement of 1848, took possession of the state power and used this power to force back at once the workers, their allies in the struggle, into their former oppressed position. Though the bourgeoisie was not able to accomplish this without uniting with the feudal party, which had been disposed of in March, without finally even surrendering power once again to this feudal absolutist party, still it has secured conditions for itself which, in the long run, owing to the financial embarrassment of the government, would place power in its hands and would safeguard all its interests, if it were possible for the revolutionary movement to assume already now a so-called peaceful development. The bourgeoisie, in order to safeguard its rule, would not even need to make itself obnoxious by violent measures against the people, since all such violent steps have already been taken by the feudal counter-revolution. Developments, however, will not take this peaceful course. On the contrary, the revolution, which will accelerate this development, is near at hand, whether it will be called forth by an independent uprising of the French proletariat or by an invasion of the Holy Alliance against the revolutionary Babylon.

And the role, this so treacherous role which the German liberal bourgeois played in 1848 against the people, will in the impending revolution be taken over by the democratic petty bourgeois, who at present occupy the same position in the opposition as the liberal bourgeois before 1848. This party, the democratic party, which is far more dangerous to

Communism and Socialism

the workers than the previous liberal one, consists of three elements:

I. Of the most advanced sections of the big bourgeoisie, which pursue the aim of the immediate complete overthrow of feudalism and absolutism. This faction is represented by the one-time Berlin compromisers, by the tax resisters.

II. Of the democratic-constitutional petty bourgeois, whose main aim during the previous movement was the establishment of a more or less democratic federal state as striven for by their representatives, the Lefts in the Frankfort Assembly, and later by the Stuttgart parliament, and by themselves in the campaign for the Reich Constitution.

III. Of the republican petty bourgeois, whose ideal is a German federative republic after the manner of Switzerland, and who now call themselves Red and Social-Democratic because they cherish the pious wish of abolishing the pressure of big capital on small capital, of the big bourgeois on the small bourgeois. The representatives of this faction were the members of the democratic congresses and committees, the leaders of the democratic associations, the editors of the democratic newspapers.

Now, after their defeat, all these factions call themselves Republicans or Reds, just as the republican petty bourgeois in France now call themselves Socialists. Where, as in Württemberg, Bavaria, etc., they still find opportunity to pursue their aims constitutionally, they seize the occasion to retain their old phrases and to prove by deeds that they have not changed in the least. It is evident, moreover, that the altered name of this party does not make the slightest difference in its attitude to the workers, but merely proves that they are now obliged to turn against the bourgeoisie, which is united with absolutism, and to seek support in the proletariat.

The petty-bourgeois democratic party in Germany is very powerful; it comprises not only the great majority of the bourgeois inhabitants of the towns, the small people in industry and trade and the guild masters; it numbers among its followers also the peasants and the rural proletariat, in so far as the latter has not yet found a support in the independent urban proletariat.

The relation of the revolutionary workers' party to the petty-bourgeois democrats is this: it marches together with them against the faction which it aims at overthrowing, it opposes them in everything whereby they seek to consolidate their position in their own interests.

Far from desiring to revolutionize all society for the revolutionary proletarians, the democratic petty bourgeois strive for a change in social conditions by means of which existing society will be made as tolerable and comfortable as possible for them. Hence they demand above all diminution of state expenditure by a curtailment of the bureaucracy and shifting the chief taxes on to the big landowners and bourgeois. Further, they demand the abolition of the pressure of big capital on small, through public credit institutions and laws against usury, by which means it will be possible for them and the peasants to obtain advances, on favorable conditions, from the state instead of from the capitalists; they also demand the establishment of bourgeois property relations in the countryside by the complete abolition of feudalism. To accomplish all this they need a democratic state structure, either constitutional or republican, that will give them and their allies, the peasants, a majority; also a democratic communal structure that will give them direct control over communal property and over a series of functions now performed by the bureaucrats.

The domination and speedy increase of capital is further to be counteracted partly by restricting the right of inheritance and partly by transferring as many jobs of work as possible to the state. As far as the workers are concerned, it remains certain above all that they are to remain wage-workers as before; the democratic petty bourgeois only desire better wages and a more secure existence for the workers and hope to achieve this through partial employment by the state and through charity measures; in short, they hope to bribe the workers by more or less concealed alms and to break their revolutionary potency by making their position tolerable for the moment. The demands of the petty-bourgeois democracy here summarized are not put forward by all of its factions at the same time and only a very few members of them consider that these demands constitute definite aims in their entirety. The further separate individuals or factions among them go, the more of these demands will they make their own, and those few who see their own program in what has been outlined above might believe that thereby they have put forward the utmost that can be demanded from the revolution. But these demands can in no wise suffice for the party

Communism and Socialism

of the proletariat. While the democratic petty bourgeois wish to bring the revolution to a conclusion as quickly as possible, and with the achievement, at most, of the above demands, it is our interest and our task to make the revolution permanent, until all more or less possessing classes have been forced out of their position of dominance, until the proletariat has conquered state power, and the association of proletarians, not only in one country but in all the dominant countries of the world, has advanced so far that competition among the proletarians of these countries has ceased and that at least the decisive productive forces are concentrated in the hands of the proletarians. For us the issue cannot be the alteration of private property but only its annihilation, not the smoothing over of class antagonisms but the abolition of classes, not the improvement of existing society but the foundation of a new one. That, during the further development of the revolution, the petty-bourgeois democracy will for a moment obtain predominating influence in Germany is not open to doubt. The question, therefore, arises as to what the attitude of the proletariat and in particular of the League will be in relation to it:

1. During the continuance of the present conditions where the petty-bourgeois democrats are likewise oppressed;

2. In the next revolutionary struggle, which will give them the upper hand;

3. After this struggle, during the period of preponderance over the overthrown classes and the proletariat.

1. At the present moment, when the democratic petty bourgeois are everywhere oppressed, they preach in general unity and reconciliation to the proletariat, they offer it their hand and strive for the establishment of a large opposition party which will embrace all shades of opinion in the democratic party, that is, they strive to entangle the workers in a party organization in which general social-democratic phrases predominate, behind which their special interests are concealed and in which the particular demands of the proletariat may not be brought forward for the sake of beloved peace. Such a union would turn out solely to their advantage and altogether to the disadvantage of the proletariat. The proletariat would lose its whole independent, laboriously achieved position and once more sink down to being an appendage of official bourgeois democracy. This union must, therefore, be most decisively rejected. Instead of once again

stooping to serve as the applauding chorus of the bourgeois democrats, the workers, and above all the League, must exert themselves to establish an independent, secret and public organization of the workers' party alongside of the official democrats and make each section the central point and nucleus of workers' societies in which the attitude and interests of the proletariat will be discussed independently of bourgeois influences. How far the bourgeois democrats are from seriously considering an alliance in which the proletarians would stand side by side with them with equal power and equal rights is shown, for example, by the Breslau democrats who, in their organ, the *Neue Oder-Zeitung*, most furiously attack the independently organized workers, whom they style Socialists. In the case of a struggle against a common adversary no special union is required. As soon as such an adversary has to be fought directly, the interests of both parties, for the moment, coincide, and, as previously, so also in the future, this connection, calculated to last only for the moment, will arise of itself. It is self-evident that in the impending bloody conflicts, as in all earlier ones, it is the workers who, in the main, will have to win the victory by their courage, determination and self-sacrifice. As previously, so also in this struggle, the mass of the petty bourgeois will as long as possible remain hesitant, undecided and inactive, and then, as soon as the issue has been decided, will seize the victory for themselves, will call upon the workers to maintain tranquillity and return to their work, will guard against so-called excesses and bar the proletariat from the fruits of victory. It is not in the power of the workers to prevent the petty-bourgeois democrats from doing this, but it is in their power to make it difficult for them to gain the upper hand as against the armed proletariat, and to dictate such conditions to them that the rule of the bourgeois democrats will from the outset bear within it the seeds of their downfall, and that their subsequent extrusion by the rule of the proletariat will be considerably facilitated. Above all things, the workers must counteract, as much as is at all possible, during the conflict and immediately after the struggle, the bourgeois endeavors to allay the storm, and must compel the democrats to carry out their present terrorist phrases. Their actions must be so aimed as to prevent the direct revolutionary excitement from being suppressed again immediately after the victory. On the contrary, they must keep it alive as long as possible. Far from opposing so-called excesses, instances of popular revenge against hated individuals or public buildings that are associated only with hateful recollections, such instances must not only be tolerated but the leadership of them taken in hand. During the struggle and after the struggle, the workers must, at every opportunity, put forward their own demands alongside of the demands of the bourgeois democrats. They must demand guarantees for the workers as soon as the democratic bourgeois set about taking over the government. If necessary they must obtain these guarantees by force and in general they must see to it that the new rulers pledge themselves to all possible concessions and promises—the surest way to compromise them. In general, they must in every way restrain as far as possible the intoxication of victory and the enthusiasm for the new state of things, which make their appearance after every victorious street battle, by a calm and dispassionate estimate of the situation and by unconcealed mistrust in the new government. Alongside of the new official governments they must establish simultaneously their own revolutionary workers' governments, whether in the form of municipal committees and municipal councils or in the form of workers' clubs or workers' committees, so that the bourgeois-democratic governments not only immediately lose the support of the workers but from the outset see themselves supervised and threatened by authorities which are backed by the whole mass of the workers. In a word, from the first moment of victory, mistrust must be directed no longer against the conquered reactionary party, but against the workers' previous allies, against the party that wishes to exploit the common victory for itself alone.

2. But in order to be able energetically and threateningly to oppose this party, whose treachery to the workers will begin from the first hour of victory, the workers must be armed and organized. The arming of the whole proletariat with rifles, muskets, cannon and munitions must be put through at once, the revival of the old Citizens' Guard directed against the workers must be resisted. However, where the latter is not feasible the workers must attempt to organize themselves independently as a proletarian guard with commanders elected by themselves and with a general staff of their own choosing, and to put themselves at the command not of the state authority but of the revolutionary community councils which the workers will have managed to get adopted. Where workers are employed at the expense of the state they must see

that they are armed and organized in a separate corps with commanders of their own choosing or as part of the proletarian guard. Arms and ammunition must not be surrendered on any pretext; any attempt at disarming must be frustrated, if necessary by force. Destruction of the influence of the bourgeois democrats upon the workers, immediate independent and armed organization of the workers and the enforcement of conditions as difficult and compromising as possible upon the inevitable momentary rule of the bourgeois democracy—these are the main points which the proletariat and hence the League must keep in view during and after the impending insurrection.

3. As soon as the new governments have consolidated their positions to some extent, their struggle against the workers will begin. Here, in order to be able to offer energetic opposition to the democratic petty bourgeois, it is above all necessary that the workers shall be independently organized and centralized in clubs. After the overthrow of the existing governments, the Central Committee will, as soon as it is at all possible, betake itself to Germany, immediately convene a congress and put before the latter the necessary proposals for the centralization of the workers' clubs under a leadership established in the chief seat of the movement. The speedy organization of at least a provincial interlinking of the workers' clubs is one of the most important points for the strengthening and development of the workers' party; the immediate consequence of the overthrow of the existing governments will be the election of a national representative assembly. Here the proletariat must see to it:

I. That no groups of workers are barred on any pretext or by any kind of trickery on the part of local authorities or government commissioners.

II. That everywhere workers' candidates are put up alongside of the bourgeois-democratic candidates, that they should consist as far as possible of members of the League, and that their election is promoted by all possible means. Even where there is no prospect whatsoever of their being elected, the workers must put up their own candidates in order to preserve their independence, to count their forces and to bring before the public their revolutionary attitude and party standpoint. In this connection they must not allow themselves to be seduced by such arguments of the democrats as, for example, that by so doing they are splitting the democratic party and making it possible for the reactionaries to win. The ultimate intention of all such phrases is to dupe the proletariat. The advance which the proletarian party is bound to make by such independent action is infinitely more important than the disadvantage that might be incurred by the presence of a few reactionaries in the representative body. If the democracy from the outset comes out resolutely and terroristically against the reaction, the influence of the latter in the elections will be destroyed in advance.

The first point on which the bourgeois democrats will come into conflict with the workers will be the abolition of feudalism. As in the first French Revolution, the petty bourgeois will give the feudal lands to the peasants as free property, that is to say, try to leave the rural proletariat in existence and form a petty-bourgeois peasant class which will go through the same cycle of impoverishment and indebtedness which the French peasant is now still going through.

The workers must oppose this plan in the interest of the rural proletariat and in their own interest. They must demand that the confiscated feudal property remain state property and be converted into workers' colonies cultivated by the associated rural proletariat with all the advantages of large-scale agriculture, through which the principle of common property immediately obtains a firm basis in the midst of the tottering bourgeois property relations. Just as the democrats combine with the peasants so must the workers combine with the rural proletariat. Further, the democrats will work either directly for a federative republic or, if they cannot avoid a single and indivisible republic, they will at least attempt to cripple the central government by the utmost possible autonomy and independence for the communities and provinces. The workers, in opposition to this plan, must not only strive for a single and indivisible German republic, but also within this republic for the most determined centralization of power in the hands of the state authority. They must not allow themselves to be misguided by the democratic talk of freedom for the communities, of self-government, etc. In a country like Germany where there are still so many relics of the Middle Ages to be abolished, where there is so much local and provincial obstinacy to be broken, it must under no circumstances be permitted that every village, every town and every province should put a new obstacle in the path of revolutionary activity, which can proceed with full force only from the center. It is not to be tolerated that the present state of affairs should be renewed, that Germans must fight separately in every town and in every province for one and the same advance. Least of all is it to be tolerated that a form of property, namely, communal property, which still lags behind modern private property and which everywhere is necessarily passing into the latter, together with the quarrels resulting from it between poor and rich communities, as well as communal civil law, with its trickery against the workers, that exists alongside of state civil law, should be perpetuated by a so-called free communal constitution. As in France in 1793 so today in Germany it is the task of the really revolutionary party to carry through the strictest centralization.

We have seen how the democrats will come to power with the next movement, how they will be compelled to propose more or less socialistic measures. It will be asked what measures the workers ought to propose in reply. At the beginning of the movement, of course, the workers cannot yet propose any directly communistic measures. But they can:

1. Compel the democrats to interfere in as many spheres as possible of the hitherto existing social order, to disturb its regular course and to compromise themselves as well as to concentrate the utmost possible productive forces, means of transport, factories, railways, etc., in the hands of the state;

2. They must drive the proposals of the democrats, who in any case will not act in a revolutionary but in a merely reformist manner, to the extreme and transform them into direct attacks upon private property; thus, for example, if the petty bourgeois propose purchase of the railways and factories, the workers must demand that these railways and factories shall be simply confiscated by the state without compensation as being the property of reactionaries. If the democrats propose proportional taxes, the workers must demand progressive taxes; if the democrats themselves put forward a moderately progressive tax, the workers must insist on a tax with rates that rise so steeply that big capital will be ruined by it; if the democrats demand regulation of state debts, the workers must demand state bankruptcy. Thus, the demands of the workers must everywhere be governed by the concessions and measures of the democrats.

If the German workers are not able to attain power and achieve their own class interests without completely going through a lengthy revolutionary development, they at least know for a certainty this time that the first act of this approaching revolutionary drama will coincide with the direct victory of their own class in France and will be very much accelerated by it.

But they themselves must do the utmost for their final victory by clarifying their minds as to what their class interests are, by taking up their position as an independent party as soon as possible and by not allowing themselves to be seduced for a single moment by the hypocritical phrases of the democratic petty bourgeois into refraining from the independent organization of the party of the proletariat. Their battle cry must be: The Revolution in Permanence.

STATUTES OF THE COMMUNIST LEAGUE

Drafted by the Central Committee in Cologne, under the direction of Marx and Engels, after the Communist split in London, September 1850. These statutes were adopted by the London branch of the Communist League, January 5, 1851, when Marx was present.

1. The aim of the Communist League is the destruction of the old society—and overthrow of the bourgeoisie—using all means of propaganda and political struggle; the spiritual, political and economic emancipation of the proletariat; the carrying out of the communist revolution. In the various stages of development which the struggle of the proletariat has to go through, the League always represents the interest of the whole movement, always attempting to unite and to organize all the revolutionary energy of the proletariat. The League remains secret and indissoluble so long as the revolution has not attained its final goal.

2. Only he can be a member who combines the following conditions:

    a. Freedom from all religion, practical renunciation of every churchly association and all ceremonies not ordered by civil law.

    b. Insight into the conditions, course of development, and final goal of the proletarian movement.

    c. Keeping away from all associations and partial efforts inimical or obstructive to the League.

    d. Ability and eagerness for propaganda, unshakable and loyal conviction, revolutionary energy.

    e. Strictest secrecy about all League affairs.

3. Eligibility for membership is decided by unanimous vote of the whole community. As a rule, new members are received by the chairmen in the presence of the assembled community. Members take an oath of absolute submission to the decisions of the League.

4. He who violates the conditions of membership is excluded. Exclusion of individuals is decided by majority vote of the community. Whole communities can be excluded by the Central Authority if so instructed by the District Community. Those excluded are denounced to the whole League and are subject to surveillance like all other suspected characters.

5. The League is organized into communities, districts, a Central Authority, and a Congress.

6. Communities consist of at least three members each, of the same locality. Each community elects a chairman, who conducts the meetings, and a deputy, who acts as treasurer.

7. The communities of each country or province are under a Chief Community, a District, which is appointed by the Central Authority. The communities are in direct contact with their districts, the districts with the Central Authority.

8. The communities meet regularly at least every fourteen days; they are in at least monthly correspondence with their districts, and the district communities at least bimonthly with the Central Authority. The Central Authority reports every three months on the state of the League.

9. The chairmen and deputies of the communities and

districts are chosen annually and are removable by their electors at any time. Members of the Central Authority are removable only by the Congress.

10. Every member of the League has to pay monthly dues, the minimum of which is determined by the Congress. Half of these dues go to the district and half to the Central Authority, and are used to cover administrative costs, distribution of propaganda, and the sending out of emissaries. The districts bear the cost of correspondence with their communities. Every three months the dues are sent to the district, which transmits half of the total income to the Central Authority and at the same time gives an accounting of income and expenditure to the communities. The Central Authority submits an accounting to the Congress. Extraordinary costs are met by extraordinary contributions.

11. The Central Authority is the executive organ of the whole League. It consists of at least three members, selected and recruited by the districts; its seat is determined by the Congress and it is accountable only to the Congress.

12. The Congress is the legislative organ of the whole League. It consists of representatives of the district assemblies, which elect one deputy for every five communities.

13. The District Assembly is the representative of the districts; it meets regularly every quarter in the district center under the chairmanship of the head of the Chief Community for consultation about district affairs. Each community sends one deputy. The district assembly for the election of League representatives meets invariably in the middle of July of every year.

Art. 5 Community
Art. 6 District
Art. 7 Central Authority
Art. 8 Congress
Art. 9 Reception into the League
Art. 10 Expulsion from the League/Money...[1]

[1] Illegible in Marx's handwriting.

14. Fourteen days after the meeting of the district election assemblies, the Congress meets at the seat of the Central Authority, if no other place has been decided upon.
15. The Congress receives from the Central Authority, which has a seat in it but no vote, an account of its whole activity and the state of the League; it declares the basic policies to be followed by the League, decides on changes in the statutes, and determines the seat of the Central Authority for the following year.
16. In urgent cases the Central Authority may call the Congress to an extraordinary session, which would then consist of the deputies elected by the districts the last time.
17. Conflicts among individual members of the same community are conclusively settled by the community; the same in districts, by the district community; and among various districts, by the Central Authority. Personal complaints about members of the Central Authority are the jurisdiction of the Congress. Conflicts among communities of the same district are decided by the district community; among communities and their district or various districts, by the Central Authority. Still, in the first instance, the convening of the district assemblies, and in the second, that of the Congress, are open as avenues for redress. The Congress also decides on all conflicts between the Central Authority and the subordinate authorities of the League.

MARGINAL NOTES TO THE PROGRAM OF THE GERMAN WORKERS' PARTY (CRITIQUE OF THE GOTHA PROGRAM)

This is one of the major documents of Marxism. With the covering letter reproduced here (dated May 5, 1875), Marx sent it to Wilhelm Bracke, asking that it be submitted to the other leaders of the Social-Democratic Workers' party (the "Eisenachers"), which was meeting with the Lassalle-founded General German Workers' Association at Gotha, May 22–27, 1875. The Gotha Congress united both groups into the Socialist Labor party, which later became the powerful German Social-Democratic party. The text here given is based on the edition of Progress Publishers, Moscow, 1968

Dear Bracke:

When you have read the following critical marginal notes on the Coalition Program, please be so good as to send them on to Geib, Auer, Bebel, and Liebknecht for examination. The manuscript must be returned to you, so that it will be at my disposal in case of necessity. I am extremely busy and have to far exceed the amount of work the doctors allow me. Hence it was in no way a "pleasure" to write such a lengthy screed. It was, however, necessary, so that the steps I will take later will not be misinterpreted by the friends in the party for whom this communication is intended.

After the Coalition Congress has been held Engels and I will publish a short explanation to the effect that we will stay away from the said program of principles altogether, and that we have nothing to do with it.

This is indispensable because of the opinion—the entirely erroneous opinion—held abroad that we secretly guide the movement of the so-called Eisenach party from here. In a recently published Russian book,[1] for example, Bakunin not only holds me responsible for all the programs, etc., of that party but also for every step Liebknecht has taken from the day of his cooperation with the People's party.

Apart from this, it is my duty not to give recognition, even by diplomatic silence, to what in my opinion is a thoroughly objectionable program that demoralizes the party.

Every step of real movement is more important than a dozen programs. If therefore it was not possible—and the conditions of the time did not permit it—to go *beyond* the

[1] Mikhail Bakunin, *Gossudarstvennost i Anarchiya*, published anonymously in Switzerland in 1873.

Eisenach program, one should simply have concluded an agreement for action against the common enemy. But if one constructs programs of principles (instead of postponing them until a prolonged period of common activity has prepared the ground), one sets up before the whole world landmarks which measure the level of party movement.

The Lassallean leaders are coming [to the Congress] because circumstances force them to do it. If it had been explained to them beforehand that there would be no haggling about principles, they would have had to be content with a program of action or a plan of organization for common action. Instead of this they are permitted to come armed with mandates, given recognition of them as binding, and thus one surrenders unconditionally to those who are in need of help. To crown the whole thing, they are holding a congress *before* the Congress of Compromise, while our own party is holding its congress *post festum*. Obviously they wanted to stifle all criticism and give our party no opportunity for reflection. We know that the mere fact of unification satisfies the workers, but it is a mistake to think this momentary success is not bought too dearly.

For the rest, the program is no good, even apart from its sanctification of the Lassallean articles of faith.

I shall be sending you in the near future the last parts of the French edition of *Capital*. The printing was held up for a considerable time by a French government ban. The thing will be ready this week or at the beginning of next week. Had you received the previous six sections? Please let me have the address of Bernhard Becker, to whom I must also send the final parts.

The bookshop of the *Volksstaat* has its peculiar ways. Up to this moment, for example, I have not received a single copy of my *Revelations About the Cologne Communist Trial*.

With best regards,

Your

KARL MARX

I

1. "Labor is the source of all wealth and all culture, and since useful labor is possible only in society and through society, the proceeds of labor belong undiminished with equal right to all members of society."

Communism and Socialism 171

FIRST PART OF THE PARAGRAPH: "Labor is the source of all wealth and all culture."

Labor is *not the source* of all wealth. *Nature* is just as much the source of use values (and it is surely of such that material wealth consists!) as labor, which itself is only the manifestation of a force of nature, human labor power. The above phrase is to be found in all children's primers and is correct insofar as it is implied that labor is performed with the appurtenant subjects and instruments. But a socialist program cannot allow such bourgeois phrases to pass over in silence the *conditions* that alone give them meaning. And insofar as man from the beginning behaves toward nature, the primary source of all instruments and subjects of labor, as an owner, treats her as belonging to him, his labor becomes the source of use values, therefore also of wealth. The bourgeois have very good grounds for falsely ascribing *supernatural creative power* to labor; since precisely from the fact that labor depends on nature it follows that the man who possesses no other property than his labor power must, in all conditions of society and culture, be the slave of other men who have made themselves the owners of the material conditions of labor. He can work only with their permission, hence live only with their permission.

Let us now leave the sentence as it stands, or rather limps. What could one have expected in conclusion? Obviously this:

"Since labor is the source of all wealth, no one in society can appropriate wealth except as the product of labor. Therefore, if he himself does not work, he lives by the labor of others and also acquires his culture at the expense of the labor of others."

Instead of this, by means of the verbal rivet "and since" a second proposition is added in order to draw a conclusion from this and not from the first one.

SECOND PART OF THE PARAGRAPH: "Useful labor is possible only in society and through society."

According to the first proposition, labor was the source of all wealth and all culture; therefore no society is possible without labor. Now we learn, conversely, that no "useful" labor is possible without society.

One could just as well have said that only in society can

useless and even socially harmful labor become a branch of gainful occupation, that only in society can one live by being idle, etc., etc.—in short, one could just as well have copied the whole of Rousseau.

And what is "useful" labor? Surely only labor which produces the intended useful result. A savage—and man was a savage after he had ceased to be an ape—who kills an animal with a stone, who collects fruits, etc., performs "useful" labor.

THIRDLY, THE CONCLUSION: "And since useful labor is possible only in society and through society, the proceeds of labor belong undiminished with equal right to all members of society."

A fine conclusion! If useful labor is possible only in society and through society, the proceeds of labor belong to society—and only so much therefrom accrues to the individual worker as is not required to maintain the "condition" of labor, society.

In fact, this proposition has at all times been made use of by the champions of the *state of society prevailing at any given time*. First come the claims of the government and everything that sticks to it, since it is the social organ for the maintenance of the social order; then come the claims of the various kinds of private property, for the various kinds of private property are the foundations of society, etc. One sees that such hollow phrases can be twisted and turned as desired.

The first and second parts of the paragraph have some intelligible connection only in the following wording:

"Labor becomes the source of wealth and culture only as social labor," or, what is the same thing, "in and through society."

This proposition is incontestably correct, for although isolated labor (its material conditions presupposed) can create use values, it can create neither wealth nor culture.

But equally incontestable is this other proposition:

"In proportion as labor develops socially, and becomes thereby a source of wealth and culture, poverty and destitution develop among the workers, and wealth and culture among the nonworkers."

This is the law of all history hitherto. What, therefore, had

Communism and Socialism

to be done here, instead of setting down general phrases about "labor" and "society," was to prove concretely how in present capitalist society the material, etc., conditions have at last been created which enable and compel the workers to lift this social curse.

In fact, however, the whole paragraph, bungled in style and content, is only there in order to inscribe the Lassallean catchword of the "undiminished proceeds of labor" as a slogan at the top of the party banner. I shall return later to the "proceeds of labor," "equal rights," etc., since the same thing recurs in a somewhat different form further on.

2. *"In present-day society, the instruments of labor are the monopoly of the capitalist class; the resulting dependence of the working class is the cause of misery and servitude in all its forms."*

This sentence, borrowed from the Rules of the International, is incorrect in this "improved" edition.

In present-day society the instruments of labor are the monopoly of the landowners (the monopoly of property in land is even the basis of the monopoly of capital) *and* the capitallists. In the passage in question, the Rules of the International do not mention either the one or the other class of monopolists. They speak of the *"monopolizer of the means of labor, that is, the sources of life."* The addition, *"sources of life,"* makes it sufficiently clear that land is included in the instruments of labor.

The correction was introduced because Lassalle, for reasons now generally known, attacked *only* the capitalist class and not the landowners. In England, the capitalist is usually not even the owner of the land on which his factory stands.

3. *"The emancipation of labor demands the promotion of the instruments of labor to the common property of society and the cooperative regulation of the total labor, with a fair distribution of the proceeds of labor."*

"Promotion of the instruments of labor to the common property" ought obviously to read their "conversion into the common property"; but this only in passing.

What are "proceeds of labor"? The product of labor or its value? And in the latter class, is it the total value of the product or only that part of the value which labor has newly added to the value of the means of production consumed?

"Proceeds of labor" is a loose notion which Lassalle has put in the place of definite economic conceptions.

What is "a fair distribution"?

Do not the bourgeois assert that the present-day distribution is "fair"? And is it not, in fact, the only "fair" distribution on the basis of the present-day mode of production? Are economic relations regulated by legal conceptions or do not, on the contrary, legal relations arise from economic ones? Have not also the socialist sectarians the most varied notions about "fair" distribution?

To understand what is implied in this connection by the phrase "fair distribution," we must take the first paragraph and this one together. The latter presupposes a society wherein the instruments of labor are common property and the total labor is cooperatively regulated, and from the first paragraph we learn that "the proceeds of labor belong undiminished with equal right to all members of society."

"To all members of society"? To those who do not work as well? What remains then of the "undiminished" proceeds of labor? Only to those members of society who work? What remains then of the "equal right" of all members of society?

But "all members of society" and "equal right" are obviously mere phrases. The kernel consists of this, that in this communist society every worker must receive the "undiminished" Lassallean "proceeds of labor."

Let us take first of all the words "proceeds of labor" in the sense of the product of labor; then the cooperative proceeds of labor are the *total social product*.

From this must now be deducted:

First, cover for replacement of the means of production used up.

Second, additional portion for expansion of production.

Third, reserve or insurance funds to provide against accidents, dislocations caused by natural calamities, etc.

These deductions from the "undiminished" proceeds of labor are an economic necessity and their magnitude is to be determined according to available means and forces, and partly by computation of probabilities, but they are in no way calculable by equity.

There remains the other part of the total product, intended to serve as means of consumption.

Communism and Socialism

Before this is divided among the individuals, there has to be deducted again, from it:

First, the general costs of administration not belonging to production.

This part will from the outset be very considerably restricted in comparison with present-day society, and it diminishes in proportion as the new society develops.

Second, that which is intended for the common satisfaction of needs, such as schools, health services, etc.

From the outset this part grows considerably in comparison with present-day society and it grows in proportion as the new society develops.

Third, funds for those unable to work, etc., in short, for what is included under so-called official poor relief today.

Only now do we come to the "distribution" which the program, under Lassallean influence, alone has in view in its narrow fashion, namely, to that part of the means of consumption which is divided among the individual producers of the cooperative society.

The "undiminished" proceeds of labor have already unnoticeably become converted into the "diminished" proceeds, although what the producer is deprived of in his capacity as a private individual benefits him directly or indirectly in his capacity as a member of society.

Just as the phrase of the "undiminished" proceeds of labor has disappeared, so now does the phrase of the "proceeds of labor" disappear altogether.

Within the cooperative society based on common ownership of the means of production, the producers do not exchange their products; just as little does the labor employed on the products appear here as the *value* of these products, as a material quality possessed by them, since now, in contrast to capitalist society, individual labor no longer exists in an indirect fashion but directly as a component part of the total labor. The phrase "proceeds of labor," objectionable also today on account of its ambiguity, thus loses all meaning.

What we have to deal with here is a communist society, not as it has *developed* on its own foundations, but, on the contrary, just as it *emerges* from capitalist society; which is thus in every respect, economically, morally, and intellectually, still stamped with the birthmarks of the old society from whose womb it emerges. Accordingly, the individual producer receives back from society—after the deductions have been made—exactly what he gives to it. What he has given to it is his individual quantum of labor. For example, the social working day consists of the sum of the individual hours of work; the individual labor times of the individual producer is the part of the social working day contributed by him, his share in it. He receives a certificate from society that he has furnished such and such an amount of labor (after deducting his labor for the common funds), and with this certificate he draws from the social stock of means of consumption as much as the same amount of labor costs. The same amount of labor which he has given to society in one form he receives back in another.

Here obviously the same principle prevails as that which regulates the exchange of commodities, as far as this is exchange of equal values. Content and form are changed, because under the altered circumstances no one can give anything except his labor, and because, on the other hand, nothing can pass to the ownership of individuals except individual means of consumption. But as far as the distribution of the latter among the individual producers is concerned, the same principle prevails as in the exchange of commodity equivalents: a given amount of labor in one form is exchanged for an equal amount of labor in another form.

Hence *equal right* here is still in principle—*bourgeois right*, although principle and practice are no longer at loggerheads, while the exchange of equivalents in commodity exchange exists only on the average and not in the individual case.

In spite of this advance, this equal right is still constantly stigmatized by a bourgeois limitation. The right of the producers is *proportional* to the labor they supply; the equality consists in the fact that measurement is made with an *equal standard,* labor.

But one man is superior to another physically or mentally and so supplies more labor in the same time, or can labor for a longer time; and labor, to serve as a measure, must be defined by its duration or intensity, otherwise it ceases to be a standard of measurement. This *equal* right is an unequal right for unequal labor. It recognizes no class differences, because everyone is only a worker like everyone else; but it tacitly recognizes unequal individual endowment, and thus productive capacity, as a natural privilege. *It is, therefore, a right of inequality, in its content, like every right.* Right by its very nature can consist only in the application of an equal standard; but unequal individuals (and they would not be different individuals if they were not unequal) are measurable only by an equal standard insofar as they are brought under an equal point of view, are taken from one definite side only, for instance, in the present case, are regarded *only as workers* and nothing more is seen in them, everything else being ignored. Further, one worker is married, another not; one has more children than another, and so on and so forth. Thus with an equal performance of labor, and hence an equal share in the social consumption fund, one will in fact receive more than another, one will be richer than another, and so on. To avoid all these defects, right, instead of being equal, would have to be unequal.

But these defects are inevitable in the first phase of communist society as it is when it has just emerged after prolonged birth pangs from capitalist society. Right can never be higher than the economic structure of society and its cultural development conditioned thereby.

In a higher phase of communist society, after the enslaving subordination of the individual to the division of labor, and therewith also the antithesis between mental and physical labor, has vanished; after labor has become not only a means of life but life's prime want; after the productive forces have also increased with the all-round development of the individual, and all the springs of cooperative wealth flow more abundantly—only then can the narrow horizon of bourgeois right be crossed in its entirety and society inscribe on its banners: From each according to his ability, to each according to his needs!

I have dealt more at length with the "undiminished" proceeds of labor, on the one hand, and with "equal right" and "fair distribution," on the other, in order to show what a crime it is to attempt, on the one hand, to force on our Party again, as dogmas, ideas which in a certain period had some meaning but have now become obsolete verbal rubbish, while again perverting, on the other, the realistic outlook, which it cost so much effort to instill into the Party but which has now taken root in it, by means of ideological nonsense about right and other trash so common among the democrats and French socialists.

Quite apart from the analysis so far given, it was in general a mistake to make a fuss about so-called distribution and put the principal stress on it.

Any distribution whatever of the means of consumption is only a consequence of the distribution of the conditions of production themselves. The latter distribution, however, is a feature of the mode of production itself. The capitalist mode of production, for example, rests on the fact that the material conditions of production are in the hands of nonworkers in the form of property in capital and land, while the masses are only owners of the personal condition of production, of labor power. If the elements of production are so distributed, then the present-day distribution of the means of consumption results automatically. If the material conditions of production are the cooperative property of the workers themselves, then there likewise results a distribution of the means of consumption different from the present one. Vulgar socialism (and from it in turn a section of the democrats) has taken over from the bourgeois economists the consideration and treatment of distribution as independent of the mode of production and hence the presentation of socialism as turning principally on distribution. After the real relation has long been made clear, why retrogress again?

4. *"The emancipation of labor must be the work of the working class, relative to which all other classes are only one reactionary mass."*

The first strophe is taken from the introductory words of the Rules of the International, but "improved." There it is said: "The emancipation of the working class must be the act of the workers themselves"; here, on the contrary, the "working class" has to emancipate—what? "Labor." Let him understand who can.

In compensation, the antistrophe, on the other hand, is a Lassallean quotation of the first water: "relative to which" (the working class) "all other classes are only one reactionary mass."

In the *Communist Manifesto* it is said: "Of all the classes that stand face to face with the bourgeoisie today, the proletariat alone is a really revolutionary class. The other classes decay and finally disappear in the face of modern industry; the proletariat is its special and essential product."

The bourgeoisie is here conceived as a revolutionary class—as the bearer of large-scale industry—relative to the feudal lords and the lower middle class, who desire to maintain all social positions that are the creation of obsolete modes of production. Thus they do not form together with the bourgeoisie "only one reactionary mass."

On the other hand, the proletariat is revolutionary relative to the bourgeoisie because, having itself grown up on the basis of large-scale industry, it strives to strip off from production the capitalist character that the bourgeoisie seeks to perpetuate. But the *Manifesto* adds that the "lower middle class" is becoming revolutionary "in view of [its] impending transfer into the proletariat."

From this point of view, therefore, it is again nonsense to say that it, together with the bourgeoisie, and with the feudal lords into the bargain, "form only one reactionary mass" relative to the working class.

Has one proclaimed to the artisans, small manufacturers, etc., and peasants during the last elections: Relative to us, you, together with the bourgeoisie and feudal lords, form only one reactionary mass?

Lassalle knew the *Communist Manifesto* by heart, as his faithful followers know the gospels written by him. If, therefore, he has falsified it so grossly, this has occurred only to put a good color on his alliance with absolutist and feudal opponents against the bourgeoisie.

In the above paragraph, moreover, his oracular saying is dragged in by main force without any connection with the botched quotation from the Rules of the International. Thus it is here simply an impertinence, and indeed not at all displeasing to Herr Bismarck, one of those cheap pieces of insolence in which the Marat of Berlin deals.

5. *"The working class strives for its emancipation first of all within the framework of the present-day national state, conscious that the necessary results of its efforts, which are common to the workers of all civilized countries, will be the international brotherhood of peoples."*

Lassalle, in opposition to the *Communist Manifesto* and to all earlier socialism, conceived the workers' movement from the narrowest national standpoint. He is being followed in this—and that after the work of the International!

It is altogether self-evident that, to be able to fight at all, the working class must organize itself at home *as a class* and that its own country is the immediate arena of its struggle, insofar as its class struggle is national, not in substance, but, as the *Communist Manifesto* says, "in form." But the "framework of the present-day national state," for instance, the German Empire, is itself in its turn economically "within the framework" of the world market, politically "within the framework" of the system of states. Every businessman knows that German trade is at the same time foreign trade, and the greatness of Herr Bismarck consists, to be sure, precisely in his pursuing a kind of *international* policy.

And to what does the German Workers' party reduce its internationalism? To the consciousness that the result of its efforts will be "the international brotherhood of peoples"—a phrase borrowed from the bourgeois League of Peace and Freedom, which is intended to pass as equivalent to the international brotherhood of the working classes in the joint struggle against the ruling classes and their governments. Not a word, therefore, about the international functions of the German working class! And it is thus that it is to challenge its own bourgeoisie—which is already linked up in brotherhood against it with the bourgeois of all other countries—and Herr Bismarck's international policy of conspiracy.

In fact, the internationalism of the program stands *even infinitely below* that of the Free Trade party. The latter also asserts that the result of its efforts will be "the international brotherhood of peoples." But it also *does* something to make trade international and by no means contents itself with the consciousness that all peoples are carrying on trade at home.

The international activity of the working classes does not in any way depend on the existence of the International Working Men's Association. This was only the first attempt to create a central organ for the activity; an attempt which was a lasting success on account of the impulse which it gave but which was no longer realizable in its first historical form after the fall of the Paris Commune.

Bismarck's *Norddeutsche* was absolutely right when it announced, to the satisfaction of its master, that the German Workers' party had sworn off internationalism in the new program.

II

"Starting from these basic principles, the German Workers' party strives by all legal means for the free state—and—socialist society: the abolition of the wage system together with the iron law of wages—and—exploitation in every form; the elimination of all social and political inequality."

I shall return to the "free" state later.

So, in future, the German Workers' party has got to believe in Lassalle's "iron law of wages"! That this may not be lost, the nonsense is perpetrated of speaking of the "abolition of the wage system" (it should read: system of wage labor), "together with the iron law of wages." If I abolish wage labor, then naturally I abolish its laws also, whether they are of "iron" or sponge. But Lassalle's attack on wage labor turns almost solely on this so-called law. In order, therefore, to prove that Lassalle's sect has conquered, the "wage system" must be abolished "together with the iron law of wages" and not without it.

It is well known that nothing of the "iron law of wages" is Lassalle's except the word "iron" borrowed from Goethe's "great, eternal iron laws." The word "iron" is a label by which the true believers recognize one another. But if I take the law with Lassalle's stamp on it, and consequently in his sense, then I must also take it with his substantiation for it. And what is that? As Lange already showed, shortly after Lassalle's death, it is the Malthusian theory of population (preached by Lange himself). But if this theory is correct, then again I cannot abolish the law even if I abolish wage labor a hundred times over, because the law then governs not only the system of wage labor but *every* social system. Basing themselves directly on this, the economists have been proving for fifty years and more that socialism cannot abolish poverty, which has its basis in nature, but can only make it *general*, distribute it simultaneously over the whole surface of society!

But all this is not the main thing. Quite apart from the false Lassallean formulation of the law, the truly outrageous retrogression consists in the following:

Since Lassalle's death there has asserted itself in our party the scientific understanding that wages are not what they appear to be—namely, the *value,* or *price, of labor*—but only a masked form for the *value,* or *price, of labor power.* Thereby the whole bourgeois conception of wages hitherto, as well as all the criticism hitherto directed against this conception, was thrown overboard once for all and it was made clear that the wage worker has permission to work for his own subsistence, that is, *to live,* only insofar as he works for a certain time gratis for the capitalist (and hence also for the latter's co-consumers of surplus value); that the whole capitalist system of production turns on the increase of this gratis labor by extending the working day or by developing the productivity, that is, increasing the intensity, of labor power, etc.; that, consequently, the system of wage labor is a system of slavery, and indeed of a slavery which becomes more severe in proportion as the social productive forces of labor develop, whether the worker receives better or worse payment. And after this understanding has gained more and more ground in our party, some return to Lassalle's dogmas although they must have known that Lassalle *did not know* what wages were, but, following in the wake of the bourgeois economists, took the appearance for the essence of the matter.

It is as if, among slaves who have at last got behind the secret of slavery and broken out in rebellion, a slave still in thrall to obsolete notions were to inscribe on the program of the rebellion: Slavery must be abolished because the feeding of slaves in the system of slavery cannot exceed a certain low maximum!

Does not the mere fact that the representatives of our party were capable of perpetrating such a monstrous attack on the understanding that has spread among the mass of our party prove by itself with what criminal levity and with what lack of conscience they set to work in drawing up this compromise program!

Instead of the indefinite concluding phrase of the paragraph, "the elimination of all social and political inequality," it ought to have been said that with the abolition of class distinctions all social and political inequality arising from them would disappear of itself.

Communism and Socialism

III

"The German Workers' party, in order to pave the way to the solution of the social question, demands the establishment of producers' cooperative societies with state aid under the democratic control of the toiling people. The producers' cooperative societies are to be called into being for industry and agriculture on such a scale that the socialist organization of the total labor will arise from them."

After the Lassallean "iron law of wages," the physic of the prophet. The way to it is "paved" in worthy fashion. In place of the existing class struggle appears a newspaper scribbler's phrase: "the social *question*," to the *"solution"* of which one "paves the way." Instead of arising from the revolutionary process of transformation of society, the "socialist organization of the total labor" "arises" from the "state aid" that the state gives to the producers' cooperative societies and which the *state*, not the worker, *"calls into being."* It is worthy of Lassalle's imagination that with state loans one can build a new society just as well as a new railway!

From the remnants of a sense of shame, "state aid" has been put—under the democratic control of the "toiling people."

In the first place, the majority of the "toiling people" in Germany consists of peasants, and not of proletarians.

Second, "democratic" means in German *"volksherrschaftlich"* ["by the rule of the people"]. But what does "control by the rule of the people of the toiling people" mean? And particularly in the case of a toiling people which, through these demands that it puts to the state, expresses its full consciousness that it neither rules nor is ripe for ruling!

It would be superfluous to deal here with the criticism of the recipe prescribed by Buchez in the reign of Louis Philippe, in opposition to the French socialists and accepted by the reactionary workers, of the *atelier*. The chief offense does not lie in having inscribed this specific nostrum in the program, but in taking, in general, a retrograde step from the standpoint of a class movement to that of a sectarian movement.

That the workers desire to establish the conditions for cooperative production on a social scale, and first of all on a national scale, in their own country, only means that they are working to revolutionize the present conditions of production, and it has nothing in common with the foundation of cooperative societies with state aid. But as far as the present cooperative societies are concerned, they are of value *only* insofar as they are the independent creations of the workers and not protégés either of the governments or of the bourgeois. . . .

I have now come to the end, for the appendix that now follows in the program does not constitute a characteristic component part of it. Hence I can be very brief here.

2. *"Normal working day."*

In no other country has the workers' party limited itself to such an indefinite demand, but has always fixed the length of the working day that it considers normal under the given circumstances.

3. *"Restriction of female labor and prohibition of child labor."*

The standardization of the working day must include the restriction of female labor, insofar as it relates to the duration, intermissions, etc., of the working day; otherwise it could only mean the exclusion of female labor from branches of industry that are especially unhealthy for the female body or are objectionable morally for the female sex. If that is what was meant, it should have been said so.

"Prohibition of child labor." Here it was absolutely essential to state the age limit.

A general prohibition of child labor is incompatible with the existence of large-scale industry and hence an empty, pious wish. Its realization—if it were possible—would be reactionary, since, with a strict regulation of the working time according to the different age groups and other safety measures for the protection of children, an early combination of productive labor with education is one of the most potent means for the transformation of present-day society.

4. *"State supervision of factory, workshop, and domestic industry."*

In consideration of the Prusso-German state it should definitely have been demanded that the inspectors are to be removable only by a court of law; that any worker can have them prosecuted for neglect of duty; that they must belong to the medical profession.

5. *"Regulation of prison labor."*

A petty demand in a general workers' program. In any case, it should have been clearly stated that there is no intention from fear of competition to allow ordinary criminals to be treated like beasts, and especially that there is no desire to deprive them of their sole means of betterment, productive labor. This was surely the least one might have expected from socialists.

6. *"An effective liability law."*

It should have been stated what is meant by an "effective" liability law.

Be it noted, incidentally, that in speaking of the normal working day the part of factory legislation that deals with health regulations and safety measures, etc., has been overlooked. The liability law comes into operation only when these regulations are infringed.

In short, this appendix also is distinguished by slovenly editing.

Dixi et salvavi animam meam. [I have spoken and saved my soul.]

SOCIALIST PROGRAM FOR GERMANY

From interview with correspondent of *Chicago Tribune*, January 5, 1879

During my visit to Dr. Marx I alluded to the platform given by J. C. Bancroft Davis in his official report of 1877 as the clearest and most concise exposition of socialism that I had seen. He said it was taken from the report of the socialist reunion at Gotha, Germany, in May, 1875. The translation was incorrect, he said, and he

Volunteered Correction

which I append as he dictated:

First: Universal, direct, and secret suffrage for all males over twenty years, for all elections, municipal and state.

Second: Direct legislation by the people. War and peace to be made by direct popular vote.

Third: Universal obligation to militia duty. No standing army.

Fourth: Abolition of all special legislation regarding press laws and public meetings.

Fifth: Legal remedies free of expense. Legal proceedings to be conducted by the people.

Sixth: Education to be by the state—general, obligatory, and free. Freedom of science and religion.

Seventh: All indirect taxes to be abolished. Money to be raised for state and municipal purposes by a direct progressive income tax.

Eighth: Freedom of combination among the working classes.

Ninth: The legal day of labor for men to be defined. The work of women to be limited, and that of children to be abolished.

Tenth: Sanitary laws for the protection of life and health of laborers, and regulation of their dwelling and places of labor, to be enforced by persons selected by them.

Eleventh: Suitable provision respecting prison labor.

In Mr. Bancroft Davis' report there is

A Twelfth Clause

the most important of all, which reads: "State aid and credit for industrial societies, under democratic direction." I asked the Doctor why he omitted this and he replied:

"When the reunion took place at Gotha, in 1875, there existed a division among the Social Democrats. The one wing were partisans of Lassalle, the others those who had accepted in general the program of the International organization, and were called the Eisenach party. That twelfth point was not placed on the platform, but placed in the general introduction by way of concession to the Lassallians. Afterwards it was never spoken of. Mr. Davis does not say that it was placed in the program as a compromise having no particular significance, but gravely puts it in as one of the cardinal principles of the program."

"But," I said, "socialists generally look upon the transformation of the means of labor into the common property of society as the grand climax of the movement."

"Yes; we say that this will be the outcome of the movement, but it will be a question of time, of education, and the institution of higher social status."

"This platform," I remarked, "applies only to Germany and one or two other countries."

"Ah!" he returned, "if you draw your conclusions from nothing but this, you know nothing of the activity of the party. Many of its points have no significance outside of Germany. Spain, Russia, England, and America have platforms suited to their peculiar difficulties. The only similarity in them is the end to be attained."

"And that is the supremacy of labor?"

"That is the emancipation of labor."

CHAPTER V

EDUCATION

Note

Marx himself was a superlatively educated man, probably the most erudite revolutionist in history. His readings as a student at the University of Berlin, discussed in his letter to his father which is included in this chapter, are overwhelming in their depth and complexity. He was at home in jurisprudence, ancient, medieval, and modern; a master of philosophy, classic and contemporary; an expert in all the intricacies of political economy. He knew Europe's great literature, which he read in the original languages.

His three daughters, brought up in England, were given an excellent education. They were exposed to literature quite early in life. "Shakespeare," his daughter Eleanor wrote, "was our house bible; at the age of six I knew whole scenes from Shakespeare by memory." Their education also included languages, singing and music lessons, even though Marx could not afford a piano. The Marx household sometimes went hungry to pay for the girls' tuition. Marx held that education should be a shared experience between parents and their children. He was opposed to forcible imposition of parental discipline. "Children," he used to say, "should educate their parents." Such a relationship, he felt, enriched education and ensured mutual respect and love. His cultured daughters rewarded him with lifelong devotion.

As for education in general, Marx, primarily concerned with the working class, believed that proletarian children should be provided with technical training, in addition to elementary schools. He was ambivalent in his attitude about compulsory education by the state, such as existed in Prussia and the United States, primarily because it meant domination by the ruling class. "Government and church," he wrote in the Gotha Program (1875), "should rather be equally excluded from any influence on the school."

REFLECTIONS OF A YOUNG MAN ON CHOOSING AN OCCUPATION*

Karl Marx's examination essay, written, at the age of seventeen, between August 10 and 16, 1835, before his graduation on September 24, 1835, from the Trier Gymnasium

Nature itself has assigned to the animal a sphere of activity in which it is to move, and the animal does so contentedly, without striving beyond it or even knowing that there is any other. To man, too, the Deity gave a general goal, that of ennobling mankind and himself, but left it up to him to seek the means by which this could be achieved; it left it up to him to choose the position in society most appropriate to him and from which he can best elevate both himself and society.

This choice is a great privilege over other creatures, but at the same time an act which can destroy a man's whole life, frustrate all his plans, and make him unhappy. To weigh this choice seriously is surely the first duty of a youth who is at the beginning of his career and who does not want to leave the most important concerns to chance.

Every person has a goal which appears great, at least to himself, and is great when the deepest convictions, the innermost voice of the heart, calls it so, because the Deity never leaves the earthling entirely without a guide; it speaks softly but surely.

This voice, however, is easily drowned out, and what we thought to be inspiration may have been the creation of a moment and can also be destroyed in a moment. Our imagination is perhaps inflamed, our senses excited; phantoms flutter before our eyes and eagerly we rush to the goal, which we presume that the Deity itself has shown us. But what we ardently press to our breast soon repels us, and we see our whole existence destroyed.

*From *Karl Marx on Education, Women and Children* by Saul K. Padover, pp. 3-6. Copyright © 1975 by Saul K. Padover. Used with permission of McGraw-Hill Book Co.

We must, therefore, seriously ask ourselves whether we are really inspired for a vocation, whether an inner voice approves of it, or whether the enthusiasm was a deception, that what we had thought to be a vocation from the Deity was only self-deceit. But how else can we manage to recognize this than by searching the source of our inspiration?

Greatness glitters, glitter stirs ambition, and ambition can easily bring forth the inspiration, or what we thought to be such; but when the fury of ambition tempts, reason can no longer restrain it, and man tumbles where his vehement impulse urges him; he no longer chooses his position, but rather chance and illusion determine it.

Then we are not called to the position in which we can most excel; it is not the one which in the long succession of years during which we may perhaps occupy it will never tire us, diminish our zeal, or cool our enthusiasm, but, instead, we shall see our wishes unfulfilled, our ideas unsatisfied, and we shall grumble against the Deity and curse mankind.

But not only ambition can stimulate a sudden inspiration for a position; we may also perhaps have embellished it with our fantasies, embellished it to reach the highest point that life can offer. We have not analyzed it, not considered the entire burden, the great responsibility it puts upon us; we have seen it only from a distance, and distance deceives.

In this, our own reason cannot be the counselor, for it is supported neither by experience nor by profound observation, while it is deceived by emotion and blinded by fantasy. To whom, then, shall we turn for support when our reason forsakes us?

Our heart calls upon our parents, who have already walked the path of life and experienced the severity of fate.

And if our inspiration still persists, if we still love the position for which we believe ourselves to be called after we have tested it coolly, perceived its burdens, and learned about its encumbrances—then may we take it up, then we are deceived neither by the inspiration nor by the rush of overeagerness.

But we cannot always avail ourselves of the position to which we believe we are called; our relations in society, to some extent, have already begun before we are able to determine them.

Even our physical nature often confronts us menacingly, and no one dare to mock its rights!

We may, to be sure, rise above it, but then we sink all the

faster; we then dare to construct a building on rotten foundations, and our entire life becomes an unfortunate struggle between the intellectual and the physical. If, however, one cannot subdue the fighting elements inside oneself, how, then, can one stand up against the wildest urges of life; how can one act calmly? Only out of calmness can great and beautiful deeds emerge; it is the only soil on which ripe fruits thrive.

Although we cannot work for long, and rarely joyfully, with a physical nature not appropriate for our position, there always arises the thought of sacrificing our own welfare to duty, of acting with weakness and yet with firmness. Nevertheless, if we have chosen a position for which we have no talents, we shall be unable to fill it worthily and shall soon recognize with shame our incompetence and tell ourselves that we are a useless creature, a member of society who cannot fill his post. The most natural consequence, then, is self-contempt, and what feeling is more painful and less capable of being cured by anything the outside world may offer? Self-contempt is a serpent that always ragingly gnaws in one's breast, sucks out the heart's lifeblood, and mixes it with the venom of hatred for humanity and despair.

A deception about our aptitude for a position, which we have examined closely, is a lapse which falls back upon us vengefully, and even though it may not be censured by the outside world, it provokes in our breast a pain more terrible than any the latter may cause.

After we have weighed everything regarding the position permitted by our condition in life, we may take up the one that guarantees us the greatest dignity, which is based on ideas of whose truth we are completely convinced, which offers the largest field to work for humanity and enables us to approach the universal goal for which every position is only a means: perfection.

Dignity is what elevates man most, what lends a higher nobility to all his acts and all his endeavors, what permits him to stand irreproachably, admired by the multitude and above it.

Only that position can impart dignity in which we do not appear as servile tools but rather create independently in our own sphere; only that position can impart dignity which requires no reprehensible acts, reprehensible even in appearance—a position which the best person can take up with noble pride. The position that guarantees this most is not always the most exalted, but it is always the superior one.

Just as a position without dignity debases us, so also we surely succumb to the burden of one which rests on ideas we later recognize as false.

Then we see no help except in self-deception, and what a desperate rescue is this that guarantees self-betrayal!

Positions which do not take hold of life but deal, rather, with abstract truths are the most dangerous for a youth whose principles are not yet matured, whose conviction is not yet firm and unshakable, although at the same time they may appear to be the loftiest when they have taken root deep in the breast and when we can sacrifice life and all strivings for the ideas thus held.

They can make happy the one who is called for them, but they destroy the one who takes them overhastily, without reflection, on the spur of the moment.

But the high opinion we have of the ideas on which our vocation is based imparts to us a higher standpoint in society, enlarges our own dignity, makes our actions unshakable.

Whoever chooses a position which he esteems highly will recoil from making himself unworthy of it; he will, therefore, act nobly because his position in society is noble.

The main principle, however, which must guide us in the selection of a position is the welfare of mankind, our own consummation. One should not think that these two interests are in hostile conflict and that the one must destroy the other, but, rather, that human nature is such that man's fulfillment can be attained only when he works for the perfection and welfare of his fellow men.

If a person works only for himself he can perhaps be a famous scholar, a great sage, a distinguished poet, but never a fulfilled, genuinely great man.

History calls those the greatest men who, while working for the universal, ennobled themselves; experience praises as the most happy the one who has made the most people happy; religion itself teaches us that the ideal, striven for by all, is the one who sacrificed himself for humanity, and who would dare contest such claims?

When we have chosen the position in which we can do most for humanity, burdens cannot bow us down, because they are only sacrifices for mankind. Then we experience no meager, narrow, egoistic joy, but our happiness belongs to millions, our deeds live on quietly but ever actively, and our ashes will be moistened by the glowing tears of noble men.

MARX'S INTELLECTUAL TRAVAIL*

This letter, the only one preserved from Marx's youth, was written to his father, on November 10, 1837, when he was a nineteen-year-old student at the University of Berlin. It is a remarkable document of a young man's spiritual and intellectual torment.

Dear Father:
There are moments in life which stand as landmarks, terminating the past and at the same time pointing firmly [in] a new direction.

At such a point of transition we feel compelled to contemplate, with the eagle eye of thought, the past and the present, in order to arrive at a true awareness of our actual situation. Indeed, world history itself loves such a retrospect, seeming to move backwards and to stand still, whereas in reality it leans back in the armchair to understand itself and to penetrate intellectually its own act, the act of the mind.

The individual, however, becomes lyrical in such moments, because metamorphosis is partly swan song, partly overture to a great new poem that tries to gain shape amidst the hazy yet brilliant colors; and yet we should erect a monument to what we have already experienced, so that it should regain in sensibility what it has lost in action; and where could we find a more sacred abode than in the hearts of our parents, the most indulgent judges, the most intimate participants, the sun of love whose fire warms our innermost strivings! What better way is there to correct, and to receive forgiveness for, what is displeasing and blameworthy in our character, than to look at it as an essentially necessary condition? In what other way can one escape the reproach of having a twisted heart than by ascribing it as much to adverse luck and to aberration of spirit as to anything else?

---

*From *Karl Marx on Education, Women and Children* by Saul K. Padover, pp. 7-16. Copyright © 1975 by Saul K. Padover. Used with permission of McGraw-Hill Book Co.

If now, at the end of a year spent here, I review the events of that period, and, in doing so, dear Father, answer the affectionate letter you wrote me from Ems, I take the liberty of examining my situation, and, in general, my view of life, which I consider an expression of reflections taking shape from many sources—science, art, and private endeavors.

When I left home, a new world had opened up for me, one of love and, at first, a love drunk with longing and empty of hope. Even the trip to Berlin, which owerwise would have enchanted me to the highest degree, would have inspired me to contemplate nature, and inflamed me to a joy of living, left me cold, and indeed, depressed me considerably. For the rocks I saw were no steeper, no bleaker than the sensations of my soul, the broad cities no livelier than my blood, the restaurant tables no more overloaded with indigestible food than the contents of my imagination, and, finally, art itself, which was not as beautiful as Jenny.

Upon arrival in Berlin, I broke with all existing connections, paid rare visits and then only with reluctance, and sought to immerse myself in science and art.

In my state of mind then, lyrical poetry was necessarily the first, at least the most pleasant, project I embarked upon, but, in accord with my position and previous development, it was purely idealistic. An equally remote otherworld, such as my love, became my heaven, my art. Everything real became blurred, and the vague had no boundaries. Attacks on the present, wide and shapeless feelings, nothing natural, everything constructed out of the blue, the complete opposite of that which is and which should be, rhetorical reflections instead of poetic ideas, but perhaps also a certain warmth of feeling and a striving for vigor—all this characterizes the poems in the first three volumes I sent to Jenny. The whole horizon of longing, which sees no limit, assumes various forms and turns "versifying" into "width."

Poetry, however, was to be merely a companion; I had to study law and I felt above all an urge to grapple with philosophy. The two were so closely connected that I studied Heineccius,[1] Thibaut,[2] and the sources uncritically and in

---

[1] Johann Gottlieb Heineccius, *Elementa iuris civilis secundum ordinem Pandectarum* (Amsterdam, 1728).

[2] Anton Friedrich Justus Thibaut, *System des Pandekten-Rechts*, Vols. I-II (Jena, 1803-05).

schoolboy fashion; thus, for example, I translated the first two books of the Pandect into German and tried to work out a philosophy of law while studying law. By way of introduction, I preceded it with some metaphysical propositions and then continued this unfortunate opus up to public law, a work of almost three hundred pages.

Above all, I was troubled by the same contradictions between the Is and the Ought that is characteristic of Idealism, and this led me to make the following hopelessly inaccurate divisions: First, the metaphysics of law, as I gratuitously termed it, that is, the principles, reflections, and definitions of concepts, divorced from all real law and all real forms of law, as in the case with Fichte,[3] but in my case more modern and less substantial. This—the unscholarly form of mathematical dogmatism, where the subject circles around the matter, reasons to and fro, without the matter itself forming into something rich and alive—obstructed an understanding of the truth from the outset. The triangle leads the mathematician to construct and to demonstrate; it remains a mere idea in space, it does not develop into anything else; it has to be set beside something else to assume different positions, and these, when juxtaposed to related ones, yield different relationships and truths. On the other hand, in all concrete expressions in the living world of ideas, such as Law, the State, Nature, and all of philosophy, the object itself has to be observed in its development, arbitrary divisions must not be intruded, and the reason of the thing itself must evolve within its own contending self and find there its own unity.

As a second part, there followed the philosophy of law, that is, according to the opinion I then held about the development of ideas in positive Roman law, as if positive law in its intellectual evolution (I do not mean in its purely finite definitions) could exist at all apart from the shape of the concept of law, which, after all, the first part should have included!

In addition, I had divided that part into formal and substantive theory of law, of which the first was meant to outline the pure form of the system in its progression and context, its structure and scope; whereas the second part was to deal with

---

[3] Johann Gottlieb Fichte, *Grundlage des Naturrechts nach Prinzipien der Wissenschaftslehre* (Jena and Leipzig, 1796).

content and the merging of form into content. There is one error which I share with Herr von Savigny, as I was to discover later when I read his erudite work on property—with the difference that what he called formal definition was something "to find the place which this or the other doctrine has in the (hypothetical) Roman system," and the material definition was that which is "the doctrine of the positive which the Romans attributed to a concept defined in this manner";—I, on the other hand, considered form as the architectonics required in the formulation of a concept, and matter as the quality required of these forms. The error was that I believed the one could and should develop independently of the other, and thus I did not arrive at true form but merely constructed a writing desk with drawers which I later filled with sand.

Concept is, after all, the mediating element between form and content. In any philosophical treatise on law, therefore, the one must be contained in the other; indeed, form should be but the continuation of content. Thus I arrived at a division that made for simple and superficial classification only, while the spirit of law and its truth were obscured by it. The whole body of law fell into contract and noncontract elements. For better illustration, I take the liberty of presenting here the schema up to the division of the *jus publicum*, which has also been treated in the formal part.

I	II
jus privatum	*jus publicum*

I. *jus privatum*
a. Conditional, contractural private law
b. Unconditional, noncontractual private law

   A. *Conditional, contractual private law*
      a. Personal law
      b. Property law
      c. Personal reality law

         a. Personal law
I. Out of encumbered contract
II. Out of assured contract
III. Out of charitable contract

I. Out of encumbered contract
2. Social contract (*societas*)
3. Hiring-out contract (*locatio conductio*)
   3. Locatio conductio
      1. Insofar as it relates to services (*operae*)
         a. Real *locatio conductio* (not meant to include Roman house- or farm-lease laws)
         b. *mandatum*
      2. Insofar as it relates to the right use (*usus rei*)
         a. Ground: *ususfructus* (but not also in the purely Roman sense)
         b. Dwellings: *habitatio*

II. *Out of the assured contract*
1. Separation or adjustment contract
2. Insurance contract

III. *Out of charitable contract*
2. *Consent contract*
1. *fidejussio* (surety)
2. *negotiorum gestio* (conducting business without mandate)

3. *Donation contract*
II. Out of assured contract
1. *donatio* (gift)
2. *gratiae promissum* (promises of favor)

b. *Property law*
I. *Out of encumbered contract*
2. *permutatio stricte sic dicta* (exchange in the original sense)
   1. Exchange proper
   2. *mutuum* (*usurae*) [loan] (interest)
   3. *emptio venditio* (buying and selling)

II. Out of the assured contract
pignus (pledge)

III. Out of the charitable contract
2. *commodatum* (lending, or loan contract)
3. *depositum* (storing of goods)

But why should I continue to fill the pages with things which I myself have rejected? Trichotomic divisions pervade the whole; it was written with tiresome prolixity and it abused the Roman concepts most barbarously in order to force them into my system. On the other hand, I thereby acquired a love for a general view of the material, at least to a certain extent.

At the end of the part on private law, I saw the falsity of the whole, which in its basis borders on Kantianism, but which deviates entirely from it in its application; and again it became clear to me that without philosophy nothing can be mastered. Thus I could once more throw myself into its arms with clear conscience, and I proceeded to write a new metaphysical system, at the end of which I was again forced to admit its incorrectness, as well as those of my own previous efforts in this direction.

In doing this, I acquired the habit of making excerpts from all the books I read—such as Lessing's *Laokoon*,[4] Solger's *Erwin*,[5] Winckelmann's history of art,[6] Luden's German history[7]—and to jot down reflections on the side. At the same time, I translated Tacitus's *Germania* and Ovid's *Libri Tristium*, and began on my own, that is, out of grammars to study English and Italian, in which I have not yet accomplished anything; I also read Klein's criminal law and his *Annals*,[8] and all the latest works of literature, the latter on the side, however.

At the end of the semester, I again sought the dances of the Muses and the music of Satyrs; and even in the last notebook which I sent you, Idealism, you will find, plays a role through forced humor (*Scorpion und Felix*) and shines through in an inept and fantastic drama (*Oulanem*), until fi-

---

[4] Gotthold Ephraim Lessing, *Laokoon: oder ueber die Grenzen der Mahlerey und Poesie* (Berlin, 1766).

[5] Karl Wilhelm Ferdinand Solger, *Erwin. Vier Gespraeche ueber das Schoene und die Kunst* (Berlin, 1815).

[6] Johann Winckelmann, *Geschichte der Kunst des Alterthums* (2 Parts; Dresden, 1764 and 1767).

[7] Heinrich Luden, *Geschichte des teutschen Volkes* (12 vols.; Gotha, 1825-1837).

[8] Ernst Ferdinand Klein, *Grundsaetze des gemeinen deutschen peinlichen Rechts nebst Bemerkung der preussischen Gesetze* (2d ed., Halle, 1799);
Annalen der Gesetzgebung und Rechtsgelehrsamkeit in den Preussischen Staaten (26 vols.; Berlin and Stettin, 1788-1809).

nally it changes entirely and moves on to mere art form, mostly without inspired objects or vibrant ideas.

And yet, these recent poems are the only ones in which, suddenly, as if by a stroke of magic—alas, the stroke was a shattering one at first—the realm of true poetry shone for me like a distant fairy palace and thus all my own creation dissolved into nothingness.

With these manifold activities during the first semester, it is small wonder that many nights were passed in wakefulness, many battles were fought, many a stimulus within and without had to be coped with, so that at the end I did not emerge very enriched; I had neglected nature, art, and the world around me, and I alienated many friends. My physical condition deteriorated, and a doctor recommended the countryside; and thus, for the first time, I traversed the whole spreading city to the Stralow gate. I did not then anticipate that my stay here would change me from a pale weakling into a physically robust man.

A curtain had fallen, my holy of holies had been torn to shreds, and new gods had to replace it.

From Idealism, which, incidentally, I had compared to and enriched with Kantianism and Fichteism, I moved to investigate the Idea in the reality itself. If the gods had formerly dwelt above the earth, they now became its center.

I had read fragments of Hegel's philosophy,[9] the grotesque, rocklike melody of which did not appeal to me. Once again I wished to dive into the sea, but with the definite intention of finding our spiritual nature as essential, concrete, and solidly rounded as the physical one; no longer would I practice the arts of fencing but hold the pure pearl up to the sunlight.

I wrote a dialogue of approximately twenty-four pages: "Cleanthes, or the Starting Point and Necessary Progress of Philosophy." It combined to a certain extent art and learning, which previously had been separated; and I plunged vigorously into the work itself, into a philosophical-dialectical de-

---

[9] Georg Wilhelm Friedrich Hegel, *Phaenomonologie des Geistes*, in his *Werke*, Vol. II (Berlin, 1832); *Wissenschaft der Logik*, in his *Werke*, Vols. III-V (Berlin, 1833-34); *Vorlesungen ueber die Geschichte der Philosophie*, in his *Werke*, Vol. XIV (Berlin, 1833); *Encyclopaedie der philosophischen Wissenschaften im Grundrisse* (3d ed., Heidelberg, 1830).

velopment of the godhead as it manifests itself as the concept itself, as religion, as nature, as history. My last theme was the beginning of the Hegelian system; and this task, for which I was somewhat prepared by my reading of natural science, Schelling,[10] and history, has caused me endless headaches, being written in such a [words crossed out in manuscript]—(since it was meant actually to constitute a new system of logic), that I myself can scarcely follow it now. This beloved offspring of mine, tended in moonlight, lures me on treacherously, like a false siren, into the arms of the enemy.

I was so angry I was unable to think at all for a couple of days, ran around like a madman in the garden close to the dirty waters of the Spree, a river of which it has been said that it "washes souls and dilutes tea" [Heinrich Heine, *Die Nordsee*]: I even joined my landlord in a hunting party, then hastened back and felt like embracing every loafer at every street corner.

Shortly thereafter I pursued only positive studies; I read Savigny's *Property*,[11] Feuerbach's and Grolmann's criminal law,[12] Cramer's *De verborum significatione*,[13] Wening-Ingenheim's pandect system,[14] and Muehlenbruch's *Doctrina Pandectarum*,[15] the last of which I have not finished. I also studied some of Lauterbach's works,[16] civil law and in particular ecclesiastical law, including the first part of Gratian's

---

[10] Friedrich Wilhelm Joseph Schelling, *Philosophische Schriften*, Vol. I (Landshut, 1809).

[11] Friedrich Carl von Savigny, *Das Recht des Besitzes* (Giessen, 1803).

[12] Johann Paul Anselm Feuerbach, *Revision der Grundsaetze und Grundbegriffe des positiven peinlichen Rechts* (2 Parts, Erfurt and Chemnitz, 1799-1800); *Lehrbuch des gemeinen in Deutschland gueltigen peinlichen Rechts* (4th ed., Giessen, 1808).

Karl von Grolmann, *Grundsaetze der Criminalrechts-Wissenschaft* (4th ed., Giessen, 1825).

[13] Andreas Wilhelm Cramer, *De verborum significatione tituli pandectarum et codicis cum variae lectionis apparatu* (Kiel, 1811).

[14] Johann Nepomuk Wening-Ingenheim, *Lehrbuch des Gemeinen Civilrechtes* (3 vols.; 4th ed., Munich, 1831-32).

[15] Christian Friedrich Muehlenbruch, *Doctrina pandectarum. Halis Saxonae 1823 bis 1825* (3 vols., 3d ed., 1838).

[16] Wolfgang Adam Lauterbach, *Collegium theorico-practicum. Ad L. Pandectarum Libros methodo synthetica* (43 vols., Tuebingen, 1690-1714).

Education   201

Concordia discordantium canonum,[17] of which I have read
virtually the whole corpus, including the appendix, and made
excerpts, and also Lancelotti's *Institutiones*.[18] Then I translated part of Aristotle's *Rhetoric,* read the famous Bacon's
(Baron Verulam) *De augmentis scientiarum*,[19] occupied myself very much with Reimarus, whose book, *Von den Kunst-
trieben der Tiere,* [20] I once had studied with great pleasure. I
also took up German law, but here I restricted my reading to
the capitularies of the Frankish kings and the popes' letters to
them. From grief over Jenny's illness and my fruitless intellectual labors, from a consuming anger over having to make
an idol of a viewpoint I hated, I fell sick, as I have already
told you, dear Father. My health restored, I burned all my
poems and sketches for short novels, etc., laboring under the
illusion that I could abandon them altogether—of which
there is as yet no evidence.

During my illness, I came to know Hegel's works, as well
as most of his disciples, from beginning to end. As a result of
several meetings with friends at Stralow, I got into a Doctors
[of Philosophy] club, which had among its members university lecturers [*Privatdozenten*] and my most intimate Berlin
friend, Dr. Rutenberg. In the course of our discussion many
an opposing opinion came to light and I clung ever more
tightly to my own world outlook, of which, in truth, I had believed myself free, but any resounding ideas I might have had
were muted; and so I was seized with a rage for irony, as so
often happens when there is that much negativism. This was
aggravated by Jenny's silence. I could not rest until I had
grasped modernity and the point of view of modern scholarship by turning out a few poor productions, such as *Der
Besuch* [The Visit], etc.

If perhaps I have failed to convey to you either a clear
idea or all the details, as well as the nuances, of the past se-

[17] In Gratian's *Corpus iuris canonici* (published in the twelfth
century).

[18] Giovanni Paolo Lancelotti, *Institutiones iuris canonici* (in
Corpus iuris canonici).

[19] Francis Bacon, *De dignitate et augmentis scientiarum* (London, 1623).

[20] Hermann Samuel Reimarus, *Allgemeine Betrachtungen ueber
die Triebe der Thiere, hauptsaechlich ueber ihre Kunst-Triebe*
(Hamburg, 1760).

mester, do please forgive me, dear Father, on account of my eagerness to speak of the present.

Herr von Chamisso sent me a measly note in which he says "he regrets that his Almanac cannot use my contributions, because it has long since gone to press." I swallowed his note in anger. Wigand, the bookdealer, forwarded my plan to Dr. [Karl] Schmidt, publisher of Wunder's Store of Good Cheese and Bad Literature. I am enclosing Wigand's letter; Schmidt has not answered yet. In the meantime, I shall by no means give up this plan, all the more so as all the famous experts on aesthetics of the Hegelian school, through the good offices of Instructor [Bruno] Bauer, who plays a great role among them, as well as my coadjutor Dr. Rutenberg, have promised to cooperate.

In regard to the question of a government career, my dear Father, I have recently made the acquaintance of Assistant Judge [Assessor] Schmidthaenner, who advised me to enter it after passing the third law examination; this would appeal to me all the more since I really prefer jurisprudence to any study of public administration. The gentleman in question told me that from the Münster District Court in Westphalia he himself and many others made it to assistant judge in three years, which, he says, is not difficult to do—provided, of course, that one works hard—since there the stages [of promotion] are not as strictly fixed as they are in Berlin and other places. If, as assistant judge, one later attains the doctorate, there are much better prospects for immediate appointment as professor extraordinary, as happened in the case of Mr. Gaertner in Bonn after he wrote a mediocre book on provincial codes of law, his only other title to fame being that he calls himself a member of the Hegelian school of law. However, my dear Father, best of fathers, would it not be possible for us to talk this over face to face? Eduard's [Karl's brother] condition, dear Mother's illness, your own indisposition, which I hope is not very serious, all makes me wish, indeed makes it virtually necessary, for me to hurry home. I would, indeed, have been there already, if I had not been in doubt about your permission, your consent.

Believe me, my dear, beloved Father, this is not a selfish wish (although I would be blissful to see Jenny again); I am, however, motivated by a thought which I may not put into words. In some respects it would be difficult for me to come, and yet, as my own sweet Jenny writes, such considerations must give way to the fulfillment of duties, which are sacred.

Whatever your decision, I implore you, dear Father, not to show this letter to Angel Mother [*Engelsmutter*], or at least not this page of it. My unexpected arrival may perhaps cheer up that great, splendid woman.

My letter to her was written long before the arrival of Jenny's dear letter, and thus, unwittingly, I may have written too much about matters that are not suitable or very little so.

In the hope that the clouds which hang over our family will gradually pass; that I may be permitted to share your sufferings and mingle my tears with yours, and in your presence perhaps demonstrate the deep affection, the boundless love, which I have often expressed poorly; in the hope that you too, dear, eternally beloved Father, mindful of the confused state of my storm-tossed soul, will forgive where the heart must often have seemed to err as my overburdened spirit stifled it; in the hope that you will soon be fully restored to health so that I shall be able to press you close to my heart and tell you all that I feel,

I remain your ever loving son, KARL.

Forgive, dear Father, the illegible handwriting and the bad style; it is nearly four o'clock; the candle has burned out completely, and my eyes are blurred; a deep restlessness has overwhelmed me; I shall not be able to mollify the specters that haunt me until I am in your dear presence.

Please greet for me my sweet, splendid Jenny. I have already read her letter twelve times, and every time I discover new charms in it. In every respect, even in style, it is the most beautiful letter I can imagine a woman writing.

EDUCATION AND ENVIRONMENT

From Engels and Marx, *The Holy Family*. The full title of this work is *The Holy Family Or Critique of Critical Critique. Against Bruno Bauer and Associates*. Published in Frankfurt in 1845, it was the first book on which Marx collaborated with Engels (in the original title page the name of the latter precedes that of the former). *The Holy Family* was a satire not only on Marx's friend the German philosopher Bruno Bauer, but also on the French social theorist Pierre Joseph Proudhon and the novelist Eugène Sue. In Marx's words, *The Holy Family* was "directed against the ideological mysticism of Hegelian and speculative philosophy in general." The text used here is from Foreign Languages Publishing House, translated by R. Dixon (Moscow, 1956), pp. 174-75.

Locke's immediate follower, Condillac, who also translated him into French, at once opposed Locke's sensualism in favor of seventeenth-century metaphysics.

In his *Essai sur l'Origine des Connaissances Humaines* [1746], he expounded Locke's ideas and proved that not only the soul, but the senses too, not only the art of creating ideas, but also the art of sensuous perception are matters of *experience* and *habit*. The whole development of man therefore depends on *education* and *environment*. It was only by *eclectic* philosophy that Condillac was supplanted in the French schools.

The difference between French and English materialism follows from the difference between the two nations. The French imparted to English materialism wit, flesh and blood, and eloquence. They gave it the temperament and grace that it lacked. They *civilized* it.

In Helvétius, who also based himself on Locke, materialism became really French. Helvétius conceived it immediately in its application to social life (Helvétius, *De l'Homme, de ses Facultés Intellectuelles et de son Éducation* [1775]). Sensuous qualities and self-love, enjoyment and correctly understood personal interests are the bases of all morality. The natural equality of human intelligence, the unity of the progress of reason and the progress of industry, the natural goodness of man, and the omnipotence of education are the main points in his system.

EDUCATION FOR THE WORKER

From "Wages," lectures delivered before the German Working Men's Association in Brussels, December 1847, and printed in the Neue Rheinische Zeitung, April 5, 6, 7 and 11, 1849

Another very favorite bourgeois proposal is *education*, especially many-sided *industrial education*.

We will not call attention to its trite contradiction, which lies in the fact that modern industry constantly replaces complicated work with more simple labor which requires no education. We will not call attention to the fact that it throws ever more children, from the age of seven up, behind the machine and makes them sources of profit not only for the bourgeois class but also for their own proletarian parents. The factory system frustrates the school laws—for example, in Prussia. We will not call attention to the fact that intellectual education, if the worker possesses it, has no direct effect at all on his wages, that education altogether depends on life conditions, that by moral education the bourgeois understands the drumming into the head of bourgeois principles, and that, finally, the bourgeois class has neither the means nor, assuming it had them, (even the desire to) apply them so as to offer the people a real education.

We confine ourselves merely to raising a purely economic point.

The actual meaning of education in the minds of the philanthropic economists is this: Every worker should learn as many branches of labor as possible, so that if, either through the application of new machinery or through a changed division of labor, he is thrown out of one branch, he can easily be accommodated in another.

ELEMENTARY EDUCATION AND CHILDREN IN FACTORIES

From *Capital*, Vol. 1, Ch. 15, Sec. 9

Factory legislation, that first conscious and methodical reaction of society against the spontaneously developed form of the process of production, is, as we have seen, just as much the necessary product of modern industry as cotton yarn, self-acting machines, and the electric telegraph. . . .

Paltry as the education clauses of the [Factory] Act appear on the whole, yet they proclaim elementary education to be an indispensable condition to the employment of children.[1] The success of those clauses proved for the first time the possibility of combining education and gymnastics[2] with manual labor, and, consequently, of combining manual labor with education and gymnastics. The factory inspectors soon found out by questioning the schoolmasters that the factory children, although receiving only one half the education of the regular day scholars, yet learned quite as much and often more.

> This can be accounted for by the simple fact that, with only being at school for one half of the day, they are always fresh, and nearly always ready and willing to receive instruction. The system on which they work, half manual labour, and half school, renders each employment a rest and a relief to the other; consequently, both are far more congenial to the child than would be the

---

[1] According to the English Factory Act, parents cannot send their children under fourteen years of age into factories under the control of the Act unless at the same time they allow them to receive elementary education. The manufacturer is responsible for compliance with the Act. "Factory education is compulsory, and it is a condition of labor." ("Rep. Insp. Fact., 31st October 1865, p. 111.)

[2] On the very advantageous results of combining gymnastics (and drilling in the case of boys) with compulsory education for factory children and pauper scholars, see the speech of N. W. Senior at the seventh annual congress of "The National Association for the Promotion of Social Science," in "Report of Proceedings, &c.," Lond. 1863, pp. 63, 64; also the "Rep. Insp. Fact., 31st October, 1865," pp. 118, 119, 120, 126, sqq.

case were he kept constantly at one. It is quite clear that a boy who has been at school all the morning cannot (in hot weather particularly) cope with one who comes fresh and bright from his work.[3]

Further information on this point will be found in Senior's speech at the Social Science Congress at Edinburgh in 1863. He there shows, amongst other things, how the monotonous and uselessly long school hours of the children of the upper and middle classes uselessly add to the labor of the teacher, "while he not only fruitlessly but absolutely injuriously wastes the time, health, and energy of the children."[4] From the factory system budded, as Robert Owen has shown us in detail, the germ of the education of the future, an education that will, in the case of every child over a given age, combine productive labor with instruction and gymnastics, not only as one of the methods of adding to the efficiency of production, but as the only method of producing fully developed human beings.

Modern Industry, as we have seen, sweeps away by technical means the manufacturing division of labor, under which

---

[3] "Rep. Insp. Fact. 31st Oct., 1865," p. 118. A silk manufacturer naively states to the Children's Employment Commissioners: "I am quite sure that the true secret of producing efficient workpeople is to be found in uniting education and labor from a period of childhood. Of course the occupation must not be too severe, nor irksome, or unhealthy. But of the advantage of the union I have no doubt. I wish my own children could have some work as well as play to give variety to their schooling." ("Ch. Empl. Comm. V. Rep.," p. 82, n. 36.)

[4] Senior, *loc. cit.*, p. 66. How Modern Industry, when it has attained to a certain pitch, is capable, by the revolution it effects in the mode of production and in the social conditions of production, of also revolutionizing people's minds is strikingly shown by a comparison of Senior's speech in 1863 with his philippic against the Factory Act of 1833; or by a comparison of the views of the congress above referred to with the fact that in certain country districts of England poor parents are forbidden, on pain of death by starvation, to educate their children. Thus, e.g., Mr. Snell reports it to be a common occurrence in Somersetshire that, when a poor person claims parish relief, he is compelled to take his children from school. Mr. Wollarton, the clergyman at Feltham, also tells of cases where all relief was denied to certain families "because they were sending their children to school!"

each man is bound hand and foot for life to a single detail operation. At the same time, the capitalistic form of that industry reproduces this same division of labor in a still more monstrous shape; in the factory proper, by converting the workman into a living appendage of the machine; and everywhere outside the factory,[5] partly reestablishing the division of labor on a fresh basis by the general introduction of the labor of women and children, and of the cheap unskilled labor.

The antagonism between the manufacturing division of labor and the methods of Modern Industry makes itself forcibly felt. It manifests itself, amongst other ways, in the frightful fact that a great part of the children employed in modern factories and manufactures are from their earliest years riveted to the most simple manipulations and exploited for years without being taught a single sort of work that would afterwards make them of use, even in the same manufactory or factory. In the English letter-press printing trade, for example, there existed formerly a system, corresponding to that in the old manufactures and handicrafts, of advancing the apprentices from easy to more and more difficult work. They went through a course of teaching till they were finished printers. To be able to read and write was for every one of them a requirement of their trade. All this was changed by the printing machine. It employs two sorts of laborers, one grown up, tenters, the other, boys mostly from 11 to 17 years of age whose sole business is either to spread the sheets of paper under the machine or to take from it the printed sheets.

---

[5] Wherever handicraft machines, driven by men, compete directly or indirectly with more developed machines driven by mechanical power, a great change takes place with regard to the laborer who drives the machine. At first the steam engine replaces this laborer, afterwards he must replace the steam engine. Consequently the tension and the amount of labor power expended become monstrous, and especially so in the case of the children who are condemned to this torture. Thus Mr. Longe, one of the commissioners, found in Coventry and the neighborhood boys of from 10 to 15 years employed in driving the ribbon looms, not to mention younger children who had to drive smaller machines. "It is extraordinarily fatiguing work. The boy is a mere substitute for steam power." ("Ch. Empl. Comm. V. Rep. 1866," p. 114, n. 6.) As to the fatal consequences of "this system of slavery," as the official report styles it, see *loc. cit.*, pp. 114 sqq.

They perform this weary task, in London especially, for 14, 15, and 16 hours at a stretch, during several days in the week, and frequently for 36 hours, with only 2 hours' rest for meals and sleep.[6] A great part of them cannot read, and they are, as a rule, utter savages and very extraordinary creatures.

> To qualify them for the work which they have to do, they require no intellectual training; there is little room in it for skill, and less for judgment; their wages, though rather high for boys, do not increase proportionately as they grow up, and the majority of them cannot look for advancement to the better-paid and more responsible post of machine minder, because while each machine has but one minder, it has at least two, and often four, boys attached to it.[7]

As soon as they get too old for such child's work, that is about 17 at the latest, they are discharged from the printing establishments. They become recruits for crime. Several attempts to procure them employment elsewhere were rendered of no avail by their ignorance and brutality, and by their mental and bodily degradation.

As with the division of labor in the interior of the manufacturing workshops, so it is with the division of labor in the interior of society. So long as handicraft and manufacture form the general groundwork of social production, the subjection of the producer to one branch exclusively, the breaking up of the multifariousness of his employment,[8] is a

[6] *Loc. cit.*, p. 3, n. 24.
[7] *Loc. cit.*, p. 7, n. 60.
[8] "In some parts of the Highlands of Scotland, not many years ago, every peasant, according to the Statistical Account, made his own shoes of leather tanned by himself. Many a shepherd and cottar too, with his wife and children, appeared at church in clothes which had been touched by no hands but their own, since they were shorn from the sheep and sown in the flaxfield. In the preparation of these, it is added, scarcely a single article had been purchased, except the awl, needle, thimble, and a very few parts of the ironwork employed in the weaving. The dyes, too, were chiefly extracted by the women from trees, shrubs and herbs." (Dugald Stewart's "Works," Hamilton Ed., Vol. VIII, pp. 327-28.)

necessary step in the development. On that groundwork each separate branch of production acquires empirically the form that is technically suited to it, slowly perfects it, and, so soon as a given degree of maturity has been reached, rapidly crystallizes that form. The only thing that here and there causes a change, besides new raw material supplied by commerce, is the gradual alteration of the instruments of labor. But their form, too, once definitely settled by experience, petrifies, as is proved by their being in many cases handed down in the same form by one generation to another during thousands of years. A characteristic feature is, that, even down into the eighteenth century, the different trades were called "mysteries" (*mystères*);[9] into their secrets none but those duly initiated could penetrate. Modern Industry rent the veil that concealed from men their own social process of production, and that turned the various spontaneously divided branches of production into so many riddles, not only to outsiders, but even to the initiated. The principle which is pursued, of resolving each process into its constituent movements, without any regard to their possible execution by the hand of man, created the new modern science of technology. The varied, apparently unconnected, and petrified forms of the industrial processes now resolved themselves into so many conscious and systematic applications of natural science to the attainment of green useful effects. Technology also discovered the few main fundamental forms of motion, which, despite the diversity of the instruments used, are necessarily taken by every productive action of the human body; just as the science of mechanics sees in the most complicated machinery nothing but the continual repetition of the simple mechanical powers.

Modern Industry never looks upon and treats the existing form of a process as final. The technical basis of that industry is therefore revolutionary, while all earlier modes of pro-

---

[9] In the celebrated *Livre des métiers* of Etienne Boileau, we find it prescribed that a journeyman on being admitted among the masters had to swear "to love his brethren with brotherly love, to support them in their respective trades, not willfully to betray the secrets of the trade, and besides, in the interests of all, not to recommend his own wares by calling the attention of the buyer to defects in the articles made by others."

duction were essentially conservative.[10] By means of machinery, chemical processes and other methods, it is continually causing changes not only in the technical basis of production, but also in the functions of the laborer, and in the social combinations of the labor process. At the same time, it thereby also revolutionizes the division of labor within the society, and incessantly launches masses of capital and of workpeople from one branch of production to another. But if Modern Industry, by its very nature, therefore necessitates variation of labor, fluency of function, universal mobility of the laborer, on the other hand, in its capitalistic form, it reproduces the old division of labor with its ossified particularizations. We have seen how this absolute contradiction between the technical necessities of Modern Industry, and the social character inherent in its capitalistic form, dispels all fixity and security in the situation of the laborer; how it constantly threatens, by taking away the instruments of labor, to snatch from his hands his means of subsistence,[11] and, by suppressing his detail functions, to make him superfluous. We have seen, too, how this antagonism vents its rage in the creation of that monstrosity, an industrial reserve army, kept in misery in order to be always at the disposal of capital; in the incessant human sacrifices from among the working class, in the most reckless squandering of labor power, and in the devastation caused by a social anarchy which turns every economic progress into a social calamity. This is the negative

[10] "The bourgeoisie cannot exist without continually revolutionizing the instruments of production, and thereby the relations of production and all the social relations. Conservation, in an unaltered form, of the old modes of production was on the contrary the first condition of existence for all earlier industrial classes. Constant revolution in production, uninterrupted disturbance of all social conditions, everlasting uncertainty and agitation, distinguish the bourgeois epoch from all earlier ones. All fixed, fast-frozen relations, with their train of ancient and venerable prejudices and opinions, are swept away, all new formed ones become antiquated before they can ossify. All that is solid melts into air, all that is holy is profaned, and man is at last compelled to face with sober senses his real conditions of life, and his relations with his kind." (F. Engels and Karl Marx: *Communist Manifesto*, London, 1848, p. 5.)

[11] "You take my life.
When you do take the means whereby I live."
                                                    Shakespeare.

side. But if, on the one hand, variation of work as present imposes itself after the manner of an overpowering natural law, and with the blindly destructive action of a natural law that meets with resistance[12] at all points, Modern Industry, on the other hand, through its catastrophes imposes the necessity of recognizing, as a fundamental law of production, variation of work, consequently fitness of the laborer for varied work, consequently the greatest possible development of his varied aptitudes. It becomes a question of life and death for society to adapt the mode of production to the normal functioning of this law. Modern Industry, indeed, compels society, under penalty of death, to replace the detail worker of today, crippled by lifelong repetition of one and the same trivial operation, and thus reduced to the mere fragment of a man, by the fully developed individual, fit for a variety of labors, ready to face any change of production, and to whom the different social functions he performs are but so many modes of giving free scope to his own natural and acquired powers.

One step already spontaneously taken toward effecting this revolution is the establishment of technical and agricultural schools, and of "*écoles d' enseignement professionnel*," in which the children of the workingmen receive some little instruction in technology and in the practical handling of the various implements of labor. Though the Factory Act, that first and meager concession wrung from capital, is limited to combining elementary education with work in the factory, there can be no doubt that when the working class comes into power, as inevitably it must, technical instruction, both theoretical and practical, will take its proper place in the working-class schools. There is also no doubt that such revo-

---

[12] A French workman, on his return from San Francisco, writes as follows: "I never could have believed, that I was capable of working at the various occupations I was employed on in California. I was firmly convinced that I was fit for nothing but letterpress printing. . . Once in the midst of this world of adventurers, who change their occupation as often as they do their shirt, egad, I did as the others. As mining did not turn out remunerative enough, I left it for the town, where in succession I became typographer, slater, plumber, &c. In consequence of thus finding out that I am fit for any sort of work, I feel less of a mollusk and more of a man." (A. Corbon, "De l'enseignement professionnel," 2ème ed., p. 50.)

Education

lutionary ferments, the final result of which is the abolition of the old division of labor, are diametrically opposed to the capitalistic form of production, and to the economic status of the laborer corresponding to that form. But the historical development of the antagonisms, immanent in a given form of production, is the only way in which that form of production can be dissolved and a new form established. "Ne sutor ultra crepidam"—this ne plus ultra of handicraft wisdom became sheer nonsense from the moment the watchmaker Watt invented the steam engine, the barber Arkwright the throstle, and the working jeweller, Fulton, the steamship.[13]

So long as Factory legislation is confined to regulating the labor in factories, manufactories, etc., it is regarded as a mere interference with the exploiting rights of capital. But when it comes to regulating the so-called "home labor,"[14] it is immediately viewed as a direct attack on the *patria potestas*, on parental authority. The tender-hearted English Parliament long affected to shrink from taking this step. The force of facts, however, compelled it at last to acknowledge that modern industry in overturning the economic foundation on which was based the traditional family, and the family labor corresponding to it, had also unloosed all traditional family ties. The rights of the children had to be proclaimed. The final report of the Ch. Empl. Comm. of 1866, states: "It is,

---

[13] John Bellers, a very phenomenon in the history of Political Economy, saw most clearly at the end of the seventeenth century the necessity for abolishing the present system of education and division of labor, which beget hypertrophy and atrophy at the two opposite extremities of society. Amongst other things he says this: "An idle learning being little better than the learning of idleness . . . Bodily labor, it's a primitive institution of God. . . . Labor being as proper for the bodies' health as eating is for its living; for what pains a man saves by ease, he will find in disease. . . . Labor adds oil to the lamp of life, when thinking inflames it. . . . A childish, silly employ" (a warning this, by presentiment, against the Basedows and their modern imitators) "leaves the children's minds silly." ("Proposals for Raising a Colledge of Industry of All Useful Trades and Husbandry." London, 1696, pp. 12, 14, 18.)

[14] "This sort of labor goes on mostly in small workshops, as we have seen in the lace-making and straw-plaiting trades, and as could be shown more in detail from the metal trades of Sheffield, Birmingham, etc.

unhappily, to a painful degree apparent throughout the whole of the evidence, that against no persons do the children of both sexes so much require protection as against their parents." The system of unlimited exploitation of children's labor in general and the so-called home labor in particular is "maintained only because the parents are able, without check or control, to exercise this arbitrary and mischievous power over their young and tender offspring. . . . Parents must not possess the absolute power of making their children mere 'machines to earn so much weekly wage.' . . . The children and young persons, therefore, in all such cases may justifiably claim from the legislature, as a natural right, that an exemption should be secured to them, from what destroys prematurely their physical strength, and lowers them in the scale of intellectual and moral beings."[15] It was not, however, the misuse of parental authority that created the capitalistic exploitation, whether direct or indirect, of children's labor; but, on the contrary, it was the capitalistic mode of exploitation which, by sweeping away the economic basis of parental authority, made its exercise degenerate into a mischievous misuse of power. However terrible and disgusting the dissolution, under the capitalist system, of the old family ties may appear, nevertheless, modern industry, by assigning as it does an important part in the process of production, outside the domestic sphere, to women, to young persons, and to children of both sexes, creates a new economic foundation for a higher form of the family and of the relations between the sexes. It is, of course, just as absurd to hold the Teutonic-Christian form of the family to be absolute and final as it would be to apply that character to the ancient Roman, the ancient Greek, or the Eastern forms which, moreover, taken together form a series in historical development. Moreover, it is obvious that the fact of the collective working group being composed of individuals of both sexes and all ages must necessarily, under suitable conditions, become a source of humane development; although in its spontaneously developed, brutal, capitalistic form, where the laborer exists for the process of production, and not the process of production for

[15]"Ch. Empl. Comm., V. Rep.," p. xxv, n. 162, and II. Rep., p xxxviii, ns. 285, 289, pp. xxv, xxvi, n. 191.

Education

the laborer, that fact is a pestiferous source of corruption slavery.[16]

The necessity for a generalization of the Factory Acts, for transforming them from an exceptional law relating to mechanical spinning and weaving—those first creations of machinery—into a law affecting social production as a whole, arose, as we have seen, from the mode in which Modern Industry was historically developed. In the rear of that industry, the traditional form of manufacture, of handicraft, and of domestic industry, is entirely revolutionized; manufactures are constantly passing into the factory system, and handicrafts into manufactures; and lastly, the spheres of handicraft and of the domestic industries became, in a, comparatively speaking, wonderfully short time, dens of misery in which capitalistic exploitation obtains free play for the wildest excesses. There are two circumstances that finally turn the scales: first, the constantly recurring experience that capital, so soon as it finds itself subject to legal control at one point, compensates itself all the more recklessly at other points;[17] secondly, the cry of the capitalists for equality in the conditions of competition, i.e., for equal restraint on all exploitation of labor.[18] On this point let us listen to two heartbroken cries. Messrs. Cooksley of Bristol, nail and chain, etc., manufacturers, spontaneously introduced the regulations of the Factory Act into their business. "As the old irregular system prevails in neighboring works, the Messrs. Cooksley are subject to the disadvantage of having their boys enticed to continue their labor elsewhere after 6 P.M. 'This,' they naturally say, 'is an injustice and loss to us, as it exhausts a portion of the boy's strength, of which we ought to have the full benefit.' "[19] Mr. J. Simpson (paper box and bag maker, London) states before the commissioners of the Ch. Empl. Comm.: "He would sign any petition for it" (legislative interference) .... "As it was, he always felt restless at night, when he had

---

[19]"Ch. Empl. Comm., V. Rep.," p. x. n. 35.

[16]"Factory labor may be as pure and excellent as domestic labor, and perhaps more so." ("Rep. Insp. Fact., 31st October, 1865," p. 129.)

[17]"Rep. Insp. of Fact., 31st October, 1865," pp. 27-32.

[18]Numerous instances will be found in "Rep. of Insp. of Fact."

his place, lest others should be working later than him and getting away his orders."[20] Summarizing, the Ch. Empl. Comm. says:

> It would be unjust to the larger employers that their factories should be placed under regulation while the hours of labor in the smaller places in their own branch of business were under no legislative restriction. And to the injustice arising from the unfair conditions of competition, in regard to hours, that would be created if the smaller places of work were exempt, would be added the disadvantage to the larger manufacturers of finding their supply of juvenile and female labor drawn off to the places of work exempt from legislation. Further, a stimulus would be given to the multiplication of the smaller places of work, which are almost invariably the least favorable to the health, comfort, education, and general improvement of the people.[21]

In its final report the Commission proposes to subject to the Factory Act more than 1,400,000 children, young persons, and women, of which number about one half are exploited in small industries and by the so-called home work.[22] It says,

---

[20] "Ch. Empl. Comm., V. Rep.," p. ix, n. 28.

[21] *Loc. cit.*, p. xxv, ns. 165 167. As to the advantages of large-scale, compared with small-scale, industries, see "Ch. Empl. Comm., III. Rep.," p. 13, n. 144, p. 25, n. 121, p. 26, n. 125, p. 27, n. 140, etc.

[22] The trades proposed to be brought under the Act were the following: Lace-making, stocking-weaving, straw-plaiting, the manufacture of wearing apparel with its numerous subdivisions, artificial flower-making, shoe-making, hat-making, glove-making, tailoring, all metal works, from blast furnaces down to needleworks, etc., paper mills, glassworks, tobacco factories, india-rubber works, braid-making (for weaving), hand-carpet-making, umbrella and parasol making, the manufacture of spindles and spools, letter-press printing, bookbinding, manufacture of stationery (including paper bags, cards, colored paper, etc), rope-making, manufacture of jet ornaments, brick-making, silk manufacture by hand, Coventry weaving, saltworks, tallow chandlers, cement works, sugar refineries, biscuit-making, various industries connected with timber, and other mixed trades.

But if it should seem fit to Parliament to place the whole of that large number of children, young persons, and females under the protective legislation above adverted to . . . it cannot be doubted that such legislation would have a most beneficent effect, not only upon the young and the feeble, who are its more immediate objects, but upon the still larger body of adult workers, who would in all these employments, both directly and indirectly, come immediately under its influence. It would enforce upon them regular and moderate hours; it would lead to their places of work being kept in a healthy and cleanly state; it would therefore husband and improve that store of physical strength on which their own well-being and that of the country so much depends; it would save the rising generation from that overexertion at an early age which undermines their constitutions and leads to premature decay; finally, it would ensure them— at least up to the age of 13—the opportunity of receiving the elements of education, and would put an end to that utter ignorance . . . so faithfully exhibited in the Reports of our Assistant Commissioners, and which cannot be regarded without the deepest pain, and a profound sense of national degradation.[23]

The Tory* Cabinet announced in the Speech from the Throne, on February 5, 1867, that it had framed the proposals of the Industrial Commission of Inquiry[24] into Bills. To get that far, another twenty years of *experimentum in corpore vili* had been required. Already in 1840 a Parliamentary Commission of Inquiry on the labor of children had been ap-

[23]*Loc. cit.*, p. xxv, n. 169.
*Here (from "The Tory Cabinet. . . ." to "Nassau W. Senior") the English text has been altered in conformity with the 4th German edition.—*Ed*.
[24]The Factory Acts Extension Act was passed on August 12, 1867. It regulates all foundries, smithies, and metal manufactories, including machine shops; furthermore glassworks, paper mills, gutta-percha and india-rubber works, tobacco manufactories, letter-press printing and bookbinding works, and, lastly, all workshops in which more than 50 persons are employed. The Hours of Labor Regulation Act, passed on August 17, 1867, regulates the smaller workshops and the so-called domestic industries.

pointed. Its Report, in 1842, unfolded, in the words of Nassau W. Senior,

> the most frightful picture of avarice, selfishness and cruelty on the part of masters and of parents, and of juvenile and infantile misery, degradation and destruction ever presented. . . . It may be supposed that it describes the horrors of a past age. But there is unhappily evidence that those horrors continue as intense as they were. A pamphlet published by Hardwicke about two years ago states that the abuses complained of in 1842 are in full bloom at the present day. It is a strange proof of the general neglect of the morals and health of the children of the working class, that this report lay unnoticed for 20 years, during which the children, "bred up without the remotest sign of comprehension as to what is meant by the term morals, who had neither knowledge, nor religion, nor natural affection," were allowed to become the parents of the present generation.[25]

The social conditions having undergone a change, Parliament could not venture to shelve the demands of the Commission of 1862, as it had done those of the Commission of 1840. Hence in 1864, when the Commission had not yet published more than a part of its reports, the earthenware industries (including the potteries), makers of paper hangings, matches, cartridges, and caps, and fustian cutters were made subject to the Acts in force in the textile industries. In the Speech from the Throne on 5th February, 1867, the Tory Cabinet of the day announced the introduction of Bills founded on the final recommendations of the Commission, which had completed its labors in 1866.

On the 15th August, 1867, the Factory Acts Extension Act, and on the 21st August, the Workshops' Regulation Act, received the Royal Assent; the former Act having reference to large industries, the latter to small.

The former applies to blast furnaces, iron and copper mills, foundries, machine shops, metal manufactories, gutta-percha works, paper mills, glassworks, tobacco manufactories, letter-press printing (including newspapers), bookbinding, in short to all industrial establishments of the above kind, in

---

[25] Senior, "Social Science Congress," pp. 55-58.

which 50 individuals or more are occupied simultaneously, and for not less than 100 days during the year.

To give an idea of the extent of the sphere embraced by the Workshops' Regulation Act in its application, we cite from its interpretation clause the following passages:

> *Handicraft* shall mean any manual labor exercised by way of trade, or for purposes of gain in, or incidental to, the making any article or part of an article, or in, or incidental to, the altering, repairing, ornamenting, finishing, or otherwise adapting for sale any article.
>
> *Workshop* shall mean any room or place whatever in the open air or under cover, in which any handicraft is carried on by any child, young person, or woman, and to which and over which the person by whom such child, young person, or woman is employed, has the right of access and control.
>
> *Employed* shall mean occupied in any handicraft, whether for wages or not, under a master or under a parent as herein defined.
>
> *Parent* shall mean parent, guardian, or person having the custody of, or control over, any . . . child or young person.

Clause 7, which imposes a penalty for employment of children, young persons, and women contrary to the provisions of the Act, subjects to fines not only the occupier of the workshop, whether parent or not, but even "the parent of, or the person deriving any direct benefit from the labor of, or having the control over, the child, young person or woman."

The Factory Acts Extension Act, which affects the large establishments, derogates from the Factory Act by a crowd of vicious exceptions and cowardly compromises with the masters.

The Workshops' Regulation Act, wretched in all its details, remained a dead letter in the hands of the municipal and local authorities who were charged with its execution. When, in 1871, Parliament withdrew from them this power, in order to confer it on the Factory Inspectors, to whose province it thus added by a single stroke more than one hundred thousand workshops, and three hundred brickworks, care was taken at the same time not to add more than eight assistants to their already undermanned staff.[26]

What strikes us, then, in the English legislation of 1867, is, on the one hand the necessity imposed on the parliament of the ruling classes of adopting in principle measures so extraordinary, and on so great a scale, against the excesses of capitalistic exploitation; and on the other hand, the hesitation, the repugnance, and the bad faith with which it lent itself to the task of carrying those measures into practice.

The Inquiry Commission of 1862 also proposed a new regulation of the mining industry, an industry distinguished from others by the exceptional characteristic that the interests of landlord and capitalist there join hands. The antagonism of these two interests had been favorable to Factory legislation, while on the other hand the absence of that antagonism is sufficient to explain the delays and chicanery of the legislation on mines.

The Inquiry Commission of 1840 had made revelations so terrible, so shocking, and creating such a scandal all over Europe, that to salve its conscience Parliament passed the Mining Act of 1842, in which it limited itself to forbidding the employment underground in mines of children under 10 years of age and females.

Then another Act, the Mines' Inspecting Act of 1860, provides that mines shall be inspected by public officers nominated specially for that purpose, and that boys between the ages of 10 and 12 years shall not be employed unless they have a school certificate, or go to school for a certain number of hours. This Act was a complete dead letter owing to the ridiculously small number of inspectors, the meagerness of their powers, and other causes that will become apparent as we proceed.

One of the most recent Blue books on mines is the "Report from the Select Committee on Mines, together with etc. Evidence, 23rd July, 1866." This Report is the work of a Parlia-

[26] The "personnel" of this staff consisted of 2 inspectors, 2 assistant inspectors, and 41 subinspectors. Eight additional subinspectors were appointed in 1871. The total cost of administering the Acts in England, Scotland, and Ireland amounted for the year 1871-72 to no more than £25,347, inclusive of the law expenses incurred by prosecutions of offending masters.

mentary Committee selected from members of the House of Commons, and authorized to summon and examine witnesses. It is a thick folio volume in which the Report itself occupies only five lines to this effect; that the committee has nothing to say, and that more witnesses must be examined!

The mode of examining the witnesses reminds one of the cross examination of witnesses in English courts of justice; where the advocate tries, by means of impudent, unexpected, equivocal and involved questions, put without connection, to intimidate, surprise, and confound the witness, and to give a forced meaning to the answers extorted from him. In this inquiry the members of the committee themselves are the cross-examiners, and among them are to be found both mine-owners and mine exploiters; the witnesses are mostly working coal miners. The whole farce is too characteristic of the spirit of capital not to call for a few extracts from this Report. For the sake of conciseness I have classified them. I may also add that every question and its answer are numbered in the English Blue books.

I. Employment in mines of boys of 10 years and upwards. In the mines the work, inclusive of going and returning, usually lasts 14 or 15 hours, sometimes even from 3, 4 and 5 o'clock A.M., till 5 and 6 o'clock P.M. The adults work in two shifts, of eight hours each; but there is no alternation with the boys, on account of the expense (ns. 80, 203, 204). The younger boys are chiefly employed in opening and shutting the ventilating doors in the various parts of the mine; the older ones are employed on heavier work, in carrying coal, etc. They work these long hours underground until their 18th or 22nd year, when they are put to miner's work proper (n. 161). Children and young persons are at present worse treated, and harder worked than at any previous period. The miners demand almost unanimously an act of Parliament prohibiting the employment in mines of children under 14. And now Hussey Vivian (himself an exploiter of mines) asks: "Would not the opinion of the workman depend upon the poverty of the workman's family?" Mr. Bruce: "Do you not think it would be a very hard case, where a parent had been injured, or where he was sickly, or where a father was dead, and there was only a mother, to prevent a child between 12 and 14 earning 1s. &d. a day for the good of the family? . . . You must lay down a general rule? . . . Are you prepared to recommend legislation which would prevent the employment of children under 12 and 14, whatever the state of their parents might be?" "Yes." Vivian: "Supposing that an enactment were passed preventing the employment of children under the age of 14, would it not be probable that ... the parents of children would seek employment for their children in other directions, for instance, in manufacture?" "Not generally I think." Kinnaird: "Some of the boys are keepers of doors?" "Yes." "Is there not generally a very great draught every time you open a door or close it?" "Yes, generally there is." "It sounds a very easy thing, but it is in fact rather a painful one?" "He is imprisoned there just the same as if he was in a cell of a jail." Bourgeois Vivian: "Whenever a boy is furnished with a lamp cannot he read?" "Yes, he can read, if he finds himself in candles. ... I suppose he would be found fault with if he were discovered reading; he is there to mind his business, he has a duty to perform, and he has to attend to it in the first place, and I do not think it would be allowed down the pit."

II. Education.—The working miners want a law for the compulsory education of their children, as in factories. They declare the clauses of the Act of 1860, which require a school certificate to be obtained before employing boys of 10 and 12 years of age, to be quite illusory. The examination of the witnesses on this subject is truly droll. "Is it (the Act) required more against the masters or against the parents?" "It is required against both I think." "You cannot say whether it is required against one more than against the other?" "No; I can hardly answer that question." "Does there appear to be any desire on the part of the employers that the boys should have such hours as to enable them to go to school?" "No; the hours are never shortened for that purpose." Mr. Kinnaird: "Should you say that the colliers generally improve their education; have you seen instances of men who have, since they began to work, greatly improved their education, or do they not rather go back, and lose any advantage that they may have gained?" "They generally become worse: they do not improve; they acquire bad habits; they get on to drinking and gambling and such-like, and they go completely to wreck." "Do they make any attempt of the kind (for providing instruction) by having schools at night?" "There are few collieries where night schools are held, and perhaps at those collieries a few boys do go to those schools; but they are so physically exhausted that it is to no purpose that they go there." "You are then," concludes the bourgeois, "against education?" "Most certainly not; but," etc. "But are they (the employers) not compelled to demand them (school certificates)?" "By law they are; but I am not aware that they are demanded by the employers." "Then it is your opinion that this provision of the Act as to requiring certificates is not generally carried out in the collieries?" "It is not carried out." "Do the men take a great interest in this question (of education)?" "The majority of them do." "Are they very anxious to see the law enforced?" "The majority are." "Do you think that in this country any law that you pass . . . can really be effectual unless the population themselves assist in putting it into operation?" "Many a man might wish to object to employing a boy, but he would perhaps become marked by it." "Marked by whom?" "By his employers." "Do you think that the employers would find any fault with a man who obeyed the law. . . ?" "I believe they would." "Have you ever heard of any workman objecting to employ a boy between 10 and 12, who could not write or read?" "It is not left to men's option." "Would you call for the interference of Parliament?" "I think that if anything effectual is to be done in the education of the colliers' children, it will have to be made compulsory by Act of Parliament." "Would you lay that obligation upon the colliers only, or all the workpeople of Great Britain?" "I came to speak for the colliers." "Why should you distinguish them (collier boys) from other boys?" "Because I think they are an exception to the rule." (n. 1638.) "In what respect?" "In a physical respect." "Why should education be more valuable to them than to other classes of lads?" "I do not know that it is more valuable; but through the overexertion in mines there is less chance for the boys that are employed there to get education, either at Sunday schools, or at the day schools." "It is impossible to look at a question of this sort absolutely by itself?" "Is there a sufficiency of schools?"—"No". . . . "If the State were to require that every child should be sent to school, would there be schools for the children to go to?" "No; but I think if the circumstances were to spring up, the schools would be forthcoming." "Some of them (the boys) cannot read and write at all, I suppose?" "The majority cannot. . . . The majority of the men themselves cannot."

COMPULSORY EDUCATION

From the Minutes of the General Council of the First International, August 10, 1869

The education question then came on for discussion, Citizen Eccarius read so much of the Geneva Resolutions as referred to training and education of children and adolescents and proposed that it be adhered to. . . .

Citizen Marx said there was a peculiar difficulty connected with this question. On the one hand, a change of social circumstances was required to establish a proper system of education; on the other hand, a proper system of education was required to bring about a change of social circumstances; we must therefore commence where we were.

The question treated at the Congress was whether education was to be national or private. National education had been looked upon as governmental, but that was not necessarily the case. In Massachusetts every township was bound to provide schools for primary education for all the children. In towns of more than 5,000 inhabitants higher schools for technical education had to be provided, in larger towns still higher. The state contributed something but not much. In Massachusetts one-eighth of the local taxes went for education, in New York one-fifth. The school committees which administered the schools were local, they appointed the schoolmasters and selected the books. The fault of the American system was that it was too much localized, the education given depended upon the state of culture prevailing in each district. There was a cry for a central supervision. The taxation for schools was compulsory, but the attendance of children was not. Property had to pay the taxes and the people who paid the taxes wanted that the money was usefully applied. Education might be national without being governmental. Government might appoint inspectors whose duty it was to see that the laws were obeyed, just as the factory inspectors looked after the observance of the factory acts, without any power of interfering with the course of education itself.

The Congress might without hesitation adopt that education was compulsory. As to children being prevented from working, one thing was certain: It would not reduce wages and people would get used to it.

The Proudhonists maintained that gratuitous education was nonsense, because the state had to pay for it; of course somebody had to pay, but not those who could least afford it. [Marx] was not in favor of gratuitous college education.

As Prussian education had been talked so much of, he would conclude by observing that the Prussian system was only calculated to make good soldiers.

UNIVERSAL FREE EDUCATION

From "Marginal Notes to the Program of the German Workers' Party" (Gotha Program) (1875), Part IV

B. "The German Workers' party demands as the intellectual and ethical basis of the state:

"I. Universal and equal elementary education by the state. Universal compulsory school attendance. Free instruction."

"Equal elementary education"? What idea lies behind these words? Is it believed that in present-day society (and it is only with this one has to deal) education can be *equal* for all classes? Or is it demanded that the upper classes also shall be compulsorily reduced to the modicum of education—the elementary school—that alone is compatible with the economic conditions not only of the wage workers but of the peasants as well?

"Universal compulsory school attendance. Free instruction." The former exists even in Germany, the second in Switzerland and in the United States in the case of elementary schools. If in some states of the latter country higher educational institutions are also "free," that only means in fact defraying the cost of the education of the upper classes from the general tax receipts. Incidentally, the same holds good for "free administration of justice" demanded under A, 5. The administration of criminal justice is to be had free everywhere; that of civil justice is concerned almost exclusively with conflicts over property and hence affects almost exclusively the possessing classes. Are they to carry on their litigation at the expense of the national coffers?

The paragraph on the schools should at least have demanded technical schools (theoretical and practical) in combination with the elementary school.

"Elementary education by the state" is altogether objectionable. Defining by a general law the expenditures on the elementary schools, the qualifications of the teaching staff, the branches of instruction, etc., and, as is done in the United States, supervising the fulfillment of these legal specifications by state inspectors, is a very different thing from appointing the state as the educator of the people! Government and church should rather be equally excluded from any influence on the school. Particularly, indeed, in the Prusso-German Empire (and one should not take refuge in the rotten subterfuge that one is speaking of a "state of the future"; we have seen how matters stand in this respect) the state has need, on the contrary, of a very stern education by the people.

But the whole program, for all its democratic clang, is tainted through and through by the Lassallean sect's servile belief in the state, or, what is no better, by a democratic belief in miracles, or rather it is a compromise between these two kinds of belief in miracles, both equally remote from socialism.

"Freedom of science" says a paragraph of the Prussian Constitution. Why, then, here?

"Freedom of conscience"! If one desired at this time of the *Kulturkampf*[1] to remind liberalism of its old catchwords, it surely could have been done only in the following form: Everyone should be able to attend to his religious as well as his bodily needs without the police sticking their noses in. But the Workers' party ought at any rate in this connection to have expressed its awareness of the fact that bourgeois "freedom of conscience" is nothing but the toleration of all possible kinds of religious freedom of conscience, and that for its part it endeavors rather to liberate the conscience from the witchery of religion. But one chooses not to transgress the "bourgeois" level.

---

[1] Cultural struggle; the reference is to Bismarck's struggle with the Catholic Church in Germany.

CHAPTER VI

HISTORY

Note

Marx was not a historian in the conventional sense and did not write history as such, but his writings are imbued with a sense of history. This is true also of his important polemical works, such as *The Class Struggles in France* (1850) and *The Eighteenth Brumaire of Louis Napoleon* (1852). Even *Capital*, his monumental work on economics, has immense historic sweep and is rooted in records of the past. He was a lifelong reader of history, studying and often annotating the works of major historical scholars in the original languages, including Russian, in which they were written.

Marx's philosophy of history is based on dialectical materialism, or what is known as the "materialist interpretation of history." This involves the fundamental idea that the determining factors in the development, relations and institutions of mankind are not mystical or ideological, but economi Human actions are rooted in men's productive activities. To procure their livelihood, human beings organize their productive forces in such a way that their activities interact throughout the economic spectrum. These material actions are the overmastering force in all social existence and relationships. Everything else in life—religion, philosophy, political ideas, social institutions—is "superstructure," resting on the economic foundations which determine the state of civilization at any given stage of history.

The productive forces and relationships are predetermined by the processes of history, and not by the caprice of will of an individual. As Marx put it in *The Eighteenth Brumaire of Louis Napoleon*:

> Men make their own history, but they do not make it as they please; they do not make it under self-selected cir-

cumstances, but under circumstances existing already, given and transmitted from the past.

The social system, or "civil society," as Hegel called it, is thus historically shaped. Class, family, ideas, institutions, all are derived from past developments. Changes do occur, but they do so within a pre-existing, inherited framework, which in turn create a new stage of development, equally rooted in the material world of production and all its relationships which alter ideas in the process.

In the *Communist Manifesto*, Marx (in collaboration with Engels) wrote:

> What else does the history of ideas prove than that intellectual production changes in character in proportion as material production is changed? ... When people speak of ideas that revolutionize society, they do but express the fact that within the old society the elements of a new one have been created.

This was the reason why Marx devoted his mature working years to research and writing in the realm of economics. In this material domain he expected to find the final answers and solutions to the problems of history and human destiny. Here he claimed to have discovered the "scientific" truth about the evolution of mankind, and its future.

To non-Marxists, Marx's claim to having "scientific" truth in history is not persuasive. They point out that ideas—religious, philosophical, scientific—cannot always be explained as economic "superstructure." Ideas may have different origins and lives of their own. They also have continuity beyond the periods of their origins and are not easily explainable as the mere results of economic production. Christianity, for example, one of the most sweeping idea-systems in history, may have had its birth among the rural poor in Palestine some two millennia ago, but how explain its widespread and powerful functioning among innumerable peoples, at all stages of economic development, all over the globe? Similarly, the materialist explanation throws no light on the rise and continuing growth of Islam in the Middle East, in Asia, in Africa, among peoples and tribes with economies that run the whole gamut of development, or non-development, from primitive to complex. Mohammedanism originated among desert nomads whose only "productive forces" were ambulating camels. Yet Christianity and Islam, as systems of ideas, have wrought monumental changes among a large portion of mankind.

Marx's "materialist interpretation" may be applicable to occasional epochs and some specific stages of history, but even then with certain reservations. The Marxian view, for instance, has been criticized for underestimating—indeed, ignoring—the role of Great Men. It must, nevertheless, be regarded as a stimulating contribution to knowledge.

WHAT HISTORY IS

From Marx and Engels, *The German Ideology* (written in 1845-46); translated from the German by Progress Publishers (Moscow, 1964), pp. 51-65

This conception of history depends on our ability to expound the real process of production, starting out from the material production of life itself, and to comprehend the form of intercourse connected with this and created by this mode of production (i.e., civil society in its various stages), as the basis of all history; and to show it in its action as State, to explain all the different theoretical products and forms of consciousness, religion, philosophy, ethics, etc., etc., and trace their origins and growth from that basis; by which means, of course, the whole thing can be depicted in its totality (and therefore, too, the reciprocal action of these various sides on one another). It has not, like the idealistic view of history, in every period to look for a category, but remains constantly on the real *ground* of history; it does not explain practice from the idea but explains the formation of ideas from material practice; and accordingly it comes to the conclusion that all forms and products of consciousness cannot be dissolved by mental criticism, by resolution into "self-consciousness" or transformation into "apparitions," "spectres," "fancies," etc., but only by the practical overthrow of the actual social relations which gave rise to this idealistic humbug; that not criticism but revolution is the driving force of history, also of religion, of philosophy and all other types of theory. It shows that history does not end by being resolved into "self-consciousness" as "spirit of the spirit", but that in it at each stage there is found a material result: a sum of productive forces, a historically created relation of individuals to nature and to one another, which is handed down to each generation from its predecessor; a mass of productive forces, capital funds and conditions, which, on the one hand, is indeed modified by the new generation, but also on the other prescribes for it its conditions of life and gives it a definite development, a special character. It shows that circumstances make men just as much as men make circumstances. This sum of productive forces, capital funds and social forms of intercourse, which every individual and generation finds in existence as something given, is the real basis of what the philosophers have conceived as "substance" and "essence of man", and what they have deified and attacked: a real basis which is not in the least disturbed, in its effect and influence on the development of men, by the fact that these philosophers revolt against it as "self-consciousness" and the "Unique." These conditions of life, which different generations find in existence, decide also whether or not the periodically recurring revolutionary convulsion will be strong enough to overthrow the basis of the entire existing system. And if these material elements of a complete revolution are not present (namely, on the one hand, the existing productive forces, on the other the formation of a revolutionary mass, which revolts not only against separate conditions of society up till then, but against the very "production of life" till then, the "total activity" on which it was based), then, as far as practical development is concerned, it is absolutely immaterial whether the *idea* of this revolution has been expressed a hundred times already, as the history of communism proves.

In the whole conception of history up to the present this real basis of history has either been totally neglected or else considered as a minor matter quite irrelevant to the course of history. History must, therefore, always be written according to an extraneous standard; the real production of life seems to be primeval history, while the truly historical appears to be separated from ordinary life, something extra-superterrestrial. With this the elation of man to nature is excluded from history and hence the antithesis of nature and history is created. The exponents of this conception of history have consequently only been able to see in history the political actions of princes and States, religious and all sorts of theoretical struggles, and in particular in each historical epoch have had to *share the illusion of that epoch*. For instance, if an epoch imagines itself to be actuated by purely "political" or "religious" motives, although "religion" and "politics" are only forms of its true motives, the historian accepts this opinion. The "idea," the "conception" of the people in question about their real practice, is transformed into the sole determining, active force, which controls and determines their practice. When the crude form in which the division of labor appears with the Indians and Egyptians calls forth the caste system in their State and religion, the historian believes that the caste system is the power which has produced this crude social form. While the French and the English at least hold by the political illusion, which is moderately close to reality, the Germans move in the realm of the "pure spirit" and make religious illusion the driving force of history. The Hegelian philosophy of history is the last consequence, reduced to its "finest expression," of all this German historiography, for which it is not a question of real, nor even of political, interests, but of pure thoughts, which consequently must appear to Saint Bruno, as a series of "thoughts" that devour one another and are finally swallowed up in "self-consciousness"[1]; and even more consistently the course of history appears to the Blessed Max Stirner, who knows not a thing about real history, as a mere tale of "knights," robbers and ghosts, from whose visions he can, of course, only save himself by "unholiness." This conception is truly religious: it postulates religious man as the primitive man, the starting-point of history; and in its imagination puts the religious production of fancies in the place of the real production of the means of subsistence and of life itself. This whole conception of history, together with its dissolution and the scruples and qualms resulting from it, is a purely *national* affair of the Germans and has only *local* interest for the Germans, as for instance the important question treated several times of late: how really we "pass from the realm of God to the realm of Man"—as if this "realm of God" had ever existed anywhere save in the imagination, and the learned gentlemen, without being aware

---

[1] Marginal note by Marx: "So-called *objective* historiography just consists in treating the historical conditions independent of activity. Reactionary character."

of it, were not constantly living in the "realm of Man" to which they are now seeking the way; and as if the learned pastime (for it is nothing more) of explaining the mystery of this theoretical bubble-blowing did not on the contrary lie in demonstrating its origin in actual earthly conditions. Always, for these Germans, it is simply a matter of resolving the nonsense of earlier writers into some other freak, i.e., of presupposing that all this nonsense has a special *sense* which can be discovered; while really it is only a question of explaining this theoretical talk from the actual existing conditions. The real, practical dissolution of these phrases, the removal of these notions from the consciousness of men, will, as we have already said, be effected by altered circumstances, not by theoretical deductions. For the mass of men, i.e., the proletariat, these theoretical notions do not exist and hence do not require to be dissolved, and if this mass ever had any theoretical notions, i.e., religion, etc., these have now long been dissolved by circumstances.

The purely national character of these questions and solutions is shown again in the way these theorists believe in all seriousness that chimeras like "the God-Man," "Man," etc., have presided over individual epochs of history (Saint Bruno even goes so far as to assert that "only criticism and critics have made history"); and when they themselves construct historical systems, they skip over all earlier periods in the greatest haste and pass immediately from "Mongolism" to history "with meaningful content," that is to say, to the history of the *Hallische* and *Deutsche Jahrbücher* and the dissolution of the Hegelian school into a general squabble. They forget all other nations, all real events, and the *theatrum mundi* is confined to the Leipzig Book Fair and the mutual quarrels of "Criticism," "Man," and "the Unique." If these theorists treat really historical subjects, as for instance the eighteenth century, they merely give a history of the ideas of the times, torn away from the facts and the practical development fundamental to them; and even that merely in order to represent that period as an imperfect preliminary stage, the as yet limited predecessor of the real historical age, i.e., the period of the German philosophic struggle from 1840 to 1844. As might be expected when the history of an earlier period is written with the aim of accentuating the brilliance of an unhistoric person and his fantasies, all the really historic events, even the really historic invasions of politics into history, receive no mention. Instead we get a narrative based not on research but on arbitrary constructions and literary gossip, such as Saint Bruno provided in his now forgotten history of the eighteenth century. These high-falutin and haughty hucksters of ideas, who imagine themselves infinitely exalted above all national prejudices, are thus in practice far more national than the beer-quaffing philistines who dream of a united Germany. They do not recognize the deeds of other nations as historical: they live in Germany, to Germany, and for Germany; they turn the Rhine-song into a religious hymn and conquer Alsace and Lorraine by robbing French philosophy instead of the French State, by Germanizing French ideas instead of French provinces. Herr Venedey is a cosmopolitan compared with the saints Bruno and Max, who, in the universal dominance of theory, proclaim the universal dominance of Germany. . . .

As far as Feuerbach is a materialist he does not deal with history, and as far as he considers history he is not a materialist. With him materialism and history diverge completely, a fact which incidentally is already obvious from what has been said.[2]

History is nothing but the succession of the separate generations, each of which exploits the materials, the capital funds, the productive forces handed down to it by all preceding generations, and thus, on the one hand, continues the traditional activity in completely changed circumstances and, on the other, modifies the old circumstances with a completely changed activity. This can be speculatively distorted so that later history is made the goal of earlier history, e.g., the goal ascribed to the discovery of America is to further the eruption of the French Revolution. Thereby history receives its own special aims and becomes "a person ranking with other persons" (to wit: "Self-Consciousness, Criticism, the Unique," etc.), while what is designated with the words "destiny," "goal," "germ," or "idea" of earlier history is nothing more

[2] The following passage is crossed out in the manuscript: "The reason why we nevertheless discuss history here in greater detail is that the words 'history' and 'historical' usually mean everything possible to the Germans except reality. A brilliant example of this is in particular Saint Bruno with his 'pulpit eloquence.'"

than abstraction formed from later history, from the active influence which earlier history exercises on later history.

The further the separate spheres, which interact on one another, extend in the course of this development, the more the original isolation of the separate nationalities is destroyed by the developed mode of production and intercourse and the division of labor between various nations naturally brought forth by these, the more history becomes world history. Thus, for instance, if in England a machine is invented, which deprives countless workers of bread in India and China, and overturns the whole form of existence of these empires, this invention becomes a world-historical fact. Or again, take the case of sugar and coffee which have proved their world-historical importance in the nineteenth century by the fact that the lack of these products, occasioned by the Napoleonic Continental System, caused the Germans to rise against Napoleon, and thus became the real basis of the glorious Wars of Liberation of 1813. From this it follows that this transformation of history into world history is not indeed a mere abstract act on the part of the "self-conscious," the world spirit, or of any other metaphysical specter, but a quite material, empirically verifiable act, an act the proof of which every individual furnishes as he comes and goes, eats, drinks, and clothes himself.

THE ROLE OF THE PAST

From *The Eighteenth Brumaire of Louis Napoleon* (1852), Pt. I

Hegel remarks somewhere that all great world-historic facts and personages appear, so to speak, twice. He forgot to add: the first time as tragedy, the second time as farce, Caussidière for Danton, Louis Blanc for Robespierre, the *Montagne* of 1848 to 1851 for the *Montagne* of 1793 to 1795, the nephew for the uncle. And the same caricature occurs in the circumstances of the second edition of the Eighteenth Brumaire.

Men make their own history, but they do not make it as they please; they do not make it under self-selected circumstances, but under circumstances existing already, given and transmitted from the past. The tradition of all dead generations weighs like an Alp on the brains of the living. And just as they seem to be occupied with revolutionizing themselves and things, creating something that did not exist before, precisely in such epochs of revolutionary crisis they anxiously conjure up the spirits of the past to their service, borrowing from them names, battle slogans, and costumes in order to present this new scene in world history in this time-honored disguise and this borrowed language. Thus Luther put on the mask of the Apostle Paul, the Revolution of 1789-1814 draped itself alternately in the guise of the Roman Republic and the Roman Empire, and the Revolution of 1848 knew nothing better to do than to parody, now 1789, now the revolutionary tradition of 1793-95. In like manner, the beginner who has learned a new language always translates it back into his mother tongue, but he assimilates the spirit of the new language and expresses himself freely in it only when he moves in it without recalling the old and when he forgets his native tongue.

When we think about this conjuring up of the dead of world history, a salient difference reveals itself. Camille Desmoulins, Danton, Robespierre, St. Just, Napoleon, the heroes as well as the parties and the masses of the old French Revolution, performed the task of their time—that of unchaining and establishing modern bourgeois society—in Roman costumes and with Roman phrases. The first one destroyed the feudal foundation and cut off the feudal heads that had grown on it. The other created inside France the only conditions under which free competition could be developed, the parceled-out land used, and the unfettered productive power of the nation employed; and beyond the French borders it swept away feudal institutions everywhere, to provide, as far as necessary, bourgeois society in France with an appropriate up-to-date environment on the European continent. Once the new social formation was established, the antediluvian colossi disappeared and with them also the resurrected Romanism— the Brutuses, the Gracchi, the publicolas, the tribunes, the senators, and Caesar himself. Bourgeois society in its sober reality bred its own true interpreters and spokesmen in the Says, Cousins, Royer-Collards, Benjamin Constants, and Guizots; its real military leaders sat behind the office desk, and the hog-headed Louis XVIII was its political chief. Entirely absorbed in the production of wealth and in peaceful competitive struggle it no longer remembered that the ghosts of the Roman period had watched over its cradle. But unheroic though bourgeois society is, it nevertheless needed heroism, sacrifice, terror, civil war, and national wars to bring it into being. And in the austere classical traditions of the Roman Republic the bourgeois gladiators found the ideals and the art forms, the self-deceptions, that they needed to conceal from themselves the bourgeois-limited content of their struggles and to keep their passion on the high plane of great historic tragedy. Similarly, at another stage of development a century earlier, Cromwell and the English people had borrowed from the Old Testament the speech, emotions, and illusions for their bourgeois revolution. When the real goal had been achieved and the bourgeois transformation of English society had been accomplished, Locke supplanted Habakkuk.

Thus the awakening of the dead in these revolutions served the purpose of glorifying the new struggles, not of parodying the old; of magnifying the given task in the imagination, not recoiling from its solution in reality; of finding once more the spirit of revolution, not making its ghost walk again.

From 1848 to 1851, only the ghost of the old revolution circulated—from Marrast, the republican in yellow [kid] gloves who disguised himself as old Bailly, down to the adventurer who hides his trivial and repulsive features behind the iron death mask of Napoleon. A whole nation, which thought it had acquired an accelerated power of motion by means of a revolution, suddenly finds itself set back into a defunct epoch, and to remove any doubt about the relapse, the old dates arise again—the old chronology, the old names, the old edicts, which had long since become a subject of antiquarian scholarship, and the old minions of the law who had seemed long dead. The nation feels like the mad Englishman in Bedlam who thinks he is living in the time of the old Pharaohs and daily bewails the hard labor he must perform in the Ethiopian gold mines, immured in this subterranean prison, a pale lamp fastened to his head, the overseer of the slaves behind him with a long whip, and at the exits a confused welter of barbarian war slaves who understand neither the forced laborers nor each other, since they speak no common language. "And all this," sighs the mad Englishman, "is expected of me, a freeborn Briton, in order to make gold for the Pharaohs." "In order to pay the debts of the Bonaparte family," sighs the French nation. The Englishman, so long as he was not in his right mind, could not get rid of his *idée fixe* of mining gold. The French, so long as they were engaged in revolution, could not get rid of the memory of Napoleon, as the election of December 10 proved. They longed to return from the perils of revolution to the fleshpots of Egypt, and December 2, 1851, was the answer. Now they have not only a caricature of the old Napoleon, but the old Napoleon himself, caricatured as would have to be in the middle of the nineteenth century.

The social revolution of the nineteenth century cannot take its poetry from the past but only from the future. It cannot begin with itself before it has stripped away all superstition about the past. The former revolutions required recollections of past world history in order to smother their own content. The revolution of the nineteenth century must let the dead bury their dead in order to arrive at its own content. There the phrase went beyond the content; here the content goes beyond the phrase.

SPANISH HISTORY

From "Insurrection in Madrid," *New-York Daily Tribune*, July 11, 1854

There is perhaps no country, except Turkey, so little known to and so falsely judged by Europe as Spain. The numberless local pronunciamentos and military rebellions have accustomed Europe to view it on a level with Imperial Rome at the era of the praetorians. This is quite as superficial an error as was committed in the case of Turkey, by those who fancied the life of the nation extinct because its official history for the past century consisted only of palace revolutions and Janissary *émeutes* [mutinies]. The secret of this fallacy lies in the simple fact that historians, instead of viewing the resources and strength of these people in their provincial and local organizations, had drawn at the source of their court almanacs. The movements of what we are used to call the State have so little affected the Spanish people that they were quite content to leave that restricted domain to the alternative passions and petty intrigues of court minions, soldiers, adventurers, and a few so-called statesmen, and they have had little cause to repent themselves of their indifference. The character of modern Spanish history deserving to receive a very different appreciation than it has until now experienced, I will take an opportunity to treat this subject. . . .

THE ROLE OF THE ARMY IN HISTORY

Letter to Frederick Engels (in Ryde), London, September 25, 1857

Dear Engels:

You will have received by now my letter from the day before yesterday with its acknowledgment of the receipt of the £5. I do not understand its delay, as I myself had mailed the letter on time.

Your "*Army*"[1] is very well done; but its size made me feel as if I had been hit over the head, for it must be harmful to you to work so much. Specifically, if I had known that you would work far into the night, I would rather have let the whole thing go to the devil.

The history of the army brings out more clearly than anything else the correctness of our conception of the connection between the productive forces and social relations. In general, the army is important for economic development. For instance, it was in the army that the ancients first fully developed a wage system. Similarly among the Romans the *peculium castrense* was the first legal form in which the right of others than fathers of families to movable property was recognized. So also the guild system among the corporation of fabri. Here, too, the first use of machinery on a large scale. Even the special value of metals and their use as money appears to have been originally based—as soon as Grimm's Stone Age was passed—on their military significance. The division of labor *within* one branch was also first carried out in the armies. The whole history of the forms of bourgeois society is very strikingly epitomized here. If someday you can find time, you must work the thing out from this point of view.

In my opinion, the only points that have been overlooked in your account are: (1) The first appearance of mercenary troops, ready for use on a large scale and at once, among the

[1] Engels' essay, "Army," in *The New American Cyclopaedia*, Vol. II, 1858.

Carthaginians (for our private use. I will look up a book on the Carthaginian armies written by a Berlin man,[2] which I came to know only later). (2) The development of the army system in Italy in the fifteenth and early sixteenth centuries. Tactical tricks, at any rate, were developed here. Extremely humorous is Machiavelli's description (which I will copy out for you) in his history of Florence of the way the condottieri fought one another. (No, when I come to see you in Brighton—when?—I would rather bring the volume of Machiavelli with me. His history of Florence is a masterpiece). And, finally (3), the Asian military system as it first appeared among the Persians and then, though modified in a great variety of ways, among the Mongols, Turks, etc. . . .

Yours,
K.M.

MATERIALIST INTERPRETATION OF HISTORY

From Preface to *Critique of Political Economy* (1859)

The subject of my professional studies was jurisprudence, which, however, I pursued as a subordinate discipline alongside philosophy and history.[1] In the year 1842-1843, as editor of the *Rheinische Zeitung*, I experienced for the first time the embarrassment of having to participate in discussions of so-called material interests. The proceedings of the Rhenish Diet on thefts of wood and parceling of landed property; the official polemic which Herr von Schaper, then president of the Rhine Province, opened against the *Rheinische Zeitung* on the conditions of the Moselle peasants[2]; and finally debates

---

[2] Wilhelm Boettlicher, *Geschichte der Carthager nach den Quellen bearbeitet* ("History of the Carthaginians, Based on the Sources," Berlin, 1827).

[1] Marx took his doctorate, not in jurisprudence but in philosophy. His dissertation, *Difference Between the Democritean and Epicurean Philosophy of Nature*, earned him a Ph.D. degree from Bonn University, 1841.

[2] For Marx's role on the *Rheinische Zeitung*, of which he was editor, see Saul K. Padover, ed., *Karl Marx on Freedom of the Press and Censorship* (New York, 1974).

on free trade and protective tariffs—all these provide the first occasion for me to occupy myself with economic questions. On the other hand, at that time, when the good will "to go ahead" greatly outweighed expert knowledge, a philosophically weak echo of French socialism and communism made itself audible in the *Rheinische Zeitung*. I declared myself against this bungling, but at the same time I had to confess in a controversy with the *Allgemeine Augsburger Zeitung* that my previous studies did not permit me even to venture any judgment on the content of the French tendencies. Instead, I eagerly seized on the illusion of the managers of the *Rheinische Zeitung*, who believed that by a weaker attitude on the part of the paper they could be saved from the death sentence imposed upon it, to withdraw from the public stage into the study.[3]

The first work which I undertook for a solution of the doubts which assailed me was a critical review of the Hegelian philosophy of law, the introduction to which appeared in 1844 in the *Deutsch-Französische Jahrbücher*, published in Paris. My investigation led to the conclusion that legal relations as well as forms of state could be neither understood by themselves nor explained by the so-called general development of the human mind, but rather are rooted in the material conditions of life, the sum total of which Hegel, following the example of Englishmen and Frenchmen of the eighteenth century, combined under the name of "civil society," the anatomy of which, however, is to be sought in political economy. The investigation of the latter, which I began in Paris, I continued in Brussels, whither I emigrated in consequence of an order of expulsion[4] by M. Guizot. The general conclusion at which I arrived and which, once reached, served as guiding thread for my studies can be briefly formulated as follows: In the social production of their life, men enter into definite relations that are indispensable and independent of their will; these relations of production correspond to a definite stage of development of their material productive forces. The sum total of these relations of production

---

[3] On March 17, 1843, Marx resigned as editor of the *Rheinische Zeitung*, which was closed by the Prussian censorship two weeks later, on April 1, 1843.

[4] Marx lived in Brussels from February 1845 to March 1848.

constitutes the economic structure of society—the real foundation, on which is built a legal and political superstructure and to which correspond definite forms of social consciousness. The mode of production in material life conditions the social, political, and intellectual life processes in general. It is not the consciousness of men that determines their existence, but, on the contrary, their social existence determines their consciousness. At a certain stage of their development, the material productive forces of society come into conflict with the existing relations of production, or—what is but a legal expression for the same thing—with the property relations within which they had been at work hitherto. From forms of development of the productive forces, these relations turn into their fetters. Then begins an epoch of social revolution. With the change of the economic foundation, the whole immense superstructure is more or less rapidly transformed. In considering such transformations, a distinction should always be made between the material transformation of the economic conditions of production, which can be determined with the precision of natural science, and the legal, political, religious, aesthetic or philosophic—in short, ideological—forms in which men become conscious of this conflict and fight it out. Just as our opinion of an individual is not based on what he thinks of himself, so can we not judge such a period of transformation by its own consciousness; on the contrary, such consciousness must rather be explained from the contradictions of material life, from the existing conflict between the social forces of production and the relations of production. No social order ever perishes before all the productive forces for which there is room in it have been developed; and new, higher relations of production never appear before the material conditions for their existence have matured within the womb of the old society itself. Mankind, therefore, always sets itself only such tasks as it can solve, for looking at the matter more closely, it will always be found that the task itself arises only when the material conditions for its solution already exist or are at least in the process of formation. In broad outlines, Asian, ancient, feudal, and modern bourgeois forms of production can be designated as progressive epochs in the economic formation of society. The bourgeois relations of production are the last antagonistic form of the social process of production—antagonistic not in the sense of individual antagonism but of one arising from the social conditions of life of individuals; at the same time the productive forces developing the womb of bourgeois society create the material conditions for the solution of that antagonism. With this social formation, therefore, the prehistory of human society comes to a close.

AGRICULTURE IN HISTORY

Letter to Frederick Engels (in Manchester), London, March 25, 1868*

Dear Fred:

I wanted to write you yesterday from the [British] Museum, but I suddenly became so unwell that I had to close the very interesting book that I held in my hand. A dark veil fell over my eyes. Then a frightful headache and a pain in the chest. I strolled home. Air and light helped, and when I got home I slept for some time. My condition is such that I really should give up all working and thinking for some time to come; but that would be difficult, even if I could afford it.

In regard to Maurer. His books are extraordinarily important.[1] Not only primeval times, but also the whole later development of the free imperial cities, the immunity of landowners, the public authority, and the struggle between the free peasantry and serfdom, are given an entirely new form.

In human history it is as in paleontology. On account of a certain judicial blindness, even the best intelligences absolutely fail to see the things that lie in front of their noses.

---

*From *Karl Marx on History and People* by Saul K. Padover, pp. 101-04. Copyright 1975 by Saul K. Padover. Used with permission of McGraw-Hill Book Co.

[1] Georg Ludwig von Maurer, *Einleitung zur Geschichte der Mark-, Hof-, Dorf-, und Stadt-Verfassung und der oeffentlichen Gewalt* ("Introduction to the History of the Border-Land, Farm, Village, and City Constitution and Public Authority,)" (Munich, 1854); *Geschichte der Dorfverfassung in Deutschland* ("History of the Village Constitution in Germany,") 2 vols., Erlangen, 1865-66); *Geschichte der Fronhöfe, der Bauernhöfe und der Hofverfassung in Deutschland* ("History of Villeinages, Peasant Farms and Farm Constitution in Germany,") 4 vols., Erlangen, 1862-63); *Geschichte der Markenverfassung in Deutschland* ("History of the Border-Lands Constitution in Germany,") Erlangen, 1856).

Later, when the moment has arrived, one is surprised to find traces everywhere of what one had failed to see. The first reaction against the French Revolution, and the period of Enlightenment bound up with it, was, of course, to regard everything medieval as romantic, and even people like Grimm[2] are not free from this. The second reaction—and this corresponds to the socialist tendency, even though those learned men have no idea that the two are connected—is to look beyond the Middle Ages into the prehistoric period of each nation. They are, therefore, surprised to find the newest in the oldest, and even egalitarian to a degree, which would have made Proudhon shudder.

To show how much they are caught up in this judicial blindness: right in my own neighborhood [in Trier], on the *Hunsruecken*, the old Germanic system survived up till the last few years. I now recall my father talking to me about it as a lawyer! Another proof: just as geologists, even the best, like Cuvier, have explained certain facts in a completely distorted way, so philologists of the importance of a Grimm have mistranslated the simplest Latin sentences because they were under the influence of Moeser[3] (who, I remember, was enchanted by the fact that among the Germans "freedom" had never existed but that *"Luft macht eigen"* [the environment makes the serf]) and others. For example, the wellknown passage in Tacitus:[4] *"arva per annos mutant, et superest ager,"* which means: they exchange the fields (*arva*) (by lot, hence also *sortes* [lot] in all the later law codes of the Barbarians) and the common land remains over (*ager* as contrasted with *arva* as public land)—is translated by Grimm, etc.: "They cultivate fresh fields every year and still there always remains (uncultivated) land!"

Likewise the passage *"Colunt discreti ac diversi"* [their tillage is individual and scattered] is supposed to prove that from times immemorial the Germans carried on cultivation on individual farms, like Westphalian *Junkers*. But in the same passage it says: *"Vicos locant non in nostrum morem connexis et cohaerentibus aedificiis: suum quisque locum spatio circumdat"* ["They do not, as we do, lay out villages with

[2] Jacob Grimm, *Deutsche Rechtsalterthümer* ("German Legal Antiquities," 2d ed., Göttingen, 1854).

[3] Justus Moeser, *Osnabrücksche Geschichte* ("Osnabrück History," Berlin and Stettin, 1780).

[4] Tacitus, *Germania*, Ch. 26.

buildings connected and joined together: each surrounds his place with a strip of land"]; and primitive Germanic villages, in the form described, still exist here and there in Denmark. Obviously Scandinavia must become as important for German jurisprudence and economics as for German mythology. And only by starting from there shall we be able to decipher our past again. For the rest, even Grimm, etc., found in Caesar[5] that the Germans always settled as *Geschlechtsgenossenschaften* [kindred associations] and not as individuals: "*gentibus cognationibusque, qui uno coiereant*" [according to clans and kindreds who settled together].

But what would old Hegel say in the next world if he heard that the word *Allgemeine* [common, or general] in German and Norse means nothing but *Gemeindeland* [communal land] and *Sundre, Besondre* [particular], nothing but the separate property divided off from the communal land? Here are the logical categories coming damn well out of "our communication" after all.

Very interesting is Fraas's *Climate and the Vegetable World in Time, a Contribution to the History of Both*,[6] particularly as it proves that climate and flora changed in historic times. He is a Darwinist before Darwin and makes even the species arise in historic times. But he is also at the same time an agronomist. He maintains that as a result of cultivation—in proportion to its degree—the "dampness" so very much beloved by the peasant is lost (hence plants, too, emigrate from South to North) and eventually the formation of steppes begins. The first effect of cultivation is useful but is eventually devastating on account of deforestation, etc. This man is as much a thoroughly learned philologist (he has written books in Greek) as he is a chemist, agronomist, etc. The sum total is that cultivation—when it progresses naturally and is not consciously controlled (as a bourgeois, of course, he does not arrive at this)—leaves deserts behind it, Persia, Mesopotamia, etc., Greece). Here again another unconscious socialist tendency!

This Fraas is also interesting for Germanism. First, Dr. Med., then inspector and teacher of chemistry and technology. Now chief of the Bavaria Veterinary Institute, university professor, head of the State agronomical experiments, etc. In

---

[5] Julius Caesar, *De Bello Gallico*, Lib. VI.
[6] Karl Fraas, *Klima und Pflanzenwelt in der Zeit, ein Beitrag zur Geschichte beider* (Landshut, 1847).

his latest writings one notices his advanced age, but he is still a jolly lad. Has knocked around a good deal in Greece, Asia Minor, Egypt! His history of agriculture is important too.[7] He calls Fourier "this pious and humanistic socialist." Of the Albanians, etc.: "Every kind of scandalous lewdness and rape."

It is necessary to look over carefully the recent and latest writings on agriculture. The physical school is opposed to the chemical school.

Don't forget to send me back the letter of Kugelmann's manufacturer.[8]

---

[7] Fraas, *Geschichte der Landwirthschaft* (Prague, 1852).

[8] Gustav Meyer, a Bielefeld manufacturer. On March 17, 1868, Marx wrote to Kugelmann: "Meyer's letter pleased me very much. Still, he partly misunderstood my theory of development. Otherwise he would have seen that I have presented *big industry* not only as the mother of antagonisms but also as the producer of the material and intellectual conditions for the solution of these antagonisms, which, indeed, cannot take place in *a comfortable way*."

CHAPTER VII

PHILOSOPHY

Note

Marx's writings on philosophy can be found primarily in his doctoral dissertation on the classic Greek atomists, Democritus and Epicurus (1841), in his long essay on "Hegel's Constitutional Law" [*Staatsrecht*], and in parts of the *Economic and Philosophic Manuscripts* (1844), which are more social-economic than philosophic. In his doctoral thesis, which dealt with the "philosophy of nature" and the gods, Marx proclaimed philosophy as "world-dominating" and, with Epicurus, as not subservient to theology. He restated this view of the superiority of philosophy as "the spiritual quintessence of its time," in one of his earliest journalistic articles (*Rheinische Zeitung*, July 14, 1842), included in this chapter.

The deepest single influence on Marx as a philosopher was Georg Wilhelm Friedrich Hegel, whose ideas dominated the University of Berlin when Marx was a student there from 1836 to 1841. While Hegel, who died in 1831, was no longer alive then, his thought had permeated widely and found expression in the lectures and writings of some of Marx's great professors, such as Eduard Gans in philosophy and Friedrich Karl von Savigny in jurisprudence. From Hegel, Marx adopted the famous dialects of Being, Not-Being and Becoming, rephrasing it as Thesis, Antithesis and Synthesis. But he turned around the Hegelian view of the universe, from subjective Idealism to objective materialism. In a postscript to the second German edition of *Capital* (1873), Marx explained how his dialectic method differed from that of Hegel:

> To Hegel, the thinking process, which, under the name of the Idea he even transforms into an independent subject, is the demiurge of the real world . . . With me, on

the contrary, the Ideal is nothing else than the material world transposed and translated in the human mind.

After Marx became a communist, at the age of about twenty-six, he gave up philosophic studies in favor of political economy and other nonphilosophic interests.

SOCRATES AND CHRIST

From notes to Marx's doctoral dissertation, *The Difference Between the Democritean and Epicurean Philosophy of Nature* (1841). The notes were written in 1838-39 (Heft, No. 6).

If there were here an anology between Socrates and Christ, it would be that Socrates is the personification of philosophy and Christ the personification of religion. Still, there is no general connection here between philosophy and religion, but the question is rather the relationship between incorporated philosophy and incorporated religion. That they relate to each other is a very vague truth, which is the general condition of the problem and not the particular ground for the answer. If in this endeavor to prove something Christian in Socrates, nothing is established about the personalities, Christ and Socrates, other than the general relationship between a philosopher and a religious teacher, this emptiness breaks forth also when the general system of the moral Socratic idea, the Platonic State, is brought into contact with the general system of the Idea and Christ as a historic individual, above all with the Church.

PHILOSOPHY ABOVE RELIGION

From Foreword of Marx's doctoral dissertation

If as an appendix a critique of Plutarch's polemic against Epicurus' theology has been added, it is because this polemic is not isolated but is representative of a species in that in itself it most strikingly presents the relation of the theologizing intellect to philosophy.

In this critique, I will not, among other things, discuss how false Plutarch's point of view is altogether when he brings philosophy before the forum of religion. For this it is sufficient to cite, in place of all argument, a passage from David Hume:

> It is certainly a kind of insult to philosophy, whose sovereign authority ought to be acknowledged on all sides, if one forces it to defend itself on every occasion because of its conclusions and to justify itself against every art and science that takes offense at it. One thinks of a king accused of high treason against his own subjects.[1]

Philosophy, so long as a drop of blood pulses in its world-dominating, absolutely free heart, will always call out against its adversaries the cry of Epicurus: "Blasphemous is not he who scorns the gods of the masses, but he who imputes the ideas of the masses to the gods."

Philosophy does not make a secret of it. The confession of Prometheus: "In a word, I entirely hate all and every god," is its own confession, its own aphorism against all divine and earthly gods who do not acknowledge human self-consciousness as the highest divinity. It allows no rival.

But to those sad March hares who rejoice over the seemingly worsened social position of philosophy, it replies again as did Prometheus to the god-serving Hermes:

> I would never change the state of my calamitous fate for your servitude; hear well, I would never change. Better it is to be the slave of this rock than to serve Father Zeus as a messenger-boy.[2]

Prometheus is the most eminent saint and martyr in the philosophic calendar.

---

[1] Hume, *A Treatise of Human Nature* (1739). Marx cited from the German translation (Halle, 1790).
[2] From Aeschylus, *Promethus*, V.

EPICURUS' NATURAL PHILOSOPHY

From the conclusion of Marx's doctoral dissertation

Democritus' astronomical views might be considered acute from the standpoint of his time. Philosophical interests cannot be derived from them. They neither go beyond the circle of empirical reflection, nor do they have any definite internal connection with the doctrine of the atom.

Epicurus' theory of the heavenly bodies and the processes connected with them, or the meteors (a condensed term for all this), on the other hand, stands in contrast not only to the opinion of Democritus but also to that of the Greek philosophers. The glorification of the heavenly body is a cult that all Greek philosophers celebrate. The system of the heavenly bodies is the first naïve and nature-determined existence of actual reason. Greek self-consciousness took the same position in the realm of the mind. It is the intellectual solar system. Hence the Greek philosophers, in worshiping the heavenly bodies, worshiped their own mind....

Epicurus concludes: Since the eternity of the heavenly bodies would disturb the ataraxy of self-consciousness, it is a necessary consequence that it should not be eternal....

We have seen how the whole Epicurean natural philosophy is pervaded by the contradiction between Being and Existence, between Form and Matter. In the heavenly bodies, however, this contradiction is eradicated, the conflicting moments are reconciled. In the celestial system, the Matter absorbed the Form and oneness into its own self and thus attained its independence. But at this point it ceases to be abstract self-consciousness. In the world of the atoms, as in the world of phenomena, Form struggles with Matter; the one negates the other, and precisely in this conflict did abstract-individual self-consciousness feel its nature realized. Abstract Form, struggling with abstract Matter, was itself. But now, when Matter reconciled itself with Form and became independent, the individual self-consciousness stepped out of its chrysalis, proclaimed itself as the true principle, and became hostile to nature, which had now become independent.

Another way of saying it is this: Insofar as Matter has absorbed in itself unity and Form, as in the case of the celestial bodies, it has ceased to be abstract oneness. It has become concrete oneness and universality, Thus in the meteors, the abstract-individual self-consciousness is confronted with its actualized contradiction—the existence and nature of what has become universal. It recognizes in it, therefore, its deadly enemy. To it is ascribed, as does Epicurus, all the anxiety and confusion of men; for the universal means precisely the dissolution of the abstract-individual. Here, therefore, the true principle of Epicurus—abstract-individual self-consciousness—is no longer concealed. It comes out of its hiding, and freed from its material masquerade, it seeks, through definition, for abstract possibility—what is possible can also be different. From the possible, the opposite is also possible—to destroy the reality of nature that has become independent. Hence the polemics against those who explain the celestial bodies as *haplos* [simple, absolute], that is, in a finite way; for the One is the Necessity and the Independent-Within-Itself.

Consequently, so long as nature expresses the individual self-consciousness and its contradiction as atom and phenomenon, the subjectivity of the latter appears only in the Form of Matter itself; where, on the other hand, it becomes independent, it reflects itself in itself, and confronts it in its own shape [*Gestalt*] as independent Form. . . .

Hence the soul of the Epicurean natural philosophy appears in the theory of the meteors. Nothing is eternal that destroys the ataraxy of the individual self-consciousness. The heavenly bodies disturb its ataraxy and its equality within itself, because they are the existing universality and because in them nature had become independent.

Hence, it is not, as *Chrysippus* believes, the gastrology of Archestratus, but the absoluteness and freedom of self-conciousness that is the principle of the Epicurean philosophy, even if the self-consciousness is conceived only under the form of oneness.

If the abstract-individual self-consciousness is posited as an abstract principle, then, to be sure, all true and real science is abolished insofar as oneness does not rule in the nature of things. But everything else that stands transcendent above human consciousness, that is, belongs to imaginary reason, also falls apart. If, however, self-consciousness, knowing itself only in the form of abstract universality, is raised to an absolute principle, then the door is opened to superstitious and unfree mysticism. Historic proof of this is found in the Stoic philosophy. Abstract-universal self-consciousness has in it the power to affirm itself in things themselves, in which it is only affirmed and never negated.

Hence Epicurus is the greatest enlightener, and he deserves the eulogy bestowed upon him by Lucretius:

> Humana ante oculos foedo quum vita jaceret,
> In terreis oppressa gravi sub relligione,
> Quae caput a coeli regionibus ostendebat,
> Horribili super aspectu mortalibus instans:
>
> Primum Grajus homo mortaleis tollere contra
> Est oculus ausus, primusque obsistere contra;
> Quem nec fama Deum nec fulmina nec minitanti
> Murmure compressit coelum. . . .
> Quare relligio pedibus subjecta vicissim
> Obteritur, nos exaequat victoria coelo.[1]

The difference between the Democritean and Epicurean natural philosophy, which we have presented at the end of the general section, has developed further and been confirmed in all spheres of nature. In Epicurus, the atomistic with all its contradictions has been developed and realized to the fullest extent as the natural science of self-consciousness. . . . In Democritus, on the other hand, the atom is merely the universal objective expression of empirical research into nature altogether. For him, therefore, the atom remains pure and abstract category, a hypothesis, which is only the result of experience and not its energetic principle, and hence remains

---

[1] Lucretius, *De Rerum Natura*:
When, before the eyes of men, disgraceful life on earth was bowed by the burden of oppressive religion, which extended its head from the high regions of heaven, and with gruesome grotesqueness frightfully threatened mankind,

a Greek first ventured to raise his mortal eye against the monster and boldly resisted it.

Neither the fable of god, nor lightning nor thunder of heaven, scared him with their threat. . . .

Thus, as in reprisal, religion lies at our feet, completely defeated,

but us, triumph raises us up to heaven.
[Trans. by SKP.]

without realization as well, since actual research into nature is no further determined by it.

EPICURUS, "THE RADICAL ENLIGHTENER"

From *The German Ideology*, pp. 149-50

To give our saint [Max Stirner] some indication of the real base on which the philosophy of Epicurus rests, it is sufficient to mention that the idea that the State rests on the mutual agreement of people, on a *contrat social*, is found for the first time in Epicurus.

The extent to which Saint Max's disclosures about the Sceptics follow the same line is already evident from the fact that he considers their philosophy more radical than that of Epicurus. The Sceptics reduced the theoretical relation of people to things to *appearance*, and in practice they left everything as of old, being guided by his appearance just as much as other are guided by actuality; they merely gave it another name. Epicurus, on the other hand, was the true radical Enlightener of antiquity; he openly attacked the ancient religion and it was from him, too, that the atheism of the Romans, insofar as it existed, was derived. For this reason, too, Lucretius praised Epicurus as the hero who was the first to overthrow the gods and trample religion underfoot; for this reason among all church elders, from Plutarch to Luther, Epicurus has always had the reputation of being the atheist philosopher *par excellence* and was called a swine; for which reason, too, Clement of Alexandria says that when Paul takes up arms against philosophy he has in mind Epicurean philosophy alone.

PHILOSOPHY, RELIGION, AND THE PRESS*

"The Leading Article in the No. 179 of the *Kölnische Zeitung*," in *Rheinische Zeitung*, July 14, 1842. This was the last of a series of three articles, the first two appearing on July 10 and 12.

---

*From *Karl Marx on Religion*, by Saul K. Padover, pp. 19-26. Copyright © 1974 by Saul K. Padover. Used with permission of McGraw-Hill Book Co.

First the question is raised: "Should philosophy discuss religious matters also in newspaper articles?"

This question can be answered only by criticizing it.

Philosophy, above all German philosophy, has a propensity to solitude, to systematic seclusion, to dispassionate self-contemplation which in its estrangement opposes it from the outset to the quickwitted and alive-to-events newspapers whose only delight is in information. Philosophy, taken in its systematic development, is unpopular; its secret weaving within itself seems to the layman to be an occupation as overstrained as it is unpractical: it is considered a professor of magic whose incantations sound pompous because they are unintelligible.

Philosophy, in accordance with its character, has never made the first step toward replacing the ascetic priestly vestments with the light, conventional garb of the newspapers. But philosophers do not grow out of the soil like mushrooms, they are the product of their time and of their people, whose most subtle, precious, and invisible sap circulates in philosophical ideas. The same spirit that builds railways by the hands of the workers builds philosophical systems in the brain of the philosophers. Philosophy does not stand outside the world any more than man's brain is outside of him because it is not in his stomach; but, of course, philosophy is in the world with its brain before it stands on the earth with its feet, whereas many another human sphere has long been rooted in the earth before it has any idea that the "head" also belongs to the world or that this world is the world of the head.

Because every true philosophy is the spiritual quintessence of its time, the time must come when philosophy not only internally by its content but externally by its appearance comes into contact and mutual reaction with the real contemporary world. Philosophy then ceases to be a definite system in presence of other definite systems, it becomes philosophy generally, in presence of the world; it becomes the philosophy of the world of the present. The formal features which attest that philosophy has achieved that importance, that it is the living soul of culture, that philosophy is becoming worldly and the world philosophical, were the same in all times: any history book will show, repeated with stereotyped fidelity, the simplest rituals which unmistakably mark philosophy's introduction into drawing rooms and priests' studies, the editorial offices of newspapers and the antechambers of courts, into the hatred and the love of the people of the time. Philosophy is introduced into the world by the clamor of its enemies, who betray their internal infection by their desperate appeals for help against the blaze of ideas. These cries of its enemies mean as much for philosophy as the first cry of a child for the anxious ear of the mother, they are the cry of life of the ideas which have burst open the orderly hieroglyphic husk of the system and become citizens of the world. The Corybantes and Cabiri, who with the roll of drums announce to the world the birth of baby Zeus, first turn against the religious section of the philosophers, partly because their inquisitorial instinct can secure a firmer hold on this sentimental side of the public, partly because the public, to which the opponents of philosophy also belong, can feel the ideal sphere of philosophy only with its ideal feelers, and the only field of ideas whose value the public believes in almost as much as in the system of material needs is that of religious ideas, and, finally, because religion polemicizes not against a definite system of philosophy but against the philosophy generally of the definite systems.

The true philosophy of the present does not differ as far as this fate is concerned from the true philosophies of the past. Indeed, this fate is a proof that history owed to the truth of philosophy.

And for six years the German papers have been drumming against the religious trend in philosophy, calumniating it, distorting it, bowdlerizing it. *Allgemeine Augsburger* sang bravuras, nearly every overture played the theme that philosophy was not worthy of being discussed by Dame Wisdom, that it was the idle bragging of youth, a fashion for blasé coteries. But in spite of all that it could not be got rid of and there was more drumming, for in its antiphilosophical caterwauling the *Augsburger* plays but one instrument, the monotonous kettledrum. All German papers, from *Berliner Politisches Wochenblatt* and *Hamburger Correspondenten* to the obscure local papers, down to *Kölnische Zeitung*, blared out about Hegel and Schelling, Feuerbach and Bauer, *Deutsche Jahrbücher*, etc. Finally the curiosity of the public was aroused and it wanted to see the Leviathan with its own eyes, all the more as semiofficial articles threatened philosophy that it would have a legal syllabus officially prescribed for it. And that was when philosophy appeared in the papers. Long had it kept silence before the self-complacent superficiality which boasted in a few stale newspaper phrases that it could blow away like soap bubbles years of study by genius, the hard-won fruits of self-sacrificing solitude, the results of that invisible but slowly extenuating struggle of contemplation; philosophy had even *protested against the newspapers* as being an inappropriate field, but in the end it had to break its silence, it became a newspaper crorespondent and—unheard-of diversion!—it suddenly occurred to the garrulous newspaper purveyors that philosophy is no food for the newspaper public and they could not refrain from drawing the attention of the governments to the dishonesty of bringing questions of philosophy and religion into the sphere of the newspapers, not to enlighten the public but to attain ulterior aims.

What is there so bad that philosophy could say about religion or about itself that your newspaper clamor had not long ago imputed to it in far worse and more frivolous terms? It only needs to repeat what you unphilosophical Capuchins have preached about it in thousands and thousands of polemics, and it has said the worst.

But philosophy speaks differently of religious and philosophical objects than you have. You speak without having studied them, it speaks after study; you appeal to the emotions, it appeals to reason; you curse, it teaches; you promise heaven and earth, it promises nothing but truth; you demand faith in your faith, it demands not faith in its results but the test of doubt; you frighten, it calms. And truly, philosophy is world-wise enough to know that its results flatter the desire for pleasure or the egoism neither of the heavenly nor of the earthly world; but the public that loves truth and knowledge for their own sakes will be able to measure itself in judgment and morality with ignorant, servile, inconsistent, and mercenary scribes.

Admittedly somebody or other, by reason of the worthlessness of his intellect or views, may misinterpret philosophy, but do not you Protestants believe that the Catholics misinterpret Christianity, do you not reproach the Christian religion with the disgraceful times of the eighth and ninth centuries, the night of St. Bartholomew, and the Inquisition? There are conclusive proofs that the hatred of the Protestant theology for philosophers arises largely out of philosophy's tolerance toward the particular confession as such. Feuerbach and Strauss were reproached more for maintaining that Catholic dogmas were Christian than for stating that the dogmas of Christianity were not dogmas of reason.

But if occasional individuals cannot digest modern philosophy and die of philosophical indigestion, that proves no more against philosophy than the occasional blowing up of a few passengers by the bursting of a boiler proves against mechanics.

The question whether philosophical and religious matters should be discussed in newspapers resolves itself in its own emptiness.

If such questions already have an interest for the public as *newspaper questions*, they have become *questions of the day*; then the point is not whether they should be discussed but where and how they should be discussed, whether within the bounds of the family and the hotels, of the schools and the churches, but not by the press; by the opponents of philosophy but not by the philosophers; whether in the obscure language of private opinion but not in the clarifying language of public reason. Then the point is whether what lives in reality belongs to the realm of the press; it is no longer a question of a particular content of the press, the question is the general one whether the press must be really the press, i.e., a free press.

From the first question we completely separate the second: "Should politics be dealt with philosophically by the newspapers in a so-called Christian state?"

If religion becomes a political quality, an object of politics, there seems to be hardly any need to mention that the newspapers not only may, but must, discuss political objects. It seems from the start that the wisdom of this world, philosophy, has more right to bother about the kingdom of this world, about the state, than the wisdom of the other world, religion. The point here is not whether the state should be philosophized about, but whether it should be philosophized about well or badly, philosophically or unphilosophically, with prejudice or without, with consciousness or without, consistently or inconsistently, in a completely rational or half-rational way. If you make religion a theory of state right, then you make religion itself a kind of philosophy.

Was it not Christianity before anything else that separated church and state?

Read Saint Augustine's *De Civitate Dei*, study the Fathers of the Church and the spirit of Christianity, and then come back and tell us which is the "Christian state," the church or the state! Does not every minute of your practical life give the lie to your theory? Do you consider it wrong to appeal to the courts when you are cheated? But the Apostle writes that that is wrong. Do you offer your right cheek when you are struck on the left, or do you not institute proceedings for assault? Yet the Gospel forbids that. Do you not claim your reasonable rights in this world? Do you not grumble at the slightest raising of a tax? Are you not furious at the slightest infringement of your personal liberty? But you have been told that the sufferings of this life are not to be compared with the bliss of the future, that suffering in patience and the bliss of hope are cardinal virtues.

Are not most of your court proceedings and the majority of civil laws concerned with property? But you have been told that your treasure is not of this world. If you base yourselves on giving to Caesar the things which are Caesar's and to God the things which are God's, do not consider the mammon of gold alone but at least just as much free reason the Caesar of this world, and the "action of free reason" is what we call philosophizing.

When at first in the Holy Alliance a quasi-religious alliance of states was to be formed and religion was to be the state motto of Europe, the Pope showed profound sense and perfect consistency in refusing to join it, for in his view the universal Christian link between nations was the Church and not diplomacy, not a worldly alliance of states [....]

Philosophy has done nothing in politics that physics, mathematics, medicine, every science, has not done within its own sphere. Bacon of Verulam declared theological physics to be a virgin vowed to God and barren; he emancipated physics from theology and she became fruitful. You no more have to ask the politician if he has faith than the doctor. Immediately before and after the time of Copernicus' great discoveries on the true solar system, the law of gravitation of the state was discovered: the center of gravity of the state was found within the state itself. As various European governments tried to apply this result with the initial superficiality of practice to the system of equilibrium of states, similarly Machiavelli and Campanella began before them, and Hobbes, Spinoza, and Hugo Grotius afterward, down to Rousseau, Fichte and Hegel, to consider the state with the eye of man and to develop its natural laws from reason and experience, not from theology, any more than Copernicus let himself be influenced by Joshua's supposed command to the sun to stand still over Gideon and the moon over the vale of Ajalon. Modern philosophy has only continued a work already started by Heraclitus and Aristotle. So it is not the reason of modern philosophy that you are polemicizing against, but the ever modern philosophy of reason. Naturally, the ignorance that yesterday or perhaps the day before discovered the age-old ideas on the state in *Rheinische* or *Königsberger Zeitung* considers the ideas of history notions which occurred overnight to certain individuals because they appear new to it and came to it overnight; it forgets that it has assumed the old role of the doctor of Sorbonne who considered it his duty to accuse Montesquieu in public because the latter was frivolous enough to maintain that the political quality, not the virtue of the Church, was the highest quality in the state; it forgets that it has assumed the role of Joachim Lange, who denounced Wolff because his doctrine of predestination would lead to desertion among soldiers and thereby to a relaxation of military discipline and finally to the collapse of the state; lastly it forgets that the Prussian *Landrecht* comes from the very school of philosophy of "that Wolff" and the Napoleonic Code comes not from the Old Testament but from the school of ideas of Voltaire, Rousseau, Condorcet, Mirabeau, and Montesquieu and from the French Revolution. Ignorance is a demon and we are afraid it will yet play us more than one tragedy; the greatest Greek poets were right when they represented it in the terrible dramas of the royal houses of Mycenae and Thebes as tragic fate.

Whereas the earlier teachers of state law construed the state out of ambition or sociability, or even reason, though not out of the reason of society but rather out of the reason of the individual, the more ideal and profound view of modern philosophy construes it out of the idea of the whole. It considers the state the great organism in which freedom of right, of morals, and of politics has to be implemented and in which in the laws of the state the individual citizen merely obeys the natural laws of his own reason, human reason. *Sapienti sat.* [Sufficient for the wise man.]

We shall conclude with a further philosophical farewell to *Kölnische Zeitung*. It was reasonable of it to take to itself a liberal "of times gone by." One can most comfortably be both liberal and reactionary at the same time, if only one is always skillful enough to address only liberals of the recent past who know no other dilemma than that of Vidocq— "prisoner or jailer." It was still more reasonable that the liberal of the recent past combated the liberals of the present. Without parties there is no development, without a parting there is no progress. We hope that with the leading article of No. 179 *Kölnische Zeitung* there has begun a new era, the era of character.

HEGEL'S DIALECTIC

From postscript to second German edition of *Capital*, written January 24, 1873

Of course the method of presentation must differ in form from the method of research. Research has to appropriate the material in detail, to analyze its various forms of development and to trace their inner connection. Only after this work is completed, can the actual movement be appropriately described. If this is done successfully, and if the life of the material is ideally mirrored, then it might appear as if one dealt with an a priori construction.

My dialectic method is fundamentally not only different from the Hegelian but is its direct antithesis. To Hegel, the thinking process, which, under the name of the Idea he even transforms into an independent subject, is the demiurge of the real world, which only forms its external phenomenon. With me, on the contrary, the Ideal is nothing else than the material world transposed and translated in the human mind.

The mystifying side of the Hegelian dialect I criticized nearly 30 years ago, at a time when it was still the fashion. But just as I was working on the first volume of *Capital*, it was the good pleasure of the tiresome, arrogant, mediocre epigones who now talk big in cultured Germany, to treat Hegel in the same way that the worthy Moses Mendelssohn in Lessing's time treated Spinoza, namely, as a "dead dog." I therefore openly avowed myself the pupil of that mighty thinker, and here and there in the chapter on the theory of value, flirted with the modes of expression peculiar to him. The mystification which the dialectic suffers in Hegel's hands, by no means prevents him from being the first to present its general forms of movement in a comprehensive and conscious manner. With him, it stands on its head. It must be turned right side up, if one is to discover the rational kernel within the mystical shell.

CHAPTER VIII
PRESS AND CENSORSHIP

Note

At the time Marx was making his debut as a professional journalist, in 1842, freedom of expression came under increasingly severe restrictions in Prussia. A new censorship decree aimed to suppress anything critical of the regime and gave sweeping powers to censors to decide not merely the content of any piece of writing but, what was more menacing, the *tendency*, or presumed intent, of the writer.

In his first major political essay, "Remarks on the Latest Prussian Censorship Instruction," included in this chapter, Marx bravely undertook an extensive critique of the government decree. The underlying argument or Marx's article was that censorship was intrinsically and irremediably faulty. A censor was an uncreative bureaucrat having no competence to dictate to a writer what he should express and how he should formulate his ideas. Truth, moreover, was not a governmental commodity to be mauled by some bureaucrat, but a universal value that belonged to mankind. Censorship, Marx argued, was logically absurd in that it made mere officeholders, untrained in philosophy, literature or science, the supreme arbiters over their intellectual superiors, the writers and thinkers. He concluded bluntly: "The real, *radical cure of the censorship* is its *abolition*. For it is a bad institution."

In May 1842, the twenty-four-year-old Marx began to write for Cologne's liberal *Rheinische Zeitung*, whose editor he soon became, a series of articles in cogent defense of freedom of the press. He eulogized the role of a free press in idealistic, almost rhapsodic terms:

> The free press is the ominpresent open eye of the spirit of the people, the embodied confidence of a people in itself, the articulate bond that ties the individual to the

state and the world. . . . The free press is the intellectual mirror in which a people sees itself. . . . It is the mind of the state that can be peddled in every cottage, cheaper than natural gas. It is universal, omnipresent, omniscient.

A newspaper with such a viewpoint could not last in autocratic Prussia. In January 1843, King Frederick William IV of Prussia issued an order to kill the *Rheinische Zeitung*. Marx then went into exile, first in Paris and then in Brussels.

When revolutions broke out in Germany in 1848, Marx returned to Cologne, where he established the *Neue Rheinische Zeitung*, subtitled *Organ of Democracy*. It was a misleading subtitle. The "new" newspaper was not a democratic organ but a communist one. For Marx was now not the liberal newspaperman of 1842-43, but an embattled communist. His interest was no longer in freedom of the press but in the overthrow of the whole "bourgeois" social order. After the suppression of the *Neue Rheinische Zeitung*, in May 1849, and his expulsion from Prussia, Marx finally made his home in London, where for a time he continued his career as a journalist but no longer as a crusader.

WHO SHOULD CENSOR?

From "Remarks on the Latest Prussian Censorship Instruction,"* Written between January 15 and February 10, 1842. Published in *Anekdota zur neuesten deutschen Philosophie und Publicistik*, February 1843.

We are not among those malcontents who even before the appearance of the latest Prussian censorship edict[1] exclaim

---

*In *Karl Marx on Freedom of the Press and Censorship* by Saul K. Padover, pp. 89-108. Copyright © 1974 by Saul K. Padover. Used with permission of McGraw-Hill Book Co.

[1] The Censorship Instruction of December 24, 1841, disapproved of limitations on literary activity but in practice sharpened the existing censorship.

"*Timeo Danaos et dona ferentes.*"[2] Rather, since an examination of laws already passed is permitted in the new instruction, even if it is not in accord with the government, we will begin with such a scrutiny. Censorship is *official criticism*; its norms are critical norms, which therefore must not be withheld from criticism, a field to which they belong.

Everybody will certainly be able to approve the *general tendency* expressed in the beginning of the Instruction: "In order to free the press even at this early date from the illegal limitation not intended by the Highest Authority, His Majesty the King, in an order addressed to the Royal State Ministry on the 10th of this month, disapproved any illegitimate censorship in the field of writing, and recognizing the value of and need for frank and reasonable publications, empowered us again to remind the censors to pay proper attention to Article II of the Censorship Edict of October 18, 1819."

Of course! Once censorship is a necessity, frank and liberal censorship is even more so.

What must arouse a certain amount of surprise right away is the date of the law in question. How so? Is it perhaps a law which conditions of the time had to minimize? This does not seem to be the case, for the censors are reminded "anew" to pay attention to it. Until 1842, therefore, the law existed, but it was not observed; for in order to free the press "even at this early date" from illegitimate limitations not intended by the Highest Authority, the law is resurrected.

The press—this is a direct consequence of these introductory remarks—has up to now been subject to illegal limitations *despite the law*.

Now does this speak against the law or against the censors?

We are hardly permitted to claim the latter. For twenty-two years illegal actions have been committed by an administration that controls the highest interest of the citizens, their minds, an administration that, even more than the Roman censors ever did, regulates not only the behavior of the individual citizen but also the behavior of the public mind. Should such unconscionable behavior and therefore disloyalty on the part of the highest civil servants be possible in the well-administered Prussian state which is so proud of its administration? Or has the state, constantly deluded, selected

---

[2] "I fear Greeks bearing gifts"—from Virgil, *Aeneid*.

the most incompetent persons for the most difficult positions? Or is it perhaps that the subject of the Prussian state has no possibility of protesting against illegal measures? Are all Prussian writers so uneducated and stupid that they are unfamiliar with laws that affect their livelihood, or are they too cowardly to demand that the laws be observed?

If we blame the censors, we compromise not only their honor but also the honor of the Prussian state and of Prussian writers.

Furthermore, because of the lawless behavior of the censors for twenty years despite the laws, the *argumentum ad hominem* is offered that the press needs other guarantees against such irresponsible individuals besides these general regulations; it has been proved that in the nature of censorship there is a basic fault that no law can remedy.

But if the censors were able men, and the law was no good, why resurrect it anew to do away with the evil it has caused?

Or is it perhaps that the objective faults of an institution are to be ascribed to individuals, so that the semblance of improvement is achieved without a real improvement? This is the kind of pseudo-liberalism that is forced to make concessions and that sacrifices people to maintain the institution, the tools, and the object. The attention of a thoughtless public is thereby diverted. Objective embitterment is turned into a matter of personalities. With a change of persons one believes a change of things is achieved. Attention is deflected from censorship itself to the individual censors, and those little writers in the service of progress-by-command hurl trivial heroics against those who have been ungraciously treated, at the same time paying high homage to the government.

We encounter still another difficulty. Some newspaper correspondents consider the Censorship Instruction a new censorship edict. They are mistaken but their error is forgivable. The Censorship Edict of October 18, 1819, was to be in force only provisionally until the year 1824—and it would have remained a provisional law to this day, except that we now learn from the present Instruction that it was never enforced.

The Edict of 1819 was an *interim* measure, the difference being that the expectation of a definite five-year term was indicated, while in the new Instruction there is no time limit; then there are expectation of *laws on freedom of the press*, while now they are *laws of censorship*.

Other newspaper correspondents consider the Censorship Instruction a renewal of the old Censorship Edict. Their error will be demonstrated in the examination of the Instruction itself.

We consider the Censorship Instruction the *anticipated spirit* of a presumed censorship law. We deduce this precisely from the spirit of the Censorship Edict of 1819, in which state laws and ordinances are of equal importance for the press. (See the Edict, Article XVI, No. 2.)

But let us return to the Instruction.

"According to this law," that is, Article II, "censorship shall not obstruct any serious and moderate pursuit of truth, nor put undue compulsion on writers, nor hinder the unrestricted sale of books."

The pursuit of truth, which is not to be impeded by censorship, is qualified as serious and moderate. Both qualifications point not to the content of the pursuit, but rather to something that lies outside the content. At the outset they divert from the pursuit of truth and bring into play an unknown third factor. If an investigation must constantly keep in mind this third factor, an exasperation supported by law, will it not lose sight of the truth? Is it not the first duty of the seeker after the truth to proceed directly at it, without glancing to the right or left? Do I not forget to speak about the substance if I must never forget to state it in a prescribed form?

Truth is as little moderate as light, and against what is it to be moderated? Against oneself? *"Verum index sui et falsi."*[8] Hence, *against falsehood?*

When moderation shapes the character of the investigation, it is more a sign of shying away from the truth than from untruth. It is a drag on every step I take. *In an investigation, it is a prescription for fear of discovering the result,* a means of keeping one from the truth.

Furthermore, truth is universal. It does not belong to me, it belongs to all; it possesses me, I do not possess it. My *style* is my property; it is my spiritual individuality. *Le style c'est l'homme.* [The style is the man.] Indeed! The law permits me to write, only I am supposed to write in a style different from mine! I may show the profile of spirit of the Censorship Edict of October 18, 1819, decorous and frank journalism

---

[8]"Truth is the test of itself and of falsehood"—Spinoza, *Ethics.*

will have sufficient elbow room, and it is to be expected that thereby a greater participation in the interests of the fatherland will be aroused and that patriotism will be enhanced.

We admit that, according to these Instructions, more than sufficient elbow room is provided for decent journalism, decent in the meaning of the censorship; the very word "elbow room" is well chosen, for that room is intended to be one that is satisfactory for a playful, shadow-boxing press. Whether this applies to *frank* journalism, and where the frankness is to come from, that we leave to the sharp eye of the reader. In regard to the expectations expressed in the Instruction, patriotism may indeed be promoted in the same way that the sending of a hangman's rope enhances Turkish nationalism; but whether the press, as moderate as it is serious, will awake some interest in the fatherland, that we leave to the press itself; a lean press cannot be fattened with stories about China. But perhaps we take the passage too seriously. Perhaps we will understand its meaning better when we regard it as merely the clasp in the chain of roses. Perhaps this liberal clasp contains a pearl of very dubious value. Let's look into it. Everything depends on the context. The enhancement of patriotism and the awakening of participation in the interests of the fatherland, which are expressed in the above passage as expectations, easily become transformed into an *order for a new restriction of the freedom* of our poor consumptive daily papers.

"In this way it is to be hoped that political literature and the daily press will recognize their tasks better than before, acquire richer material and a more dignified tone, and abstain in the future from playing on the curiosity of their readers by reporting meaningless items taken from foreign newspapers, gossip, and personalities written by malevolent or poorly informed correspondents—a tendency that it is the undoubted function of the censorship to combat."

In this indicated way, it is to be hoped that political literature and the daily press will recognize their task better, etc. However, better recognition cannot be commanded; it is a fruit still to be expected, and hope is hope. But the Instruction is much too practical to content itself with hopes and pious wishes. While the press is given hope for its future betterment *by this new comfort*, it is at the same time deprived by the benevolent Instruction of a right that it presently possesses. It loses what it still has, the hope of its betterment. The press fares like poor Sancho Panza, from whom the court physician withheld all food so that an upset stomach would not make him incapable of performing the duties required by the Duke.

At the same time we cannot let the opportunity pass without challenging the Prussian writer for his appropriation of this sort of decorous style. The preface of the Instruction reads: "In this way it is to be hoped that . . ." The "that" governs a whole series of regulations, that is, that political literature and the daily press recognize their tasks better than before, that they acquire a more dignified tone, etc., etc., that they abstain from printing meaningless reports from foreign newspapers, etc. All these regulations are still placed in the realm of hope; but the conclusion, connected to the preceding by a dash—"a tendency that it is the undoubted function of the censorship to combat"—saves the censor the tedious job of waiting for the hoped-for improvement of the daily press and empowers him, rather, to strike out anything disagreeable without further ado. The *internal cure* is replaced by an *amputation*.

"But to achieve this goal it is necessary that great caution be employed in the licensing of new journals and new editors, so that the daily press is entrusted into the hands of completely irreproachable men, whose scientific competence, rank, and character guarantee the seriousness of their endeavors and their loyalty."

Before we go into details, a general observation is in order. The licensing of new editors, that is, all future editors, is left entirely to the "great caution" exercised by government authorities—the censorship—whereas the old censorship, though under certain restrictions, left the choice of the editor *up to the publisher*:

"Article IX. The Superior Censorship Office is empowered to inform the publisher of a newspaper that the editor in question is not the type to inspire confidence, in which case the publisher is obliged either to appoint a new editor or, if he wishes to keep him, must set up bond for him, the amount to be determined by one of the State Ministers mentioned above at the recommendation of the said Superior Censorship Office."

In the new Censorship Instruction an entirely different depth, one might say a romanticism of the spirit, is expressed. While the old Censorship Edict prescribes external and prosaic bonds, which are therefore legally definable and by which even a displeasing editor could be licensed, the Instruction, on the contrary, deprives the publisher of a newspaper of any personal preference and leaves it to the preventive wisdom of the government, the great caution and the intellectual profundity of the authorities, to decide the internal, subjective criteria that cannot be defined from the outside. But when the imprecision, the sensitive inwardness, and the subjective extravagance of romanticism turn to the realm of the purely external—in the sense that the external fortuitousness no longer appears in its prosaic exactitude and limitation but in a wondrous glory and in illusory depth and splendor—the Instruction, too, will hardly escape this romantic fate.

The editors of the daily press, in which category all journalism falls, are to be completely irreproachable men. Scientific competence is stated to be the first guarantee of such complete irreproachableness. Not the slightest doubt is raised whether the censor possesses scientific competence to judge any sort of scientific competence. If it is true that Prussia has such a multitude of scientific geniuses who are known to the government—each city has at least one censor—why don't these encyclopedic brains show up as writers themselves? If these officials, overwhelming in number, mighty by virtue of their science and their genius, would rise for once and crush those wretched writers who are active in only one genre of writing, and even there without officially tested qualifications, the confusions of the press could be ended better than by censorship. Why do these clever men keep silent when, like the Roman geese, they could save the Capitol by their cackle? They must be men of too much modesty. The scientific public does not know them, but the government does.

And if those men are men such as no state could ever find, for never has a state known entire classes consisting of universal geniuses and polyhistorians, how much more gifted must be those who choose them! What secret science must the latter possess to be able to attest the scientific qualifications of officials who are otherwise unknown to the republic of science! The higher we climb in this *bureaucracy of intelligence*, the more wondrous are the minds we meet. Practically speaking, for a state possessing such pillars of a perfect press, is it worth the effort to appoint these men guardians of a deficient press, to use the perfect as a means for debasing the imperfect?

The more censors you employ, the more chances of improvement you take away from the realm of the press. You remove healthy people from your army to make them doctors for the sick.

Stamp the ground as Pompey did, and an armored Pallas Athena will spring out of every government building. The shallow daily press will collapse entirely before the official press. The existence of light suffices to refute darkness. Let your light shine and do not hide it under a bushel. Instead of the deficient censorship, whose sterling value is problematical even to you, give us a perfect press which is obedient to you, of which the Chinese state has been the model for centuries.

But is it not an intellectual criterion to make "scientific competence" the necessary requirement for the writers of the daily press, instead of the conventional requirement of privileged favoritism; isn't this a criterion of essence rather than of person?

Unfortunately, the Censorship Instruction interrupts our panegyric. Alongside the guarantee of scientific competence one finds requirements of rank and character. Rank and character!

Character, placed immediately after rank, seems to be almost a mere effluence of rank. Let us, above all, take a look at rank. It is so boxed in between scientific competence and character that one is almost tempted to doubt its good conscience.

The general requirement of scientific competence, how liberal! The special requirement of rank, how illiberal! Since scientific competence and character are very indefinite, while rank, on the contrary, is definite, why shouldn't we conclude that logically and necessarily the indefinite will lean on the definite and find support and content there? Would it be a great mistake of the censor to interpret the Instruction as saying that the external form of scientific competence and of character, as they appear in the world, constitute rank, the more since the censor's own rank assures him that this is the government's view? Without this interpretation it is, to say the least, completely incomprehensible why scientific competence and character are not sufficient guarantees in themselves, and why rank is made a necessary third requirement. Since these requirements are seldom if ever combined, the censor is in a dilemma over which to choose, for after all, somebody has to edit newspapers and periodicals. Scientific competence and character, in the absence of rank, because of their indefiniteness, can be a problem for the censor, since he must understandably wonder how such qualities can exist apart from rank. On the other hand, may the censor have doubts about character and science where rank is concerned? In such a case he would place less confidence in the judgment of the state than in himself, while in the opposite case he would place more confidence in the writer than in the state. Should a censor be so tactless and so wrong-headed? This should not be expected and it certainly was not expected. Rank, because it is the decisive criterion in case of doubt, is altogether the absolutely decisive one.

We have already seen that the Instruction conflicts with the Censorship Edict because of its orthodoxy, so now it does also because of its romanticism, which at the same time is always purposeful poetry. The money bond, which is a prosaic and real guarantee, becomes abstract, and this abstraction transforms itself into an entirely real and individual rank which acquires a magical, fictitious significance. The significance of the guarantee changes in the same way. No longer does the publisher select the editor, for whom he vouches to the authorities; the authorities select the editor, for whom they vouch to themselves. The old Edict expects the editor's work to be safeguarded by the bond the publisher puts up. The Instruction, on the other hand, does not concern itself with the editor's work, but with his person. It calls for a definite personal individuality which the publisher's money is to provide. The new Instruction is just as external as the old Edict; but where the latter expresses and delimits what is naturally prosaic and definite, the former lends an extremely fortuitous and imaginary spirit, and expresses what is merely individual in the poignancy of the universal.

But if the romantic Instruction in regard to the editor gives a tone of the most blithe indefiniteness to what is externally most definite, so it also gives the tone of legal definiteness to the most vague indefiniteness about the censor.

"Equal caution must be applied in appointing the censor, so that the office of censorship is put in the hands of men of proven character and ability, who are fully in accord with the honor of having confidence placed in them. Such men must be right-thinking and at the same time sharp-eyed, who understand how to separate form from substance, and overlook with sure tact minor objections that are not justified by the sense and tendency of the article as a whole."

What rank and character are for the writer, proven character is for the censor, since rank is assumed for him. More important is the fact that while scientific competence is required in the writer, only ability, without further modification, is required in the censor. The old Edict, which, politics apart, is rationalistic, requires in Article III "scientifically trained" and even "enlightened" censors. Both predicates are omitted in the Instruction; and in place of competence in the writer, which signifies a definite, trained, actual competence, in the censor only a predisposition to competence, a general ability, is expected. This means that a *predisposition to competence* is to *censor real competence*, despite the fact that in nature the situation is reversed. Finally, we note in passing that the competence of the censor is not defined in detail as to the actual content, hence, of course, its character becomes ambiguous.

Furthermore, the office of censorship is to be given to men "who fully deserve the honor of having confidence placed in them." No further discussion is needed for this pleonastic pseudo directive which says that only trustworthy men are to be appointed, that they will fully deserve the honored confidence, the honored trust placed in them, a very complete trust, of course, etc.

Finally, the censors are to be men who are "right-thinking and sharp-eyed, who understand how to separate form from substance and overlook with sure tact minor objections that are not justified by the sense and tendency of the article as a whole."

On the other hand, the Instruction further prescribes: "In regard to this" (that is, the investigation of the tendency) "the censors have to pay special attention to the form and the tone of the language used and must not permit publication of writings insofar as their tendency is harmful because of passion, violence, and presumptuousness."

On the one hand, then, the censor is to judge the *tendency from the form*, and on the other the *form from the tendency*. As previously the content had already entirely disappeared as a criterion for censorship, so now the form also disappears. If the tendency is good, then offenses against form are to be overlooked. Even if the article is not altogether very serious and moderate, even if it appears to be violent, passionate, and presumptuous, who would thereby be intimidated by the rough exterior? One must know how to separate the *form* from the *substance*. Any semblance of definiteness must be eliminated; the Instruction must end with a *complete contradiction of itself*; because anything that reveals tendency is actually first qualified by the tendency and can be recognized only by the tendency. The violence of the patriot is sacred zeal, his passion is the susceptibility of a lover, his presumptuousness is dedicated participation too boundless to be moderate.

All objective norms have been abandoned; the personal relationship is left, and the tact of the censor has to be called a guarantee. What, then, can the censor violate? Tact. And tactlessness is no crime. What is the writer threatened with? His existence. What state had ever made the existence of a whole class dependent on the tact of individual officials?

Let us say it again: *All objective norms have been abandoned.* For the writer, tendency is made the final content, ordered and prescribed, the object being a formless opinion. The tendency as subject, as opinion of the opinion, is at the discretion of, and is sole guide for, the censor.

Although the censor's arbitrariness—and the justification of mere opinion is justification of arbitrariness—is concealed behind the semblance of concrete directives, the Instruction, on the other hand, clearly asserts the arbitrariness of the Superior Censorship Office, which is given complete confidence. This confidence placed in the director is the ultimate guarantee of the press. Thus the essence of censorship in general is based on a police state's arrogant conceit about its officials. The public's sense and good will is not trusted with even the simplest thing; but for the officials even the impossible is to be possible.

This basic fault runs through all our institutions. Thus, for example, in criminal proceedings judge, plaintiff, and defendant are united in *one person*. This combination is contrary to all the laws of psychology. But the official is above the psychological laws to which the public is subject. Nevertheless, a deficient governmental principle may be excused; but it becomes inexcusable when it is not honest enough to be consistent. The difference between the *responsibility* of the officials and that of the public should correspond to the difference between officials and public; but it is precisely here, where only results could justify the principle and make it lawful within its own sphere, that it is abandoned and replaced with its opposite.

HUMAN IMPERFECTION AND PRESS FREEDOM

From "Debates on Freedom of the Press and Publication," *Rheinische Zeitung*, May 12, 1842*

The speaker [in the Rhineland Landtag] placed himself *à la hauteur des principes* [at the height of principles]. To combat freedom of the press, one must defend the permanent immaturity of the human species. . . .

If the immaturity of the human species is the mystical argument against freedom of the press, then, at any rate, censorship is a highly understandable measure against the immaturity of the human species. What develops is imperfect. Development only ends with death. Hence the real conclusion from this would be to kill man to save him from this state of imperfection. So at least the speaker concludes, in order to kill freedom of the press. For him, true education consists in keeping man swaddled in the cradle throughout his life, because as soon as he begins learning to walk he falls down, and he learns to walk only by falling down. But if we all remain swaddled children, who will swaddle us? If we all lie in the cradle, who will rock it? If we are all jailed, who will be the keeper?

Man is by nature imperfect, as an individual and in the mass. . . . What follows from this? That the reasoning of our speaker is imperfect, governments are imperfect, the Landtags are imperfect, freedom of the press is imperfect, every sphere of human activity is imperfect. If, therefore, one of these spheres should not exist because of its imperfection, then nobody has the right to exist, and man altogether has no right to exist.

---

*In *Karl Marx on Freedom of the Press and Censorship* by Saul K. Padover, pp. 21-22. Copyright ©1974 by Saul K. Padover. Used with permission of McGraw-Hill Book Co.

From "Debates on the Freedom of the Press and Publication," *Rheinische Zeitung*, May 15, 1842*

From the standpoint of the Idea, it is self-evident that freedom of the press has an entirely different justification from censorship, in that the former is itself an aspect of the Idea, of freedom, a positive good; whereas censorship is an aspect of unfreedom, a polemic of the viewpoint of semblance as against the viewpoint of essence, a mere negation.

No! No! No! the speaker cries out meantime. I don't blame the appearance, I blame the essence. Freedom is the infamy of press freedom. Freedom gives possibility to evil. Hence freedom is evil. . . .

Does not freedom of the press exist in the land of censorship? The press in general is a consummation of human freedom. Hence where there is a press there is freedom of the press.

In the land of censorship, to be sure, the state has no freedom of the press, but a member of the state, the *government*, does have it. Apart from the fact that official government publications have complete freedom of the press, doesn't the censor exercise absolute freedom of the press every day, if not directly, then indirectly? . . .

Freedom is so very much of the essence of man that even its opponents realize it, in that they fight its reality; they want to appropriate the most costly jewel, which they will not consider the jewel of human nature.

No man fights against freedom; at most, he fights against the freedom of others. Hence every kind of freedom has always existed, at one time as a particular prerogative, at another, as a general right. . . .

One does not ask whether freedom of the press should exist, for it always exists. One asks whether freedom of the press is the privilege of individual men or whether it is the privilege of the human spirit. One asks whether the non-right of the one side should be the right of the other. One asks whether "freedom of the mind" has a greater right than "freedom against the mind."

---

*In *Karl Marx on Freedom of the Press and Censorship* by Saul K. Padover, pp. 21-22. Copyright © 1974 by Saul K. Padover. Used with permission of McGraw-Hill Book Co.

If, however, a free press and freedom of the press are to be rejected as the consummation of "universal freedom," the censorship and a censored press are even more the consummation of a particular freedom, for how can the species be good if the genus is bad? If the speaker had been consistent, he would have rejected, not the free press, but the press. According to him, the press would be good only if it were not the product of freedom, that is, not a human product. Either animals or gods would be completely entitled to the press.

CENSORSHIP AND PRESS LAW

From "Debates on the Freedom of the Press and Publication," *Rheinische Zeitung*, May 15, 1842*

In a press law, freedom punishes. In a censorship law, freedom is punished. The censorship law is a suspect law against freedom. The press law is a vote of confidence which the press gives itself. The press law punishes the misuse of freedom. The censorship law punishes freedom as a misuse. It treats freedom as a criminal. . . .

A press law is a real law because it is the positive essence of freedom. It regards freedom as the normal condition of the press, the press as an essence of freedom, and therefore comes in conflict with abuse by the press only in the exceptional cases when it opposes its own principle and thereby suspends itself. . . .

Thus the press law, far from being a repressive measure against freedom of the press, is merely a means to discourage repetition of violation through a penalty; one should, rather, view the lack of press legislation as the exclusion of freedom of the press from the sphere of lawful freedom, for lawfully recognized freedom exists in the state as law. Laws are not repressive measures against freedom, any more than the law of gravity is a repressive measure against movement; the law of gravity propels the eternal motions of the heavenly bodies but, as a law of falling, kills me if I violate it by trying to

---

*In *Karl Marx on Freedom of the Press and Censorship* by Saul K. Padover, p. 29. Copyright © 1974 by Saul K. Padover. Used with permission of McGraw-Hill Book Co.

dance in the air. Rather, laws are positive, clear, universal norms, in which freedom has won an impersonal theoretical existence independent of the caprice of any individual. A law text is the Bible of freedom of a people.

The press law is therefore the legal recognition of freedom. It is *law*, because it is the positive Being of freedom. It must therefore be in existence even if it is never applied, as in North America, whereas censorship can never become lawful, any more than slavery, even if it exists a thousand times as law.

From "Debates on the Freedom of the Press and Publication," *Rheinische Zeitung*, May 19, 1842*

We have shown how the press law is a right and the censorship a wrong. But the censorship itself admits that it is not an end in itself, that it is not a good in and by itself, that therefore it rests on the principle: "The end sanctifies the means." But an end that needs unholy means is no holy end, and cannot the press also adopt the principle and boast: "The end sanctifies the means"?

The censorship is thus no law but a police measure, but it is itself a *bad police measure*, because it does not achieve what it wants and it does not want what it achieves.

If the censorship law wants to *prevent* freedom as something displeasing, it achieves its opposite. In the country of censorship, every forbidden piece of writing—that is, printed without the censor—is an event. It passes as a martyr, and there is no martyr without a halo and devout followers. It passes as an exception, and the more freedom continues to be of value to man, the more it becomes an exception to the general unfreedom. Every mystery corrupts. Where public opinion is a mystery to itself, it is from the outset corrupted by all writings that formally break through the mysterious bounds. The censorship makes all forbidden writing, good or bad, extraordinary writing, while freedom of the press robs all writing of special importance. . . .

---

*In *Karl Marx on Freedom of the Press and Censorship* by Saul K. Padover, p. 31. Copyright © 1974 by Saul K. Padover. Used with permission of McGraw-Hill Book Co.

The free press is the omnipresent open eye of the spirit of the people, the embodied confidence of a people in itself, the articulate bond that ties the individual to the state and the world, the incorporated culture which transfigures material struggles into intellectual struggles and idealizes its raw material shape. It is the ruthless confession of a people to itself, and it is well known that the power of confession is redeeming. The free press is the intellectual mirror in which a people sees itself, and self-viewing is the first condition of wisdom. It is the mind of the state that can be peddled in every cottage, cheaper than natural gas. It is universal, omnipresent, omniscient. It is the ideal world, which constantly gushes from the real one and streams back to it ever richer and animated anew.

THE VOICE OF THE PEOPLE

From "The Relation of the Mosel Region to the Cabinet Order of December 24, 1841, and the More Free Movement of the Press Effected Thereby," in *Rheinische Zeitung*, January 19, 1843*

To solve the difficulties, the administration and the administered both need a third element, which is political without being bureaucratic, an element that does not derive from bureaucratic presuppositions, that is, civic without being directly entangled in private interests and their needs. This complementary element, composed of a political head and a civic heart, is a *free press*. In the realm of the press the administration and the administered can criticize each other's principles and demands as equals, no longer in a subordinate relationship but with equal political worth, no longer as *persons* but as *intellectual powers*, with a basis of reason. The "free press," as it is the product of public opinion, also produces public opinion, and it alone has the power to make a special interest into a general interest; it alone has the power to make the distress of the Mosel region an object of general at-

---

*In *Karl Marx on Freedom of the Press and Censorship* by Saul K. Padover, pp. 76-77. Copyright © 1974 by Saul K. Padover. Used with permission of McGraw-Hill Book Co.

tention and general sympathy in the Fatherland; it alone has the power to alleviate the misery, if for no other reason than that it distributes the feeling of misery among all.

The press relates itself to the conditions of the people as *intelligence*, but it relates itself to them equally as *mood*; its language, therefore, is not merely the wise language of judgment that hovers over conditions but also the affective language of the conditions themselves, a language which cannot and should not be expected in bureaucratic reports. Finally, the free press carries the people's misery to the foot of the throne, not in a bureaucratically approved form but in its own medium, before which the distinction between administration and administered disappears and which results in a more equally near-standing and more equally far-standing citizenry.

THE HARSH CENSORSHIP

From "The Prussian Press Bill," in *Neue Rheinische Zeitung*, July 20, 1848*

Herr Hansemann has proposed an interim press law. . . .

We reported the main points of this press law a few days ago. Hardly have we had the chance to prove, through the libel action, that Articles 367 and 369 of the *Code Pénal* are in the most glaring contradiction to press freedom, when Herr Hansemann moves not only to extend them to the entire monarchy [Prussia] but also to sharpen them threefold. . . .

We find the prohibition, punishable with a three-month to three-year penalty, against accusing anyone of things that are legally punishable or of "exposing him to public contempt"; we find the prohibition against stating the truth in any way other than by "valid documentary evidence"; in short, we again find the classic monuments of Napoleonic press despotism. . . .

From the day this law goes into effect, the Prussian officials can sleep in peace. If Herr Pfuel burns the hands and ears of Poles in Höllenstein, and the press reports it—four and a half months to four and a half years in prison! If cit-

---

* In *Karl Marx on Freedom of the Press and Censorship* by Saul K. Padover, pp. 121-22. Copyright © 1974 by Saul K. Padover. Used with permission of McGraw-Hill Book Co.

izens are jailed by an oversight, although it is known that they are innocent, and the press reports it—four and a half months to four and a half years in prison! If district officers [*Landräte*] turn themselves into reactionary traveling salesmen and signature collectors for royalist addresses, and the press exposes this—four and a half months to four and a half years in prison!

From the day this law goes into effect, the officials can commit any despotism, any tyranny, any illegality, with impunity; they can coolly flog or order to be flogged, arrest and hold without a hearing; the only effective control, the press, has been made ineffective. The day this law goes into effect the bureaucracy can celebrate a festival of joy; it can become more mighty, more unrestrained, more strong than it was before March.

In fact, what remains of freedom of the press when what deserves public contempt can no longer be exposed to public contempt?

THE DUTY OF A REVOLUTIONARY PRESS

Speech before the Court of Assizes in Cologne, February 7, 1849; published in *Neue Rheinische Zeitung*, February 14, 1849. As editor of this newspaper, Marx was tried for publishing derogatory remarks about Prussian government officials. He and his co-defendants (Frederick Engels and Hermann Korff) were acquitted by the jury amid jubilation of those present.

Gentlemen of the Jury! Today's proceedings have a certain importance because Articles 222 and 367 of the *Code Pénal*, referred to in the indictment of the *Neue Rheinische Zeitung*, are the only ones in Rhineland law[1] available to the government in connection with direct incitement to revolt....

I, for my part, assure you, gentlemen, I prefer to follow

---

[1] Marx, whose father was a lawyer, had, among other things, studied law at the University of Berlin.

the great world events, to analyze the course of history, rather than tussle with local idols, with gendarmes and courts. No matter how great these gentlemen [the Prussian officials who felt themselves insulted] may consider themselves in their own imaginations, they are *nothing*, altogether *nothing* in the titanic struggles of the present time. I regard it as a real sacrifice when we decide to break a lance with *these* opponents. But once and for all it is the duty of the press to speak up for the oppressed in its immediate vicinity. And also, gentlemen, the house of servitude has its own proper support in the subordinate political and social authorities that directly confront the private life of the person, the living individual. It does not suffice to fight general conditions and the higher authorities. The press must decide to enter the lists against *this* particular gendarme, *this* procurator, *this* district administrator. On what was the March [1848] Revolution shattered? It reformed only the highest political summit, it left the foundations of that summit untouched—the old bureaucracy, the old army, the old courts, the old judges who were born, trained, and grew gray in the service of absolutism. The first duty of the press, therefore, is *to undermine all the foundations of the existing political system*. (Applause in court.)

CHAPTER IX

RELIGION

Note

Marx's religious views, including his sharp criticism of Christianity and strong antipathy for Judaism, were shaped by his family background and by the theological currents that prevailed in Germany in his youth. A descendant of generations of rabbis, his father had him baptized a Lutheran at the age of six in order to enable him to enter public school. Marx was raised in a family that was only nominally Christian and educated in schools that had a traditional bias against Judaism. After attending the university and studying contemporary German theological radicals, such as Ludwig Feuerbach and Bruno Bauer, he came to reject all religions, but retained a special animus for that of his ancestors, as can be seen in his essay, "On the Jewish Question," the full text of which is included in this Chapter.

It is this essay that has led critics of Marx to accuse him, not without justification, of anti-semitism. In it he re-echoed the ancient anti-Semitic charges, then widespread in Christian Europe, that Judaism was a Mammon-oriented religion and the Jews its money-worshiping votaries. He argued that Judaism had corrupted society through its profit-motive and that the only way to achieve human emancipation was to eliminate "Jewishness."

Marx's position on the subject was based, not merely on historically prevalent prejudice, but also on a lack of knowledge of the lives and faith of the people from whom he descended. Even a cursory study reveals that Jews did not worship Mammon but an all-pervasive Deity symbolizing universal human qualities of justice, mercy and truth. As an educated man, Marx should have known that the Talmud, the ancient source of Jewish wisdom and behavior, ordained humane practices in all activities; hunting and cruelty to servants and animals, for example, were forbidden to Jews, although they were widely practiced by Christians, high and low. In fact, Marx's indisputable ethical passion in general has often been regarded by his admirers as messianically Jewish in nature. Marx himself chose to ignore the fact that the founders and earliest practitioners of Judaism were not money-minded tradesmen but shepherds and simple country people who were moved by an overwhelming sense of a monotheistic Deity. Insofar as Marx's Jewish contemporaries pursued money affairs, they did so out of necessity and not out of religious compulsion, primarily in countries—Czarist Russia and Poland, for example—where, virtually all other means of livelihood, including farming, were closed to them.

Marx was likewise hostile to Christianity in both its practice and philosophy. His antipathy applied to church, clergy, and governments that called themselves Christian (as did that of Prussia in his day). An example of his "aversion," as he called it in a letter to Ferdinand Lassalle, is his attack on the so-called "social principles of Christianity." He wrote:

> The social principles of Christianity justified slavery in antiquity, glorified medieval serfdom. . . .
> The social principles of Christianity transfer the . . . settlement of all infamies to heaven, and thereby justify the continuation of these infamies on earth. . . .
> The social principles of Christianity declare all vile acts of the oppressors against the oppressed to be either just punishment for original sin and other sins, or suffering that the Lord in His infinite wisdom has destined for those redeemed.
> The social principles of Christianity preach cowardice, self-contempt, abasement, submission, humility—in brief, all the characteristics of the *canaille*. . . .
>
> The social principles of Christianity are hypocritical.[1]

As for religion in general, Marx's position can be found in the essay on Hegel's "Philosophy of Law," excerpts of which are contained in this Chapter. In it, he followed Feuerbach's

[1] "The Communism of the *Rheinischer Beobachter*," in *Deutsche-Bruesseler-Zeitung*, September 12, 1847.

anthropological view that "man makes religion, religion does not make man." Religion, he asserted, was an illusion, the product of human imagination. It is man's search for a "supernatural being in the fantastic reality of heaven," where he actually finds no reality but only a "reflection of himself." Religion, Marx stated, was the "sigh of the distressed creature," being both an escape from the misery of this world and a protest against this wretchedness.

Since religion is mere illusion, it cannot solve man's problems. It can only aggravate them. To achieve real happiness for man, it is necessary to abolish the illusory happiness of religion, by eliminating the conditions that require such illusions. In this sense, Marx characterized religion as "the *opium* of the people." This attitude towards religion can be found in communist countries today.

Marx concerned himself with religious questions only in his early years, when he was interested in philosophy, which then included theology. The older Marx did not write on the subject, which he came to regard as boring. He adverted to religion only insofar as it affected politics. In an interview in the *Chicago Tribune* (January 5, 1879), he said: "As socialism grows, religion will disappear. Its disappearance must be done by social development, in which education must play a great role."

A. RELIGION IN GENERAL

PROOF OF THE EXISTENCE OF GOD

From "Critique of the Plutarchian Polemic Against Epicurus' Theology," Appendix in Notes and Comments in Marx's doctoral dissertation, *Difference Between the Democritean and Epicurean Philosophy of Nature* (1841)

Finally we remind Herr Schelling of the concluding words of the letter cited above: "It is time to announce freedom of the mind to the better part of mankind, and no longer to tolerate that it laments the loss of its fetters."[1]

If this was already true in 1795, what of the year 1841?

To take the occasion here of recalling a theme that has become almost notorious—the *proof of the existence of God*—Hegel entirely turned around, that is, rejected, these theological proofs in order to justify them. What kinds of clients are these whom the lawyer cannot save from being condemned without killing himself? For example, Hegel interprets the end of the world as God in the image: "Because the accidental is *not*, God or the Absolute is." The theological proof alone puts it in reverse: "Because the accidental has true Being, God is." God is the guarantee of the accidental world. Obviously the reverse can also be said.

The proofs of the existence of God are either nothing but hollow tautologies—for example, the ontological proof means only that "what I really conceive is a true conception for me," and has an effect on me; in this sense all the gods, heathen as well as Christian, possess a real existence. Did not the old Moloch rule? Was not the Delphic Apollo a real power in the life of the Greeks? Here Kant's *Critique* [*of Pure Reason*] also means nothing. If somebody imagines that he possesses a hundred Taler, and if this notion is not merely a subjective wish but one he believes in, then the hundred imagined Taler have the same value as a hundred real ones. He will, for example, incur debts in his imagination and they will have the same effect as the debts that humanity has contracted with its gods. On the contrary, Kant's example could have strengthened the ontological proof. Real Taler have the same existence as imagined gods. Does a real Taler have existence elsewhere than in the imagination, even if it is in a universal or fairly common imagination of humanity? Introduce paper money into a country where its usage is not known and everybody will laugh at your subjective imagination. Bring your gods to a land where other gods prevail and it will be proved to you that you suffer from imaginings and abstractions. Rightly so. He who brought the old Greeks a different god would have had to find proof of his existence. Because for the Greeks he did not exist. *What a particular country is*

---

[1] Friedrich Wilhelm Joseph von Schelling, *Philosophische Briefe über Dogmatismus und Kriticismus* ("Philosophic Letters on Dogmatism and Criticism," 1795), p. 129.

for particular foreign gods, that the country of reasons is for god altogether—a territory in which his existence ceases to be.

Or else the proofs of the existence of a god are nothing but the *proofs of the existence of actual human self-consciousness, logical explication of the same*. For example, the ontological proof. What is the direct Being in which this is conceived? Self-consciousness.

In this sense, all the proofs of the existence of a god are proofs of *nonexistence, refutations* of all conceptions of a god. Real proofs would sound the reverse of this. "Because nature is badly contrived, God is." "Because the world is irrational, God is." "Because thought is not, God is." However, what does all this say except that *to him to whom the world is irrational, and who is therefore himself irrational, God is? Or irrationality is the existence of God.*

RELIGION AND ANIMALS

From "Debates on Freedom of the Press and Publication," *Rheinische Zeitung*, May 8, 1842

The speaker blames the Swiss press for having adopted the "beastly" party names of the "horn-and-claw men," in brief for speaking Swiss to the Swiss, who live with oxen and cows in a certain patriarchal harmony. . . .

In regard to the "beastly" party names we remark that religion itself dignifies the "beastly" as symbol of the spiritual. Our speaker will in any case reject the Indian press, which in religious enthusiasm celebrates the cow Sabala and the ape Hanuman. He will reproach the Indian press for the Indian religion, as he reproached the Swiss press for the Swiss character. But there is one press which he will hardly subject to censure; we mean the *holy press*, the Bible; and doesn't the latter divide all mankind into two great parties, the *goats* and the *sheep*? Does not God himself characterize his own relationship to the houses of Judah and Israel in the following way: I am a moth to the house of Judah and a mite to the house of Israel? Or, what is closer to us seculars, isn't there a princely literature which transforms all of anthropology into zoology—we mean the heraldic literature? That contains more curiosities than the horn-and-claw men.

CRITICISM OF RELIGION IS THE PRESUPPOSITION OF ALL CRITICISM*

From "Toward the Critique of Hegel's Philosophy of Law. Introduction," written at the end of 1843 and early 1844; published in *Deutsch-Französische Jahrbücher*, 1844

For Germany, the criticism of religion has been essentially completed, and the criticism of religion is the presupposition of all criticism.

The profane existence of error is compromised when its heavenly *oratio pro aris et focis* [prayer for altar and hearth] has been refuted. Man, who in his search for a supernatural being in the fantastic reality of heaven found only a reflection of himself, will no longer be inclined to find only the semblance of his own self, a nonhuman being, where he seeks and must seek his true reality.

The basis of irreligious criticism is: *Man makes religion,* religion does not make man. And indeed, religion is the self-awareness and self-regard of man who either has not yet found or has already lost himself again. But man is not an abstract being, crouching outside the world. Man is the *world of men,* the state, society. This state, this society, produce religion, which is an inverted world consciousness because they are an inverted world. Religion is the general theory of that world, its encyclopedic compendium, its logic in popular form, its spiritual *point d'honneur* [point of honor], its enthusiasm, its moral sanction, its solemn complement, its general ground of consolation and justification. It is the fantastic realization of the human *being* because the human *being* possesses no true reality. The struggle against religion is therefore indirectly the struggle against that world whose spiritual aroma is religion.

Religious misery is in one way the expression of real misery, and in another a protest against real misery. Religion

*In *Karl Marx on Religion* by Saul K. Padover, pp. 35-37. Copyright © 1974 Saul K. Padover. Used with permission of McGraw-Hill Book Co.

is the sigh of the afflicted creature, the soul of a heartless world, as it is also the spirit of spiritless conditions. It is the *opium* of the people.

The abolition of religion as the *illusory* happiness of the people is the demand for their *real* happiness. The demand to abandon the illusions about their condition is the *demand to give up a condition that requires illusions*. Hence criticism of religion is in embryo a *criticism of this vale of tears* whose halo is religion.

Criticism has plucked the imaginary flowers from the chain, not for the purpose of enabling man to wear the existing chain without fantasy or consolation, but to make him cast off the chain and pluck the living flower. The criticism of religion disillusions man so that he thinks, acts, and shapes his reality like a disillusioned man who has come to his senses, so that he revolves around himself and thereby around his real sun. Religion is only the illusory sun that revolves around man so long as he does not revolve around himself.

It is, therefore, the task of history, after the otherworldly truth has disappeared, to establish *the truth of this world*. It is the immediate task of philosophy, which stands in the service of history, to expose human self-alienation in its *unholy form* after it has been unmasked in its *holy form*. Criticism of heaven thus is transformed into criticism of earth, *criticism of religion* into *criticism of law,* and *criticism of theology* into *criticism of politics.* . . .

The weapon of criticism, to be sure, cannot replace the criticism of weapons; material force must be overthrown by material force, but theory itself also becomes a material force as soon as the masses grip it. Theory is capable of gripping the masses when it demonstrates *ad hominem* [in man], and it demonstrates *ad hominem* when it becomes radical. To be radical is to grasp things by the root. But for man, the root is man himself. The clear proof of the radicalism of German theory, and hence of its practical energy, is that it issues from the decisive, *positive* suspension of religion. The criticism of religion ends with the doctrine that *man is the highest being for man,* hence with the *categorical imperative to overthrow all conditions* in which man is a degraded, enslaved, abandoned, contemptible being—conditions that cannot be better described than by the exclamation of a Frenchman on the occasion of a projected dog tax: "Poor dogs! They want to treat you like human beings!"

Even historically, theoretical emancipation has a specifically practical significance for Germany. For Germany's revolutionary past is theoretical—it is the Reformation. As the revolution then began in the brain of the monk, so now it begins in the brain of the philosopher.

Luther, to be sure, vanquished the bondage of *devotion* when he replaced it with the bondage of *conviction*. He shattered faith in authority while he restored the authority of faith. He transformed parsons into laymen and laymen into parsons. He freed man from outward religiosity while he made religiosity the innerness of man. He emancipated the body from its chain while he put chains on the heart.

But while Protestantism was not the true solution, it was the true formulation of the problem. It was no longer, therefore, a question of the struggle of the layman against the *parson outside himself*, but of a struggle with *his own inner parson*, his *parson nature*. And if the Protestant transformation of German laymen into parsons emancipated the lay popes, the princes with their clergy, the privileged, and the philistines, so the philosophical transformation of the priestly Germans into men will emancipate the *people*. But little as the emancipation will stop with the princes, just as little will the secularization of estates stop with the *robbery of the church* that was set in motion by hypocritical Prussia above all. At that time the Peasant War, the most radical fact of German history, was wrecked by theology. Today, when theology itself is wrecked, the most unfree fact of German history, our *status quo*, will be shattered by philosophy. On the eve of the Reformation official Germany was the most absolute vassal of Rome. On the eve of its revolution Germany is the absolute vassal of something less than Rome—of Prussia and Austria, of bumpkin-Junkers and philistines. . . .

One fine day Germany will find itself at the *niveau* [level] of European decline before ever having reached the *niveau* of European emancipation. It will then be compared to a fetishist wasting away from the diseases of Christianity.

HEGEL AND "RELIGION AS ALIENATED HUMAN SELF-CONSCIOUSNESS"

From "Critique of the Hegelian Dialectic and Philosophy as a Whole," *Economic and Philo-*

sophic Manuscripts of 1844, pp. 148-53. Marx wrote this in Paris in 1844 but the work remained unpublished until 1932, when the Moscow Institute of Marxism-Leninism brought out the papers, despite their incompleteness and missing pages, in book form under the title *Economic and Philosophic Manuscripts of 1844*. This selection is based on the edition of Progress Publishers (Moscow, 1959), translated by Martin Milligan.

Second, this implies that self-conscious man, insofar as he has recognized and annulled and superseded the spiritual world (or his world's general spiritual mode of being) as self-alienation, nevertheless again confirms this in its alienated shape and passes it off as his true mode of being—reestablishes it, and pretends to be at home in his other-being as such. Thus, for instance, after annulling and superseding religion, after recognizing religion to be a product of self-alienation, he yet finds confirmation of himself in *religion as religion*. Here is the root of Hegel's false positivism, or of his merely apparent criticism: this is what Feuerbach designated as the positing, negating, and reestablishing of religion or theology—but it has to be grasped in more general terms. Thus reason is as much at home in unreason as unreason. The man who has recognized that he is leading an alienated life in politics, law, etc., is leading his true human life in this alienated life as such. Self-affirmation, in contradiction with itself—in contradiction both with the knowledge of and with the essential being of the object—is thus true knowledge and life.

There can therefore no longer be any question about an act of accommodation on Hegel's part vis-à-vis religion, the state, etc., since this is *the* lie of his principle.

If I *know* religion as alienated human consciousness, then what I know in it as religion is not my self-consciousness, but my alienated self-consiousness confirmed in it. It therefore know my own self, the self-consciousness that belongs to its very nature, confirmed not in religion but rather in annihilated and superseded religion.

In Hegel, therefore, the negation of the negation is not the confirmation of the true essence, effected precisely through negation of the pseudoessence. With him the negation of the negation is the confirmation of the pseudoessence, or of the self-estranged essence in its denial; or it is the denial of this pseudoessence as an objective being dwelling outside man and independent of him, and its transformation into the subject.

A peculiar role, however, is played by the act of superseding, in which denial and preservation—denial and affirmation—are bound together.

Thus, for example, in Hegel's *Philosophy of Right*, private right superseded equals morality, morality superseded equals the family, the family superseded equals civil society, civil society superseded equals the state, the state superseded equals world history. In the actual world, private right, morality, the family, civil society, the state, etc., remain in existence, only they have become *moments* of man—states of his existence and being—which have no validity in isolation, but dissolve and engender one another, etc. They have become *moments of motion*.

In their actual existence this mobile nature of theirs is hidden. It first appears and is made manifest in thought, in philosophy. Hence my true religious existence is my existence in the *philosophy of religion*; my true political existence is my existence, my existence in *philosophy*. Likewise the true existence, existence in the *philosophy of nature*; my true artistic existence, existence in the *philosophy of art*; my true *human* existence, my existence in *philosophy*. Likewise the true existence of religion, the state, nature, art, is the philosophy of religion, of nature, of the state, and of art. If, however, the philosophy of religion, etc., is for me the sole true existence of religion, then, too, it is only as a *philosopher of religion* that I am truly religious, and so I deny real religious sentiment and the really religious man. But at the same time I assert them, in part within my own existence or within the alien existence which I oppose to them—for this is only their philosophic expression—and in part I assert them in their own original shape, for they have validity for me as merely the apparent other-being, as allegories, forms of their own true existence (i.e., of my philosophical existence) hidden under sensuous disguises.

In just the same way, quality superseded equals quantity, quantity superseded equals measure, measure superseded equals essence, essence superseded equals appearance, appearance superseded equals actuality, actuality superseded equals the concept, the concept superseded equals objectivity, objectivity superseded equals the absolute Idea, the absolute Idea superseded equals nature, nature superseded equals subjective mind, subjective mind superseded equals ethical objective mind, ethical mind superseded equals art, art superseded equals religion, religion superseded equals absolute knowledge.

On the other hand, this act of superseding is a transcending of the thought entity; thus private property as a thought is transcended in the thought of morality. And because thought imagines itself to be directly the other of itself, to be sensuous reality—and therefore takes its own action for sensuous, real action—this superseding in thought, which leaves its object standing in the real world, believes that it has really overcome it. On the other hand, because the object has now become for it a moment of thought, thought takes it in its reality too to be self-confirmation of itself—of self-consciousness, of abstraction.

From the one point of view the existent which Hegel supersedes in philosophy is therefore not real religion, the real state, or real nature, but religion itself already become an object of knowledge, i.e., dogmatics; the same with jurisprudence, political science, and natural science. From the one point of view, therefore, he stands in opposition both to the real thing and to immediate, unphilosophic science or the unphilosophic conceptions of this thing. He therefore contradicts their conventional conceptions.

On the other hand, the religious man, etc., can find in Hegel his final confirmation.

It is now time to lay hold of the positive aspects of the Hegelian dialectic within the realm of estrangement:

(a) Annulling as an objective movement of retracing the alienation into self. This is the insight, expressed within the estrangement, concerning the appropriation of the objective essence through the annulment of its estrangement; it is the estranged insight into the real objectification of man, into the real appropriation of his objective essence through the annihilation of the estranged character of the objective world, through the annulment of the objective world in its estranged mode of being—just as atheism, being the annulment of God, is the advent of theoretical humanism; and communism, as the annulment of private property, is the justification of real human life as man's possession and thus the advent of practical humanism (or just as atheism is humanism mediated with itself through the annulment of religion, while communism is humanism mediated with itself through the annulment of private property). Only through the annulment of this mediation—which is itself, however, a necessary premise—does positively self-deriving humanism, *positive humanism*, come into being.

But atheism and communism are no flight, no abstraction; they are not a losing of the objective world begotten by man—of man's essential powers given over to the realm of objectivity; they are not a returning in poverty to unnatural, primitive simplicity. On the contrary, they are but the first real coming-to-be, the realization become real for man, of man's essence—of the essence of man as something real.

Thus by grasping the positive meaning of self-referred negation (if even again in estranged fashion) Hegel grasps man's self-estrangement, the alienation of man's essence, man's loss of objectivity and his loss of realness as finding of self, change of his nature, his objectification and realization. In short, within the sphere of abstraction, Hegel conceives labor as man's act of self-genesis—conceives man's relation to himself as an alien being and the manifesting of himself as an alien being to be the coming-to-be of *species consciousness* and *species life*.

(b) However, apart from, or rather in consequence of, the perverseness already described, this act appears in Hegel:

First of all as a merely formal, because abstract, act, because the human essence itself is taken to be only an *abstract, thinking essence*, conceived merely as self-consciousness. And,

Second, because the conception is formal and abstract, the annulment of the alienation becomes a confirmation of the alienation; or, again, for Hegel this movement of self-genesis and self-objectification in the form of self-alienation and self-estrangement is the absolute, and hence final, *expression of human life*—of life with itself as its aim, of life at rest in itself, of life that has attained oneness with its essence.

This movement in its abstract form as dialectic is therefore regarded as truly human life, and because it is nevertheless an abstraction—an estrangement of human life—it is regarded as a divine process, but as the divine process of man, a process traversed by man's abstract, pure, absolute essence that is distinct from him.

Third, this process must have a bearer, a subject. But the subject first emerges as a result. This result—the subject knowing itself as absolute self-consciousness—is therefore God—*absolute spirit*—*the self-knowing and self-manifesting Idea*. Real man and real nature become mere predicates, symbols of this esoteric, unreal man and of this unreal nature. Subject and predicate are therefore related to each other in absolute inversion—a mystical subject-object or a subjectivity reaching beyond the object—the absolute subject as a process, as subject alienating itself and returning from alienation into itself, but at the same time retracting this alienation into itself, and the subject as this process; a pure, restless revolving within itself.

First, the formal and abstract conception of man's act of self-genesis or self-objectification.

Hegel having posited man as equivalent to self-consciousness, the estranged object—the estranged essential reality of man—is nothing but consciousness, the thought of estrangement merely, estrangement's abstract and therefore empty and unreal expression, negation. The annulment of the alienation is therefore likewise nothing but an abstract, empty annulment of that empty abstraction—the *negation of the negation*. The rich, living, sensuous, concrete activity of self-objectification is therefore reduced to its mere abstraction, *absolute negativity*—an abstraction which is again fixed as such and thought of as an independent activity—as sheer activity. Because this so-called negativity is nothing but the abstract, empty form of that real living act, its content can in consequence be merely a formal content begotten by abstraction from all content. As a result there are general, abstract forms of abstraction pertaining to every content and on that account indifferent to, and consequently valid for, all content—the thought forms or logical categories torn from *real* mind and from *real* nature.

MEN ARE THE PRODUCERS OF THEIR OWN CONCEPTIONS

From *The German Ideology*, pp. 29-30, 37-38, 42-43 of the Progress Publishers edition

(Moscow, 1964), translated from the German by S. Ryazanskaya

The entire body of German philosophical criticism from Strauss to Stirner[1] is confined to criticism of *religious* conceptions.[2] The critics started from real religion and actual theology. What religious consciousness and a religious conception really meant was determined variously as they went along. Their advance consisted in subsuming the allegedly dominant metaphysical, political, juridical, moral, and other conceptions under the class of religious or theological conceptions; and similarly in pronouncing political, juridical, moral consciousness as religious or theological, and the political, juridical, moral man—"*man*" in the last resort—as religious. The dominance of religion was taken for granted. Gradually every dominant relationship was pronounced a religious relationship and transformed into a cult, a cult of law, a cult of the state, etc. On all sides it was only a question of dogmas and belief in dogmas. The world was sanctified to an ever increasing extent, till at last our venerable Saint Max [Stirner] was able to canonize it *en bloc* and thus dispose of it once for all. . . .

The production of ideas, of conceptions, of consciousness, is at first directly interwoven with material activity and the material of men, the language of real life. Conceiving, thinking, the mental intercourse of men, appear at this stage as the direct efflux of their material behavior. The same applies to mental production as expressed in the language of politics, law, morality, religion, metaphysics, etc., of a people. Men are the producers of their conceptions, ideas, etc.—real, active men, as they are conditioned by a definite development of their productive forces and of the intercourse correspond-

---

[1] David Friedrich Strauss, *Das Leben Jesu* (*The Life of Jesus*) (1835-36), and Max Stirner (Johann Caspar Schmidt), *Der Einzige und sein Eigentum* (*The Individual and His Property*) (Leipzig, 1845).

[2] The passage following this sentence is crossed out in the manuscript: " . . . claiming to be the absolute redeemer of the world from all evil. Religion was continually regarded and treated as the archenemy, as the ultimate cause of all relationships repugnant to these philosophers."

ing to these, up to its furthest forms. Consciousness can never be anything but conscious existence, and the existence of men is their actual life process. If in all ideology men and their circumstances appear upside-down as in a camera obscura, this phenomenon arises just as much from their historical life process as the inversion of objects on the retina does from their physical life process.

In direct contrast to German philosophy, which descends from heaven to earth, here we ascend from earth to heaven. That is to say, we do not set out from what men say, imagine, conceive, nor from men as narrated, thought of, imagined, conceived, in order to arrive at men in the flesh. We set out from real, active men, and on the basis of their real life process we demonstrate the development of the ideological reflexes and echoes of this life process. The phantoms formed in the human brain are also, necessarily, sublimates of their material life process, which is empirically verifiable and bound to material premises. Morality, religion, metaphysics, all the rest of ideology and their corresponding forms of consciousness, thus no longer retain the semblance of independence. They have no history, no development; but men, developing their material production and their material intercourse, alter, along with this their real existence, their thinking and the products of their thinking. Life is not determined by consciousness, but consciousness by life. In the first method of approach the starting point is consciousness taken as the living individual; in the second method, which conforms to real life, it is the real living individuals themselves, and consciousness is considered solely as *their* consciousness. . . .

For the animal, its relationship to others does not exist as a relationship. Consciousness is therefore from the very beginning a social product, and remains so as long as men exist at all. Consciousness is at first, of course, merely consciousness concerning the *immediate* sensuous environment and consciousness of the limited connection with other persons and things outside the individual who is growing self-conscious. At the same time it is consciousness of nature, which first appears to men as a completely alien, all-powerful and unassailable force, with which men's relations are purely animal and by which they are overawed like beasts; it is thus a purely animal consciousness of nature (natural religion).

We see here immediately: this natural religion or this particular relation of men to nature is determined by the form of society, and vice versa. Here, as everywhere, the identity of nature and man appears in such a way that the restricted relation of men to nature determines their restricted relation to one another, and their restricted relation to one another determines men's restricted relation to nature, just because nature is as yet hardly modified historically; and on the other hand, man's consciousness of the necessity of associating with the individuals around him is the beginning of the consciousness that he is living in society at all. This beginning is as animal as social life itself at this stage. It is mere herd consciousness, and at this point man is distinguished from sheep only by the fact that with him consciousness takes the place of instinct or his instinct is a conscious one. This sheeplike or tribal consciousness receives its further development and extension through increased productivity, the increase of needs, and, what is fundamental to both of these, the increase of population. With these there develops the division of labor, which was originally nothing but the division of labor in the sexual act, then that division of labor which develops spontaneously or "naturally" by virtue of natural predisposition (e.g., physical strength), needs, accidents, etc., etc. Division of labor becomes truly such only from the moment when a division of material and mental labor appears.[3] From this moment onward consciousness *can* really flatter itself that it is something other than consciousness of existing practice, that it *really* represents something without representing something real; from now on consciousness is in a position to emancipate itself from the world and to proceed to the formation of "pure" theory, theology, philosophy, ethics, etc. But even if this theory, theology, philosophy, ethics, etc. comes into contradiction with existing relations, this can occur only because existing social relations have come into contradiction with existing forces of production. . . .

---

[3] Marginal note by Marx: "The first form of ideologists, *priests*, is concurrent."

MATERIALISM

From *The Holy Family*, pp. 167-77

"Spinozism dominated the eighteenth century in its later French variety, which made matter into substance, as well as in deism, which conferred on matter a more spiritual name. . . Spinoza's French school and the supporters of deism were but two sects disputing over the true meaning of his system. . . . The simple fate of this Enlightenment was its sinking into romanticism after being obliged to surrender to the reaction which began after the French movement."

That is what criticism says.

To the critical history of French materialism we shall oppose a brief outline of its profane, voluminous history. We shall admit with due respect the abyss between history as it really happened and history as it happened according to the decree of "absolute criticism," the creator equally of the old and of the new. And finally, obeying the prescriptions of criticism, we shall make the "Why?," "Whence?," and "Whither?" of critical history the "objects of a persevering study."

"Speaking exactly and in the prosaic sense," the French Enlightenment of the eighteenth century, in particular French materialism, was not only a struggle against the existing political institutions and the existing religion and theology; it was just as much an open struggle against the metaphysics of the seventeenth century, and against all metaphysics, in particular that of Descartes, Malebranche, Spinoza, and Leibniz. Philosophy was opposed to metaphysics as Feuerbach, in his first decisive attack on Hegel, opposed sober philosophy to drunken speculation. Seventeenth-century metaphysics, beaten off the field by the French Enlightenment—to be precise, by French materialism of the eighteenth century—was given a victorious and solid restoration in German philosophy, particularly in speculative German philosophy of the nineteenth century. After Hegel linked it in so masterly a fashion with all subsequent metaphysics and with German idealism, and founded a metaphysical universal kingdom, the attack on speculative metaphysics in general again corresponded, as in the eighteenth century, to the attack on theology. It will be defeated forever by materialism, which has now been perfected by the work of speculation itself and coincides with humanism. As Feuerbach represented materialism in the theoretical domain, French and English socialism and communism in the practical field represented materialism which coincided with humanism.

"Speaking exactly and in the prosaic sense," there are two trends in French materialism; one traces its origin to Descartes, the other to Locke. The latter is mainly a French development and leads directly to socialism. The former, mechanical materialism, merges with what is properly French natural science. The two trends cross in the course of development. We have no need here to go deep into the French materialism which comes direct from Descartes, any more than into the French Newton school or the development of French natural science in general.

We shall therefore just note the following:

Descartes in his physics endowed matter with self-creative power and conceived mechanical motion as the act of its life. He completely separated his physics from his metaphysics. Within his physics matter is the only substance, the only basis of being and of knowledge.

Mechanical French materialism followed Descartes' physics in opposition to his metaphysics. His followers were by profession antimetaphysicists, i.e., physicists.

The school begins with the physician Leroy, reaches its zenith with the physician Cabanis, and the physician Lamettrie it its center. Descartes was still living when Leroy, like Lamettrie in the eighteenth century, transposed the Cartesian structure of animals to the human soul and affirmed that the soul is a modus of the body and ideas are mechanical motions. Leroy even thought Descartes had kept his real opinion secret. Descartes protested. At the end of the eighteenth century Cabanis perfected Cartesian materialism in his treatise, *Rapport du physique et du moral de l'homme*.

Cartesian materialism still exists today in France. It had great success in mechanical natural science which, "speaking exactly and in the prosaic sense," will be least of all reproached with romanticism.

Metaphysics of the seventeenth century, represented in France by Descartes, had materialism as its antagonist from its very birth. It personally opposed Descartes in Gassendi, the restorer of Epicurean materialism. French and English materialism was always closely related to Democritus and Ep-

Religion 299

icurus. Cartesian metaphysics had another opponent in the English materialist Hobbes. Gassendi and Hobbes were victorious over their opponent long after their death, when metaphysics was already officially dominant in all French schools.

Voltaire observed that the indifference of Frenchmen to the disputes between Jesuits and Jansenists in the eighteenth century was due less to philosophy than to Law's financial speculation. And, in fact, the downfall of seventeenth-century metaphysics can be explained by the materialistic theory of the eighteenth century only as far as that theoretical movement itself is explained by the practical nature of French life at the time. That life was turned to the immediate present, worldly enjoyment and worldly interests, the *earthly* world. Its antitheological, antimetaphysical, and materialistic practice demanded corresponding antitheological, antimetaphysical, and materialistic theories. Metaphysics had in practice lost all credit. Here we have only to indicate briefly the theoretical process.

In the seventeenth century, metaphysics (cf. Descartes, Leibniz, and others) still had an element of positive, profane content. It made discoveries in mathematics, physics, and other exact sciences which seemed to come within its pale. This appearance was done away with as early as the beginning of the eighteenth century. The positive sciences broke off from it and determined their own separate fields. The whole wealth of metaphysics was reduced to beings of thought and heavenly things, although this was the very time when real beings and earthly things began to be the center of all interest. Metaphysics had gone stale. In the very year in which Malebranche and Arnauld, the last great French metaphysicians of the seventeenth century, died, Helvétius and Condillac were born.

The man who deprived seventeenth-century metaphysics of all credit in the domain of theory was Pierre Bayle. His weapon was skepticism, which he forged out of metaphysics' own magic formulas. He at first proceeded from Cartesian metaphysics. As Feuerbach was driven by the fight against speculative theology to the fight against speculative philosophy precisely because he recognized in speculation the last prop of theology, because he had to force theology to turn back from pretended science to coarse, repulsive faith, so Bayle too was driven by religious doubt to doubt about metaphysics which was the support of that faith. He therefore critically investigated metaphysics from its very origin. He became its historian in order to write the history of its death. He mainly refuted Spinoza and Leibniz.

Pierre Bayle not only prepared the reception of materialism and the philosophy of common sense in France by shattering metaphysics with his skepticism. He heralded atheistic society, which was soon to come to existence, by proving that a society consisting only of atheists is possible, that an atheist can be a respectable man, and that it is not by atheism but by superstition and idolatry that man debases himself.

To quote the expression of a French writer, Pierre Bayle was "the last metaphysician in the seventeenth-century sense of the word and the first philosopher in the eighteenth-century sense."

Besides the negative refutation of seventeenth-century theology and metaphysics, a positive, antimetaphysical system was required. A book was needed which would systematize and theoretically justify the practice of life of the time. Locke's treatise on the origin of human reason came from across the Channel as if in answer to a call. It was welcomed enthusiastically, like a long-awaited guest.

To the question: Was Locke perchance a follower of Spinoza? "profane" history may answer: Materialism is the native son of Great Britain. Even Britain's scholastic Duns Scotus wondered: "Can matter think?"

In order to bring about that miracle he had recourse to God's omnipotence, i.e., he forced theology itself to preach materialism. In addition he was a nominalist. Nominalism is a main component of English materialism and is in general the first expression of materialism.

The real founder of English materialism and all modern experimental science was Bacon. For him natural science was true science and physics based on perception was the most excellent part of natural science. Anaxagoras with his *homoeomeria* and Democritus with his atoms are often the authorities he refers to. According to his teaching the senses are infallible and are the source of all knowledge. Science is experimental and consists in applying a rational method to the data provided by the senses. Induction, analysis, comparison, observation, and experiment are the principal requisites of rational method. The first and most important of the inherent qualities of matter is motion, not only mechanical and mathematical movement, but still more impulse, vital life spirit, tension, or, to use Jakob Boehme's expression, the throes of matter. The primary forms of matter are the living, individualizing forces of being inherent in it and producing the distinctions between the species.

In Bacon, its first creator, materialism contained latently and still in a naïve way the germs of all-round development. Matter smiled at man with poetical sensuous brightness. The aphoristic doctrine itself, on the other hand, was full of the inconsistencies of theology.

In its further development materialism became one-sided. Hobbes was the one who systematized Bacon's materialism. Sensuousness lost its bloom and became the abstract sensuousness of the geometrician. Physical motion was sacrificed to the mechanical or mathematical, geometry was proclaimed the principal science. Materialism became hostile to humanity. In order to overcome the antihuman incorporeal spirit in its own field, materialism itself was obliged to mortify its flesh and become an ascetic. It appeared as a *being of reason*, but it also developed the implacable logic of reason.

If man's senses are the source of all his knowledge, Hobbes argues, proceeding from Bacon, then conception, thought, imagination, etc., are nothing but phantoms of the material world more or less divested of its sensuous form. Science can only give a name to these phantoms. One name can be applied to several phantoms. There can even be names of names. But it would be a contradiction to say, on the one hand, that all ideas have their origin in the world of the senses and to maintain, on the other hand, that a word is more than a word, that besides the beings represented, which are always individual, there exist also general beings. An incorporeal substance is just as much a contradiction as an incorporeal body. Body, being, substance are one and the same real idea. One cannot separate the thought from matter which thinks. Matter is the subject of all changes. The word "infinite" is meaningless unless it means the capacity of our mind to go on adding without end. Since only what is material is perceptible, knowable, nothing is known of the existence of God. I am sure only of my own existence. Every human passion is a mechanical motion ending or beginning. The objects of impulses are what is called good. Man is subject to the same laws as nature; might and freedom are identical.

Hobbes systematized Bacon, but did not give a more precise proof of his basic principle that our knowledge and our ideas have their source in the world of the senses.

Locke proved the principle of Bacon and Hobbes in his essay on the origin of human reason.

Just as Hobbes did away with the theistic prejudices in Bacon's materialism, so Collins, Dodwell, Coward, Hartley, Priestley, and others broke down the last bounds of Locke's sensualism. For materialists, at least, deism is no more than a convenient and easy way of getting rid of religion.

We have already mentioned how opportune Locke's work was for the French. Locke founded the philosophy of *bon sens*, common sense; i.e., he said indirectly that no philosopher can be at variance with the healthy human senses and reason based on them.

Locke's immediate follower, Condillac, who also translated him into French, at once opposed Locke's sensualism to seventeenth-century metaphysics. He proved that the French had quite rightly rejected metaphysics as the mere bungling of fancy and theological prejudice. He published a refutation of the systems of Descartes, Spinoza, Leibniz and Malebranche.

In his *Essai sur l'origine des connaissances humaines* he expounded Locke's ideas and proved that not only the soul, but the senses too, not only the art of creating ideas, but also the art of sensuous perception, are matters of experience and habit. The whole development of man therefore depends on education and environment. It was only by eclectic philosophy that Condillac was ousted from the French schools.

The difference between French and English materialism follows from the difference between the two nations. The French imparted to English materialism wit, flesh and blood, and eloquence. They gave it the temperament and grace that it lacked. They civilized it.

In Helvétius, who also based himself on Locke, materialism became really French. Helvétius conceived it immediately in its application to social life (Helvétius, *De l'homme, de ses facultés intellectuelles et de son éducation*). Sensuous qualities and self-love, enjoyment and correctly understood personal interests, are the bases of morality. The natural equality of human intelligence, the unity of progress of reason and progress of industry, the natural goodness of man, and the omnipotence of education are the main points in his system.

In Lamettrie's works we find a combination of Descartes'

system and English materialism. He makes use of Descartes' physics in detail. His *Man Machine* is a treatise after the model of Descartes' beast-machine. The physical part of Holbach's *Système de la nature, ou des lois du monde physique et du monde moral* is also a result of the combination of French and English materialism, while the moral part is based substantially on the moral of Helvétius. Robinet (*De la Nature*), the French materialist who had the most connection with metaphysics and was therefore praised by Hegel, refers explicitly to Leibniz.

We need not dwell on Volney, Dupuis, Diderot, and others any more than on the physiocrats, having already proved the dual origin of French materialism from Descartes' physics and English materialism and the opposition of French materialism to seventeenth-century metaphysics and to the metaphysics of Descartes, Spinoza, Malebranche, and Leibniz. The Germans could not see this opposition before they came into the same opposition with speculative metaphysics.

As Cartesian materialism merges into natural science proper, the other branch of French materialism leads direct to socialism and communism.

There is no need of any great penetration to see from the teaching of materialism on the original goodness and equal intellectual endowment of men, the omnipotence of experience, habit, and education, and the influence of environment on man, the great significance of industry, the justification of enjoyment, etc., how necessarily materialism is connected with communism and socialism. If man draws all his knowledge, sensation, etc., from the world of the senses and the experience gained in it, the empirical world must be arranged so that in it man experiences and gets used to what is really human and that he becomes aware of himself as man. If correctly understood interest is the principle of all morality, man's private interest must be made to coincide with the interest of humanity. If man is not free in the materialist sense, i.e., free not through the negative power to avoid this or that, but through the positive power to assert his true individuality, crime must not be punished in the individual, but the antisocial source of crime must be destroyed, and each man must be given social scope for the vital manifestation of his being. If man is shaped by his surroundings, his surroundings must be made human. If man is social by nature, he will develop his true nature only in society, and the power of his nature must be measured not by the power of separate individuals but by the power of society.

This and similar propositions are to be found almost literally even in the oldest French materialists. This is not the place to assess them. *Fable of the Bees; or, Private Vices, Public Benefits,* by Mandeville, one of the early English followers of Locke, is typical of the social tendencies of materialism. He proves that in modern society vice is indispensable and useful. This was by no means an apology for modern society.

Fourier proceeds immediately from the teaching of the French materialists. The Babouvists were coarse, uncivilized materialists, but mature communism too comes directly from French materialism. The latter returned to its mother country, England, in the form Helvétius gave it. Bentham based his system of correctly understood interest on Helvétius' morality, and Owen proceeded from Bentham's system to found English communism. Exiled to England, the Frenchman Cabet came under the influence of communist ideas there and on his return to France became the most popular, although the most superficial, representative of communism. Like Owen, the more scientific French communists, Dézamy, Gay, and others, developed the teaching of materialism as the teaching of real humanism and the logical basis of communism.

THESES ON FEUERBACH

Written in spring 1845 in Brussels, published by Engels in an appendix of his *Ludwig Feuerbach and the End of Classical German Philosophy* (1888)

1.

The chief defect on all hitherto existing materialism (including that of Feuerbach) is that the object, the reality, sensuousness, is conceived only in the form of the *object* or the perception [*Anschauung*]; but not as human sensuous activity, practice; not subjectively. Therefore the active side, abstract in opposition to materialist, was developed by idealism—

which, of course, does not know the real, sensuous activity as such. Feuerbach wants sensuous objects—objects really differentiated from thought-objects; but he does not conceive human activity itself objective activity. In *Essence of Christianity,* therefore, he considers only the theoretical attitude as the genuinely human, while the practice is conceived and established only in its dirty-Jewish aspect. Thus he does not grasp the significance of "revolutionary," of "practical-critical" activity.

2.

The question whether objective truth can be attributed to human thinking—is not a question of theory, but a practical one. In practice, man must prove truth, that is, reality and power, the "this-sidedness" of his thinking. The dispute over the reality or nonreality of thought—which is isolated from practice—is a purely scholastic question.

3.

The materialist doctrine concerning the transformation of conditions of education forgets that circumstances are changed by men and that the educator must himself be educated. Hence this doctrine must necessarily divide society into two parts, of which one dominates over it.

The coincidence of the changing of circumstances and of human activity or self-changing can be conceived and rationally understood only as revolutionary practice.

Feuerbach starts out from the fact of religious self-alienation, the duplication of the world into a religious and a secular one. His work consists in the dissolution of the religious world in its secular foundation. But the fact that the secular foundation lifts itself and establishes an independent realm in the clouds can be explained only by the self-dismemberment and the self-contradiction of this secular basis. These, therefore, must be understood in themselves, as well as in their own contradiction, before being revolutionized in practice. Thus, for example, after the earthly family is discovered to be the mystery of the holy family, the former must first itself be destroyed in theory and practice.

4.

Feuerbach, not satisfied with abstract thinking, wants contemplation; but he does not conceive sensuousness as practical, human-sensuous activity.

5.

Feuerbach resolves the religious essence into human essence. But human essence is not an abstraction innate in each individual. In its reality it is the *ensemble* of social relations.

Feuerbach, who does not go into criticism of the real essence, is therefore compelled:

1. to abstract from the historic process and to establish the religious spirit by itself, and to postulate an abstract—isolated—human individuality.

2. The essence can, therefore, be conceived as a "species," as inner and mute, which unites many individuals naturally with the generality.

7.

Feuerbach, therefore, does not see that the "religious spirit" is in itself a social product and that the abstract individual whom he analyzes belongs to a definite form of society.

8.

All social life is essentially practical. All mysteries, which lead to theories about mysticism, find their rational solution in human practice and in the comprehension of this practice.

9.

The highest point reached by intuitive materialism, that is, materialism which does not comprehend sensuousness as practical activity, is the idea of single individuals and of civil society.

10.

The standpoint of the old materialism is civil society; the standpoint of the new is the human society or socialized humanity.

11.

Philosophers have merely interpreted the world in various ways: the point, however, is to change it.

B. CHRISTIANITY

THE UNION OF THE FAITHFUL WITH CHRIST*

> Marx wrote this composition on August 17, 1835, at the age of seventeen, as one of the essays on religion required for graduation from the Trier Gymnasium. Marx's religious teacher, Johann Abraham Kuepper, the Protestant minister who had also prepared him for baptism, commented on it: "An essay rich in thought, glowing, forceful, deserving of every praise, even though the Essence of the Union [with Christ] under consideration is not given and the Reason for it is conceived only one-sidedly and its Necessity demonstrated only meagerly."

Before we consider the Reason and Essence and the effects of the Union of Christ with the faithful, let us see whether this Union is necessary, whether it is determined by the nature of man, whether or not it may in itself achieve the goal for which God has created him out of the Void.

If we turn to history, the great teacher of humanity, we will find there engraved with an iron stylus that all nations, even those that attained the highest levels of culture, gave birth to the greatest men, produced the most splendid arts, had the most complex scientific problems—nevertheless could not shake off the fetters of superstition, had no proper conception of themselves or the Deity, could not cleanse their morality of alien admixtures and unworthy limitations. Even their virtues were more the product of a rough kind of greatness, of unrestrained egoism, of a passion for fame and bold deeds, than a striving for true perfection.

*From *Karl Marx on Religion* by Saul K. Padover, pp. 3-6. Copyright © 1974 by Saul K. Padover. Used with permission of McGraw-Hill Book Co.

And the ancient peoples, the savages, among whom the teaching of Christ had not yet spread, show an inner unrest, a fear of the wrath of their gods, an inner conviction of their unworthiness, while at the same time they bring sacrifices to their gods to atone for their sins.

Yes, the greatest sage of antiquity, the divine Plato, in more than one passage expresses a deep yearning for a higher Being whose appearance would fulfill the unsatisfied longing for truth and light.

Thus the history of nations teaches us the necessity of the Union with Christ.

To be sure, even when we study the history of the individual and the nature of man, we always see a divine spark in his breast, an enthusiasm for the Good, a striving for perception, a longing for truth—but the sparks of the eternal are smothered by the flame of lust. The enthusiasm for virtue is stifled by the tempting voice of sin, which is made ridiculous when the full power of life is felt. The striving for perception is replaced by the inferior striving for worldly goods; the longing for truth is extinguished by the sweet-smiling power of the lie; and so man stands, the only creature that does not fulfill its goal, the only member in all Creation not worthy of the God that created him. But the benevolent Creator does not hate his handiwork; he wanted to elevate it to his own level and He sent us his Son, through whom He calls to us: "Now ye are clean through the word which I have spoken unto you. Abide in me, and I in you [John 15:3-4]."

Now that we have seen how the history of nations and the consideration of the individual prove the necessity of a union with Christ, let us consider the last and most difficult proof of all the word of Christ himself.

And where does He express the necessity of the union more clearly than in the beautiful comparison between the vine and the branch, where He calls himself the vine and us the branch? The branch cannot bear fruit of itself, and likewise, says Christ, you can do nothing without Him. He states this even more strongly when he says: "I am the vine, ye are the branches: He that abideth in me, and I in him, the same bringeth forth much fruit: for without me ye can do nothing. If a man abide not in me, he is cast forth as a branch, and is withered [John 15:5-6]."

But it should be kept in mind that this applies only to those who have succeeded in understanding the word of

Christ; as for others, who have not been able to comprehend Him, we cannot judge the decree of the Lord over such nations and individuals.

Our heart, our reason, history itself, and the word of Christ, all call to us loudly and decisively that a union with him is an absolute necessity, that without Him we cannot attain our goal, that without Him we are rejected by God, and that only He can save us.

Thus penetrated by the conviction that this union is an absolute necessity, we are eager to learn the meaning of this high gift, this ray of light from the loftier world which falls upon our ear and ringingly raises us to heaven, and to discuss its inner Being and its Essence.

Once we have comprehended the necessity of the union, the basis for it—our need for salvation, our sinfully inclined nature, our uncertain reason, our corrupted heart, our unworthiness in God's presence— is clearly revealed before our eyes, and we need search no more.

But who could express the essence of the union more beautifully than did Christ in his comparison of the vine and the branch? Who, even in great treatises, could lay before the eye the innermost parts that are at the basis of this union better than Christ did in these words: "I am the true vine, and my Father is the husbandman [John 15:1]." "I am the vine, ye are the branches [John 15:5]."

If the branch were sentient, how joyously would it look to the gardener who tends it, who anxiously clears it of weeds and ties it to the vine from which it derives nourishment and sap for its beautiful blossoms.

In the union with Christ, therefore, we turn, before everything, our loving eye toward God, feel for Him an ardent gratitude, sink joyfully on our knees before Him.

Then, after a beautiful sun has risen through our union with Christ, when we feel our total unworthiness and at the same time exult over our salvation, then only can we love God, who formerly appeared to us as an offended lord but is now a forgiving father and a benevolent teacher.

But the branch, if it were sentient, would not only look up to the vine dresser, but would also fervently cling to the vine stock and feel the closest relation to the branches around it; it would love the other branches, because a gardener tends them and a stock gives them vigor.

Thus the union with Christ means a most intimate and vital companionship with Him, keeping Him before our eyes and in our hearts, and being permeated by the highest love, so that we can turn our hearts toward our brothers, united with us through Him, and for whom He had sacrificed himself.

But this love for Christ is not fruitless; it fills us not only with the purest reverence and highest respect for Him, but also has the effect of making us keep his commandments in that we sacrifice ourselves for each other and are virtuous, but virtuous only out of love for Him: "Of sin, because they believe not in me; Of righteousness, because I go to my Father, and ye see me no more; Of judgment, because the prince of this world is judged. I have yet many things to say unto you, but ye cannot bear them now. Howbeit when he, the Spirit of truth, is come, he will guide you into all truth: for he shall not speak of himself; but whatsoever he shall hear, that shall he speak: and he will shew you things to come. He shall glorify me; for he shall receive of mine, and shall shew it unto you [John 16:9-14]."

This is the great chasm which separates and elevates Christian virtues from others; this is one of the greatest effects brought out in men by the union with Christ.

Virtue is not the gloomy caricature found in the Stoic philosophy; it is not the child of the harsh doctrines of duty found among all heathen nations. It is, rather, the consequence of the love for Christ, love for a divine Being; and when it derives from such a pure source, it appears free of everything earthly and is truly divine. Then every repulsive aspect is submerged, everything earthly suppressed, everything crude extinguished, and virtue is more enlightened as it becomes milder and more humane.

Never before had human reason been able to present it so; previously virtue had been limited, an earthly quality.

Once a man has attained this virtue, this union with Christ, he will quietly and calmly bear the blows of fortune, bravely meet the storms of passions, and fearlessly endure the rage of evil—for who could then oppress him, who could deprive him of his Savior?

His prayers will then be answered, for he prays only for the union with Christ, that is, only for the divine, and how can it fail to elevate and to comfort when one proclaims the Savior himself? "Nevertheless I tell you the truth; it is expedient for you that I go away: for if I go not away, the Comforter will not come unto you; but if I depart, I will send him unto you [John 16:7]."

And who would not gladly endure pain, knowing that through his abiding in Christ and through his works, God Himself is honored, that his consummation elevates the Lord of Creation? "And when he is come, he will reprove the world of sin, and of righteousness, and of judgment [John 15:8]."

Thus the union with Christ imparts an inner exaltation, comfort in suffering, calm trust, and a heart full of love for humankind, open to everything noble, everything great, not out of ambition but for the sake of Christ. Thus the union with Christ imparts a joyousness which the Epicurean in his frivolous philosophy and the deep thinker in his most arcane science have vainly tried to snatch at, but which the soul can attain only through its unrestrained and childlike Union with Christ and God, which alone makes life more beautiful and exalted. "Of judgment, because the prince of this world is judged [John 16:11]."

THE SOCIAL PRINCIPLES OF CHRISTIANITY*

From "The Communism of the *Rheinischer Beobachter*," in *Deutsche-Brüsseler-Zeitung*, September 12, 1847.

"What is the alpha and omega of the Christian faith? The dogma of original sin and salvation. And therein lies the link of solidarity among humanity at its highest potential; one for all and all for one."

Happy people! The *cardinal question* is solved forever. The proletariat will find two inexhaustible life sources under the double wings of the Prussian eagle and the Holy Ghost: first, the income tax surplus over and above the ordinary and extraordinary needs of the state, which surplus is equal to null; and second, the revenues from the heavenly domains of original sin and salvation, which are likewise equal to null. Both

---

*From *Karl Marx on Religion* by Saul K. Padover, pp. 93-94. Copyright © 1974 by Saul K. Padover. Used with permission of McGraw-Hill Book Co.

of these nulls provide a splendid ground for the one-third of the nation that has no land for its subsistence, and a powerful support for another third which is in decline. In any case, imaginary surpluses, original sin, and salvation will satisfy the hunger of the people in quite a different way from the long speeches of the liberal deputies!

It is said further: "In the 'Our Father' we pray: 'lead us not into temptation.' And what we ask for ourselves we must also practice toward our neighbors. But our social conditions do indeed tempt man, and excessive misery incites to crime."

And *we*, the gentlemen bureaucrats, judges, and consistorial counsellors of the Prussian State, exercise this respect [for our fellow men] by joyfully wracking people on the wheel, beheading, imprisoning, and flogging, and thereby "leading" the proletarians "into temptation," so that later they too can wrack, behead, imprison, and flog us. And that will not fail to happen.

"Such conditions," the consistorial councilor declares, "a Christian State *must not* tolerate; it must find a remedy for them."

Yes, with absurd babble about society's duties of solidarity, with imaginary surpluses and blank checks drawn on God the Father, Son, and Company.

"We can also be spared the already tedious talk about communism," our observant consistorial councilor remarks. "If those whose calling it is would only develop the social principles of Christianity, the communists would soon become silent."

The social principles of Christianity have now had eighteen hundred years to develop, and need no further development by the Prussian consistorial councilors.

The social principles of Christianity justified slavery in antiquity, glorified medieval serfdom, and, when necessary, also know how to defend the oppression of the proletariat, although they may do so with a piteous face.

The social principles of Christianity preach the necessity of a ruling and an oppressed class, and for the latter they have only the pious wish that the former will be benevolent.

The social principles of Christianity transfer the consistorial councilors' settlement of all infamies to heaven, and thereby justify the continuation of these infamies on earth.

The social principles of Christianity declare all vile acts of the oppressors against the oppressed to be either just punishment for original sin and other sins, or suffering that the Lord in his infinite wisdom has destined for those redeemed.

The social principles of Christianity preach cowardice, self-contempt, abasement, submission, humility—in brief, all the qualities of the *canaille*; and the proletariat, not wishing to be treated as *canaille*, needs its courage, its self-respect, its pride, and its sense of independence even more than its bread.

The social principles of Christianity are hypocritical, but the proletariat is revolutionary.

So much for the social principles of Christianity.

CHRISTIAN SOCIALISM

From *Communist Manifesto* (1848)

As the parson has ever gone hand in hand with the landlord, so has clerical socialism with feudal socialism.

Nothing is easier than to give Christian asceticism a socialist tinge. Has not Christianity declaimed against private property, against marriage, against the state? Has it not preached, in the place of these, charity and poverty, celibacy and mortification of the flesh, monastic life and Mother Church? Christian Socialism is but the holy water with which the priest consecrates the heartburnings of the aristocrat.

CHANGING RELIGIOUS IDEAS

From *Communist Manifesto* (1848)

When people speak of ideas that revolutionize society, they do but express the fact that within the old society the elements of a new one have been created, and that the dissolution of the old ideas keeps even pace with the dissolution of the old conditions of existence.

When the ancient world was in its last throes, the ancient religions were overcome by Christianity. When Christian ideas succumbed in the eighteenth century to rationalist ideas, feudal society fought its death battle with the then revolutionary bourgeoisie. The idea of religious liberty and freedom of conscience merely gave expression to the sway of free competition within the domain of knowledge.

THE ANTI-CHURCH MOVEMENT

"Anti-Church Movement—A Demonstration in Hyde Park," published in the *Neue Oder-Zeitung*, June 28, July 5, 1855. This text is based on a translation in Marx and Engels, *On Britain*, published by the Foreign Languages Publishing House, Moscow, 1962 (and ed.).

It is an old and historic maxim that obsolete social forces, nominally still in possession of all attributes of power and continuing to vegetate after the basis of their existence has long rotted away under their feet, inasmuch as the heirs are quarreling among themselves even bfore the obituary notice has been printed and the will read—that these forces once more summon all their strength before their last death struggle, pass from the defensive to the offensive, make demands instead of retreating, and try to draw the most extreme conclusions from premises which have not only been put in question but are already condemned. Such is now the English oligarchy. Such is the church, its twin sister. Countless attempts at reorganization have been made within the Established Church, both the High and the Low, attempts to come to an understanding with the Dissenters and thus to confront the profane mass of the nation with a compact force. There has been a rapid succession of religious coercive measures. The pious Earl of Shaftesbury, formerly known as Lord Ashley, lamented in the House of Lords the fact that in England alone five million people are altogether alienated not only from the church but also from Christianity in general. "*Compelle intrare*" ["Force them to enter"], replies the Established Church. It leaves it to Lord Ashley and other such dissenting, sectarian, and overexcited pietists to pull out of the fire the chestnuts it means to eat.

The first measure of religious coercion was the Beer Bill,

which shut down all places of public entertainment on Sundays, except between 6:00 and 10:00 P.M. The bill was smuggled through the House at the end of a sparsely attended session, after the pietists had bought the support of the big London beer-pub owners by guaranteeing them that the license system, that is, the monopoly of big capital, would continue. Then came the Sunday Trading Bill, which has now passed its third reading in the Commons and separate clauses of which have just been debated by the Committee of the Whole. This new coercive measure also had the assured support of big capital, because only small shopkeepers keep open on Sunday and the owners of the big stores are quite ready to do away with the Sunday competition of the small shops through parliamentary means. In both cases there is a conspiracy between the church and monopoly capital, but in both cases there are religious penal laws against the lower classes to assuage the consciences of the upper classes. The Beer Bill affected the aristocratic clubs as little as the Sunday Trading Bill did the Sunday pursuits of genteel society. The workers receive their wages late on Saturday; hence they are the only ones for whom shops open on Sunday. They are the only ones who are compelled to do their shopping, small as it is, on Sundays. Hence the new bill is directed only against them. In the eighteenth century the French aristocracy said: For us, Voltaire; for the people, the Mass and the Tithe. In the nineteenth century the English aristocracy says: For us, pious phrases; for the people, Christian practice. The classical saints of Christianity castigated *their* bodies for the salvation of the souls of the masses; the modern, educated saints castigate the *body of the masses* for the salvation of their own souls.

This alliance between a dissolute, degenerate, and pleasure-seeking aristocracy and a church propped up by the filthy profit calculus of beer magnates and monopolistic wholesalers led yesterday to a mass demonstration in Hyde Park, the like of which London has not seen since the death of George IV, the "first gentleman of Europe." We were spectators from beginning to end, and we do not think we exaggerate in saying that the *English revolution began yesterday in Hyde Park*. The latest news from the Crimea acted as an effective ferment on this "unparliamentary," "extraparliamentary," and "antiparliamentary" demonstration.

Lord Robert Grosvenor, the author of the Sunday Trading

Bill, when reproached on the score that it was a law against the poor and not against the rich classes, replied: "The aristocracy to a large extent refrains from using its servants and horses on Sundays."

In the last days of the past week one could read on the walls of London a Chartist poster in big letters:

> New Sunday Bill prohibiting newspapers, shaving, smoking, eating and drinking and all kinds of recreation and nourishment, both corporal and spiritual, which the poor people still enjoy at the present time. An open-air meeting of artisans, workers and "the lower orders" generally of the capital will take place in Hyde Park on Sunday afternoon to see how religiously the aristocracy is observing the Sabbath and how anxious it is not to use its servants and horses on that day, as Lord Robert Grosvenor said in his speech. The meeting is called for three o'clock on the right bank of the Serpentine on the side toward Kensington Gardens. Come and bring your wives and children in order that they may profit by the example their "betters" set them!

It should be kept in mind that what Longchamps is to Parisians, the road along the Serpentine in Hyde Park is to English high society—the place where of an afternoon, particularly on Sunday, they parade their splendid carriages and horses with all their trappings, followed by swarms of lackeys. It will be realized from the above poster that the struggle against clericalism in England assumes the same character as every other serious struggle there—that of a *class struggle* of the poor against the rich, the people against the aristocracy, the "lower orders" against their "betters."

At three o'clock approximately 50,000 people had gathered at the announced spot on the right bank of the Serpentine in Hyde Park's vast meadows—and from the approaches on the other bank this swelled to at least 200,000. One could see smaller groups of milling people being shoved about from place to place. The large number of constables present were obviously trying to deprive the organizers of the meeting of what Archimedes had asked for to move the earth, namely, a place to stand on. Finally, a large crowd made a firm stand, and [James] Bligh, the Chartist, constituted himself chairman on a small eminence in the midst of the throng. He had hardly begun his harangue when Police Inspector Banks, at the head of forty truncheon-swinging constables, informed him that the park was the private property of the Crown and that no meeting was permitted to be held there.

After some *pourparlers*, with Bligh attempting to demonstrate to Banks that parks were public property and the latter answering that he had strict orders to arrest him if he persisted in his intentions, Bligh shouted amidst the immense roar of the crowds surrounding him: "Her Majesty's police declare that Hyde Park is private property of the Crown and that Her Majesty is unwilling to let her land be used by the people for their meetings. So let's move to Oxford Market."

With the ironic cry, "God save the Queen!" the throng broke up to move to Oxford Market. But meanwhile [James] Finlen, a member of the Chartist executive committee, rushed to a tree some distance away, followed by a crowd which quickly formed so tight and compact a circle around him that the police abandoned their attempt to get through to him. "Six days a week," he said, "we are treated like slaves, and now Parliament wants to rob us of the little bit of freedom we still have on the seventh. These oligarchs and capitalists allied with the sanctimonious parsons want to do penance by mortifying us instead of themselves for the unconscionable murder of the sons of the people in the Crimea."

We left the group to approach another, where a speaker stretched out on the ground harangued his audience from this horizontal position. Suddenly shouts sounded on all sides: "Let's go to the road, let's go to the carriages!" Meanwhile, the heaping of insults on horse riders and occupants of carriages had already begun. The constables, who constantly received reinforcements from the city, drove the promenading pedestrians off the carriage road. They thus helped to make both sides of the road become deeply lined with people, from Apsley House up Rotten Row along the Serpentine as far as Kensington Gardens—a distance of more than a quarter of an hour's walk. The spectators consisted of about two-thirds workers and one-third members of the middle class, all with women and children. The involuntary actors, elegant ladies and gentlemen, "commoners and lords," in their tall coaches-and-four with liveried lackeys fore and aft, joined by a few mounted elderly fellows slightly flushed by port wine, this time did not pass in review but were made to run the gantlet. A Babel of jeering, taunting, discordant shouts, in which no language is as rich as English, soon bore down upon them from both sides. As it was an improvised concert, instruments were lacking. The chorus, therefore, had only its own organs at its disposal and had to confine itself to vocal music. And a diabolic concert it was: a cacophony of grunting, hissing, whistling, squeaking, snarling, growling, croaking, shrieking, groaning, rattling, howling, gnashing sounds! A music that could drive one mad and move a stone. To this must be added outbursts of genuine Old English humor peculiarly mixed with long-contained boiling wrath. "Go to church!" were the only articulate sounds that could be distinguished. One lady appeasingly offered a prayer book in orthodox binding from her carriage in her outstretched hand. "Give it to your horses to read!" came the thundering reply, echoing a thousand voices. When the horses started to shy, buck, and finally run away, jeopardizing the lives of their elegant burdens, the derisive cries grew louder, more menacing, more ruthless. Noble lords and ladies, among them Lady Granville, wife of a Minister and President of the Privy Council, were forced to alight and make use of their own legs. When elderly gentlemen, wearing broad-brimmed hats and otherwise so appareled as to betray their special claim to perfection in religion, rode by, the strident outbursts of fury were extinguished, as if in obedience to a command, by irrepressible laughter. One of those gentlemen lost his patience. Like Mephistopheles, he made an indecent gesture, sticking out his tongue at the enemy. "He is a windbag, a parliamentary man! He fights with his own weapons!" someone shouted on one side of the road. "He is a saint! He is singing psalms!" was the antistrophe from the opposite side. In the meantime the metropolitan telegraph had informed all police stations that a riot was about to break out in Hyde Park and the police were ordered to the theater of military operations. Soon one detachment of police after another marched at short intervals through the double file of people, from Apsley House to Kensington Gardens, each received with the popular ditty:

Where are the geese?
Ask the police!

This was a hint at a notorious theft of geese recently committed by a constable in Clerkenwell.

The spectacle lasted three hours. Only English lungs could

perform such a feat. During the performance one heard among various groups such opinions as: "This is only the beginning," "That is the first step," "We hate them," etc. While rage was to be read on the faces of the workers, such smiles of blissful self-satisfaction covered the physiognomies of the middle classes as we had never seen there before. Shortly before the end, the demonstration increased in violence. Canes were raised against the carriages and through the endless dissonance one could hear the cry: "You rascals!" During the three hours zealous Chartists, men and women, plowed their way through the crowd and distributed leaflets which stated in big type:

Reorganization of Chartism!
A big public meeting will take place next Tuesday, June 26, in the Literary and Scientific Institute in Friar Street, Doctors' Commons, to elect delegates to a conference for the reorganization of Chartism in the capital. Admission free.

Most of the London papers today carry only a brief report of the events in Hyde Park. No editorials as yet, except in Lord Palmerston's *Morning Post*. "A spectacle," the editorial says, "both disgraceful and dangerous in the extreme has taken place in Hyde Park, an open violation of law and decency—an illegal interference by physical force in the free action of the legislature. The scene must not be allowed to be repeated next Sunday, as has been threatened."

At the same time, however, it declares that the "fanatical" Lord Grosvenor is solely "responsible" for this mischief, being the man who had provoked the "just indignation of the people"! As if Parliament had not adopted Lord Grosvenor's bill in three readings! Or perhaps he too brought his influence to bear "by physical force on the free action of the legislature?"

THE MEDIEVAL CHURCH AND MONEY

From Heft VII, in *Grundrisse der Kritik der Politischen Oekonomie,* written 1857-58. The text here is based on a translation by S.W. Ryazanskaya for the new edition, *A Contribution to the Critique of Political Economy* (Progress Publishers, Moscow, 1970).

The imposition by the Popes of church tax estimates in practically all Catholic Christian countries contributed not a little to the development of the entire monetary system in industrial Europe and, in consequence, to the genesis of various attempts at circumventing the Church's command (against interest). The Pope made use of the Lombards for the exaction of investiture moneys and other dues from the archbishoprics. These leading usurers and pawnbrokers were under papal protection. Known as long ago as the middle of the twelfth century, they called themselves "official *usurarii,*" "Roman episcopal money dealers," in England. Some bishops of Basel, among others, pawned to Jews episcopal rings, silken garments, all the Church paraphernalia, for trifling sums, on which they paid interest. But bishops, abbots, priests themselves also practiced usury with Church paraphernalia by pawning them to Tuscan money dealers from Florence, Siena, and other cities for a portion of the gain....

When money is the *universal equivalent, the general power of purchasing,* everything is purchasable, everything is exchangeable for money. But a thing can be transformed into money only when it is alienated, when the possessor has divested himself of it. Everything external or of indifference to the individual is therefore alienable. The so-called *inalienable, eternal* possessions and the immovable, fixed property relationships corresponding to them thus break down before money. Furthermore, when money itself is in circulation merely to be exchanged for gratification, etc.—for values that can in the end be dissolved in purely personal gratifications—everything becomes valuable only to the extent that it exists for the individual. The independent value of things—its relativity, its exchangeability—except in so far as it exists merely for other things, is thereby dissolved. Everything is sacrificed to egoistical gratification. For just as everything is alienable for money, so everything is obtainable with money. Everything is to be had for "cash money," since, in existing externally to the individual, it is to be caught by fraud, violence, etc. Hence everything is acquirable by everybody, and it is a matter of accident as to what the individual may or may not acquire, since it depends only on the money in his possession. Thereby the individual by himself is placed as the lord of everything. There are no absolute values, since value as such is relative to money. There is nothing inalienable, since everything is alienable through money. There is nothing higher, more sacred, etc. since everything is acquirable with money. The *"res sacrae"* ["holy things"] and *"religiosae,"* which could be *"in nullius bonis,"* *"nec aestimationem recipere, nec ubliquari alienarique posse"* ["could neither have money estimation nor be put aside"], which are exempt from *"commercio hominum"* ["commercial man"], do not exist before money—as all are equal before God. Beautiful, how the Roman Church in the Middle Ages is itself the chief propagandist of money.

As the Church law against usury had long lost all meaning, Martin also abolished the word itself in 1425 . . . In no country in the Middle Ages was there a general rate of interest. Only the priests were strict. Uncertainty of judicial institutions for the security of loans. Hence the higher the interest rate in individual cases. The scanty circulation of money, the necessity to pay in cash, since the exchange business is still undeveloped. Hence great variation in the consideration of interest and the notion of usury. In the times of Charlemagne, it was considered usurious only when a hundred percent was charged. In Lindau and Bodensee, 1344, native citizens charged 216⅔ percent. In Zurich the city council set the legal rate of interest at 43⅓ percent . . . In Italy, 40 percent occasionally had to be paid, although from the twelfth to the fourteenth centuries the usual rate did not exceed 20 percent . . . Verona ordered the legal rate at 12½ percent . . . Frederick II in his decree . . . 10 percent, but applying only to Jews. He would not deign to speak for Christians. In Rhenish Germany in the thirteenth century 10 percent was the usual.

CHRISTIANITY AND THE MATERIAL CONDITIONS OF SOCIETY

From *Capital*, Vol.I, Ch.1, Sec.4

For a society of commodity producers, whose general social relationship of production consists of retaining their relation to their products as commodities, and hence as values, and thereby reducing their private labor to a form of homogeneous human labor—for such a society, Christianity with its *cultus* of abstract man, particularly in its bourgeois developments, Protestantism, Deism, etc., is the most suitable form of religion. In the modes of production of ancient Asia, of Antiquity, etc., we find that the conversion of products into commodities, and hence the existence of men as mere producers of commodities, plays a subordinate role, which, however, increases in importance as the ancient communities approach closer and closer to the stage of their decline. Trading nations proper exist in the ancient world only in its interstices, like the gods of Epicurus in Intermundia, or like the Jews in the pores of Polish society. These ancient social organisms of production are extraordinarily more simple and transparent than the bourgeois ones, but they are based either on the immaturity of the individual man, who has not yet severed the umbilical cord that unites him naturally with his own species, or on direct master-and-servant relationships. They are conditioned by a lower stage of development of the productive power of labor and the correspondingly encompassing relationships of men within their material life-generating processes, and hence to each other and to nature. This actual narrowness is reflected ideally in the ancient worship of nature and in folk religions. The religious reflex of the real world can vanish altogether only when the relationships of practical everyday life offer men daily visible and reasonable relationships to each other and to nature. The shape of the life process of society, that is, the material process of production, strips off its misty veil only when it is put forth as a product of freely associated men, under their conscious control according to plan. This, however, requires a material groundwork of society, or a series of material conditions of existence which, in their turn, are the natural product of a long and painful process of development.

Political economy has, to be sure, analyzed, even if incompletely, value and its magnitude, and discovered the hidden content in these forms. It has never asked the question why that content assumes that form, and why labor is represented by the value of its product and the labor time by the magnitude of that labor product. Formulas which carry on their forehead the inscription that they belong to a state of society in which the productive process has mastery over man, and man does not yet have mastery over the productive process—such formulas appear to the bourgeois consciousness as much a self-evident necessity of nature as productive labor itself. Hence prebourgeois forms of the social organism of production are treated by them in much the same way as the Church Fathers treated pre-Christian religions.

PROTESTANT PARSONS AND THE POPULATION THEORY

From *Capital*, Vol. I, Ch. 25, Sec. 1, fn. 2

If the reader reminds me of Malthus, whose *Essay on Population* appeared in 1798, I remind him that this work in its first form is nothing more than a schoolboyish, superficial plagiary of Defoe, Sir James Stewart, Townsend, Franklin, Wallace, etc., and does not contain a single sentence thought out by himself. The great sensation this pamphlet caused was due solely to party interest. The French Revolution had found passionate defenders in the United Kingdom; the "principle of population," slowly worked out in the eighteenth century, and then in the midst of a great social crisis proclaimed with drums and trumpets as the infallible antidote to the teachings of Condorcet, etc., was greeted with jubilance by the English oligarchy as the great destroyer of all hankerings after human development. Malthus, hugely astonished at his success, gave himself to stuffing into his book materials superficially compiled, and adding to it new matter, not discovered but annexed by him. Note further: Although Malthus was a parson of the High Church of England, he had taken the monastic vow of celibacy. This was one of the conditions of a fellowship in the Protestant University at Cambridge: "We do not allow the members of the Colleges to be married; as soon as one takes a wife he ceases forthwith to be a member of the College." (*Reports of Cambridge University Commission*, p. 172.) This circumstance favorably distinguishes Malthus from the other Protestant parsons, who have by themselves shuffled off the Catholic command of priestly celibacy and have taken "Be fruitful and multiply" as their special mission, so that they generally contribute everywhere to an increase of population to a really indecent degree, while at the same time they preach to the workers the "principle of population." It is characteristic that the economical burlesque of the Fall of Man, Adam's apple, the "urgent appetite," the "checks which tend to blunt the shafts of Cupid," as Parson Townsend merrily puts it—that this ticklish point was and is monopolized by the Reverends of Protestant theology, or rather of the Protestant church. With the exception of the Venetian monk Ortes, an original and clever writer, most of the population-theory teachers are Protestant parsons. For example, Bruckner, *Théorie du Système animal*, in which the whole subject of modern population theory is exhausted, and to which the passing quarrel between Quesnay and his pupil, Mirabeau *père*, furnished ideas on the same topic; then Parson Wallace, Parson Townsend, Parson Malthus and his pupil the arch-Parson Thomas Chalmers, to say nothing of the lesser Reverend scribblers in this line. Originally political economy was studied by philosophers like Hobbes, Locke, Hume; by businessmen and statesmen like Thomas More, Temple, Sully, De Witt, North, Law, Vanderlint, Cantillon, Franklin; and in theory particularly, and with the greatest success, by medical men like Petty, Barbon, Mandeville, Quesnay. Even in the middle of the eighteenth century, the Reverend Mr. Tucker, an important economist of his time, apologized for occupying himself with Mammon. Later, and with this very "principle of population," the hour of the Protestant parsons struck. As if he had a presentiment of their business bungling, Petty, who treats population as the basis of wealth, and was, like Adam Smith, an outspoken enemy of the parsons, says: "That religion best flourishes when the Priests are most mortified, as was before said of the Law, which best flourisheth when lawyers have least to do." He therefore advises the Protestant parsons, if they will not once and for all follow the Apostle Paul and "mortify" themselves by celibacy, "not to breed more Churchmen than the benefices, as they are now shared out, will receive, that is to say, if there be places for about twelve thousand in England and

Wales, it will not be safe to breed up twenty-four thousand ministers, for then the twelve thousand which are unprovided for will seek ways to get themselves a livelihood, which they cannot do more easily than by persuading the people that the twelve thousand incumbents do poison or starve their souls, and misguide them in their way to Heaven." (Petty, *A Treatise of Taxes and Contributions*, p. 57.) Adam Smith's position vis-à-vis the Protestant priesthood of this time is characterized by the following. In *A Letter to A. Smith, LL.D, on the Life, Death and Philosophy of His Friend, David Hume. By One of the People Called Christians* (4th ed, Oxford, 1784), Dr. Horne, High Church Bishop of Norwich, reproves Adam Smith because in a published letter to Mr. Strahan he "embalmed his friend David" (Hume) because he told the public how "Hume amused himself on his deathbed with Lucian and whist," and because he even had the impudence to write of Hume: "I have always considered him both in his lifetime and since his death, as approaching as nearly to the idea of perfectly wise and virtuous man, as, perhaps, the nature of human frailty will permit." The Bishop cries out angrily: "Is it right in you, sir, to hold up to our view as 'perfectly wise and virtuous' the character and conduct of one who seems to have been possessed with an incurable antipathy to all that is called religion; and who strained every nerve to explode, suppress, and extirpate the spirit of it among men, that its very name, if he could effect it, might no more be had in remembrance?" (Loc. cit, p. 8.) "But let not the lovers of truth be discouraged. Atheism cannot be of long continuance" (p. 17). Adam Smith "had the atrocious wickedness to propagate atheism through the land ... Upon the whole, Doctor, your meaning is good; but I think you will not succeed this time. You would persuade us, by the example of David Hume, Esq., that atheism is the only cordial for low spirits, and the proper antidote against the fear of death ... You may smile over Babylon in ruins and congratulate the hardened Pharaoh on his overthrow in the Red Sea." (Loc. cit, pp. 21-22.) One orthodox individual among A. Smith's college visitors writes after his death: "Smith's well-placed affection for Hume ... hindered him from being a Christian. When he met with honest men whom he liked ... he would believe almost anything they said. Had he been a friend of the worthy ingenious Horrox he would have believed that the moon sometimes disappeared in a clear sky without the interposition of a cloud ... He approached to republicanism in his political principles." (*The Bee*, by James Anderson, 18 vols, Edinburgh, 1791-1793, Vol. 3, pp. 166, 165.) Parson Thomas Chalmers suspects Adam Smith of having invented the category of "unproductive laborers" specifically out of malice against the Protestant parsons, in spite of their blessed work in the vineyard of the Lord.

RELIGION AND THE MONETARY SYSTEM

From *Capital*, Vol. III, Ch. 35, Conclusion

The monetary system is essentially a Catholic institution, the credit system essentially Protestant. "The Scotch hate gold." In the form of paper, the monetary existence of commodities is only a social existence. It is *faith* that brings salvation. Faith in money value as the immanent spirit of commodities, faith in the mode of production and its predestined order, faith in the individual agents of production as mere personifications of self-converting capital. But the credit system does not emancipate itself from the basis of the monetary system any more than Protestantism has emancipated itself from the foundations of Catholicism.

C. JEWS AND JUDAISM

"ON THE JEWISH QUESTION"*

Written in the fall of 1843 and published in *Deutsch-Französische Jahrbücher*, 1844. This article is a review of two books by Marx's friend Bruno Bauer: *Die Judenfrage* ("The Jewish Question," Brunswick, 1843) and *Die Fahigkeit der heutigen Juden und Christen, frei zu werden* ("The Capacity of Today's

---

*Karl Marx on Religion by Saul K. Padover, pp. 169-92. Copyright 1974 Saul K. Padover. Used with permission of McGraw-Hill Book Co.

Jews and Christians to Become Free," Zurich and Winterthur, 1843).

The German Jews desire emancipation. What kind of emancipation do they desire? *Civil, political* emancipation.

Bruno Bauer answers them: Nobody in Germany is politically emancipated. We [Christians] are also unfree. How shall we liberate you? You Jews are egoists when you demand a special emancipation for yourselves as Jews. As Germans, you should work for the political emancipation of Germany; as men, for the emancipation of mankind; and you should feel the particular form of your oppression and your shame not as an exception to the rule but rather as its confirmation.

Or do Jews desire to be put on an equal footing with the Christian subjects? If so, they recognize the Christian state as legitimate, as the regime of general subjection. Why should they be displeased with their special yoke when they are pleased with the general yoke? Why should the German interest himself in the emancipation of the Jew when the Jew does not interest himself in the emancipation of the German?

The Christian state recognizes only *privileges*. In it the Jew has the privilege of being a Jew. As a Jew he has rights that Christians do not have. Why does he desire rights that he does not have and that Christians enjoy?

When the Jew wants to be emancipated from the Christian state, he asks that the Christian state abandon its religious prejudice. Does he, the Jew, abandon *his* religious prejudice? Has he, then, the right to demand of another this abdication of religion?

opposition to the dominant religion. But Jew, too, can be-

By its very nature the Christian state cannot emancipate the Jew; but, Bauer adds, the Jew by his very nature cannot the Jew Jewish, both are equally incapable of giving or receiving emancipation.

The Christian state can behave toward the Jew only in the manner of the Christian state, that is, in a privileged way, in that it permits the separation of the Jew from the rest of the subjects and makes him feel the pressure of other separated spheres all the more heavily, since the Jew stands in religious be emancipated. So long as the state remains Christian and

have toward the state only in a Jewish manner, that is, as an alien, in that he contraposes his chimerical nationality to actual nationality, his illusory law to actual law, imagining himself justified in his separation from humanity, abstaining on principle from participation in historical movement, looking to a future that has nothing in common with the general future of mankind, regarding himself as a member of the Jewish people and the Jewish people as a chosen people.

On what basis, then, do you Jews desire emancipation? Because of your religion? It is the mortal enemy of the religion of the state. As citizens? There are no citizens in Germany. As men? You are not men, any more than those to whom you appeal.

After giving a critique of former positions and solutions, Bauer formulates the question of Jewish emancipation in a new way. What, he asks, is the nature of the Jew who is to be emancipated, and the Christian state which is to emancipate him? He answers with a critique of the Jewish religion, analyzes the religious antagonism between Judaism and Christianity, and explains the essence of the Christian state, all this with dash, acuteness, wit, and thoroughness, in a style as precise as it is meaty and energetic.

How, then, does Bauer solve the Jewish question? What is the result? The formulation of a question is its solution. The critique of the Jewish question is the answer to the Jewish question. The résumé is as follows:

The most persistent form of antagonism between the Jew and the Christian is *religious* antagonism. How does one solve an antagonism? By making it impossible. And how is a religious antagonism made impossible? By *abolishing religion*. As soon as Jew and Christian recognize their respective religions as nothing more than *different stages of evolution of the human spirit,* as different snakeskins shed by history, and recognize *man* as the snake who wore them, they will no longer find themselves in religious antagonism but only in a critical, scientific, and human relationship. *Science* constitutes their unity. Contradictions in science, however, are resolved by science itself.

The German Jew is particularly affected by the lack of political emancipation in general and by the pronounced Christianity of the state. In Bauer's view, however, the Jewish question has a universal significance, independent of specific

German conditions. It is the question of the relation of religion to the state, of the *contradiction between religious bias and political emancipation*. The emancipation from religion is presented as a condition both for the Jew who wants to be politically emancipated and for the state which is to emancipate him and is to be emancipated itself as well. . . .[1]

Bauer thus demands, on the one hand, that the Jew give up Judaism and man in general give up religion, to be emancipated *as a citizen*. On the other hand, he holds that the consequence of the *political* abolition of religion is simply the abolition of religion altogether. The state that makes religion a presupposition is not yet a true or real state.

"The religious view, to be sure, gives the state guarantees. But what state? What kind of state?"

At this point Bauer's one-sided conception of the Jewish question becomes apparent.

It by no means suffices to inquire: Who should emancipate? Who should be emancipated? Criticism has to concern itself was a third question. It must ask: *What kind of emancipation* is involved? What are the underlying conditions of the desired emancipation? Criticism of *political emancipation* itself was at first the final critique of the Jewish question and its true resolution in the "universal question of the age."

Since Bauer does not raise the question to this level, he falls into contradictions. He presents conditions that are not rooted in the essence of political emancipation. He raises questions that are not relevant to his problem, and he solves problems that leave his questions unanswered. When Bauer says of the opponents of Jewish emancipation that "their mistake simply lay in their assuming the Christian state to be the only true state and not subjecting it to the same criticism they applied to Judaism," we find his error to be that he subjects *only* the "Christian state," and not the state in general, to criticism, that he fails to examine the *relation between political emancipation and human emancipation*, and hence he posits conditions that are explainable only by his uncritical confusion of political emancipation with universal human emancipation. While Bauer asks the Jews whether from their standpoint they have the right to demand political emancipation, we on the contrary ask: Has the standpoint of political emancipation the right to demand from the Jews the abolition

[1] Several quotations from Bauer are omitted.

of Judaism and from men in general the abolition of religion altogether?

The Jewish question has a different aspect, varying according to the state in which the Jew finds himself. In Germany, where there is no political state and no state as such exists, the Jewish question is a purely *theological* question. The Jew finds himself in *religious* opposition to a state that acknowledges Christianity as its foundation. This state is theology *ex professo* [by profession]. Criticism is here criticism of theology, a double-edged criticism—critique of Christian and critique of Jewish theology. But however *critical* we may be, we are still moving in the realm of theology.

In France, a constitutional state, the Jewish question is a question of constitutionalism, a question of the incompleteness of political emancipation. As the semblance of a state religion is preserved there—even if only by the meaningless and contradictory formula of a *religion of the majority*—the relation of the Jews to the state also retains the semblance of a religious, theological antithesis.

Only in the free states of North America—at least in one part of them—does the Jewish question lose its theological significance and become a truly *secular* question. Only where the political state exists in its full development can the relation to the political state by the Jew, or the religious man in general, appear in its proper and pure form—that is, the relation of religion to the state. Criticism of this relation ceases to be theological criticism the moment the state abandons a *theological* posture toward religion and relates itself to religion as a state, that is, *politically*. Criticism then becomes *criticism of the political state*. At this point, where the question ceases to be *theological*, Bauer's criticism ceases to be critical.

"In the United States there exists neither a state religion nor a religion declared to be that of the majority, nor a preeminence of one faith over another. The state is foreign to all cults." (Gustave-Auguste de Beaumont, *Marie ou l'esclavage aux États-Unis* [Brussels, 1835].) There are even some North American states where "the constitution does not impose religious beliefs or sectarian practice as a condition of political rights" (op. cit., p. 225). Yet "no one in the United States believes that a man without religion can be an honest man" (op. cit., p. 224).

Nevertheless, North America is preeminently the land of religiosity, as Beaumont, De Tocqueville, and the Englishman

Hamilton assure us unanimously. The North American states, however, serve us only as an example. The question is: What is the relation of *complete* political emancipation to religion? If we find even in a country with complete political emancipation that religion not only exists but is fresh and vital, we have proof that the existence of religion is not incompatible with the full consummation of the state. Since, however, the existence of religion implies a deficiency, the source of this deficiency can be sought only in the nature of the state itself. We no longer take religion to be the *foundation* but only the *manifestation* of secular narrowness. We therefore explain religious prejudice in free citizens as coming from their secular prejudice. We do not claim that they must do away with their religious prejudice to elevate their secular limitations. We do claim that they will eliminate their religious prejudice as soon as they have elevated their secular limitations. We do not convert secular questions into theological ones. We convert theological questions into secular ones. After history has been, for much too long, resolved into superstition, we now resolve superstition into history. The question of the *relation of political emancipation to religion* becomes for us a question of the *relation of political emancipation to human emancipation*. We criticize the religious weakness of the political state by criticizing the political state, apart from its religious weakness, in its secular construction. The contradiction between the state and a particular religion, such as Judaism, we humanly resolve in the contradiction between the state and particular secular elements, and the contradiction between the state and religion in general into the contradiction between the state and its presuppositions in general.

The political emancipation of the Jew, the Christian, the religious man in general, is the *emancipation of the state* from Judaism, from Christianity, from *religion* in general. In a form and manner corresponding to its own nature, the state as such emancipates itself from religion when it emancipates itself from the state religion, that is, when the state as a state recognizes no religion but rather recognizes itself simply as the state. The political emancipation from religion is not the completed and consistent emancipation from religion because political emancipation is not the completed and consistent form of *human* emancipation.

The limits of political emancipation are seen at once in the fact that the state can liberate itself from a limitation without man really being free from it, without the state becoming a free state and man becoming a free man. Bauer himself tacitly admits this when he sets this stipulation for political emancipation:

"Every religious privilege in general, including also the monopoly of a privileged church, must be abolished, and if a few or many or even the overwhelming majority still feel obliged to fulfill their religious obligations, such a practice must be left to them as a purely private matter."

The *state* can thus emancipate itself from religion, even if the *overwhelming majority* is still religious. And the overwhelming majority does not cease to be religious by being religious *in private*.

But the attitude of the state, particularly the free state, to religion is still only the attitude of the *human beings* who make up the state. Hence it follows that man frees himself from a limitation *politically, through the state*, when, in contradiction with himself, he overcomes the limitation in an *abstract, limited,* and partial manner. It follows, furthermore, that when man frees himself *politically*, he does so indirectly, through an *intermediary*, even if the intermediary is necessary. Finally, it follows that man, even when he proclaims himself an atheist through the medium of the state, that is, when he proclaims the state to be atheistic, is still captive to religion because he recognizes his atheism indirectly, through an intermediary. Religion is merely the indirect recognition of man, through a *mediator*. The state is the mediator between man and the freedom of man. As Christ is the mediator on whom man unburdens all his own divinity and his whole *religious burden*, so also the state is the mediator on which man places all his unholiness and his whole *human burden*.

The political elevation of man above religion shares all the defects and all the advantages of political elevation in general. If the state as state, for example, abolishes private property, man proclaims private property is abolished politically as soon as he does away with property qualifications for active and passive voting eligibility, as has been done in many North American states. Hamilton interprets this fact quite correctly from a political point of view: "The great majority of the people have won a victory over property owners and financial wealth." Is not private property abolished in idea when the have-nots come to legislate for the haves? Property qualification is the last political form for recognizing private property.

Nevertheless, the political annulment of private property not only does not abolish private property but even presupposes it. The state abolishes distinctions of *birth, rank, education,* and *occupation* in its own fashion when it declares them to be *nonpolitical*, when it proclaims that every member of the community participates *equally* in popular sovereignty without regard for these distinctions, and when it treats all elements of the actual life of the nation from the standpoint of the state. Nonetheless, the state permits private property, education, and occupation to operate and manifest their particular nature as private property, education, and occupation in their *own* ways. Far from removing the *factual* distinctions, the state does rather exist only by presupposing them, is aware of itself, as a *political state* and makes its universality effective only in opposition to these elements. Hegel therefore correctly defines the relation of the *political state* to religion when he says:

"If the state is to be realized as a self-aware ethical actuality of the spirit, it must be distinct from the form of authority and faith; this distinction, however, emerges only insofar as the ecclesiastical sphere comes to a division within itself; only thus has the state attained universality of thought, the principle of its form, transcending particular churches and bringing it into existence." (Hegel's *Philosophy of Law*, 1st ed., p. 346.)

Exactly! Only thus, by being *above* the *particular* elements, does the state constitute itself as a universality.

In its nature the perfected political state is man's *species life* in contrast to his material life. In civil society all the presuppositions of this egoistic life remain outside the sphere of the state, but as qualities of civil society. Where the political state has reached full development, man leads a double life, a heavenly and an earthly life, not only in thought and consciousness but also in reality, as a *communal being* in the life of the *political community* and as a *private person* in the life of *civil society*, treating other men as means, reducing himself to a means, and becoming the plaything of alien powers. The political state is related spiritually to civil society as heaven is to earth. It stands in the same opposition to civil society and transcends it in the same way religion transcends the limitation of the profane world; that is, by recognizing, restoring, and letting itself be dominated by it. In his innermost essence, in civil society man is a profane being. Here, where he counts as an actual individual to himself and others, he is a fictitious phenomenon. On the other hand, in the state, where man counts as a species being, he is an imaginary member of an imagined sovereignty, stripped of his actual individual life and filled with an unreal universality.

The conflict in which man, as a believer in a particular religion, finds himself with his own citizenship, a member of the community along with other men, reduces itself to a secular split between the political state and the civil society. For man as bourgeois, "life in the state is only a semblance or a momentary exception to the real nature of things and to the general rule." The bourgeois, to be sure, like the Jew, participates in the life of the state only sophistically in the same way the *citoyen* remains only sophistically a Jew or bourgeois; but this sophistry is not personal. It is the sophistry of the political state itself. The difference between the religious person and the citizen is the difference between the shopkeeper and the citizen, between the day laborer and the citizen, between the landowner and the citizen, between the *living individual* and the *citizen*. The contradiction between the religious person and the political person is the same as that between the bourgeoisie and the *citoyen*, between the member of civil society and his political lion skin.

This secular conflict, to which the Jewish question ultimately reduces itself—the relation between the political state and its presuppositions, whether the latter be material elements, such as private property, etc., or spiritual elements, such as education and religion, the conflict between the *general* interest and the *private* interest, the split between the *political state* and the *civil society*—these secular contradictions are untouched by Bauer, while he polemicizes against their *religious* expression.

"It is precisely its basis, its necessity, that assures the maintenance of civil society and guarantees its necessity, that exposes its maintenance to constant dangers, sustains in it an element of uncertainty, and produces in civil society a constantly alternating mixture of poverty and riches, misery and prosperity, and change in general."

Consider his entire section, "Civil Society," which is constructed along the main lines of Hegel's philosophy of law. Civil society in its opposition to the political state is recognized as necessary because the political state is recognized as necessary.

Political emancipation is indeed a great step forward; it is not, to be sure, the final form of human emancipation in general, but it is the final form of human emancipation *within* the prevailing world order. It goes without saying that we are here speaking of actual, practical emancipation.

Man emancipates himself politically from religion in that he banishes it from the sphere of public law into private right. It is no longer the spirit of the state, where man—even if in a limited fashion, in a particular form and in a particular sphere—associates as a species being in community with other men; it has become the spirit of civil society, the sphere of egoism, the *bellum omnia contra omnes* [war of all against all]. It is no longer the essence of *community* but the essence of *division*. It has become an expression of *separation* of man from his *community*, from himself and other men— as it was originally. It is now only the abstract acknowledgment of particular perversity, of private whim, of caprice. The endless splits of religion in North America, for example, already give it the external form of a purely individual matter. It has been thrown among numerous private interests and exiled from the commonwealth as a community. But one must not be deceived about the scope of political emancipation. The division of man into *public* and *private persons*, the displacement of religion from the state into civil society, is not merely a step in political emancipation but its *fulfillment*, which abolishes man's actual religiosity as little as it seeks to abolish it.

The breaking up of human beings into Jew and citizen, into Protestant and citizen, into religious man and citizen— this splintering is not a lie *against* citizenship or a circumvention of political emancipation; it is *political emancipation itself*, the political mode of emancipation from religion. To be sure, in periods when the political state as such is forcibly born from civil society, when men strive to liberate themselves under the form of political self-liberation, the state can and must go so far as to *abolish* religion to the point of *destroying* it, but only in the way it abolishes private property by setting a maximum, by confiscation, by progressive taxation, or only in the way it abolishes life by the guillotine. In moments of special concern for itself, political life seeks to repress its presuppositions, civil society and its elements, and to constitute itself as the actual, consistent life species of man. But it can do that only in violent contradiction to its own life conditions by declaring the revolution to be *permanent*, and this the political drama is bound to end with the restoration of religion, private property, and all elements of civil society, just as war ends with peace.

Indeed, the perfected Christian state is not the so-called Christian state professing Christianity as its foundation, as its state religion that excludes all others; it is, rather, the *atheistic* state, the *democratic* state, the state that classifies religion as among the other elements of civil society. The state that is still theological and still officially prescribes belief in Christianity has not yet dared to proclaim itself *as a state* and has not yet succeeded in expressing in secular and human form, in its *actuality* as a state, the *human* foundation whose supreme expression is Christianity. The so-called Christian state is simply only a *nonstate*, for it is not Christianity as a religion but only the *human background* of the Christian religion that can realize itself in actual human creations.

The so-called Christian state is the Christian denial of the state, but in no way the political actualization of Christianity. The state that still professes Christianity in the form of religion does not profess it in political form because it still behaves religiously toward religion, that is, it is not the *actual expression* of the human basis of religion because it still provokes the unreality and the imaginary form of this human core. The so-called Christian state is an *imperfect* state, and the Christian religion serves as supplement and as sanctification of its imperfection. Religion, therefore, becomes necessarily its means to an end, and the state is a hypocrite. There is a great difference between a perfected state that counts religion as one of its prerequisites because of a lack in the general nature of the state, and an imperfect state which, in its particular existence and deficiency, proclaims religion as its foundation. In the latter cases, religion becomes *imperfect politics*. In the former case, the imperfection of even perfected politics is revealed in religion. The so-called Christian state needs the Christian religion to complete itself *as a state*. The democratic state, the real state, needs no religion for its political fulfillment. It can, rather, divorce itself from religion because in it is fulfilled the human basis of religion in a secular way. The so-called Christian state, on the other hand, behaves politically toward religion and religiously toward

Religion

politics. As it reduces political forms to mere appearance, so also does it reduce religion to a mere appearance.

To elucidate this contradiction, let us consider Bauer's construct of the Christian state, a construct that derives from his view of the Christian-Germanic state. . . .[2]

Bauer goes on to show how the people of a Christian state constitute a non-nation; they have no will of their own, but have, rather, their true existence in their ruler, to whom they are subject but who, however, is alien to them by origin and nature, that is, given to them by God without their own consent; furthermore, the laws of this people are not their own doing but are positive revelations. Bauer shows how the supreme ruler requires privileged mediators with his own people, the masses; how the masses themselves split into a multitude of distinct spheres formed and determined by chance, and differentiated from each other by their interests, particular passions and prejudices, but given the privilege of isolating themselves from each other.

But Bauer himself says: "Politics, if it is to be nothing more than religion, cannot be politics any more than cleaning cooking pans, if it is to be treated religiously, can be regarded as an economic matter."

In the Christian-Germanic state, however, religion is an "economic matter," just as an "economic matter" is religion. In the Christian-Germanic state the dominance of religion is the religion of domination.

The separation of the "spirit of the Gospel" from the "letter of the Gospel" is an *irreligious* act. The state that permits the Gospel to speak in the words of politics or in any other words than those of the Holy Spirit commits a sacrilege, if not in the eyes of men at least in the eyes of its own religion. The state that acknowledges Christianity as its highest rule and the Bible as its charter must be confronted with the words of Holy Writ, for the Writ is holy in every word. This state, as well as the human rubbish on which it is based, falls into a painful and, from the standpoint of religious consciousness, insoluble contradiction, in the light of the teaching of the Gospel, which "it not only does not follow, but also cannot do so unless it wants to dissolve itself completely as a state." And why does it not want to dissolve itself completely? It cannot answer this question either for itself or for others. In

[2] A quotation from Bauer is omitted.

its own consciousness, the official Christian state is an *ought* whose realization is unattainable, which knows how to legitimize the actuality of its existence only by lying, and hence always remains a subject of doubt, unreliable and problematic. Criticism is thus completely right in forcing the state bases on the Bible into a mental derangement in which it no longer knows itself whether it is illusion or reality, in which the infamy of its secular purposes, for which religion serves as its cloak, irreconcilably conflicts with the integrity of its religious consciousness, to which religion appears as the purpose of the world. Such a state can free itself from its inner torment only by becoming the myrmidon of the Catholic Church. In the face of that church, which claims secular power as its servant, the state, the secular power claiming domination over the religious spirit, is impotent.

In the so-called Christian church, what counts, indeed, is *alienation*, but not *man*. The only man who does count, the *king*, is a being who is specifically differentiated from other men, who is personally religious and directly connected with heaven, with God. The relations prevailing here are still *religious* relations. The religious spirit is still not yet secularized.

But the religious spirit cannot actually be secularized, for what is it, in fact, but the *unsecular* form of a stage in the evolution of the human spirit? The religious spirit can be actualized only if the stage of evolution of the human spirit, whose religious expression it is, emerges into and assumes its *secular* form. This is what occurs in the democratic state. The basis of the democratic state is not Christianity but the human basis of Christianity. Religion remains the ideal, unsecular consciousness of its members, because it is the ideal form of the stage of human development fulfilled in the democratic state.

The members of the political state are religious because of the dualism between individual life and the life of the species, between the life of civil society and political life; they are religious inasmuch as man regards his true life as the political life remote from his actual individuality; they are religious inasmuch as religion is here the spirit of civil society, the expression of separation and alienation of man from man. Political democracy is Christian in that it regards man—not merely one man but every man—as *sovereign*, as the highest being; but this means that in his uncivilized and unsocial aspect, in his fortuitous existence, and just as he is, corrupted by the entire organization of our society, lost to himself, alienated, oppressed by the domination of inhuman relations and elements—in a word, man who is not yet an *actual* species being. The sovereignty of man, although an alien being distinct from actual men, which is the chimera, the dream, and the postulate of Christianity, is a tangible and present reality, a secular maxim, in democracy.

In the perfected democracy, the religious and theological consciousness appears to itself all the more religious and theological for being seemingly without political significance or earthly purposes, secluded from the world—an expression of reason's limitation, a product of caprice and fantasy, an actual life in the beyond. Christianity here achieves the *practical* expression of its universal religious significance in that the most varied views are grouped together as a form of Christianity, the more so since the state does not require anyone to profess Christianity, or any other religion in general. (See Beaumont, op. cit.) [In a democracy] the religious consciousness revels in the wealth of religious contradictions and multiplicity.

We have thus shown: Political emancipation from religion permits religion, although not a privileged religion, to continue. The contradiction in which the adherent of a particular religion finds himself in relation to his citizenship is only *one aspect* of the universal *secular contradiction between the political state and civil society*. The fulfillment of the Christian state is a state that acknowledges itself as a state and ignores the religion of its members. The emancipation of the state from religion is not the emancipation of actual man from religion.

We thus do not say with Bauer to the Jews: You cannot be politically emancipated without radically emancipating yourselves from Judaism. Rather we tell them: Because you can be politically emancipated without completely and consistently renouncing Judaism, *political emancipation* itself is not thereby *human* emancipation. If you Jews want to be politically emancipated without emancipating yourselves humanly, the incompleteness and contradiction lies not only in you but in the *essence* and *category* of political emancipation. If you are encompassed in this category, you share a general bias. Just as the state *evangelizes* when, in spite of being a state, it behaves toward the Jew in a Christian way, so the Jew *politicizes* when, in spite of being a Jew, he demands civil rights.

But if man, even if he is a Jew, wants to be politically emancipated and acquire civil rights, can he claim and acquire the so-called rights of man? Bauer denies it. . . .[3]

According to Bauer, man must sacrifice the "privilege of faith" to be able to acquire the universal rights of man. Let us for a moment consider these so-called rights of man, and particularly those rights in their most authentic form, the form they have among their discoverers, the North Americans and the French. In part, those rights are *political* that can be exercised only in community with others. Participation in the community, and particularly in the *political* community, the *state*, constitutes their substance. They belong in the category of political freedom, of civil rights, which, as we have seen, by no means presupposes the consistent and positive abolition of religion, including Judaism. There remains now for consideration the other part, the rights of man insofar as they are distinct from the rights of the citizen.

Among these one finds freedom of conscience, the right to practice one's chosen religion. The *privilege of faith* is expressly recognized either as a right of man or as a consequence of a right of man, freedom. . . .[4]

The incompatibility of religion with the rights of man is so little implied in the concept of the rights of man that the right to be religious according to one's liking, and to practice one's own particular religion, is explicitly included among the rights of man. The privilege of religion is a universal human right.

The rights of man as such are distinguished from the rights of the citizen, from civil rights. Who is this *man* distinguished from the *citizen*? None other than the *member of civil society*. Why is the member of civil society called "man," simply man, and why are his rights called the rights of man? How can we explain this fact? By the relation of the political state to civil society and by the nature of political emancipation.

First of all, let us note that the so-called rights of man as distinguished from the rights of the citizen are only the rights of a member of civil society, that is, of egoistic man, man separated from other men and from the community. The

---

[3] A quotation from Bauer is omitted.
[4] Quotations from the French *Declaration of the Rights of Man* and from some American state constitutions are omitted.

most radical constitution, the [French] Constitution of 1793, may be quoted:

Declaration of the Rights of Man and of the Citizen. Article 2. "These rights, etc." (the natural and imprescriptible rights) "are: equality, liberty, security, property."

What is this *liberty?*

Article 6. "Liberty is the power belonging to each man to do anything which does not impair the rights of others," or, according to the *Declaration of the Rights of Man* of 1791: "Liberty consists of the power to do anything which does not harm others."

Liberty is thus the right to do and perform anything that does not harm others. The limit within which each can act without harming others is determined by law just as the boundary between two fields is marked by a stake. What is involved here is the liberty of man as an isolated monad, withdrawn into himself. Why, according to Bauer, is the Jew not capable of aquiring human rights? "So long as he remains a Jew, the limited nature which makes him a Jew must triumph over the human nature which should link him as a man with other men and most separate him from non-Jews."

But liberty as a right of man is not based on the association of man with man, but rather on the separation of man from man. It is the *right* of this separation, the *right* of the *limited* individual, limited to himself.

The practical application of the right of liberty is the right of *private property.*

Of what does the right of private property consist? Article 16 (Constitution of 1793): "The right of property is that belonging to every citizen to enjoy and dispose of his goods, his revenues, the fruit of his labor and of his industry, as he wills."

The right of private property is thus the right to enjoy and dispose of one's possessions as one wills, without regard for other men and independently of society. Individual freedom, as well as its application, constitutes the foundation of civil society. It lets every man find in other men not the *realization* but rather the *limitation* of his own freedom. It proclaims above all the right of man "to enjoy and dispose of his goods, his revenues, the fruit of his labor and of his industry, *as he wills.*"

There still remain the other rights of man, equality and security.

Equality, here used in its nonpolitical sense, is nothing but the equality of the above-mentioned liberty, namely: that every man is equally viewed as a self-sufficient monad. The Constitution of 1795 defines the concept of equality, according to its significance, as follows:

Article 3: "Equality consists in the fact that the law is the same for all, whether it protects or whether it punishes."

And security?

Article 8 (Constitution of 1793): "Security consists in the protection accorded by society to each of its members for the preservation of his person, his rights and his property."

Security is the supreme concept of civil society, the concept of the police, the concept that the whole society exists only to guarantee to each of its members the preservation of his person, his rights, and his property. In this sense, Hegel calls civil society "the state of necessity and rationality."

Civil society does not raise itself above its own egoism through the concept of security. Rather, security is the *guarantee* of egoism.

Thus none of the so-called rights of man goes beyond egoistic man, man withdrawn into himself, his private interest and his private choice, and separated from the community as a member of civil society. Far from viewing man here in his species being, his species being itself, society, appears rather to be an external framework for the individual, as a limitation of its original independence. The only bond that unites men is natural necessity, need, and private interest, the maintenance of their property and their egoistic persons.

It is quite curious that a nation just beginning to liberate itself, to tear down all barriers among the various members, and to build a political community, should solemnly proclaim (Declaration of 1791) the justification of the egoistic man, separated from his fellow men and from the community, and should even repeat this proclamation at a moment when only the most heroic sacrifice, which is urgently required, can save the nation, when the sacrifice of all the interests of civil society is made the order of the day and egoism has to be punished as a crime (*Declaration of the Rights of Man* of 1793). This becomes even more curious when we observe how the political liberators reduce citizenship, the *political community*, to a mere *means* for the preservation of these so-called rights of man and that the citizen is thus declared to be the servant of the egoistic man, the sphere in which man acts as a member of the community is degraded below that in which he acts as a fractional being, and finally man as bourgeois rather than man as citizen is considered to be the *proper* and *authentic* man.

"The goal of all political association is the preservation of the natural and imprescriptible rights of man" (*Declaration of the Rights of Man*, 1791, Article 2). "Government is instituted to guarantee man's enjoyment of his natural and imprescriptible rights" (*Declaration*, etc., of 1793, Article 1).

Thus even at the moment of its youthful enthusiasm, fired by the urgency of circumstances, political life is proclaimed to be a mere *means* whose goal is life in civil society. Revolutionary practice, to be sure, stands in flagrant contradiction to its theory. While security, for example, is proclaimed to be one of the rights of man, the violation of the privacy of the mails is publicly established as the order of the day. While the "*unlimited* freedom of the press" (Constitution of 1793, Article 122) as a consequence of the rights of man and individual freedom is guaranteed, freedom of the press is completely destroyed because "freedom of the press should not be permitted if it compromises public liberty" (Robespierre *jeune*, in *Parliamentary History of the French Revolution*, by Buchez and Roux, Vol. 28, p. 159). This means, therefore, that the human right of liberty ceases to be a right when it comes into conflict with political life, while theoretically political life is only the guarantee of the rights of man, the rights of individual men, and should be abandoned once it contradicts its *goal*, which is the rights of man. But the practice is only the exception, and the theory is the rule. Even if we choose to regard revolutionary practice as the correct expression of this relationship, the puzzle is still to be solved as to why, in the consciousness of the political emancipators, the relationship is turned upside down and the end appears as the means, and the means as the end. This optical illusion of their consciousness would always remain the same puzzle, even though a psychological and theoretical puzzle.

The enigma is easily solved.

Political emancipation is at the same time the *dissolution* of the old society on which rests the sovereign power, the state as alienated from the people. The political revolution is the revolution of civil society. What was the character of the old society? One word characterizes it: *Feudalism*. The old civil society had a *directly political* character—that is, the elements of civil life, such as property, for example, the family, or the mode and manner of work, were raised into elements of political life in the form of landlordism, estates, and corporations. In this form they determined the relationship of the particular individual to the *state as a whole*, that is, his political relationship, his separation and exclusion from other parts of society. For the feudal organization of national life had not raised ownership and labor to the level of social elements, but rather completed their separation from the state as a whole and established them as separate societies within society. Thus the life functions and life conditions of civil society always remained political, even if political in the feudal sense, that is, they excluded the individual from the state as a whole and transformed the special relationship between his corporation and the state into his own general relationship to national life, just as they transformed his specific civil activity and situation into a general activity and situation. As a consequence of this organization, there necessarily appears the unity of the state, as well as its consciousness, will, and activity—the general political power—likewise as the special business of the ruler and his servants, separated from the people.

The political revolution, which overthrew this domination and raised political affairs into people's affairs, and made the political state *everybody's* business—that is, an actual state—necessarily destroyed all estates, corporations, guilds, and privileges which had been the various expressions of the separation of the people from their community. The political revolution thereby abolished the political character of civil society. It shattered civil society into its constituent parts, on the one hand *individuals* and on the other the *material* and *spiritual elements* which constituted the vital contents and civil situation of these individuals. It released the political spirit, which had been broken, fragmented, and lost, as it were, in various cul-de-sacs of feudal society; it gathered up this scattered spirit, liberated it from its entanglements with civil life, and turned it into the sphere of the community, the general concern of the people ideally independent of these particular elements of civil life. A definite activity and situation in life now sank to a merely individual signficance.

These no longer partook of the general relationship of the individual to the state as a whole. Public affairs as such became, rather, the general affairs of every individual and the political function became his general function.

But the fulfillment of the idealism of the state was at the same time the fulfillment of the materialism of civil society. The casting off of the political yoke was at the same time the casting off of the bond that had kept the egoistic spirit of civil society in fetters. Political emancipation was at the same time the emancipation of civil society from politics, from the very *semblance* of apolitical content.

Feudal society was dissolved into its foundation, into *man*. But into man as he actually was as its foundation, into *egoistical* man.

This man, the member of civil society, is now the basis and presupposition of the political state. He is recognized by it as such in the rights of man.

But the freedom of egoistic man and the recognition of this freedom is rather the recognition of the unbridled movement of the spiritual and material elements which form his life's content.

Thus man was not freed from religion; he received religious freedom. He was not freed by property. He received freedom of property. He was not freed by the egoism of occupation, but received freedom of occupation.

The constitution of the political state and the dissolution of civil society into independent individuals—whose relations are law just as the relations of estates and guilds were privilege—is accomplished in *one and the same act*. As a member of civil society, man is nonpolitical man but necessarily appears to be natural man. The rights of man appear as natural rights because self-conscious activity is concentrated in the political act. Egoistic man is the passive and preexisting result of the dissolved society, an object of immediate certainty, hence a *natural* object. The political revolution dissolves civil life into its constituent elements without revolutionizing those elements or subjecting them to criticism. It regards civil society—the world of needs, labor, private interests, private rights—as the basis of its existence, as a presupposition that needs no further ground, and hence as its *natural* basis. Finally, man, as a member of civil society, is regarded as *authentic man*, man as distinct from *citizen*, because he is man in his sensuous, individual, and most intimate existence, while political man is only the abstract and artificial man, man as an allegorical, moral person. Actual man is recognized only in the form of an egoistic individual; authentic man only in the form of abstract citizen.

The abstraction of the political man is correctly depicted by Rousseau: "Whoever dares to undertake the construction of a nation must feel himself capable of changing, so to speak, human nature and transforming each individual, who is himself a complete but isolated whole, into a part greater than himself from which he somehow derives his life existence, substituting a partial and moral existence for physical and independent existence. It is necessary to deprive man of his own powers and to give him alien powers which he cannot use without the aid of others." (*Social Contract*, Book II, London, 1782, p. 67.)

All emancipation is *restoration* of the human world and of the relationships of *men themselves*.

Political emancipation is the reduction of man to a member of civil society, to an egoistic, independent individual on the one hand, and to a citizen, a moral person, on the other.

Only when the actual, individual man has taken back into himself the abstract citizen and in his everyday life, his individual work, and his individual relationships has become a *species being*—only when he has recognized and organized his own powers as *social* powers so that social force is no longer separated from him in the form of *political* power, only then is human emancipation complete.

II

Here Bauer deals with the relation between the Jewish and Christian religions and their relation to criticism. Their relation to criticism is their relation to "the capacity to become free."

Thus: "The Christian has only one stage to surmount, namely, his religion, in order to abandon religion in general" and thus become free; "the Jew, on the other hand, has to break not only with his Jewish nature but also with the development of the completion of his religion, a development that has remained alien to him".

Thus Bauer transforms the question of Jewish emancipation into a purely religious one. The theological scruple as to whether Jew or Christian has the better prospect of salvation

Religion

is here reproduced in the enlightened form: Which of the two is *more capable of emancipation?* Thus the question is no longer: Does Judaism or Christianity emancipate? But, on the contrary: What makes more free, the negation of Judaism or the negation of Christianity?

"If they want to be free, the Jews should not embrace Christianity but Christianity in dissolution and religion generally in dissolution, that is, enlightenment, criticism [of religion] and its results, free humanity".

For the Jew, what is still involved here is *professing a faith,* not Christianity, but rather Christianity in dissolution.

Bauer demands that the Jew break with the essence of the Christian religion, a demand which, as he says himself, does not follow from the development of the Jewish essence.

When Bauer, at the end of his *Jewish Question,* interpreted Judaism merely as a crude religious criticism of Christianity and hence gave it "only" a religious significance, it was to be expected that he would also transform the emancipation of the Jews into a philosophical-theological act.

Bauer conceives the *ideal* abstract essence of the Jew, his *religion,* as his *whole* nature. Hence he correctly concludes: "The Jew contributes nothing to mankind if he disregards his narrow law," if he eliminates all his Judaism.

The relation of Jews and Christians thus becomes the following: The sole interest of the Christian in the emancipation of the Jew is a general human interest, a *theoretical* interest. Judaism is an offensive fact to the religious eye of the Christian. As soon as the Christian's eye ceases to be religious, this fact ceases to be offensive. In and for itself, the emancipation of the Jew is not the business of the Christian.

The Jew, on the other hand, in order to emancipate himself, not only has to do his own work but also at the same time to go through the work of the Christian—the *Critique of the Synoptics* [by Bruno Bauer] and the *Life of Jesus* [by David Friedrich Strauss]. "They can look after themselves: they will determine their own destiny; but history does not allow itself to be mocked."

We will try to break the theological formulation of the question. The question concerning the Jew's capacity for emancipation becomes for us the question: What particular *social* element is to be overcome in order to abolish Judaism? For the modern Jew's capacity for emancipation is the relation of Judaism to the emancipation of the modern world. This relation follows necessarily from the particular position of Judaism in today's enslaved world.

Let us consider the actual, secular Jew; not the *Sabbath Jew*, as Bauer does, but the *everyday Jew*.

Let us not look for the secret of the Jew in his religion, but let us look for the secret of religion in the actual Jew.

What is the secular basis of Judaism? Practical need, self-interest.

What is the worldly cult of the Jew? Haggling. What is his worldly god? Money.

Very well! Emancipation from haggling and money, and thus, from practical and real Judaism, would be the self-emancipation of our age.

An organization of society which would abolish the preconditions of haggling and thus its opportunity for existence would render the Jew impossible. His religious consciousness would dissolve like stale smoke in the actual life-giving air of society. On the other hand, when the Jew recognizes this practical nature of his as invalid and strives to eliminate it, he simply works away from his previous development toward general *human emancipation* and turns against the highest practical expression of human self-alienation.

Thus we perceive in Judaism a general contemporary antisocial element, which has been carried to its present apex by a historical development to which the Jews have zealously contributed—an apex at which it must necessarily dissolve itself.

The emancipation of the Jews, in the final analysis, is the emancipation of mankind from *Judaism*.

The Jew has already emancipated himself in a Jewish way. "The Jew who is only tolerated in Vienna, for example, determines the fate of the whole empire through his financial power. The Jew, who may be without rights in the smallest German state, decides the destiny of Europe. While corporations and guilds exclude the Jew or are unfavorable to him, audacity in industry mocks the obstinacy of these medieval institutions." (B. Bauer, *The Jewish Question*, p. 114.)

This is no isolated fact. The Jew has emancipated himself in a Jewish way not only by acquiring financial power but also because, with and without him, *money* has become a world power, and the practical Jewish spirit has become the practical spirit of Christian nations. The Jews have emancipated themselves insofar as the Christians have become Jews.

"The pious and politically free inhabitant of New England," Colonel Hamilton, for example, reports, "is a kind of Laocoön who does not even make the slightest effort to free himself from the serpents which strangle him. Mammon is his idol to whom he prays not only with his lips but with all the power of his body and soul. In his eyes, the world is nothing but a stock exchange, and he is convinced that here below he has no other destiny than to become richer than his neighbors. Haggling dominates his every thought, exchange of things constitutes his only recreation. When he travels, he carries, so to speak, his shop or office on his back and talks of nothing but interest and profit. If he loses sight of his own business for a moment, it is only in order to sniff out that of others."

Yes, the practical domination of Judaism over the Christian world in North America has achieved such clear and common expression that the very *preaching of the Gospel,* the Christian ministry, has become an article of commerce and the bankrupt merchant takes to the Gospel while the minister who has become rich goes into business.

"That man whom you see at the head of a respectable congregation began as a merchant; his business having failed, he became a minister; the other one started with the ministry, but as soon as he had acquired a sum of money, he left the pulpit for business. In the eyes of many, the religious ministry is a true commercial career" (Beaumont, op. cit., pp. 185, 186).

According to Bauer, it is "a hypocritical situation when the Jew is deprived of political rights in theory while he wields enormous power in practice and exercises his political influence wholesale which is denied to him in retail" (*The Jewish Question,* p. 114).

The contradiction existing between the practical political power of the Jew and his political rights is the contradiction between politics and financial power in general. While the former is ideally superior to the latter, in actual fact it has become its serf.

Judaism has persisted alongside Christianity not only as the religious critique of Christianity, not only as the incorporated doubt about the religious origin of Christianity, but equally because the practical Jewish spirit, Judaism, has perpetuated itself in Christian society and even attained its highest development there. The Jew, who exists as a special member of civil society, is only the special manifestation of civil society's Judaism.

Judaism has survived not in spite of history but by means of history.

Out of its own entrails, civil society constantly produces the Jew.

What, actually was the foundation, in and of itself, of the Jewish religion? Practical need, egoism.

Hence the Jew's monotheism is in reality the polytheism of many needs, a polytheism that makes even the toilet an object of divine law. *Practical need, egoism* is the principle of *civil society* and appears purely as such as soon as civil society has fully delivered itself of the political state. The god of *practical need and self-interest* is *Money*.

Money is the jealous god of Israel before whom no other god may exist. Money degrades all the gods of mankind—and converts them into commodities. Money is the universal, self-sufficient *value* of all things. Hence it has robbed the whole world, the human world as well as nature, of its proper worth. Money is the alienated essence of man's labor and life, and this alien essence dominates him as he worships it.

The god of the Jews has been secularized and has become the god of the world. The bill of exchange is the actual god of the Jew. His god is only an illusory bill of exchange.

The view of nature achieved under the rule of private property and money is an actual contempt for and practical degradation of nature, which, to be sure, does exist in the Jewish religion but only in imagination.

In this sense, Thomas Muenzer declared it to be intolerable "that every creature should be turned into property, the fish in the water, the birds in the air, the plants on the earth—the creature must also become free."[5]

[5] Quoted from Thomas Muenzer's anti-Luther pamphlet, *Hoch verursachte Schutzrede und Antwort wider das geistlose, sanftlebende Fleisch zu Wittenberg, welches mit verkehrter Weise durch den Diebstahl der heiligen Schrift die erbaermliche Christenheit also ganz jaemmerlich besudelt bat* ("Highly Motivated Defense Speech and Reply Against the Insipid Soft-living Flesh at Wittenberg, Which in a Topsy-Turvy Way, Through the Theft of Holy

What is contained abstractly in the Jewish religion—contempt for theory, for art, for history, for man as an end in himself—is the *actual conscious* standpoint and virtue of the money-man. The species relation itself, the relation between man and woman, etc., becomes an object of commerce! The woman is haggled away.

The chimerical nationality of the Jew is the nationality of the merchant, of the money-man in general.

The Jew's unfathomable and unbounded law is only the religious caricature of baseless and bottomless morality and law in general, the caricature of merely *formal* rites with which the world of self-interest surrounds itself.

Here, too, the highest relation of man is the *legal* relation, the relation to laws which apply to him not because they are laws of his will and nature, but because they are in force and because defection from them will be avenged.

Jewish Jesuitism, the same practical Jesuitism that Bauer finds in the Talmud, is the relationship of the world of self-interest to the laws governing it, whose cunning is the chief art of that world.

Yes, the movement of that world within its laws is necessarily an abrogation of the law.

Judaism could not develop further as religion, could not develop further theoretically, because the perspective of practical need is limited by its very nature and is soon exhausted.

By its very nature, the religion of practical need could not find fulfillment in theory but only in practice, precisely because practice is its truth.

Judaism could create no new world; it could only draw world creations and world conditions into the compass of its own activity because practical need, whose rationale is self-interest, remains passive and does not extend itself willingly but only finds itself extended by the continuous development of social conditions.

Judaism reaches its apex with the perfection of civil society; but civil society achieves perfection only in the Christian world. Only under the reign of Christianity, which makes all national, natural, moral, and theoretical relationships *external* to man, could civil society separate itself completely from po-

---

Scriptures, Has Quite Miserably Befouled Wretched Christianity," 1524).

litical life, sever all man's species ties, substitute egoism and selfish need for those ties, and dissolve the human world into a world of atomistic individuals confronting each other in mutual hostility.

Christianity arose out of Judaism. It has again dissolved itself into Judaism.

From the beginning, the Christian was the theorizing Jew; the Jew is, therefore, the practical Christian, and the practical Christian has again become a Jew.

Christianity overcame real Judaism only in appearance. It was too *noble*, too spiritual, to eliminate the crudeness of practical need except by elevating it into the heavens.

Christianity is the sublime thought of Judaism, and Judaism is the common practical application of Christianity; but this application could become universal only after Christianity as the completed religion had *theoretically* completed the alienation of man from himself and from nature.

Only then could Judaism attain universal dominion and convert divested man and divested nature into *alienable* and salable objects subservient to egotistic need, dependent on haggling.

Selling is the practice of alienation [of property]. As long as man is religiously captivated, knows his nature only as objectified, and thus makes it into an alien, illusory being, so under the dominion of egoistic need he can only act practically, only produce objects practically, by subordinating his products, as well as his activity, to the domination of an alien being, bestowing upon it the significance of an alien being—Money.

The Christian salvation-egoism in its practical fulfillment necessarily becomes the material egoism of the Jew, heavenly need is converted into earthly need, subjectivism into self-interest. We do not explain the Jew's tenacity from his religion but rather from the human basis of his religion, from practical need, from egoism.

Since the Jew's real nature has been generally actualized and secularized in civil society, civil society could not convince the Jew of the unreality of his religious nature, which is precisely the ideal perception of practical need. Hence not only in the Pentateuch or the Talmud but also in present society do we find the nature of the contemporary Jew, not as an abstract being but also as a highly empirical one, not only as the Jew's own narrowness but also as the Jewish narrowness of society.

As soon as society succeeds in abolishing the empirical esence of Judaism—haggling and its presuppositions—the Jew becomes impossible, because his consciousness no longer has an object, because the subjective basis of Judaism—practical need—is humanized, because the conflict between individual-sensuous existence and man's species existence is abolished.

The *social* emancipation of the Jew is the *emancipation of society from Judaism.*

CHAPTER X
SCIENCE AND TECHNOLOGY

Note

From the time that Marx wrote his doctoral dissertation, in 1841, until the end of his life, his interest in natural science never ceased. The dissertation dealt with the "natural philosophy" of the classic Greek thinkers Democritus and Epicurus, particularly with the theory of the atoms. Thenceforth he kept abreast with the growth and expansion of the natural sciences. As early as 1856, in a speech in London, he stated that the real nineteenth-century revolutionary forces were not the firebrand orators inciting to rebellion, but steam and electricity.

As can be seen from the selections in this chapter, Marx's range of scientific interest and knowledge included astronomy, electricity, mathematics, and physics. In his own library he had several dozen books, which he annotated, on scientific agriculture, chemistry and statistics. He read widely in scientific anthropology. When Charles Darwin's *On the Origin of Species* came out in 1859, Marx was one of the first to hail it as a confirmation of his own theories of materialism.

Marx had a special interest in and talent for higher mathematics. When beset by illnesses and worries, he found refuge in algebra and infinitesimal calculus. In the last years of his life he was preparing a book on higher mathematics.

Technology held a particular fascination for him. In preparation for *Capital*, he went to great lengths to study machinery and its significance in industry, often consulting his friend Frederick Engels, a manufacturer, about technical details. Machinery, he remarked, was "gifted with the wonderful power of shortening and fructifying human labor." As he wrote in *Capital* (Vol.I, Ch.15, Sec.1, fn.13), technology was man's way of dealing with nature, causing basic transformations in production and social relations.

SCIENCE: THE REAL NINETEENTH CENTURY REVOLUTION

Speech at a Chartist banquet, April 14, 1856; published in the Chartist weekly, The People's Paper, *April 19, 1856. Marx gave this "little speech in English," as he informed Engels (April 16, 1856).*

The so-called revolutions of 1848 were but poor incidents—small fractures and fissures in the dry crust of European society. However, they revealed the abyss. Beneath the apparently solid surface they betrayed oceans of liquid matter, only needing expansion to rend into fragments continents of hard rock. Noisily and confusedly they proclaimed the emancipation of the proletariat, *i.e.*, the secret of the nineteenth century, and of the revolution of that century. That social revolution, it is true, was no novelty invented in 1848. Steam, electricity, and the self-acting mule were revolutionists of a rather more dangerous character than even citizens Barbès, Raspail, and Blanqui. But although the atmosphere in which we live weighs upon everyone with a 20,000-pound force, do you feel it? No more than European society before 1848 felt the revolutionary atmosphere enveloping and pressing it from all sides. There is one great fact, characteristic of this our nineteenth century, a fact which no party dares deny. On the one hand, there have started into life industrial and scientific forces which no epoch of former human history had ever suspected. On the other hand, there exist symptoms of decay far surpassing the horrors recorded of the latter times of the Roman Empire. In our days everything seems pregnant with its contrary. Machinery, gifted with the wonderful power of shortening and fructifying human labor, we behold starving and overworking it. The newfangled sources of wealth, by some strange weird spell, are turned into sources of want. The victories of art seem bought by the loss of character. At the same pace that mankind masters nature, man seems to become enslaved to other men or to his own infamy. Even the pure light of science seems unable to shine but on the dark background of ignorance. All our invention and progress seem to result in endowing material forces with intellectual life, and in stultifying human life into a material force. This antagonism between modern industry and science on the one hand, modern misery and dissolution on the other hand; this antagonism between the productive powers and the social relations of our epoch is a fact, palpable, overwhelming, and not to be controverted. Some parties may wail over it; others may wish to get rid of modern arts, in order to get rid of modern conflicts. Or they may imagine that so signal a progress in industry wants to be completed by as signal a regress in politics. On our part, we do not mistake the shape of the shrewd spirit that continues to mark all these contradictions. We know that to work well the newfangled forces of society, they only want to be mastered by newfangled men—and such are the workingmen. They are as much the invention of modern time as machinery itself. In the signs that bewilder the middle class, the aristocracy, and the poor prophets of regression, we do recognize our brave friend Robin Goodfellow,[1] the old mole that can work in the earth so fast, that worthy pioneer—the Revolution. The English workingmen are the first-born sons of modern industry. They will then, certainly, not be the last in aiding the social revolution produced by that industry, a revolution, which means the emancipation of their own class all over the world, which is as universal as capital rule and wages slavery. I know the heroic struggles the English working class have gone through since the middle of the last century—struggles no less glorious because they are shrouded in obscurity and burked by the middle-class historian. To revenge the misdeeds of the ruling class, there existed in the Middle Ages, in Germany, a secret tribunal called the *"Vehmgericht."* If a red cross was seen marked on a house, people knew that its owner was doomed by the *"Vehm."* All the houses of Europe are now marked with the mysterious red cross. History is the judge—its executioner, the proletarian.

ELECTRICITY AND AGRICULTURE

From letter to Frederick Engels (in Manchester), London, May 5, 1851

[1] A Character in Shakespeare's *A Midsummer Night's Dream.*

Science and Technology

Dear Engels:

I am sending you, under separate cover, a copy of the article on the application of electricity to agriculture,[1] in English. Be so kind as to write me by return mail:

(1) What you think of the subject.
(2) Explain the matter to me, since I did not quite understand it, in plain German.

A field is divided into rectangles, 76 yards long and 40 yards wide, and containing, therefore, just one acre each. The above is the plan of such a rectangle.

At each of the points A, B, C, and D pegs are driven into the ground; the external lines represent strong iron wires, extending from and fastened to each of the 4 pegs, and communicating with each other, so as to form a square or wire, sunk 3 inches below the surface; at the Points E and F, 15-foot-high poles are fixed in the ground; a wire is connected with the cross wire beneath the surface at the Point E—carried up the pole and along the center of the square to the top of the pole at F, down which it is conducted and fixed to the cross wire beneath the surface at that point. We must remark here that the squares must be formed, to run from North to South, so that the wire passing from E to F shall be at right angles with the Equator. It is well known that a considerable body of electricity is generated in the atmosphere, and constantly traveling from East to West with the motion of the earth. This electricity is attracted by the wire suspended under the surface of the ground, from the points, A, B, C and D . . . any quantity of electricity could be generated, that might be required, by placing under the ground at the point G, a bag

---

[1] "Electricity and Agriculture," in *The Economist*, April 26 and May 3, 1845.

of charcoal, and plates of zinc at the Point H, and to connect the two by a wire passing over two poles similar to those at E and F and crossing the longitudinal wire passing from those points. The cost at which this application can be made is computed at one pound per acre, and it is reckoned to last 10-15 years, the wires being carefully taken up and replaced each year.

The poles are made of dry wood. As the area increases the cost diminishes. . . . The mode in which the plot is laid out is as follows. With a mariners' compass and measured lengths of common string, lay out the places for the wooden pins, to which the *buried* wire is attached (by passing through a small staple). Care must be taken to lay the length of the buried wire due north and south by compass, and the breadth due east and west. This wire must be placed from two to three inch-degrees in the soil. The lines of the buried wire are then completed. The *suspended* wire must be attached and in contact with the buried wires at both of its ends. A wooden pin with a staple must therefore be driven in, and the two poles (one 14 feet and other 15 feet) being placed by the compass due north and south, the wire is placed over them, and fastened to the wooden stake, but touching likewise at this point the buried wire. The suspended wire must [not] be drawn too tight, otherwise the wind will break it.[2]

Voilà l'affaire.[3]

---

[2] The whole letter beginning with "A field is divided . . ." was written in English, probably as a paraphrase of the article in *The Economist*.

[3] "This is the story." Engels replied, May 9, 1851: "The electricity story is simple, insofar as the construction is concerned." Then he explained its structure in detail, and stated: "I find the success of the thing somewhat dubious."

Science and Technology 359

ELECTRICITY

From letter to Frederick Engels, London, November 8, 1882

Dear Fred:

What do you say to Deprez's experiment at the Munich Electricity Exposition?[1] Almost a year has already passed since Longuet had promised to get for me the works of Deprez (especially in proof that electricity permits the transmission of power for long distances through simple telegraph wires).[2] Specifically, an intimate friend of Deprez, D'Arsonval, is a collaborator on the journal, *Justice,* and has published a number of things on Deprez's researches. Longuet forgot every time, as usual.

DARWIN'S NATURAL SELECTION

From letter to Frederick Engels (in Manchester), London, December 19, 1860

Dear Frederick:

. . . In my time of trial [illness]—during the last four weeks—I have read all sorts of things. Among others, Darwin's book on *Natural Selection.*[1] Although it is developed in a crude English way, this is the book that contains the natural-history foundation for our viewpoint [historical materialism]. In contrast, A. Bastian's *Der Mensch in der Geschichte*[2] (three thick volumes; the fellow is a young Bre-

---

[1] At the international Electro-Technical Exposition in Munich, the French physicist Marcel Deprez demonstrated long-distance transmission of electricity from Munich to Miesbach, a distance of about 40 kilometers.

[2] Deprez published his writings on electricity in 1881 and 1882, in the journals, *La Lumière Électrique* and *Électricité.*

[1] Darwin, *On the Origin of Species by Means of Natural Selection* (1859).

[2] Bastian, *Der Mensch in der Geschichte, Zur Begründung einer psychologischen Weltanschauung* ("Man in History. On the Founding of a Psychological Conception of the World," 3 vols., Leipzig, 1860).

men physician who toured around the world for a number of years), with its attempt at a "natural-history" presentation of psychology and a psychological presentation of history, is poor, confused, and formless. The only useful things in it are some ethnographic oddities here and there. In addition, a lot of pretentiousness and an atrocious style. . . .

Yours,
K.M.

From letter to Frederick Engels (in Manchester), London, June 18, 1862

Dear Engels:

... I am amused at Darwin, into whom I looked again, when he says that he applies the "Malthusian" theory *also* to plants and animals, as if the joke in Herr Malthus did not consist of the fact that he did *not* apply it to plants and animals but only to human beings—in geometrical progression—in contrast to plants and animals. It is remarkable how Darwin has discerned anew among beasts and plants his English society with its division of labor, competition, disclosure of new markets, "discoveries," and the Malthusian "struggle for existence." It is Hobbes's *bellum omnium contra omnes*,[1] and it reminds me of Hegel's *Phenomenology*, wherein bourgeois society figures as a "spiritual animal kingdom," while in Darwin the animal kingdom figures as bourgeois society.

From letter to Frederick Engels (in Manchester), London, August 7, 1866

Dear Fred:

... A very important work which I will send you (but on condition that you return it, as it does not belong to me) as soon as I have finished making the necessary notes, is: P. Trémaux, *Origine et Transformations de l'Homme et des autres Êtres* (Paris, 1865). Despite shortcomings that strike me, it is a *very important* advance over Darwin. The two main points in it are: the crossbreedings do not, as is believed, pro-

[1] "War of all against all."

duce a different but, on the contrary, a typical unity of the species. In contrast, the formation of the earth does *differentiate* (not in itself, but as main basis). Progress, which in Darwin is purely accidental, is here a necessity, on the basis of the periods of developments of the earth; degeneration, which Darwin cannot explain, is here simple; similarly, the rapid extinction of mere transitional forms, compared with the slowness of the development of the species type, so that the gaps in paleontology, which bother Darwin, are here a necessity. Similarly, fixity is developed as a necessary law (apart from the individual variations, etc.) in the once-constituted species. The difficulties of hybridization in Darwin are here, on the contrary, supports of the systems, as it is demonstrated that in fact a species is constituted only when crossbreeding with another one ceases, becomes fruitful or possible, etc.

In its historical and political application, the book is much more important and copious than Darwin. For certain questions, such as nationality, etc., a natural basis is found in this work alone. For example, the author corrects the Pole Duchinski, whose findings in regard to the geological differences between Russia and the West Slavs he confirms to the extent that, contrary to the Pole's belief, the Russians are no Slavs but rather Tartars, etc., and that in the predominant soil formation of Russia the Slav became Tartarized and Mongolized. ...

THE MEANING OF MACHINERY

From letter to Frederick Engels (in Manchester), London, January 28, 1863

Dear Frederick:

... In my last letter[1] I asked you about the selfactor [automatic spinning machine]. Specifically, the question was this: How did the spinning machine work *before* the selfactor? I understand the selfactor, but not the preceding situation.

---

[1] Marx to Engels, January 24, 1863: "I have never understood how the selfactors changed spinning, or rather, since steampower had already been introduced, how the spinner operated before that."

I am adding something to the section on machinery [in *Capital*],[2] There are some curious questions which I ignored in my first treatment. In order to get a clear understanding of it, I have reread all my notebooks (extracts) on technology and am also attending a practical (and experimental) course for workers by Professor Willis (in Jermyn Street, at the Geological Institute, where Huxley also used to give his lectures). It is the same for me with mechanics as with languages. I understand the mathematical laws but the simplest technical reality, which demands perception, is harder for me than for the biggest blockheads.

You may or may not know, since the matter is in itself of no importance, that there is a conflict of views on how a *machine* differs from a *tool*. The English (mathematical) mechanists, in their crude way, call a *tool a simple machine* and a *machine a complicated tool*. Still, the English technologists, who pay a little more attention to economics (and are followed by many, by most, English economists), base their distinction on the fact that in one case the *motive power* derives from human beings, in the other from a *natural force*. The German jackasses, who are great at such trifles, have, therefore, concluded that, for instance, a *plow* is a machine and that the most complicated spinning jenny, etc., insofar as it is worked by hand, is not. But there is no question that if we look at the machine in its *elementary* form, the industrial revolution does not emerge from the *motive power*, but from that part of the machinery which the Englishman calls the *working machine*—not, for example, from the substitution of the foot, which moves the spinning wheel, by water or steam, but by the transformation of the immediate spinning process itself and the displacement of that part of human labor which was not merely an "exertion of power" (as in treading the wheel), but was directly applied to the working up of the raw material. Leaving out the purely *historical* development of machinery, but considering machinery as the basis of present methods of production, there is little question but that the *working machine* alone (for example, the sewing machine) is the decisive factor; for as soon as this process has been mechanized, everyone nowadays knows, the thing can be moved by hand, water power, or steam engine according to its size.

[2]Marx was then working on *Capital*, published in 1867. Chapter XIII, Sec. 1, of that work contains a section "The Development of Machinery."

Science and Technology

For the mere mathematicians these are indifferent questions, but they become very important when one wants to prove the connection between human social relations and the development of these material methods of production.

The rereading of my technological-historical excerpts has led me to the view that, apart from the discoveries of gunpowder, the compass, and the printing press—these necessary preconditions of bourgeois development—the two material bases on which the preparations for machine industry were organized within manufacture, from the sixteenth to the middle of the eighteenth century (the period in which manufacture was developing from handicraft to large scale industry), were the *clock* and the *mill* (at first the corn mill, that is, a water mill), both inherited from antiquity. (The water mill was introduced into Rome from the Near East in the time of Julius Caesar.) The clock is the first automatic machine applied to practical purposes, and the whole theory of production of regular motion was developed on it. In the nature of things, it is itself based on the connection between part-artistic handicraft and direct theory. Cardano, for example, wrote on (and gave practical formulae for) the construction of clocks. German writers of the sixteenth century called clock-making "learned (non-guild) handicraft," and from the development of the clock it would be possible to show how different from handicraft has been the relation between learning and practice, and from [*modern*] large-scale industry, for example. There is also no doubt that in the eighteenth century the idea of applying automatic (moved by springs) devices to production was first suggested by clocks. It can be proved historically that Vaucanson's experiments in this field have had an extraordinary influence on the imagination of the English inventors.

In the *mill*, on the other hand, from the very beginning, as soon as the water-mill was produced, one finds the essential differences in the organism of a machine. Mechanical driving power. The prime motor, on which it depends. Transmissions mechanism. Finally, the working machine, which deals with the material. Each of those organisms is independent of the others. The theory of *friction* and with it the investigations into the mathematical forms of wheelwork, cogs, etc., were all made at the mill; ditto here first the theory of measurement of the degree of motive power, of the best way of applying it, etc. Practically all the great mathematicians since the middle of the seventeenth century, insofar as they occupied themselves with practical mechanics and theorized about them, start with the simple corn-grinding water mill. Indeed, this was why the word *mill* came to be applied during the manufacturing period to all mechanical motive power adapted to practical purposes.

But with the mill, as with the pressing machines, the forge, the plow, etc., the actual work of hammering, crushing, grinding, pulverizing, etc., was performed from the very first *without* human labor, even though the moving force was human or animal. Hence this kind of machinery is very ancient, at least in its origins, and actual mechanical propulsion was formerly applied to it. Hence it is also practically the only machinery found in the manufacturing period. The *industrial revolution* begins as soon as mechanism is employed where, since ancient times, the final result has always required human labor; not, that is to say, where, as with the tools just mentioned, the actual material to be worked on has, from the *beginning, never* been touched by the human hand, but where, from the nature of the thing, man has not from the very first acted as mere *power*. If one is to follow the German jackasses in calling the use of animal power (which is just as much *voluntary* movement as human power) machinery, then the use of this kind of locomotive is at any rate much older than the simplest handicraft tool.

ROMAN ARITHMETIC

From letter to Lion Philips, Marx's uncle (in Zalt-Bommel), London, April 14, 1864

Dear Uncle:

... In the [British] Museum I looked into Boethius' *De Arithmetica* (an author of the period of the People's Migration) on the subject of the Roman division (naturally he knew *no other*). From this, and from some other writings which I compared, I deduce the following: moderate accounts, such as household and business, were never recorded on the calculating slate with figures but with weights and other similar symbols. On that slate they put several parallel lines, marking, by weight or other physical indications, Ones on the first line, Tens on the second, Hundreds on the third, Thousands on the fourth, etc. Such calculating boards were used practically throughout the whole Middle Ages and are still in use by the Chinese today. As regards higher mathematical calculations, the Romans, insofar as these appear among them, used the multiplication table or the one-times-one of Pythagoras, at that time, indeed, still inconvenient and ponderous, for it consisted partly of its own characters and partly of letters from the Greek (later Roman) alphabet. As the whole division dissolved in analyses of the dividends in factors and the multiplication table was carried to considerably high figures, it had to suffice to divide such expressions as MDXL, etc. Every figure, such as M, for example, had to be reduced into factors, which it formed with the divisor, and the results were then added up. Thus, for instance, M divided by two equals D (500); D divided by two equals 250, etc. That in major calculations the old method encountered insurmountable obstacles can be seen from the cunning devices to which the extraordinary mathematician Archimedes had to take recourse.

THEORY OF LIGHT

From letter to Lion Philips, (in Zalt-Bommel), London, April 14, 1864

Dear Uncle:

... In regard to the "Darkness of the Outer Space," this necessarily arises from the theory of light. As colors appear only as a result of refraction of light waves from bodies, and as in the *intermediate spaces* between the heavenly bodies there is neither *atmosphere* nor any other substances, they must be pitch black. They let all the light rays pass through, which is another way of saying that they are dark. Moreover, the space outside the atmospheres of the planets, etc., is damned *"kond en kil,"*[1] which is also the reason why the higher reaches of our own atmosphere are ice-cold in summer and winter, particularly because of the thinness, hence the weightlessness, of those strata. But

Sollte diese Qual uns quälen
Da sie unsre Lust vermehrt?[2]

[1] Dutch for "cold and frosty."
[2] From Goethe's *Westöstlicher Diwan*: "Suleika." Freely translated: "Should this pain torment us, As it increases our pleasure?"

But why light and heat, *where there is no eye to see the one*, and no organic matter to feel the other?[3] The worthy Epicurus already had the very sensible idea of banishing the Gods to the *intermundi* (that is, the *empty* intermediate spaces), and in truth, R's[4] "perfect dogs" belong in those cold, cool, pitch-dark *"stoffelooze wereldruimte."*[5]

ASTRONOMY

From letter to Frederick Engels, August 19, 1865

Dear Fred:

... In my state of ill health, I can do little writing, and then only by fits and starts. In the meantime I fool around, although even reading is not compatible with influenza. "On occasion," I again "pursued" a little astronomy, among other things. And here I want to mention something that was new, at least to me, but has probably been known to you for some time. You know Laplace's theory of the creation of the Celestial System and how he explains the rotation of the various bodies around each other. Starting from there, a Yankee, Kirkwood, discovered a kind of law on the *difference* in the rotation of the planets, which had hitherto seemed abnormal. The law is this: *"The square of the number of times* that each planet rotates during one revolution in its orbit, is proportioned to the *cube of the breadth of a diameter of its sphere of attraction."*[1]

Specificially, between two planets there is a point where their force of attraction is in equilibrium; hence a body remains motionless at this point. On the other hand, on each side of this point, a body will fall to one or the other planet. This point, therefore, forms the limit for the *sphere of attraction*[1] of the planet. This sphere of attraction again is the measure of the width of the gaseous ring, from which, according to Laplace, the planet was formed at the time of its first separation from the general gaseous mass. Thereform

---

[3] The italicized words were written by Marx in English.
[4] A. Roodhuizen, a Dutch clergyman married to Marx's cousin, Antoinette Philips.
[5] Dutch: "immaterial outer spaces."
[1] Marx quoted this in English and supplied the italics.

Kirkwood concluded that, if Laplace's hypothesis was correct, there must exist a definite relation between the velocity of the planet's rotation and the breadth of the ring from which it was formed, or its sphere of attraction. And this he has expressed in the above law, based on analytical calculations.

Old Hegel made some very good jokes about the "sudden change" that took place in the centripetal and centrifugal force precisely at the moment when one achieves preponderance over the other. For example, the centrifugal force is greatest near the sun; *thus*, says Hegel, the centrifugal force is the greatest, since it overcomes the *maximum of centripetal* force, and vice versa. Moreover, the forces are in *equilibrium* in the middle distance of the apses. *Hence* they can *never again* get out of this equilibrium, etc. For the rest, in his polemic,[2] Hegel concludes that Newton, with his "proofs," added nothing to Kepler, had the "idea" of movement—something that is now pretty universally recognized.

From letter to Frederick Engels, August 22, 1865

... In regard to Kirkwood's law, there is no doubt that it explains the difference in the rotatory movements, for example, between those of Jupiter and those of Venus, etc., which had hitherto appeared to be accidental. But I do not know *how* he discovers and proves the law itself, but in my next visit to the British Museum I will locate his original work and report it to you. The only "problem" in the thing seems to be the mathematical determination of the sphere of attraction of each planet. What is *hypothetical* is probably only the acceptance of Laplace's theory as a point of departure.

---

[2] George Wilhelm Friedrich Hegel, *Vorlesungen über die Naturphilosophie als der Encyklopädie der Philosophischen Wissenschaften im Grundrisse* ("Lectures on Natural Philosophy as the Encyclopedia of Philosophic Sciences in Outline"), in *Werke*, Vol. VII, First Part (2nd ed., Berlin, 1847).

DIFFERENTIAL CALCULUS

Appendix to letter to Frederick Engels (in Manchester), London, end 1865/ early 1866

During my last visit to Manchester,[1] you asked me for an explanation of differential calculus. In the following example the thing will become entirely clear to you. The whole differential calculus, to begin with, arose from the task of drawing a *tangent* through any point to any curve. I will illustrate this for you.

Assume the line *nAo* is any curve the nature of which (whether parabola, ellipse, etc.) we do *not* know and where at point m a tangent is to be drawn.

Ax is the axis. We drop the perpendicular *mP* (the ordinate) on the abscissa *Ax*. Assume then that point *n* is the infinite *next* point to the curve near *m*. If I should drop a perpendicular *np* on the axis, then *p* must be the infinite next point to *P* and *np* the infinite next parallel line to *mP*. Now drop an infinite small perpendicular *mR* on *np*. Assume now the abscissa $AP \ldots x$ and the ordinate $mP \ldots y$, $np = mP$ (or Rp) is enlarged by an infinite small increment [n R], or [n R] = dy (differential from y) and mR ($= Pp$) = dx. Since the piece of the tangents *mn* is infinitely small, it coincides with the corresponding part of the curve itself. I may therefore consider *mnR* as a △ (triangle), and the △ *mnR* and *mTP* are similar triangles. Hence: dy ($= nR$): dx ($= mR$) = y (mP): PT (which is the subtangent of

---

[1] Marx visited Engels from October 20 to November 2, 1865.

the Tm). Thus the subtangent $PT = y \dfrac{dx}{dy}$. This is now the *general differential equation* for all tangential points of *all* curves. Should I now continue to operate further with this equation and determine the magnitude of the subtangent PT (if I have it, I need only to connect the points T and m by a straight line to establish the tangent), I have to know which is the *specific character* of the curve: Corresponding to its character (as parabola, ellipse, zissoid, etc.), it has a *definite general* equation for its ordinate and abscissa at each of the points one knows from algebraic geometry. If, for example, the curve mAo is a parabola, then I know that y^2 ($y =$ is the ordinate of any point) $= ax$, where a is the parameter of the parabola and x the y ordinate of the corresponding abscissa.

If I put this value of y in the equation $PT = \dfrac{ydx}{dy}$, I must first seek and find dy, that is, the differential of y (the expression that y assumes in its infinite small growth). If $y^2 = ax$, I know from the differential calculus that $d(y^2) = d(ax)$ (I must of course differentiate both sides of the equation) yields $2y = adx$ (that is always called differential). Thus $dx = \dfrac{2ydy}{a}$. If I put this value of dx into the formula $PT = \dfrac{ydx}{dy}$, I get $PT = \dfrac{2y^2dy}{ady} = \dfrac{2y^2}{ady} = (day^2 = ax)\dfrac{2ax}{a} = 2x$. Or the subtangent of every point m in the parabola $=$ the double abscissa of the same point. The differential magnitudes disappear in the operation.

TECHNOLOGY

From *Capital*, Vol. I, Pt. IV, Ch. 15, Sec. 1, fn. 3

A critical history of technology would show how little any of the inventions of the eighteenth century are the work of a single individual. Hitherto there is no such book. Darwin has interested us in the history of Nature's Technology, i.e., in the formation of the organs of plants and animals, which organs serve as instruments of production for sustaining life. Does not the history of the productive organs of man, of organs that are the material basis of all social organization, deserve equal attention? And would not such a history be easier to compile, since, as Vico says, human history differs from natural history in this, that we have made the former, but not the latter? Technology discloses man's mode of dealing with nature, the process of production by which he sustains his life, and thereby also lays bare the mode of formation of his social relations, and of the mental conceptions that flow from them. Every history of religion even, that fails to take account of this material basis, is uncritical. It is, in reality, much easier to discover by analysis the earthly core of the misty creations of religion, than, conversely, it is to develop from the actual relations of life the corresponding celestialized forms of those relations. The latter method is the only materialistic, and therefore the only scientific, one. The weak points in the abstract materialism of natural science, a materialism that excludes history and its process, are at once evident from the abstract and ideological conceptions of its spokesmen whenever they venture beyond the bounds of their own specialty.

TECHNOLOGY AND INDUSTRY

From *Capital,* Vol.I, Ch.15, Sec.9

Modern Industry rent the veil that concealed from men their own social process of production, and that turned the various spontaneously divided branches of production into so many riddles, not only to outsiders, but even to the initiated. The principle which is pursued, of resolving each process into its constituent movements, without any regard to their possible execution by the hand of man, created the new modern science of technology. The varied, apparently unconnected, and petrified forms of the industrial processes now resolved themselves into so many conscious and systematic applications of natural science to the attainment of given useful effects. Technology also discovered the few main fundamental forms of motion, which, despite the diversity of the instruments used, are necessarily taken by every productive action of the human body; just as the science of mechanics sees in the most complicated machinery nothing but the continual repetition of the simple mechanical powers.

Modern Industry never looks upon and treats the existing form of a process as final. The technical basis of that industry is therefore revolutionary, while all earlier modes of production were essentially conservative. By means of machinery, chemical processes and other methods, it is continually causing changes not only in the technical basis of production, but also in the functions of the laborer, and in the social combinations of the labor process. At the same time, it thereby also revolutionizes the division of labor within the society.

CHAPTER XI

THE STATE

Note

Marx, the philosopher of world revolution, never really developed a full theory of the state or a genuine analysis of the meaning of and structure of power. His writings in this area are mostly indirect. In his early years he believed that the highest end of a community was the "democratic state" with its sense of freedom, which expressed the "self-worth of men." He was critical of the then prevailing European states which claimed to be "Christian" and were based on oppressive theocratic dogmas.

After he became a communist, Marx changed his idea of the state. He no longer viewed it as an institution of universal freedom, which he now referred to as "vulgar democracy," but as an instrument of class domination, as he elaborated it in the Gotha Program included in this chapter. The state, he wrote, cannot be separated from the ruling class. In a capitalist system, he wrote, the machinery of government is in the hands of the bourgeoisie. In a future communist society, power would be wielded by the working class, which would develop its own conception and function of the state.

THE CHRISTIAN STATE

From "The Leading Article in No.179 of the *Kölnische Zeitung*,"* in *Rheinische Zeitung*, July 14, 1842

---

*In *Karl Marx on Religion* by Saul K. Padover, pp. 23-25. Copyright © 1974 Saul K. Padover. Used with permission of McGraw-Hill Book Co.

The State

The truly religious state is the theocratic state; the prince of such states must be either the God of religion, Jehovah himself, as in the Jewish state, God's representative, the Dalai Lama, as in Tibet, or finally, as Goerres correctly demands of Christian states in his last work, they must all submit to a church which is an "infallible church." For if, as in Protestantism, there is no supreme head of the church, the domination of religion is nothing but the religion of domination, the cult of the will of the government.

Once a state includes several confessions with equal rights, it cannot be a religious state without violating particular confessions; it cannot be a church which condemns adherents of another confession as heretics, which makes every piece of bread dependent on faith, which makes dogma the link between separate individuals and existence as citizens of the state. Ask the Catholic inhabitants of "poor green Erin," ask the Huguenots before the French Revolution: they did not appeal to religion, for their religion was not the religion of the state; they appealed to the "Rights of Humanity," and philosophy interprets the Rights of Humanity and demands that the state be the state of human nature.

But the half, the limited, rationalism, which is as unbelieving as it is theological, says that the universal Christian spirit, irrespective of confessional differences, must be the spirit of the state! It is the greatest irreligiousness, the wantonness of worldy reason, to separate the general spirit of religion from the positive religion; this separation of religion from its dogmas and institutions is equal to asserting that the universal spirit of right must reign in the state irrespective of the definite laws and the positive institutions of right.

If you presume to stand so high above religion as to have the right to separate the general spirit of religion from its positive definition, what reproach have you to make to the philosophers if they want to make the separation complete and not a halfway one, if they proclaim not the Christian, but the human, spirit the universal spirit of religion?

Christians live in states with differing constitutions, some in a republic, some in an absolute, some again in a constitutional monarchy. Christianity does not decide on the *correctness* of the constitutions, for it knows no distinction between constitutions; it teaches, as religion must: Submit to the authority, for *all authority* is ordained by God. The correctness of state constitutions is therefore to be judged not according to Christianity, nor according to the nature, the essence of the state itself, not according to the nature of Christian society, but according to the nature of human society.

The Byzantine state was the properly religious state, for there dogmas were matters of state, but the Byzantine state was the worst of all states. The states of the *ancien régime* were the most Christian states, nonetheless they were states of "the will of court."

There is a dilemma that "sound" common sense cannot solve. Either the Christian state corresponds to the concept of the state as a realization of rational freedom, and then nothing else can be demanded for it to be a Christian state than that it be a reasonable state; then it is enough to develop the state out of the reason of human relations, a work accomplished by philosophy. Or the state of rational freedom cannot be developed out of Christianity: then you will yourselves concede that this development does not lie in the tendency of Christianity, for Christianity does not wish for a bad state, and any state which is not the embodiment of rational freedom is a bad state.

Answer the dilemma as you like, you will have to concede that the state is not to be constituted from religion but from the reason of freedom. Only the crassest ignorance can assert that the theory of making the state concept independent is a passing whim of modern philosophers.

THE POLITICAL STATE

From letter to Arnold Ruge, September 1843

Reason has always existed, but not always in reasonable form. Hence the critic can choose any form of theoretical and practical consciousness and develop the true reality in its "ought" and final goal out of its own forms of existing reality. In regard to real life, the political state, even where it is not yet permeated with socialist demands, contains the demands of reason in all its *modern* forms. And it does not stop with that. Everywhere it subordinates reason to reality. But everywhere also it falls into the contradiction between its ideal destiny and its presuppositions.

Out of this conflict of the political state within itself, therefore, social truth can develop everywhere. Just as *religion* is the index to the theoretical struggles of mankind, so the *political state* is the index to its practical ones. Hence the political state expresses within its form *sub specie rei publicae* [as a special political form] all social conflicts, needs, truths, etc. It is therefore definitely not beneath the *hauteur des principes* [level of principles] to make the most specialized political questions—say, the difference between a *ständisch* [estate] system and a representative system—the object of criticism. For this question expresses only in a *political* way the difference between government by the people and the rule of private property. Hence the critic not only can but must enter into these political questions (which in the view of the crude socialists is beneath all dignity). In demonstrating the advantage of the representative system over the estate one, the critic interests a large part of the people in a *practical* subject. In raising the representative system out of its own political form to a general form and validating the true significance that lies at its foundation, he forces that part to rise above itself, for its victory is at the same time its loss.

THE RELIANCE OF THE STATE ON ADMINISTRATION*

From "Critical Marginal Notes on the Article, 'The King of Prussia and Social Reform. By a Prussian,'" *Vorwärts!* August 7 and 10, 1844. The "Prussian" was Arnold Ruge, with whom Marx had recently broken over the *Deutsch-Französische Jahrbücher*, for which Ruge, its co-publisher with Marx, refused further financial support.

No government in the world has issued ordinances on pauperism without an agreement with its officials. The English Parliament even sent commissioners to all European countries

Karl Marx on Revolution by Saul K. Padover, pp. 14-16. Copyright © 1971 by Saul K. Padover. Used with permission of McGraw-Hill Book Co.

to get information about the various administrative remedies for pauperism. Insofar as states have occupied themselves with pauperism, they have confined themselves to administrative and charitable measures or have done even less.

Can the state act differently?

The state will never find the cause of social want in the "state and the organization of society," as the "Prussian" requires of his King. When there are political parties, each finds the cause of every evil in the fact that its counterpart, instead of itself, is at the helm of the state. Even radical and revolutionary politicians seek the cause of the evil not in the *nature* of the state, but in a specific *form of state*, which they want to replace with another form of state.

The state and the organization of society, from a *political* standpoint, are not two different things. The state is the organization of society. Insofar as the state admits social evils, it attributes them either to natural laws, which no human power can change, or to private life, which is independent of the state, or to the inadequacy of the administration, which is dependent on it. Thus England finds poverty rooted in the law of nature, according to which the population always exceeds the means of subsistence. From another side, England explains pauperism as the consequence of the ill will of the poor, just as the King of Prussia explains it as caused by the un-Christian spirit of the rich and the Convention explains it as a result of a suspect, counter-revolutionary attitude of the property owners. Hence England punishes the poor, the King of Prussia admonishes the rich, and the Convention decapitates property owners.

Finally, *all* states seek the cause of their ills in *accidental* or *intentional* defects of administration, and therefore they seek the remedy in administrative measures. Why? Precisely because the administration is the organizing activity of the state.

The state cannot transcend the contradiction between the aim and good intentions of the administration, on the one hand, and its means and resources, on the other, without transcending itself, for it is based on this contradiction. It is based on the contradiction between *public* and *private* life, on the contradiction between general interests and particular interests. Hence the administration must confine itself to a formal and negative activity, for where private life and work begin, there its power ceases. Indeed, as against the consequences which spring from the unsocial nature of this civil life, of private property, trade, industry, and the mutual plundering of different civil groups—as against these consequences, impotence is the natural law of administration. This dismemberment, this debasement, this *slavery of civil society* is the natural foundation on which the modern state rests, just as the *civil society of slavery* was the natural foundation on which in antiquity the state rested. The existence of the state and the existence of slavery are indivisible. The state of antiquity and the slavery of antiquity—patent classical antitheses—were no less closely welded than the modern state and the modern world of huckstering—sanctimonious Christian antitheses. If the modern state wanted to do away with the impotence of its administration, it would have to do away with the present form of private life. If it wanted to do away with private life, it would have to do away with itself, because it exists *only* in contrast to that life. No living person, however, believes that the shortcomings of his existence are rooted in principle, or essence, of his life, but in circumstances *outside* his life. Suicide is unnatural. Hence the state cannot believe in the inner impotence of its administration, that is, of its own self. It can notice only formal, accidental defects and seek to remedy them. If such modifications are fruitless, then the social ill is either a natural imperfection independent of mankind, a *law of God*, or else the will of private individuals is too corrupted to meet the good objectives of the administration. And what perverse private individuals! They grumble against the government whenever it restricts freedom, and they demand that the government prevent the necessary consequences of that freedom!

The more powerful the state, and hence the more political a country is, the less it is inclined to seek the basis and understanding of the general principle of social ills in the principle of the state itself, and hence in the existing organization of society, of which the state is the active, self-conscious, and official expression. Political thought is political precisely because it operates within the confines of politics. The more acute and more vigorous it is, the more it is incapable of understanding social ills. The classical period of political thought is the French Revolution. Far from perceiving the source of social defects in the principle of the state, the heroes of the French Revolution see the source of social defects in the political abuses. Thus Robespierre sees in great poverty and great wealth only an obstacle to pure democracy. He wants, therefore, to establish a general Spartan frugality. The principle of politics is the *will*. The more one-sided and hence the more perfected the political thought is, the more he believes in the omnipotence of the will; the more blind he is to the natural and intellectual restrictions on the will, the more incapable he is of discovering the source of social ills. No further proof is needed against the foolish hope of the "Prussian," whereby "political thought" is called upon "to discover the root of social misery in Germany."

THE FRENCH BOURGEOIS STATE

From *The Civil War in France*, written in April and May 1871 and published in English as a brochure in June 1871. This pamphlet, published in the name of the First International in defense of the Paris Commune, is considered by communists "a most important work of scientific communism."

On the dawn of the eighteenth of March, Paris arose to the thunderburst of *"Vive la Commune!"* What is the Commune, that sphinx so tantalizing to the bourgeois mind?

"The proletarians of Paris," said the Central Committee in its manifesto of March 18, "amidst the failures and treasons of the ruling classes, have understood that the hour has struck for them to save the situation by taking into their own hands the direction of public affairs. . . .They have understood that it is their imperious duty and their absolute right to render themselves masters of their own destinies, by seizing upon the governmental power."

But the working class cannot simply lay hold of the ready-made state machinery and wield it for its own purposes.

The centralized state power, with its ubiquitous organs of standing army, police, bureaucracy, clergy, and judiciary—organs wrought after the plan of a systematic and hierarchic division of labor—originates from the days of absolute monarchy, serving nascent middle-class society as a mighty weapon in its struggles against feudalism. Still, its development remained clogged by all manner of medieval rubbish, seignorial rights, local privileges, municipal and guild monopolies, and provincial constitutions. The gigantic broom of the French Revolution of the eighteenth century swept away all these relics of bygone times, thus clearing simultaneously the social soil of its last hindrances to the superstructure of the modern state edifice raised under the First Empire, itself the offspring of the coalition wars of the old semifeudal Europe against modern France. During the subsequent regimes the government, placed under parliamentary control—that is, under the direct control of the propertied classes—not only became a hotbed of huge national debts and crushing taxes; with its irresistible allurements of place, pelf, and patronage, it not only became the bone of contention between the rival factions and adventurers of the ruling classes; but its political character changed simultaneously with the economic changes of society. At the same pace at which the progress of modern industry developed, widened, intensified the class antagonism between capital and labor, the state power assumed more and more the character of the national power of capital over labor, of a public force organized for social enslavement, of an engine of class depotism. After every revolution marking a progressive phase in the class struggle, the purely repressive character of the state power stands out in bolder and bolder relief. The Revolution of 1830, resulting in the transfer of government from the landlords to the capitalists, transferred it from the more remote to the more direct antagonists of the workingmen. The bourgeois republicans who, in the name of the Revolution of February, took the state power, used it for the June massacres, in order to convince the working class that "social" republic meant the republic insuring their social subjection, and in order to convince the royalist bulk of the bourgeois and landlord class that they might safely leave the cares and emoluments of government to the bourgeois "republicans." However, after their one heroic exploit of June, the bourgeois republicans had, from the front, to fall back to the rear of the party of Order—a combination formed by all the rival fractions and factions of the appropriating class in their now openly declared antagonism to the producing classes. The proper form of their joint-stock government was the parliamentary republic, with Louis Bonaparte for its President. Theirs was a regime of avowed class terrorism and deliberate insult toward the "vile multitude." If the parliamentary republic, as M. Thiers said, "divided them" (the different fractions of the ruling class) "least," it opened an abyss between that class and the whole body of society outside their spare ranks. The restraints by which their own divisions had under former regimes still checked the state power were removed by their union: and in view of the threatening upheaval of the proletariat, they now used that state power mercilessly and ostentatiously as the national war engine of capital against labor. In their uninterrupted crusade against the producing masses they were, however, bound not only to invest the executive with continually increased powers of repression, but at the same time to divest their own parliamentary stronghold—the National Assembly—one by one, of all its own means of defense against the Executive. The Executive, in the person of Louis Bonaparte, turned them out. The natural offspring of the party of Order republic was the Second Empire.

The Empire, with the *coup d'état* for its certificate of birth, universal suffrage for its sanction, and the sword for its scepter, professed to rest upon the peasantry, the large mass of producers not directly involved in the struggle of capital and labor. It professed to save the working class by breaking down parliamentarism, and with it the undisguised subserviency of government to the propertied classes. It professed to save the propertied classes by upholding their economic supremacy over the working class; and finally it professed to unite all classes by reviving for all the chimera of national glory. In reality, it was the only form of government possible at a time when the bourgeoisie had already lost, and the working class had not yet acquired, the faculty of ruling the nation. It was acclaimed throughout the world as the savior of society. Under its sway, bourgeois society, freed from political cares, attained a development unexpected even by itself. Its industry and commerce expanded to colossal dimensions; financial swindling celebrated cosmopolitan orgies; the misery of the masses was set off by a shameless display of gorgeous, meretricious, and debased luxury. The state power, apparently soaring high above society, was at the same time itself the greatest scandal of that society and the very hotbed of all its corruptions. Its own rottenness, and the rottenness of the society it had saved, were laid bare by the bayonet of Prussia, herself eagerly bent upon transferring the supreme seat of that regime from Paris to Berlin. Imperialism is at the same time the most prostitute and the ultimate form of the state power which nascent middle-class society had commenced to elaborate as a means of its own emancipation from feudalism, and which full-grown bourgeois society had finally transformed into a means for the enslavement of labor by capital.

WHAT IS "THE FREE STATE"?

From *Critique of the Gotha Program* (1875), Sec. IV

A. "The free basis of the state."

First of all, according to [section] II, the German Workers' party strives for "the free state."

Free state—what is this?

It is by no means the aim of the workers, who have got rid of the narrow mentality of humble subjects, to set the state free. In the German Empire the "state" is almost as "free" as in Russia. Freedom consists in converting the state from an organ superimposed upon society into one completely subordinate to it, and today, too, the forms of state are more free or less free to the extent that they restrict the "freedom of the state."

The German Workers' party—at least if it adopts the program—shows that its socialist ideas are not even skin-deep; in that, instead of treating existing society (and this holds good for any future one) as the *basis* of the existing state (or of the future state in the case of future society), it treats the state rather as an independent entity that possesses its own intellectual, ethical, and libertarian bases.

And what of the riotous misuse which the program makes of the words "present-day state," "present-day society," and of the still more riotous misconception it creates in regard to the state to which it addresses its demands?

"Present-day society" is capitalist society, which exists in all civilized countries, more or less free from medieval admixture, more or less modified by the particular historical development of each country, more or less developed. On the other hand, the "present-day state" changes with a country's frontier. It is different in the Prusso-German Empire from what it is in Switzerland, and different in England from what it is in the United States. The "present-day state" is therefore a fiction.

Nevertheless, the different states of the different civilized countries, in spite of their motley diversity of form, all have this in common, that they are based on modern bourgeois society, only one more or less capitalistically developed. They have, therefore, also certain essential characteristics in common. In this sense it is possible to speak of the "present-day state" in contrast with the future, in which its present root, bourgeois society, will have died off.

The question then arises: What transformation will the state undergo in communist society? In other words, what social functions will remain in existence there that are analogous to present state functions? This question can only be answered scientifically, and one does not get a flea-hop nearer to the problem by a thousand-fold combination of the word people with the word state.

Between capitalist and communist society lies the period of the revolutionary transformation of the one into the other. Corresponding to this is also a political transition period in which the state can be nothing but *the revolutionary dictatorship of the proletariat*.

Now the program does not deal with this nor with the future state of communist society.

Its political demands contain nothing beyond the old democratic litany familiar to all: universal suffrage, direct legislation, popular rights, a people's militia, etc. They are a mere echo of the bourgeois People's party, of the League of Peace and Freedom. They are all demands which, insofar as they are not exaggerated in fantastic presentation, have already been *realized*. Only the state to which they belong does not lie within the borders of the German Empire, but in Switzerland, the United States, etc. This sort of "state of the future" is a present-day state, although existing outside the "framework" of the German Empire.

But one thing has been forgotten. Since the German Workers' party expressly declares that it acts within "the present-day national state," hence within its own state, the Prusso-German Empire—its demands would indeed otherwise be largely meaningless, since one only demands what one has not got—it should not have forgotten the chief thing, namely, that all those pretty little gewgaws rest on the recognition of the so-called sovereignty of the people and hence are appropriate only in a *democratic republic*.

Since one has not the courage—and wisely so, for the circumstances demand caution—to demand the democratic republic, as the French workers' programs under Louis Philippe and under Louis Napoleon did, one should not have resorted, either, to the subterfuge, neither "honest" nor decent, of demanding things which have meaning only in a democratic republic from a state which is nothing but a police-guarded military despotism, embellished with parliamentary forms, alloyed with a feudal admixture, already influenced by the bourgeoisie and bureaucratically carpentered, and then to assure this state into the bargain that one imagines one will be able to force such things upon it "by legal means."

Even vulgar democracy, which sees the millennium in the democratic republic and has no suspicion that it is precisely in this last form of state of bourgeois society that the class struggle has to be fought out to a conclusion—even it towers mountains above this kind of democratism which keeps within the limits of what is permitted by the police and not permitted by logic.

That, in fact, by the word "state" is meant the government machine, or the state insofar as it forms a special organism separated from society through division of labor, is shown by the words "the German Workers' party demands as the economic basis of the state: a single progressive income tax," etc. Taxes are the economic basis of the government machinery and of nothing else. In the state of the future, existing in Switzerland, this demand has been pretty well fulfilled. Income tax presupposes various sources of income of the various social classes, and hence capitalist society. It is, therefore, nothing remarkable that the Liverpool financial reformer, bourgeois headed by Gladstone's brother, are putting forward the same demand as the program.

CHAPTER XII

WOMEN AND CHILDREN

Note

Marx's opinion of women and children reflected his personal life. His marriage had its roots in a passionate romance. He and Jenny von Westphalen met when they were children in Trier, Germany, fell in love while at school, and married in 1843 when he was twenty-five and she was twenty-nine years old. Their married life, despite cruel economic hardships, was one of deep companionship and affection. Jenny's devotion to her husband and his ideas was total, and she in turn was the only woman in his life. Thirteen years after their marriage, on June 21, 1856, Marx, when away from home, was still capable of writing to his wife: "I have you vividly before me, and I carry you on my hands, and I kiss you from head to foot, and I fall on my knees before you, and I groan, 'Madame, I love you.' "

Marx had a genuine compassion for women and affection for children. He treated his own wife and three daughters not only with tenderness but also with respect for their minds. He depended upon his wife for literary, artistic and political opinions, as he did also in the case of his housekeeper, Helene Demuth, with whom he was in the habit of playing chess. He raised his three children to be women of culture and intellectual independence; they, in turn, repaid him with lifelong admiration and trust. He loved to play with children, his own and others.

His indignation at the exploitation and abuse of working-class children and women was boundless. In his *Capital,* some of the passages of which are included in this chapter, he went to great length to detail their mistreatment under capitalism. A just system, he felt, was characterized by a humane treatment of women. "Social progress," he wrote to Dr. Ludwig Kugelmann (December 12, 1868), "can be measured accurately by the social status of the beautiful sex (the ugly ones included)."

THE DIVORCE LAW DRAFT*

In *Rheinische Zeitung,* December 19, 1842

Cologne, December 18.

In connection with the proposed divorce law,[1] the *Rheinische Zeitung* has taken a completely isolated position, the untenability of which has hitherto not been proven by any one. The *Rheinische Zeitung* agrees with the bill, insofar as it finds the existing Prussian marriage law unethical, the numerous and frivolous grounds for divorce inadmissible, and the existing proceedings not commensurate with the dignity of the matter—criticism that is applicable to the Old-Prussian court proceedings altogether. On the other hand, the *Rheinische Zeitung* raises the following main objections to the new bill: (1) that it substitutes mere revision for reform, since the Prussian statute law has been retained as fundamental, giving rise to considerable awkwardness and uncertainty; (2) that marriage is treated by the legislature, not as an ethical but as a religious and ecclesiastical institution, and thus the secular nature of marriage has not been recognized; (3) that the legal proceedings are very deficient and consist of an external composition of contradictory elements; (4) that, on the one hand, there is police severity contradicting the concept of marriage, and, on the other hand, there is too much indulgence toward so-called grounds of equity; (5) that the whole conception of the bill leaves much to be desired in logical consistency, precision, clarity, and thoroughness.

Insofar as the opponents of the bill point to these deficiencies, we agree with them, but we can in no way approve their

---

*In *Karl Marx on Education, Women and Children,* by Saul K. Padover, pp. 50-53. Copyright © 1975 Saul K. Padover. Used with permission of McGraw-Hill Book Co.

[1] On October 20, 1842, the *Rheinische Zeitung* published the draft of a proposed divorce law, secretly prepared under the direction of Marx's University of Berlin professor, Friedrich Karl von Savigny. The publication of the draft led to wide discussion, and to the suppression of the *Rheinische Zeitung,* of which Marx was the editor.

unconditional apology for the former system. We repeat again the statement we made earlier: "If the legislature cannot decree morality, it can even less recognize immorality as legal."[2] When we ask for the basis of the argument of these opponents (who are not opponents of the ecclesiastical view and of the other deficiencies mentioned), they always talk about the unhappiness of spouses bound to each other against their will. They take a eudaemonical position; they think of only two individuals, and forget the family; they forget that nearly every divorce is a separation of a family, and, even from a purely legal viewpoint, children and their property ought not to be dependent on arbitrary whims. If marriage were not the basis of the family, it would be no more the subject of legislation than is friendship. Those opponents, therefore, consider only the individual will, or rather the caprice of the spouses, but they do not consider the will of the marriage, the ethical substance of this relationship. The legislator, however, must regard himself as a naturalist. He does not make the laws; he does not invent them; he only formulates them; he expresses the inner laws of spiritual relationships in conscious, positive laws. If one must reproach the legislator with the grossest arbitrariness when he replaces the essence of the matter with his personal whims, so also he himself has no less the right to reproach private persons with the grossest arbitrariness when they wish to substitute their own caprices for the essence of the matter. Nobody is forced to enter into marriage, but everybody must be forced to obey the laws of marriage once he enters into it. A person entering marriage does not make or invent it, any more than a swimmer invents nature and the laws of water and gravity. Marriage, therefore, cannot accommodate itself to his arbitrariness, but his arbitrariness must accommodate itself to marriage, He who breaks a marriage arbitrarily maintains that arbitrariness and lawlessness are the laws of marriage, for no reasonable person would have the presumptuousness to consider his acts to be privileged acts, acts appropriate to him alone; rather, he will pass them off as legal acts appropriate to all. What, then, do you oppose? Legislation by arbitrariness. But you surely will not want to make arbitrari-

[2] "The Draft of the New Marriage Law," in supplement to *Rheinische Zeitung*, November 15, 1842.

ness into law at the moment you accuse the legislator of arbitrariness.

Hegel says: "In itself, in accordance with its concept, marriage is indissoluble, but *only* in itself; that is, only in accordance with its concept."[3] This says nothing that is intrinsic to marriage. All ethical relationships are by their concepts indissoluble, as one can easily be convinced by assuming their truth. A true State, a true marriage, a true friendship—these are indissoluble; but no State, no marriage, no friendship corresponds completely to its concept; and, like actual friendship, even in the family, and like the actual State in world history, so actual marriage in the State is dissoluble. No ethical existence corresponds to its essence, or at least does not have to correspond to it. In nature itself there is dissolution and death, where a Being no longer fully corresponds to its destiny. Just as world history decides whether a State is so much at variance with the idea of the State that it no longer deserves to continue, so does the State decide under what conditions an existing marriage has ceased to be a marriage. Divorce is nothing but the declaration that the marriage is dead and that its existence is only pretense and deception. It is obvious that neither the arbitrariness of the legislator nor that of the private person but only the essence of the matter can decide whether or not a marriage is dead, but a death certificate, as is well known, depends on the facts of the case and not on the wishes of the interested parties. But if, in connection with physical death, you demand significant and undeniable proof, should not also the legislator have to substantiate, by indubitable symptoms, an ethical death, since to preserve the life of ethical relationships is not only his right but also his duty, the duty of its self-preservation?

The *certainty* that the conditions of ethical relationships no longer correspond to their existence, as objectively substantiated by science and general insight, will, of course, be present only when law is the conscious expression of the people's will formulated with their knowledge and consent. Let us add a word about making divorce easier or more difficult: Do you consider a natural body healthy, sound, and truly organized if any external shock, any injury, would destroy it? Would you not feel offended if it were established as an axiom that your

[3] Hegel, *Grundlinien der Philosophie des Rechts*, Appendix 163.

friendship could not withstand the smallest accidents and must dissolve at any vagary? But in regard to marriage, the legislator can only determine when it *may* be dissolved, although it is already dissolved in its essence. The judicial dissolution can be only the recording of the inner dissolution. The viewpoint of the legislator is the viewpoint of necessity. Thus, the legislator honors marriage, recognizes its ethical essence, when he considers it strong enough to survive many conflicts without injuring it. Compliance with the wishes of individuals would be transformed into injustice against the essence of individuals; against their ethical reason which is embodied in ethical relationships.

Finally, we can call it only rashness when States with strict divorce laws (among which the Rhineland is *proud* to be included) are accused by some of hypocrisy. Only a person with a horizon that does not extend beyond the surrounding ethical corruption can venture such accusations, which the Rhineland, for example, finds ridiculous and at most considers as proof that even the notion of ethical relationships can be lost and any ethical fact can be taken as a fairy tale and a lie. This is the immediate consequence of laws and have not been dictated by a high regard for man—a mistake that cannot be eliminated by passing from material contempt to ideal contempt, and by demanding unconscious obedience to supra-ethical and supra-natural authority instead of conscious subordination to ethico-natural forces.

THE COMMUNITY OF WOMEN

From *Economic and Philosophic Manuscripts of 1844* (based on the translation by Progress Publishers, Moscow, 1959), pp. 93–95

... COMMUNISM IS:

(1) In its first form only a generalization and consummation of this relationship. It shows itself as such in a twofold form: on the one hand, the dominion of material property bulks so large that it seeks to destroy everything which is not capable of being possessed by all as private property. It seeks to abstract by force from talent, etc. For it the sole purpose of life and existence is direct, physical possession. The category of laborer is not done away with, but extended to all

Women and Children

men. The relationship of private property persists as the relationship of the community to the world of things. Finally, this movement of counterposing universal private property to private property finds expression in the bestial form of counterposing to marriage (certainly a form of exclusive private property) the community of women, in which a woman becomes a piece of communal and common property. It may be said that this idea of the community of women gives away the secret of this as yet completely crude and thoughtless communism. Just as the woman passes from marriage to general prostitution,[1] so the entire world of wealth (that is, of man's objective substance) passes from the relationship of exclusive marriage with the owner of private property to a state of universal prostitution with the community. In negating the personality of man in every sphere, this type of communism is really nothing but the logical expression of private property, which is this negation. General envy constituting itself as a power is the disguise in which avarice reestablishes itself and satisfies itself, only in another way. The thoughts of every piece of private property—inherent in each piece as such—are at least turned against all wealthier private property in the form of envy and the urge to reduce to a common level, so that this envy and urge even constitute the essence of competition. The crude communism is only the consummation of this envy and of this leveling down proceeding from the preconceived minimum. It has a definite, limited standard. How little this annulment of private property is really an appropriation is in fact proved by the abstract negation of the entire world of culture and civilization, the regression to the unnatural simplicity of the poor and undemanding man who has not only failed to go beyond private property, but has not yet even attained to it.

The community is only a community of labor, and an equality of wages paid out by the communal capital—the community as the universal capitalist. Both sides of the relationship are raised to an imagined universality—labor as a

---

[1] Prostitution is only a *specific* expression of the *general* prostitution of the *laborer,* and since it is a relationship in which not the prostitute alone, but also the one who prostitutes, fall—and the latter's abomination is still greater—the capitalism, etc., also comes under this head—K.M.

state in which every person is put, and capital as the acknowledged universality and power of the community.

In the approach to woman as the spoil and handmaid of communal lust is expressed the infinite degradation in which man exists for himself, for the secret of this approach has its unambiguous, decisive, plain, and undisguised expression in the relation of man to woman and in the manner in which the direct and natural procreative relationship is conceived. The direct, natural, and necessary relation of person to person is the relation of man to woman. In this natural relationship of the sexes man's relation to nature is immediately his relation to man, just as his relation to man is immediately his relation to nature—his own natural function. In this relationship, therefore, there is sensuously manifested, reduced to an observable fact, the extent to which the human essence has become nature to man, or to which nature has to him become the human essence of man. From this relationship one can therefore judge man's whole level of development. It follows from the character of this relationship how much man as a species being, as man, has come to be himself and to comprehend himself; the relation of man to woman is the most natural relation of human being to human being. It therefore reveals the extent to which man's natural behavior has become human, or the extent to which the human essence in him has come to be nature to him. In this relationship there is revealed, too, the extent to which man's need has become a human need; the extent to which, therefore, the other person as a person has become for him a need—the extent to which he in his individual existence is at the same time a social being. The first positive annulment of private property—crude communism—is thus merely one form in which the vileness of private property, which seeks to set itself up as the positive community, comes to the surface.

FAMILY

From Marx and Engels, *The German Ideology* (1945–46), Ch. III, Sec. D ("Hierarchy")

One cannot in general speak of *"the"* family. Historically, the bourgeoisie gives the family the character of the bourgeois family, wherein boredom and money are the binding links, and to which also belongs the bourgeois dissolution of the family, which does not prevent it from constantly continuing its existence. Its dirty existence corresponds to the holy concept of it in official phraseology and universal hypocrisy. Where the family is actually abolished, as in the proletariat, just the opposite of what "Stirner" thinks occurs. There the concept of the family does not exist at all, but here and there, to be sure, family affection, based on extremely real relations, can be found. In the eighteenth century, the concept of the family was dissolved by the philosophers, because the actual family was already in the process of dissolution at the highest pinnacles of civilization. The internal family bond was dissolved, including the separate components constituting the concept of the family, for example, obedience, piety, marital fidelity, etc.; but the real body of the family: property relation, the excluding relation toward other families, forced living together—relations produced by the existence of children, the structure of modern towns, the formation of capital, etc.—remained, although much disturbed, because the existence of the family is made necessary by its connection with the mode of production that is independent of the will of bourgeois society. This indispensability has been strikingly shown during the French Revolution, when for a moment the family was legally as good as abolished. The family continues to exist even in the nineteenth century, only the process of its dissolution has become more universal, not in regard to concept but because of the more developed industry and competition; it [the family] still exists, despite the fact that its dissolution has long been declared by French and English socialists, and this has at last penetrated to the German church fathers by way of French novels.

THE BOURGEOIS FAMILY

From the *Communist Manifesto* (1848). Pt. II

Abolition of the family. Even the most radical flare up at this infamous proposal of the Communists.

On what foundation is the present family, the bourgeois family, based? On capital, on private gain. In its completely developed form this family exists only among the bourgeoisie. But this state of things finds its complement in the practical absence of the family among the proletarians, and in public prostitution.

The bourgeois family will vanish as a matter of course when its complement vanishes, and both will vanish with the vanishing of capital.

Do you charge us with wanting to stop the exploitation of children by their parents? To this crime we plead guilty.

But, you will say, we destroy the most hallowed of relations when we replace home education by social.

And your education! Is not that also social, and determined by the social conditions under which you educate, by the intervention, direct or indirect, of society by means of schools, etc.? The Communists have not invented the intervention of society in education; they do but seek to alter the character of that intervention, and to rescue education from the influence of the ruling class.

The bourgeois claptrap about the family and education, about the hallowed co-relation of parent and child, becomes all the more disgusting, the more by the action of Modern Industry all family ties among the proletarians are torn asunder, and their children transformed into simple articles of commerce and instruments of labor.

But you Communists would introduce community of women, screams the whole bourgeoisie in chorus.

The bourgeois sees in his wife a mere instrument of production. He hears that the instruments of production are to be exploited in common, and, naturally, can come to no other conclusion than that the lot of being common to all will likewise fall to the women.

He has not even a suspicion that the real point aimed at is to do away with the status of women as mere instruments of production.

For the rest, nothing is more ridiculous than the virtuous indignation of our bourgeois at the community of women which, they pretend, is to be openly and officially established by the Communists. The Communists have no need to introduce community of women; it has existed almost from time immemorial.

Our bourgeois, not content with having the wives and daughters of their proletarians at their disposal, not to speak of comon prostitutes, take the greatest pleasure in seducing each others' wives.

Bourgeois marriage is in reality a system of wives in common, and thus, at the most, what the Communists might possibly be reproached with is that they desire to introduce, in susbtitution for a hypocritically concealed, an openly legalized community of women. For the rest, it is self-evident that the abolition of the present system of production must bring with it the abolition of the community of women springing from that system, i.e., of prostitution both public and private.

CHILD PSYCHOLOGY

From *"Debatten über Pressefreiheit und Publikation der Landständischen Verhandlungen,"* in *Rheinische Zeitung,* May 5, 1842

... It is well known that the first theoretical activity of the mind, oscillating halfway between sensateness and thinking, is *counting*. Counting is the child's first free theoretical act of reason....

Space is the first thing the size of which impresses the child. It is the size of the world that the child first experiences. Hence it considers a grown man to be a great man....

But the theoretical thinking of a child is quantitative: hence its judgment and its practical thought is practical-sensate. The sensate quality is the first tie that connects it with the world. The practical sense, preferably the nose and mouth, are the first organs with which it judges the world....

The child, of course, stops with its sensate perception; it sees only the particular. For the child, the invisible nerve threads that connect the particular with the general ... do not exist. The child believes the sun revolves around the earth; the general revolves around the particular. Hence the child does not believe in the *spirit* [*Geist*] but in *spirit*. ...

JUVENILE AND CHILD LABOR

"Instructions for the Delegates of the Provisional General Council [of the First International]. The Different Questions." Written in English at the end of August 1866; published in The International Courier, *February 20 and March 13, 1867.*

We consider the tendency of modern industry to make children and juvenile persons of both sexes cooperate in the great work of social production as a progressive, sound, and legitimate tendency, although under capital it was distorted into an abomination. In a rational state of society *every child whatever*, from the age of 9 years, ought to become a productive laborer in the same way that no able-bodied adult person ought to be exempted from the general law of nature, viz.: to work in order to be able to eat, and work not only with the brain but with the hands too.

However, for the present, we have only to deal with the children and young persons of both sexes [belonging to the working people. They ought to be divided][1] into three *classes*, to be treated differently; the first class to range from 9 to 12; the second, from 13 to 15 years; and the third to comprise of ages of 16 and 17 years. We propose that the employment of the first class in any workshop or housework be legally restricted to *two*; that of the second, to *four*; and that of the third, to *six* hours. For the third class, there must be a break of at least one hour for meals or relaxation.

It may be desirable to begin elementary school instruction before the age of 9 years; but we deal here only with the most indespensable antidotes against the tendencies of a social system which degrades the working man into a mere instrument for the accumulation of capital, and transforms parents by their necessities into slaveholders, sellers of their own children. The *right* of children and juvenile persons must be vindicated. They are unable to act for themselves. It is, therefore, the duty of society to act on their behalf.

[1] These words were ommitted in the newspaper text.

Women and Children   395

If the middle and higher classes neglect their duties toward their offspring, it is their own fault. Sharing the privileges of these classes, the child is condemned to suffer from their prejudices.

The case of the working class stands quite different. The working man is no free agent. In too many cases he is even too ignorant to understand the true interest of his child, or the normal conditions of human development. However, the more enlightened part of the working class fully understands that the future of its class, and, therefore, of mankind, altogether depends upon the formation of the rising working generation. They know that, before everything else, the children and juvenile workers must be saved from the crushing effects of the present system. This can only be effected by converting *social reason* into *social force*, and, under given circumstances, there exists no other method of doing so than through *general laws*, enforced by the power of the state. In enforcing such laws the working class does not fortify governmental power. On the contrary, they transform that power, now used against them, into their own agency. They effect by a general act what they would vainly attempt by a multitude of isolated individual efforts.

Proceeding from this standpoint we say that no parent and no employer ought to be allowed to use juvenile labor except when combined with education.

By education we understand three things.

Firstly: *Mental education.*

Secondly: *Bodily education*, such as is given in schools of gymnastics, and by military exercise.

Thirdly: *Technological training*, which imparts the general principles of all processes of production, and, simultaneously, initiates the child and young person in the practical use and handling of the elementary instruments of all trades.

A gradual and progressive course of mental, gymnastic, and technological training ought to correspond to the classification of the juvenile laborers. The costs of the technological schools ought to be partly met by the sale of their products.

The combination of paid productive labor, mental education, bodily exercise, and polytechnic training will raise the working class far above the level of the higher and middle classes.

It is self-understood that the employment of all persons

from [9] and to 17 years (inclusively) in nightwork and all health-injuring trades must be strictly prohibited by law.

WOMEN AND CHILDREN IN INDUSTRY

From Capital, *Vol. I, Ch. 15, Sec. e. The text used here is from the third German edition, translated by Samuel Moore and Edward Aveling, published by Charles H. Kerr & Co., Chicago, 1906, as revised by Ernest Untermann.*

The cheapening of labor power, by sheer abuse of the labor of women and children, by sheer robbery of every normal condition requisite for working and living, and by the sheer brutality of overwork and night work, meets at last with natural obstacles that cannot be overstepped. So also, when based on these methods, do the cheapening of commodities and capitalist exploitation in general. So soon as this point is at last reached—and it takes many years—the hour has struck for the introduction of machinery, and for the thenceforth rapid conversion of the scattered domestic industries and also of manufactures into factory industries.

An example, on the most collossal scale, of this movement is afforded by the production of wearing apparel. This industry, according to the classification of the Children's Employment Commission, comprises straw-hat makers, ladies'-hat makers, cap-makers, tailors, milliners and dressmakers, shirt-makers, corset-makers, glove-makers, shoemakers, besides many minor branches, such as the making of neckties, collars, etc. In 1861, the number of females employed in these industries, in England and Wales, amounted to 586,299; of these, 115,242 at the least were under 20, and 16,650 under 15 years of age. The number of these workwomen in the United Kingdom in 1861 was 750,334. The number of males employed in England and Wales in hat-making, shoe-making, glove-making and tailoring was 437,969; of these, 14,964 under 15 years, 89,285 between 15 and 20, and 333,117 over 20 years. Many of the smaller branches are not included in these figures. But take the figures as they stand; we then have for England and Wales alone, according to the census of 1861, a total of 1,024,277 persons, about as many as are absorbed by agriculture and cattle breeding. We begin to understand what becomes of the immense quantities of goods conjured up by the magic of machinery, and of the enormous masses of workpeople, which that machinery sets free.

The production of wearing apparel is carried on partly in manufactories in whose workrooms there is but a reproduction of that division of labor, the *membre disjecta* of which were found ready to hand; partly by small master-handicraftsmen; these, however, do not, as formerly, work for individual consumers but for manufactories and warehouses, and to such an extent that often whole towns and stretches of country carry on certain branches, such as shoemaking, as a specialty; finally, on a very great scale by the so-called domestic workers, who form an external department of the manufactories, warehouses, and even the workshops of the smaller masters.[1]

The raw material, etc., is supplied by mechanical industry, the mass of cheap human material (*taillable à merci et miséricorde*)[2] is composed of the individuals "liberated" by mechanical industry and improved agriculture. The manufactures of this class owed their origin chiefly to the capitalist's need to have at hand an army ready equipped to meet any increase of demand.[3] . . . At last the critical point was reached. The basis of the old method, sheer brutality in the exploitation of the workpeople accompanied more or less by a systematic division of labor, no longer sufficed for the expanding markets and for the still more rapidly expanding competition of the capitalists. The hour struck for the advent of machinery. The decisively revolutionary machine, the machine which attacks in an equal degree the whole of the numberless branches of this sphere of production—dressmaking, tailoring, shoemaking, sewing, hat-making, and many others—is the sewing machine.

---

[1] In England millinery and dressmaking are for the most part carried on on the premises of the employer, partly by workmen who live there, partly by women who live off the premises.—K.M.

[2] "Delivered to mercy and charity."

[3] Mr. White, a commissioner, visited a military clothing manufactory that employed 1,000 to 1,200 persons, almost all females, and a shoe manufactory with 1,300 persons; of these nearly one half were children and young persons.—K.M.

Its immediate effect on the workpeople is like that of all machinery, which, since the rise of modern industry, has seized upon new branches of trade. Children of too tender an age are sent adrift. The wage of the machine hands rises compared with that of the houseworkers, many of whom belong to the poorest of the poor. That of the better-situated handicraftsmen, with whom the machine competes, sinks. The new machine hands are exclusively girls and young women. With the help of mechanical force they destroy the monopoly that male labor had of the heavier work, and they drive off from the lighter work numbers of old women and very young children. The overpowering competition crushes the weakest of the manual laborers. The fearful increase in death from starvation during the last ten years in London runs parallel with the extension of machine sewing.[4] The new workwomen turn the machines by hand and foot, or by hand alone, sometimes sitting, sometimes standing, according to the weight, size, and special make of the machine, and expend a great deal of labor power. Their occupation is unwholesome, owing to the long hours, although in most cases they are not so long as under the old system. Wherever the sewing machine locates itself in narrow and already overcrowded workrooms, it adds to the unwholesome influences. "The effect," says Mr. Lord, "on entering low-ceiled workrooms in which 30 to 40 machine hands are working is unbearable. . . . The heat, partly due to the gas stoves used for warming the irons, is horrible. . . . Even when moderate hours of work, i.e., from 8 in the morning till 6 in the evening, prevail in such places, yet 3 or 4 persons fall into a swoon regularly every day."[5]

From *Capital*, Vol. I, Ch. 15, Sec. 8c

In the hardware manufactures of Birmingham and the neighborhood, there are employed, mostly in very heavy work, 30,000 children and young persons, besides 10,000

---

[4] An instance. The weekly report of deaths by the Registrar-General, dated 26th February, 1864, contains 5 cases of death from starvation. On the same day *The Times* reports another case. Six victims of starvation in one week!—K.M.

[5] Children's Employment Commission, Second Report, 1864, p. lxvii, n. 406-991; p. 84, n. 124; p. lxxiii, n. 441; p. 68, n. 6; p. 84, n. 126; p. 78, n. 85; p. 76, n. 695 p. lxxii, n. 483.

women. There they are to be seen in the unwholesome brass-foundries, button factories, enameling, galvanizing, and lacquering works. Owing to the excessive labor of their workpeople, both adult and nonadult, certain London houses where newspapers and books are printed have got the ill-omened name of "slaughterhouses." Similar excesses are practiced in bookbinding, where the victims are chiefly women, girls, and children; young persons have to do heavy work in rope walks and night work in salt mines, candle manufactories, and chemical works; young people are worked to death at turning the looms in silk weaving, when it is not carried on by machinery. One of the most shameful, the most dirty, and the worst paid kinds of labor, and one on which women and young girls are by preference employed, is the sorting of rags. It is well known that Great Britain, apart from its own immense store of rags, is the emporium for the rag trade of the whole world. They flow in from Japan, from the most remote States of South America, and from the Canary Islands. But the chief sources of their supply are Germany, France, Russia, Italy, Egypt, Turkey, Belgium, and Holland. They are used for manure, for making bed-flocks, for shoddy, and they serve as the raw material of paper. The rag sorters are the medium for the spread of smallpox and other infectious diseases, and they themselves are the first victims. A classical example of overwork, of hard and inappropriate labor, and of its brutalizing effects on the workman from his childhood upwards, is afforded not only by coal mining and miners generally, but also by tile- and brick-making, in which industry the recently invented machinery is, in England, used only here and there. Between May and September the work lasts from 5 in the morning till 8 in the evening, and where the drying is done in the open air it often lasts from 4 in the morning till 9 in the evening. Work from 5 in the morning till 7 in the evening is considered "reduced" and "moderate."

Both boys and girls of 6 and even 4 years of age are employed. They work for the same number of hours, often longer, than the adults. The work is hard and the summer heat increases the exhaustion. In a certain tile field at Mosley, e.g., a young woman 24 years of age was in the habit of making 2,000 tiles a day, with the assistance of two little girls, who carried the clay for her, and stacked the tiles. These girls carried daily 10 tons up the slippery sides of the clay pits, from a depth of 30 feet, and then for a distance of 210 feet.

It is impossible for a child to pass through the purgatory of a tile-field without great moral degradation. . . . The low language, which they are accustomed to hear from their tenderest years, the filthy, indecent, and shameless habits, amidst which, unknowing, and half wild, they grow up, make them in afterlife lawless, abandoned, dissolute. . . . A frightful source of demoralization is the mode of living. Each molder, who is always a skilled laborer, and the chief of a group, supplies his seven subordinates with board and lodging in his cottage. Whether members of his family or not, the men, boys, and girls all sleep in the cottage, which contains generally two, exceptionally three rooms, all on the ground floor, and badly ventilated. These people are so exhausted after the day's work that neither the rules of health or cleanliness, nor of decency are in the least observed. Many of these cottages are models of untidiness, dirt, and dust. . . . The greatest evil of the system that employs young girls on this sort of work consists in this, that, as a rule, it chains them fast from childhood for the whole of their afterlife to the most abandoned rabble. They become rough, foul-mouthed boys, before Nature has taught them that they are women. Clothed in a few dirty rags, the legs naked far above the knees, hair and face besmeared with dirt, they learn to treat all feelings of decency and of shame with contempt. During mealtimes they lie at full length in the fields, or watch the boys bathing in a neighboring canal. Their heavy day's work at length completed, they put on better clothes, and accompany the men to the public houses.

That excessive insobriety is prevalent from childhood upwards among the whole class is only natural.

The worst is that the brick-makers despair of themselves. You might as well, said one of the better kind to a chaplain of Southallfield, try to raise and improve the devil as a brickie, sir!

THE INFLUENCE OF MACHINERY ON CHILD AND WOMAN LABOR

From Minutes of the General Council of the First International, July 28, 1868

The discussion of the proposition, "The influence of machinery in the hands of capitalists," was opened by Citizen Marx. He said what strikes us most is that all the consequences which were expected as the inevitable result of machinery have been reversed. Instead of diminishing the hours of labor, the working day was prolonged to sixteen and eighteen hours. Formerly, the normal working day was ten hours....

It was not until 1833 that the hours of labor for children were limited to twelve. In consequence of overwork there was no time left whatever for mental culture. They also became physically deteriorated; contagious fevers broke out among them, and this induced a portion of the upper class to take the matter up. The first Sir Robert Peel was one of the foremost in calling attention to the crying evil, and Robert Owen was the first mill owner who limited the hours of labor in his factory. The ten hours' bill was the first law which limited the hours of labor to ten and a half per day for women and children, but it applied only to certain factories....

Another consequence of the use of machinery was to force women and children into the factory. The woman has thus become an active agent in our social production. Formerly female and children's labor was carried on within the family circle. I do not say that it is wrong that women and children should participate in our social production. I think every child above the age of nine ought to be employed at productive labor a portion of its time, but the way in which they are made to work under existing circumstances is abominable....

To conclude for the present, machinery leads on one hand to associated organized labor, on the other to the disintegration of all formerly existing social and family relations.

CHILD LABOR

From interview with correspondent of the *New York Herald,* August 3, 1871

The recent exposé of children as young as four years working in the *back*fields is a case in point. Here are children—girls and boys of from eight to ten years old—carrying forty pounds of earth upon their heads a distance of fourteen miles a day, living in the mud like beasts until they have almost lost the semblance of the human form divine; and yet the men who have grown rich from the blood and sweat and toil and suffering of these poor, miserable little creatures—these men who call themselves respectable, who go to church on Sundays in their carriages—come to me and talk about the sacredness of private property forsooth! So talked the cotton planter of the South. So talks every heavy-handed infamy that has ever disgraced humanity.

FEMALE AND CHILD LABOR

From "Marginal Notes to the Program of the German Workers' Party" (Gotha Program) (1875), Pt. IV

The standardization of the working day must include the restriction of female labor, insofar as it relates to the duration, intermissions, etc., of the working day; otherwise it could only mean the exclusion of female labor from branches of industry that are especially unhealthy for the female body or are objectionable morally for the female sex. If that is what was meant, it should so have been said.

"Prohibition of child labor." Here it was absolutely essential to state the age limit.

A general prohibition of child labor is incompatible with the existence of large-scale industry and hence an empty, pious wish. Its realization—if it were possible—would be reactionary, since, with a strict regulation of the working time according to the different age groups and other safety measures for the protection of children, an early combination of productive labor with education is one of the most potent means for the transformation of present-day society.

SELECTED BIBLIOGRAPHY

(In English)
ONE-VOLUME COLLECTIONS

MARX'S NON-ECONOMIC BOOKS IN ENGLISH TRANSLATION

The Difference Between the Democritean and Epicurean Philosophy of Nature, Ph.D. dissertation, 1841, in N. D. Livergood, *Activity in Marx's Philosophy*. The Hague, 1967.

Critique of Hegel's "Philosophy of Right," 1844, ed. by J. O. Malley. Cambridge, 1970.

Economic and Philosophic Manuscripts of 1844. Moscow, 1959; New York, 1964.

The Holy Family, with Engels, 1845. Moscow, 1956.

The German Ideology, with Engels, 1846. Moscow, 1964.

The Poverty of Philosophy, 1847. Moscow, 1955.

The Class Struggles in France, 1848–50. 1850. Moscow, 1969.

The Eighteenth Brumaire of Louis Napoleon, 1852. New York, 1963.

The Civil War in France, 1871. Moscow, 1968.

ONE-VOLUME COLLECTIONS

Avineri, S. *Karl Marx on Colonialism and Modernization*. New York, 1969.

Bottomore, T. B. *Karl Marx: Selected Writings in Sociology and Social Philosophy*. New York, 1956.

Easton, L. D., and Guddat, K. H. *Writings of the Young Marx on Philosophy and Society*. New York, 1967.

McLellan, D. *Karl Marx: Early Texts*. New York, 1971.

Padover, S. K. *Karl Marx on Revolution.* New York, 1971.

Padover, S. K. *Karl Marx on America and the Civil War.* New York, 1972.

Padover, S. K. *Karl Marx on the First International.* New York, 1973.

Padover, S. K. *Karl Marx on Freedom of the Press and Censorship.* New York, 1974.

Padover, S. K. *Karl Marx on Religion.* New York, 1974.

Padover, S. K. *Karl Marx on Education, Women and Children.* New York, 1975.

Padover, S. K. *Karl Marx on History and People.* New York, 1977.

BIOGRAPHIES

Berlin, I. *Karl Marx: His Life and Environment.* Oxford, 1939.

McLellan, D. *Marx Before Marxism.* New York, 1970.

McLellan, D. *Karl Marx: His Life and Thought.* New York, 1974.

Mehring, F. *Karl Marx.* English trans., Ann Arbor, 1962.

Padover, S. K. *Karl Marx: An Intimate Biography.* New York, 1978.

Payne, R. *Marx.* London, 1968.

Stepanova, E. *Karl Marx: Short Biography.* Moscow, 1956.

INTERPRETATIONS

Althusser, L. *For Marx.* New York, 1970.

Bober, M. M. *Karl Marx's Interpretation of History.* Cambridge, Mass., 1927.

Garaudy, R. *Karl Marx, The Evolution of His Thought.* New York, 1967.

Lefebvre, H. *The Sociology of Marx*. New York, 1968.

Lichtheim, G. *Marxism, An Historical and Critical Study*. New York, 1961.

Tucker, R. C. *The Marxian Revolutionary Idea*. New York, 1969.

BIOGRAPHIC INDEX

Aeschylus (*525–456* B.C.), Greek dramatist, 35, 248n

Alexander I (*1777–1825*), Czar of Russia, 1801–1825, 31, 135n

Alexander II (*1818–1881*), Czar of Russia, 1855–1881, 94n

Anaxagoras (*c. 500–c. 428* B.C.), classical Greek philosopher, 300

Anderson, James (*1739–1808*), Scottish economist, 326

Annenkov, Pavel Vassilyevich (*1812–1887*), liberal Russian landowner, 6, 111 & n

Apelles (*4th century* B.C.), classical Greek painter, 29n

Archestratus (*4th century* B.C.), classical Greek poet, 250

Archimedes (*c. 287–212* B.C.), classical Greek mathematician and physicist, 316, 365

Aristotle (*384–322* B.C.), classical Greek philosopher, 106, 201, 258

Arkwright, Sir Richard (*1732–1792*), British inventor, 92, 213

Arnauld, Antoine (*1612–1694*), French philosopher, 299

Ashley (*see* Shaftesbury)

Auer, Ignace (*1846–1907*), German Social Democratic leader, 169

Augustine, Saint (*354–430*), Doctor of the Church, 256–57

Aveling, Edward (*1851–1898*), English socialist, co-translator of Marx's *Capital*, 396

Babeuf, François Noel (*1760–1797*), French revolutionist, 148, 304

Bacon, Francis (*1561–1626*), English philosopher and statesman, 201 & n, 257, 301–02

Biographic Index

Bailly, Jean Sylvain *(1736–1793)*, guillotined French revolutionist, 236

Bakunin, Michael *(1814–1876)*, Russian anarchist, 19, 169 & n

Balzac, Honoré de *(1799–1850)*, French novelist, 21, 28

Banks, George *(1788–1856)*, Tory member of Parliament, 317

Barbès, Armand *(1809–1870)*, French revolutionist, condemned to life imprisonment in 1848, amnestied in 1854, 65, 355

Barbon, Nicholas *(1640–1698)*, English economist, 324

Basedow, Johann Bernhard *(1724–1790)*, German pedagogical writer, 213n

Bastian, Adolf *(1862–1905)*, German ethnographer, 359–60 & n

Bastiat, Frédéric *(1801–1850)*, French economist, 129 & n

Bauer, Bruno *(1809–1882)*, Young Hegelian German philosopher, friend of Marx during his Berlin University days, 202, 204, 232–33, 254, 281, 326–51

Bauer, Heinrich (n.d.), German shoemaker, Communist League member, emigrated to Australia, 1851, 154

Bayle, Pierre *(1647–1706)*, French rationalist philosopher, 299–300

Beaumelle, Laurent de la *(1726–1773)*, French anti-Voltaire journalist, 37

Beaumont, Gustave Auguste de *(1802–1866)*, French writer who traveled with de Tocqueville in America, 330, 339, 349

Bebel, August *(1840–1913)*, leading founder of the German Social Democratic Party, 97, 169

Becker, Bernhard *(1826–1882)*, German editor and labor leader, 170

Bellers, John *(1654–1725)*, English economist, 213n

Bentham, Jeremy *(1748–1832)*, English philosopher, founder of Utilitarianism, 28–29, 304

Beresford, William (b. *1798*), Tory politician, member of Parliament, 51

Berkeley, Francis Henry Fitzhardinge *(1794–1870)*, Liberal member of Parliament, 56

Bernstein, Eduard *(1850–1932)*, German Social Democratic theorist, 99n

Berry, Marie Caroline de (*1798–1870*), French duchess, mother of Comte de Chambord, Legitimist Pretender to French throne, 35

Bismarck, Otto von (*1815–1898*), Prussian Prime Minister, *1862–1871*; German Imperial Chancellor, *1871–1890*, 36, 179–80, 226n

Blanc, Louis (*1811–1898*), French revolutionist and socialist, 234

Blanqui, Louis Auguste (*1805–1881*), French communist, spent 36 years of his life in prison, 65, 355

Bligh, James, an active Chartist, 316–17

Boehme, Jakob (*1575–1624*), German mystic, 301

Boethius, Anicius Manlius Severinus (*c.480–524* A.D.), Roman philosopher, 364

Boettlicher, Johann Friedrich Wilhelm (*1798–1850*), German philologist, 239

Boileau, Étienne (*1200–1269*), royal Captain of Paris, 210n

Bolte, Friedrich (n.d.), German cigar maker, emigrated to U.S., member of First International, and of New York *Arbeiter-Zeitung* editorial board, 95

Bonaparte, Louis (*see* Napoleon III)

Boxhorn, Marcus Zuerius (*1612–1653*), Dutch historian, 91n

Bracke, Wilhelm (*1842–1880*), German publisher, a founder of the Social Democratic Party, 19, 97, 99, 168–69

Brissot de Warville, Jacques (Jean) Pierre (*1754–1793*), French revolutionist, Jacobin, later Girondist, 125 & n

Brontë, Charlotte (*1816–1855*), English novelist, 22

Bruckner, John (*1726–1804*), English Protestant theologian, 324

Buchez, Philippe Joseph Benjamin (*1796–1865*), French republican historian, journalist and politician, 183, 343

Buelow-Cummerow, Ernst Gottfried Georg von (*1755–1851*), Prussian journalist and politician, 105

Buridan, Jean (fl. *1328*), French Scholastic philosopher, rector of the University of Paris, 59

Cabanis, Pierre Jean Georges (*1757–1808*), French physician and materialist philosopher, 298

Cabet, Étienne (*1788–1856*), French utopian communist, author of *Voyage en Icarie* (1840), 108–09 & n, 128, 131, 304

Biographic Index 409

Caesar, Julius (*c.102–44* B.C.), Roman general and statesman, 235, 244 & n, 257, 363

Campanella, Thomas (*1568–1639*), Italian utopian communist, 257

Cantillon, Richard (*1680–1734*), English economist and businessman, 324

Cardano, Geronimo (*1501–1576*), Italian physician and mathematician, 363

Cardwell, Edward, Viscount (*1813–1886*), British Liberal statesman, 47

Carlyle, Thomas (*1795–1881*), Scottish essayist and historian, 29–31

Castlereagh, Robert Stewart, viscount (*1769–1822*), British statesman, 92

Caussidière, Marc (*1808–1865*), French socialist émigré in London after 1848 revolution, 234

Chalmers, Thomas (*1780–1847*), Scottish theologian and economist, 324, 326

Chamisso, Adelbert von (*1781–1838*), German poet, 202

Charlemagne (*742–814*), King of the Franks, 321

Charles VI (*1685–1740*), Holy Roman Emperor, 1711–1740, 91n

Chateaubriand, François René de (*1786–1848*), French author, 31–32

Chrysippus (*c.280–c.205* B.C.), Greek Stoic philosopher, 250

Clement of Alexandria (*c.150–c.215*), a Greek Church Father, Gnostic, 252

Cobbett, William (*c.1763–1835*), English journalist and reformer, 30

Collins, Anthony (*1679–1729*), English materialist philosopher, 302

Condillac, Étienne Bonnot de (*1715–1780*), French philosopher, Deist, 204, 299, 302

Condorcet, Marie Jean Antoine Nicolas, marquis de (*1743–1794*), French philosopher and revolutionist, 124n, 258, 323

Considérant, Victor (*1808–1893*), French Fourierist socialist, 106

Constant, Benjamin (*1767–1830*), Swiss-born French writer, 235

Cook, Joseph, of Boston, 96

Cooke, George Wingrove (*1814–1865*), English historian, 45

Copernicus, Nicholas *(1475–1543)*, Polish astronomer, founder of modern astronomy, 257–58

Corbon, Claude Anthime *(1808–1891)*, French republican politician, 212n

Cousin, Victor *(1792–1862)*, French philosopher, 235

Coward, William *(c.1656–1725)*, English materialist philosopher, 302

Cramer, Andreas Wilhelm *(1760–1833)*, German jurist and philosopher, 200 & n

Cromwell, Oliver *(1599–1658)*, Lord Protector of England, 1653–1658, 30 & n, 97, 236

Crossley, Francis *(1817–1872)*, English manufacturer, member of Parliament, 52, 57

Danton, Georges Jacques *(1759–1794)*, French Revolutionary orator who was guillotined, 30, 234, 235

D'Arsonval, Jacques Arsène *(1851–1940)*, French physiologist and physicist, 359

Darwin, Charles *(1809–1882)*, author of *On the Origin of Species* (1859), admired by Marx, 244, 354, 359–61, 369–70

Davis, John Chandler Bancroft *(1822–1907)*, American diplomat, envoy in Berlin, *1874–1877*, 185–86

Defoe, Daniel *(1660–1731)*, English author, famous for his *Robinson Crusoe* (1719), 323

Democritus *(c.460–c.370 B.C.)*, classical Greek philosopher, one of main subjects of Marx's Ph.D. dissertation, 2n, 15, 246, 283, 300, 354

Demuth, Helene *(1823–1890)*, the Marx family lifelong housekeeper and friend, 384

Deprez, Marcel *(1843–1918)*, French physicist, 359 & n

Derby, Edward, earl of *(1799–1869)*, Tory statesman, Prime Minister, *1858–1859, 1866–1868*, 53

Descartes, René *(1596–1650)*, French philosopher and scientist, 297–98, 302–03

Dézamy, Théodore *(1803–1850)*, French utopian communist, 108, 304

Dickens, Charles *(1812–1870)*, English novelist, 22

Diderot, Denis *(1713–1784)*, French philosopher, leader of the Enlightenment, 35

Dodwell, Henry *(d.1784)*, English Deist, 302.

Duchinski, Franciszek *(1817–1893)*, Polish historian and ethnographer, 361

Biographic Index

Duncker, Franz Gustav *(1822–1888)*, Berlin publisher of Marx's *Critique of Political Economy*, 18

Dunoyer, Barthélemy Charles Pierre Joseph *(1786–1862)*, French economist, 128

Duns Scotus, John *(d.1308)*, Scottish Scholastic philosopher, 300

Eccarius, Georg Johann *(1818–1889)*, German refugee tailor in London, general secretary of First International, 224

Edwards, Henry, Tory member of Parliament, 52, 57

Enfantin, Barthélemy Prosper *(1796–1864)*, French Saint-Simonian socialist, 107

Engels, Frederick *(1820–1895)*, Marx's lifelong friend and collaborator, 4–10, 13, 15–16, 18, 20, 29, 31, 32, 39, 42, 57, 97, 102, 133, 188, 152, 154, 165, 169, 203, 211n, 229, 238, 279, 304, 314, 354-55, 357-58n, 361 & n, 366, 368

Epicurus *(341–270 b.c.)*, classical Greek philosopher, one of the subjects of Marx's Ph.D. dissertation, 2n, 15, 247–52, 283, 311, 322, 354, 366

Euler, Leonhard *(1707–1803)*, Swiss pioneer mathematician, 12

Everet, *(18th century)*, English inventor, 92

Favre, Jules *(1809–1880)*, French politician, negotiated peace treaty with Germany in 1871, 37

Feuerbach, Johann Paul Anselm von *(1775–1833)*, German jurist, father of Ludwig Feuerbach, 56, 200 & n

Feuerbach, Ludwig *(1804–1872)*, German materialist philosopher who influenced Marx, 3, 110, 233, 254, 281–83, 289, 298–99, 304–05

Fichte, Johann Gottlieb *(1762–1814)*, German nationalist philosopher, 195 & n, 199, 257

Finlen, James (n.d.), prominent English Chartist, 317

Flerovsky, N. (pseudonym for Bervi, Vassily) *(1829–1918)*, Russian economist and sociologist, 11

Fourier, François Marie Charles *(1772–1837)*, French utopian socialist theorist, 102, 106, 108, 112, 122, 148, 150, 245, 304

Fraas, Karl Nikolaus *(1810–1875)*, German botanist and agronomist, 244–45 & n

Franklin, Benjamin *(1706–1790)*, American statesman and scientist, 323–24

Frederick I (Barbarossa) (*1123–1190*), Holy Roman Emperor, *1155–1190*, 58
Frederick II (*1194–1250*), Holy Roman Emperor, *1220–1250*, 58, 321
Frederick II (the Great) (*1712–1786*), King of Prussia, *1740–1786*, 60
Frederick William IV (*1795–1861*), King of Prussia, *1840–1861*, 59–60, 67, 262
Fréron, Elie (*1719–1776*), French anti-Voltaire journalist, 37
Fritzsche, Friedrich Wilhelm (*1825–1905*), German labor leader and editor, 97
Frost, John (*1784–1877*), Chartist, banished to Australia in 1839, returned in 1856, 56
Fulton, Robert (*1765–1815*), American inventor, builder of steamboats, 213n

Gaertner, Gustav Friedrich (d.*1841*), German jurist, Bonn University professor, 202
Gans, Eduard (*c.1797–1839*), Hegelian professor of law at Berlin University, where Marx attended his lectures, 246
Garnier, Germain de (*1754–1821*), French Physiocratic economist, 24 & n
Gaskell, Elizabeth (Cleghorn Stevenson) (*1810–1865*), English novelist, 22
Gassendi, Petrus (Pierre), (*1592–1655*) French materialist philosopher, 298–99
Gay, Jules (*1807–c.1876*), French utopian communist, 304
Geib, August (*1842–1879*), Hamburg bookdealer, a founder of the German Social Democratic Party, 169
Geiser, Bruno (*1846–1898*), German Social Democratic journalist, 97
George IV (*1762–1830*), British king, *1820–1830*, 315
George, Henry (*1839–1897*), American economist, founder of Single Tax movement, 33–34
Gladstone, Robert (*1811–1877*), English businessman, brother of Prime Minister Gladstone, 383
Gladstone, William Ewart (*1809–1898*), British Prime Minister, *1868, 1880–1885, 1892–1894*, 47, 96
Goerres, Johannes Joseph von (*1776–1848*), German historian, 372–73
Goethe, Johann Wolfgang von (*1749–1832*), German poet and dramatist, 35, 79, 181, 365
Gracchi:—Gaius Sempronius (*153–121* B.C.) and Tiberius

Biographic Index

Sempronius *(163–133 B.C.)* Gracchus, Roman statesmen, 235

Graham, Sir James Robert George *(1792–1861)*, British Tory statesman, 47

Granville, Lady Maria Luise Dalberg *(d.1860)*, wife of British Whig statesman, George Leveson-Gower, Earl Granville *(1815–1891)*, 318

Gratian *(12th century)*, Italian monk, founder of canon law, 200-01 & n

Grey, Sir Henry George, earl of *(1802–1894)*, British Whig statesman, 52

Grimm, Jakob *(1785–1863)*, German philologist, a founder of modern philology, 238, 243 & n, 244–45

Grolmann, Karl Ludwig Wilhelm von *(1775–1829)*, German jurist, 200 & n

Grosvenor, Robert, lord *(1801–1895)*, English Whig statesman, 315–16, 319

Grotius, Hugo *(1583–1645)*, Dutch jurist, pioneer in international law, 257

Gruen, Karl *(1817–1887)*, German journalist, spokesman of so-called true socialism, 39, 126

Guizot, François Pierre Guillaume *(1787–1874)*, French statesman and historian, 30 & n, 35–36, 135, 235, 240

Hamilton, Thomas *(1789–1842)*, Scottish author of *Men and Manners in America* (1833), 330–32, 349

Hansemann, David Justus *(1790–1864)*, Cologne banker, Prussian Minister of Finance, 1848, 278–79

Harney, George Julian *(1817–1897)*, English Chartist, editor of *Northern Star* and *Red Republican*, 133

Hartley, David *(1705–1757)*, English physician and materialist philosopher, 302

Hasenclever, Wilhelm *(b. 1844)*, German labor journalist and Reichstag deputy, 97

Hegel, Georg Wilhelm Friedrich *(1770–1831)*, German philosopher whose ideas had a profound influence on Marx, 3, 31, 60, 66, 70, 112, 114, 125–126, 199 & n, 200–02, 204, 228, 231–32, 234, 240, 244, 246–47, 254, 257, 259–60, 282, 284, 286, 288–93, 297, 303, 333–34, 342, 360, 367 & n, 387

Heine, Heinrich *(1797–1856)*, German poet, friend of Marx in Paris, 3, 29, 200

414   THE ESSENTIAL MARX

Heineccius, Johann Gottlieb (*1681–1741*), German jurist, 194–95 & n

Helvétius, Claude Adrien (*1715–1771*), French philosopher, Encyclopedist, 29, 128, 204, 299, 302–04

Hengstenberg, Ernst von (*1802–1869*), German theologian, Berlin University professor, 61

Hennequin, Victor Antoine (*1816–1854*), French Fourierist socialist, 106

Heraclitus (*c.535–c.475* B.C.), classical Greek philosopher, 258

Hermes, Carl Heinrich (*1800–1856*), German journalist, an editor of *Koelnische Zeitung*, 248

Hobbes, Thomas (*1588–1679*), English philosopher and political theorist, 257, 299, 301–02, 324, 360

Hoechberg, Karl (*1853–1885*), German socialist writer, editor of the Social Democratic journal, *Zukunft*, 99n

Horne, George (*1730–1792*), Bishop of Norwich, 325

Hume, David (*1711–1776*), English philosopher, historian and economist, 248 & n, 324–25

Hume, Joseph (*1777–1855*), English radical member of Parliament, 56

Huxley, Thomas Henry (*1825–1895*), English biologist, 362

Jean Paul (pseudonym for Richter, Johann Paul Friedrich) (*1763–1825*), German satirist, 31

Jones, Ernest Charles (*1819–1869*), English Chartist, publisher of *Notes to the People* and *The People's Paper*, London Chartist weeklies, 52–57

Kant, Immanuel (*1724–1804*), German philosopher, 124–26, 198–99, 284

Kelley-Wischnewetzky, Florence (*1859–1932*), American socialist, 4n

Kepler, Johannes (*1571–1630*), German astronomer, discoverer of the laws of planetary motion, 35, 367

King, Peter John Locke (*1811–1885*), radical member of Parliament, 56

Kirkwood, Daniel (*1814–1895*), American professor of astronomy at Indiana University, 366–67

Klein, Ernst Ferdinand (*1743–1810*), German jurist, 198 & n

Korff, Hermann (n.d.), ex-Prussian officer, manager of *Neue Rheinische Zeitung* under Marx's editorship, 279

Biographic Index

Kosegarten, Wilhelm *(1792–1868)*, German pro-feudalism writer, 106

Kuepper, Johann Abraham *(1779–1850)*, Lutheran pastor, Marx's religious teacher in Trier, 307

Kugelmann, Ludwig *(1828–1902)*, Hanover physician, friend of Marx, 244 & n, 384–85

Lafargue, Laura (*see* Marx, Laura)

Laffitte, Jacques *(1767–1844)*, French banker and politician, 35

Lamartine, Alphonse Marie Louis de *(1790–1869)*, French poet and politician, 131–33

Lamettrie (La Mettrie), Julien Offray de *(1709–1751)*, French materialist philosopher, 298, 302–03

Lancelotti, Giovanni Paolo *(1511–1591)*, Italian jurist, specialist on canon law, 91, 201 & n

Lange, Friedrich Albert *(1828–1875)*, German philosopher, 181

Lange, Joachim *(1670–1744)*, German theologian, 258

Laplace, Pierre Simon, marquis de *(1749–1827)*, French astronomer and mathematician, 366–67

Lassalle, Ferdinand *(1825–1864)*, German lawyer and labor leader, founder of General German Workers Association, 169, 173–75, 178–79, 181–84, 186, 226, 282

Lauterbach, Wolfgang Adam *(1618–1678)*, German jurist, 200 & n

Law, John *(1671–1729)*, Scottish financier and economist, 299, 324

Leibniz (Leibnitz), Gottfried Wilhelm von *(1649–1716)*, German philosopher and mathematician, 12, 297–300, 302–03

Lenin, Nikolai (Ulyanov, Vladimir Ilyich) *(1870–1924)*, Russian communist statesman, first premier of the Soviet Union, 6

Leopold I *(1790–1865)*, king of the Belgians, 1831–1865, 7

Leroux, Pierre *(1791–1871)*, French Saint-Simonian socialist, 106

Le Roy (De Roy), Henry *(1598–1679)*, Dutch physician and philosopher, 298

Lessing, Gotthold Ephraim *(1719–1781)*, German dramatist, exponent of the Enlightenment, 198 & n, 259

Liebknecht, Wilhelm *(1826–1900)*, a leading founder of the

German Social Democratic Party, friend and follower of Marx, 97, 169
Linguet, Simon Nicolas Henri (*1736–1794*), French economist, 130 & n
Locke, John (1632–1704), English philosopher and political theorist, 204, 236, 298, 300, 302, 324
Longuet, Charles (*1839–1903*), French socialist, husband of Marx's daughter Jenny, 19–20, 359
Louis XVIII (*1755–1824*), King of France, *1815–1824*, 31, 235
Louis Philippe (*1773–1850*), King of France, *1830–1848*, 3, 35–37, 85, 183, 383
Lucian (*2d century*), Greek satirist, 325
Lucretius (Titus Lucretius Carus) (*c.99–c.55* B.C.), Roman poet, 251–52
Luden, Heinrich (*1780–1847*), professor of history, Jena University, 198 & n
Luther, Martin (*1483–1546*), German leader of the Protestant Reformation, 235, 252, 281, 288, 350n

M'Douall, Peter Murray (*1814–1854*), a Chartist leader, 106
MacFarlane, Helen (n.d.), first translator of the *Communist Manifesto* into English, 17, 123
Machiavelli, Niccolò (*1469–1527*), Florentine author and statesman, 239, 257
MacLaurin, Colin (*1698–1746*), Scottish mathematician, 12
MacMahon, Marie Edmé Maurice de (*1808–1893*), marshal of France, president of France, *1873–1879*, 97
Malebranche, Nicolas (*1638–1715*), French Cartesian philosopher, 297, 299, 302–03
Malthus, Thomas Robert (*1766–1834*), English economist and demographer, 47, 124, 181, 323–24, 360
Mandeville, Bernard (*1670–1733*), English satirist, 304, 324
Marat, Jean Paul (*1743–1793*), Swiss-born French revolutionary journalist, assassinated, 179
Marrast, Armand (*1801–1852*), mayor of Paris, *1848–1849*, editor, 236
Martin V (Oddone Colonna) (*1368–1431*), pope, *1417–1431*, 321
Marx, Edgar (*1847–1855*), Marx's son, 5n, 16–17
Marx, Eduard (*1826–1837*), Marx's younger brother, 202
Marx, Eleanor (Tussy) (*1855–1898*), Marx's youngest daughter, 8, 17, 188

Biographic Index

Marx, Franziska *(1851–1852)*, Marx's infant daughter, 17

Marx, Heinrich *(1777–1838)*, Marx's father, 15, 193

Marx, Henriette *(1787–1863)*, Marx's mother, 15, 202–03

Marx, Jenny von Westphalen *(1814–1881)*, Marx's wife, 19, 194, 201–03, 384

Marx, Jenny *(1844–1882)*, Marx's oldest daughter, 5n, 15, 19, 34

Marx, Karl (personal) *(1818–1883)*, 2–13, 18–19, 34–35

Marx, Laura *(1845–1911)*, Marx's second daughter, wife of Paul Lafargue, 5n, 8, 11, 16, 18

Maurer, Georg Ludwig von *(1790–1872)*, German historian, 242 & n

Meissner, Otto Karl *(1819–1902)*, Hamburg publisher of Marx's *Capital*, 18

Mendelssohn, Moses *(1729–1786)*, German-Jewish philosopher, 259

Metternich, Klemens, prince von *(1773–1859)*, Austrian statesman, dominant figure of the Holy Alliance, 135

Mevissen, Gustav von *(1815–1899)*, a Cologne banker active in politics, 61

Meyer, Sigfrid *(c.1840–1872)*, German socialist engineer, emigrated to U.S. in 1866, 11 & n

Milton, John *(1608–1674)*, English poet, 26

Mirabeau, Honoré Gabriel Riquetti, marquis de *(1749–1791)*, leader in the French Revolution, 35, 258, 324

Moeser, Justus *(1720–1794)*, German historian, 243 & n

Moll, Josef *(1812–1849)* Cologne communist, watchmaker, 154–55

Montesquieu, Charles de Secondat, baron *(1689–1755)*, French political philosopher, 258

Moore, Samuel *(c.1830–1911)*, English lawyer, co-translator of *Capital*, 134, 396

More, Sir Thomas *(1478–1535)*, English statesman, author of *Utopia*, 324

Mueller, Adam Heinrich, von *(1779–1829)*, anti-Adam Smith German economist, 91n

Muenzer, Thomas *(c.1489–1525)*, German Anabaptist leader, 350 & n

Napoleon I *(1769–1821)*, Emperor of the French, *1804–1815*, 36, 131, 234–37, 278

Napoleon III *(1808–1873)*, Emperor of the French, *1852–1870*, 36–38, 97, 130–31, 234–37, 379–80, 383

Nero, Claudius Caesar (*37–68* A.D.), Roman emperor, 85
Newton, Sir Isaac (*1642–1727*), English physicist, 298, 367
Nieuwenhuis, Ferdinand Domela (*1846–1919*), Dutch Social Democratic leader, 100
Nonnotte, Claude François (*1711–1793*), French Jesuit, anti-Voltairean, 37
North, Sir Dudley (*1641–1691*), English economist, 324

Orsini, Felice (*1819–1858*), Italian revolutionist, executed for attempting to assassinate Napoleon III, 97
Ortes, Giammaria (*1713–1790*), Venetian monk whom Marx described as "one of the great economic writers of the 18th century," 324
Ovid (Publius Ovidius Naso) (*43* B.C.–*c.17* A.D.), Roman poet, 198
Owen, Robert (*1771–1858*), English manufacturer and utopian socialist, 88, 148, 150, 304, 401

Padover, Saul K. (*1905–   *), political scientist and biographer, editor of the Karl Marx Library, 12n, 66n, 75n, 95n, 97n, 100n, 103n, 107n, 111n, 123n, 133n, 189n, 193n, 239n, 242n, 252n, 262n, 273n, 275n, 276n, 277n, 278n, 286n, 307n, 311n, 326n, 373n, 383n
Palmerston, Henry John Temple, viscount (*1784–1856*), British statesman, Prime Minister, *1855–1858*, *1859–1865*, 88 & n, 319
Paul, Saint (*c.5–c.67* A.D.), Apostle, 235, 252, 324
Peel, Sir Robert (*1788–1850*), British statesman, Prime Minister, *1834–1835*, *1841–1846*, 42–43 & n, 47–48, 401
Péreire, Isaac (*1806–1880*), French banker, founder of the joint-stock bank, Crédit Mobilier, 61
Peter I (the Great) (*1672–1725*), Czar of Russia, *1682–1725*, 130
Petty, Sir William (*1623–1687*), English statistician, described by Marx as "founder of modern Political Economy," 324–25
Pfuel, Ernst Heinrich Adolf von (*1779–1866*), Prussian general, Prime Minister in *1848*, 278
Philips, Antoinette (Nannette) (*c.1837–1885*), Marx's cousin, 34, 35n
Philips, Lion (*1794–1866*), Dutch businessman, Marx's uncle, 34, 364–65

Plato (*c.427–c.347* B.C.), classical Greek philosopher, 107, 247, 308

Plutarch (*c.46–c.120* A.D.), Greek biographer and essayist, 247–48, 252, 283

Pompey (Cneius Pompeius Magnus) (*106–48* B.C.), Roman general, 269

Pompignan, Jean Jacques de (*1709–1784*), French anti-Voltaire poet, 37

Priestley, Joseph (*1733–1804*), English scientist and theologian, 302

Prometheus, a Titan in classical Greek religion, 248

Proudhon, Pierre Joseph (*1809–1865*), French social theorist, criticized by Marx, 3, 5 & n, 15, 73, 102, 106, 108, 111–32, 147, 204, 225, 243

Pythagoras (*c.582–c.507* B.C.), classical Greek philosopher, 365

Quesnay, François (*1694–1774*), French physician and founder of the Physiocratic school of economics, 324

Raspail, François Vincent (*1794–1878*), French scientist, socialist, 65, 355

Raumer, Friedrich von (*1781–1873*), German historian, 130

Reimarus, Hermann Samuel (*1694–1768*), German theologian and philosopher, 201 & n

Ricardo, David (*1772–1823*), English economist, 33, 127

Riego, Rafael de (*1785–1823*), a Spanish officer, leader in the 1820–1823 revolution, executed, 31

Robespierre, Maximilien (*1758–1794*), French revolutionist, guillotined on July 28, 234–35, 343, 377

Robinet, Jean François Eugène (*1825–1899*), French physician and historian, 303

Roodhuizen, A., Dutch pastor, husband of Marx's cousin, Antoinette Philips, 366 & n

Rossi, Pellegrino Luigi Eduardo (*1787–1848*), Italian economist, 26

Rousseau, Jean Jacques (*1712–1778*), Geneva-born French philosopher, 130–31, 172, 257–58, 346

Roux-Lavergne, Pierre Célestin (*1802–1874*), French historian, 343

Royer-Collard, Pierre Paul (*1763–1845*), French philosopher and politician, 235

Ruge, Arnold (*1802–1880*), German editor and writer, co-publisher with Marx of *Deutsch-Französische Jahrbücher*, 15, 102, 107, 374–75

Russell, John, lord *(1792–1878)*, British Whig statesman, Prime Minister, *1846–1852, 1865–1866*, 53

Rutenberg, Adolf *(1808–1869)*, Young Hegelian journalist, Marx's friend at Berlin University, 201–02

Saint Bruno *(see* Bauer, Bruno)

Saint-Just, Louis de *(1767–1794)*, French revolutionist, guillotined with Robespierre on July 28, 235

Saint-Simon, Claude Henri, comte de *(1760–1825)*, French social philosopher, 102, 148

Sainte-Beuve, Charles Augustin *(1804–1869)*, French literary critic, 32 & n

Samuel, *(11th century,* B.C.*)* high priest and judge of Israel, 93

Sand, George (pseudonym for Amandine Dupin) *(1804–1876)*, French novelist, 74

Savigny, Friedrich Karl von *(1779–1861)*, professor of jurisprudence at Berlin University when Marx was a student there, 196, 200 & n, 246, 385n

Say, Jean Baptiste *(1767–1832)*, French economist, 235

Schaper, von, German government official, governor of the Rhine Province, *1842–1845*, 239

Schapper, Karl *(1812–1870)*, German communist refugee in London, 154

Schelling, Friedrich Wilhelm Joseph von *(1775–1854)*, German philosopher, 200 & n, 254, 283–84 & n

Schlosser, Friedrich Christoph *(1776–1861)*, German historian, 13 & n

Schmidt, Karl, manager of the Leipzig publishing firm, Julius Wunder, 202

Schmidthaenner, Dr., a German judiciary official, 202

Schramm, Karl August, anti-Marx editor of *Jahrbuch für Sozialwissenschaft und Sozialpolitik*, 99 & n

Schweitzer, Johann Baptist von *(1834–1875)*, German editor, president of the General German Workers Association, 123

Scotus *(see* Duns Scotus)

Senior, Nassau William *(1790–1864)*, English economist, 87, 206–07 & n, 217n, 218 & n

Shakespeare, William *(1564–1616)*, 22, 35, 188, 356n

Sidmouth, Henry Addington, viscount *(1757–1844)*, British Tory statesman, Prime Minister, *1801–1804*, 92

Biographic Index

Sièyes, Emmanuel Joseph (*1748–1836*), pamphleteer during the French Revolution, 105

Sismondi, Jean Charles de (*1773–1842*), Swiss economist and historian, 93

Smith, Adam (1723–1790), Scottish economist, author of the *Wealth of Nations* (1776), admired by Marx, 24–25 & n, 115, 324–26

Smith, Edward (*c.1818–1874*), English physician, medical inspector, 82

Socrates (*469–399* B.C.) classical Greek philosopher, 247

Solger, Karl Wilhelm Ferdinand (*1780–1819*), professor of philosophy at Berlin University, 198 & n

Sorge, Friedrich Adolph (*1828–1906*), German-born communist in U.S., friend and correspondent of Marx, 33

Spartacus (d.*71* B.C.), Roman gladiator, leader of a slave revolt, 35

Spinoza, Baruch (Benedict) (*1632–1677*), Dutch-Jewish philosopher, 257, 259, 265n, 297–300, 302–03

Stahl, Friedrich Julius (*1802–1861*), German jurist, Berlin University professor, 61

Steuart (Stewart), Sir James (*1712–1780*), English Mercantilist economist, 323

Stewart, Dugald (*1753–1828*), Scottish economist, 209n

Stirner, Max (pseudonym for Johann Caspar Schmidt) (*1806–1856*), German philosopher, satirized by Marx and Engels in *The German Ideology*, 39, 231, 233, 252, 294 & n, 391

Strahan, William (*1715–1785*), English publisher of David Hume and Adam Smith, 325

Strauss, David Friedrich (*1808–1874*), German Young Hegelian philosopher, 255–56, 294 & n, 347

Sulla, Lucius Cornelius (*138–78* B.C.), Roman general, dictator, *82–79* B.C., 37

Sully, Maximilien de Béthune, duc de (*1560–1641*), French statesman, main adviser to Henry IV, 324

Swinton, John (*1829–1901*), Scottish-born New York journalist, editor of the weekly *John Swinton's Paper*, 33

Tacitus (*c.55–c.117* A.D.), Roman historian, 198, 243 & n

Temple, Sir William (*1628–1699*), English diplomat, 324

Thackeray, William Makepeace (*1811–1863*), English novelist, 22

Thibaut, Anton Friedrich Justus (*1772–1840*), German jurist and historian, 194 & n

Thierry, Jacques Nicolas Augustin (*1795–1856*), French historian, 57

Thiers, Louis Adolphe (*1797–1877*), French historian and statesman, President of the Republic, *1871–1873*, 35–37, 128, 379

Tocqueville, Alexis de (*1805–1859*), French politician and writer, author of *Democracy in America* (1835), 330

Torrington, George Byng, viscount (*1812–1884*), British statesman, Whig, 56

Townsend, Joseph (*1739–1816*), English sociologist, Malthusian, 323–24

Tremenheere, Hugh Seymour (*1804–1893*), British government official, author of reports on labor conditions, 84

Tshernyshevsky, Nicolai Gavrilovich (*1828–1889*), Russian philosopher and critic, 11

Tucker, Josiah (*1712–1799*), English clergyman and economist, 324

Tupper, Martin (*1810–1889*), an English versifier, 28–29, 35

Tussy (*see* Marx, Eleanor)

Ure, Andrew (*1778–1857*), English chemist and economist, 87

Vanderlint, Jacob (d.*1740*), English economist, 324

Vaucanson, Jacques de (*1709–1782*), a French inventor, 363

Venedey, Jacob (*1805–1871*), a German radical journalist and politician, 233

Vico, Giovanni Battista (*1688–1744*), Italian philosopher and sociologist, 370

Victoria (*1819–1901*), Queen of the United Kingdom, *1837–1901*, 94

Vidocq, François Eugène (*1775–1857*), French criminal and police agent, 259

Villèle, Jean Baptiste (*1773–1854*), French statesman, Premier, *1822-1827*, 31

Virgil (*70–19* B.C.), Roman poet, 263n

Vogt, Karl (*1817–1895*), German scientist in Switzerland, attacked by Marx in pamphlet, *Herr Vogt* (1860), 18

Volney, Constantin de (*1757–1820*), French philosopher, 303

Voltaire, François Marie Arouet de (*1694–1778*), French

man of letters, satirist, leading figure of the Enlightenment, 37–38, 129–31, 258, 299, 315

Wallace, Robert *(1697–1771)*, English Malthusian statistician, 323–24

Watt, James *(1736–1819)*, Scottish inventor of the steam engine, 213

Weitling, Christian Wilhelm *(1808–1871)*, German tailor, utopian communist, 103n, 108

Wening (Wenning)-Ingenheim, Johann Nepomuk von *(1790–1831)*, German jurist, 200 & n

Westphalen, Jenny von *(1814–1881)*, wife of Marx, 15, 19 (*see also* Marx, Jenny)

Weydemeyer, Joseph *(1818–1866)*, German communist, emigrated to U.S., Union Army officer during Civil War, 63

Wigand, Otto *(1795–1877)*, German publisher in Leipzig, 202

Williams, Zephania *(c.1794–1874)*, English Chartist, organizer of Welsh miners, 56

Willis, Robert *(1800–1875)*, English scholar and lecturer before labor audiences, 362

Winckelmann, Johann Joachim *(1717–1768)*, German pioneer archaeologist, historian of classical art, 198 & n

Witt, Jan de *(1625–1672)*, Dutch republican leader, 324

Wolff, Christian von *(1679–1754)*, German philosopher, 29, 258

Wolff, Wilhelm (Lupus) *(1809–1864)*, German communist refugee in England, friend of Marx and Engels, 154

Wood, Sir Charles (later, Lord Halifax) *(1800-1885)*, British Whig statesman, 52–53, 55–57

Wunder, Julius (n.d.), Leipzig book dealer, 202

Zeus, presiding god of the classical greek pantheon, ruler of the heavens, 248, 254

SUBJECT INDEX

Ability and needs, 177
Action, 169
Actors, 21, 27 (*see also* Theatre)
Administration, 61, 375-78 (*see also* The State)
Advocati, 46-47
Aesthetics (*see* Art)
Africa, 85
Agricultural chemistry, 12, 139 (*see also* Chemistry)
Agriculture, 44, 78, 152-53, 242-45, 354, 356-59, 397 (*see also* Farmers; Peasants)
Albania, 245
Algiers, 12
Alienation, 287, 289, 291-93, 305, 314, 321, 338-39, 348, 352
Alsace-Lorraine, 233
Ambition, 190
America (*see* United States)
America, general, 136, 145, 150, 233
American Revolution (1776), 97
Anekdota zur neuesten deutschen Philosophie und Publicistik, 262
Animal kingdom, 360
Animals and religion, 285-86
Anthropology, 283, 285-86, 354

Anti-Church movement, 314-19 (*see also* Church of England; Religion)
Antinomies, 124-26
Anti-Renters (U.S.), 34 & n, 150
Anti-semitism (*see* Jews; Judaism)
Apothecary, 25, 31
Apparel industry, 396-97
Aristocracy, 40-41, 45-47, 50, 57, 59-62, 69, 76-77, 94, 137, 315-17, 356 (*see also* Ruling class)
Arithmetic (*see* Mathematics)
Army, Armies, 103, 152, 238, 378
Art, Artists, 21-29, 199, 241, 290 (*see also* Music; Painting)
Artisans, 80, 106 (*see also* Guils; Handicrafts)
Asia, 78-79, 228, 239, 241, 245, 322
Assassination, 97
Astronomy, 249-57, 354, 365-67
Ataraxy, 245-50
Atelier (*see* Workshops, national)
Atheism, 251, 292, 300, 325, 332 (*see also* Religion)
Atoms (*see* Epicurus)

425

Augsburger Allgemeine Zeitung, 103-07, 240, 254
Austria, 96, 288
Authors, 27-37 (*see also* Novelists)

Bandmühle, 91 n (*see also* Machines)
Bank of France, 100-01
Bankocracy, 46
Banks, 153
Bavaria, 245
Beer Bill, 314-15 (*see also* Temperance)
Belgium, 399
Bengal, 77-78 (*see also* India)
Berlin, 61 (*see also* Prussia)
Berlin University, 14-15, 61, 188, 193, 246, 279n
Berliner Politische Wochenblatt, 105, 254
Besuch (Der), 201
Bible, 236, 258, 288, 337-38, 349
Bien Publique (Le), 133 & n
Blue Books, 82 & n, 84, 220-21 (*see also* Factory inspectors)
Bonaparte (*see* Napoleon I; Napoleon III)
Bonn University, 14, 239n
Book industry, 399 (*see also* Publishers)
Books, 26-27 (*see also* Authors)
Bourgeois, Bourgeoisie, 5, 29-30, 40-41, 43, 45-49, 51-52, 57-62, 68-69, 73, 75-76, 98-101, 116, 119-20, 122, 125, 130, 134, 136-51, 155-65, 179-80, 205, 211n, 235-36, 238, 241-42, 313-14, 322, 334, 360, 372, 378-81, 390-93 (*see also* Middle Class)
Bourgeois prejudice, 145
Brazil, 118

Bread, 83n
British Constitution, 43, (*see also* England)
British Empire, 45, 78, 86 (*see also* Colonies)
British Museum, 8-9, 242, 364, 367
Brussels, 3-7, 15-16, 240 (*see also* Belgium)
Bureaucracy, Bureaucrats, 58-60, 69, 158, 268-69, 272, 278, 280, 378 (*see also* Administration)
Byzantium, 374

Caesarism, 92, (*see also* Caesar, Julius: in Biographic Index)
Calculus, 368-69 (*see also* Mathematics)
California, 6, 34n, 213n
Cambridge University, 323-24
Canals, 153
Canterbury, archbishop, 93
Capital (Marx), 4, 9-11, 18-21, 24, 28-39, 90, 170, 206, 227, 259, 322-26, 354, 362 & n, 369-71, 396-400
Capital, Capitalism (wealth), 26-27, 33-34, 50, 54, 61, 88, 91, 93, 95, 129, 136, 141, 146, 157-58, 164, 173, 179, 182, 214, 372, 382, 389n (*see also* Money)
Capitalist production, 26-28
Capitalist society (*see* Capitalism)
Carding machines, 92 (*see also* Weaving)
Carthaginians, 239 & n
Cash nexus, 137
Caste system, 79, 231 (*see also* Classes)
Catholics, Catholicism, Catholic church, 76, 226n, 255-56,

Subject Index

320-21, 326, 338, 373 (*see also* Church and State)
Censorship, 2 & n, 7, 67, 240 & n, 261-79 (*see also* Newspapers; Press)
Ceylon, 77
Chancery, court, 49
Charlatanism, 130
Chartism, Chartists, 30 & n, 42-57, 64, 76, 80n, 86, 150, 316, 319, 355
Chemistry, 12, 354
Chicago Tribune, 12 & n, 96, 103, 185, 283
Child, Children, 23-24, 56, 85, 87 & n, 132, 188, 273, 384-402 (*see also* Psychology)
Child labor, 103, 184, 186, 205-24, 394-402
China, 136, 234, 266, 269
Christ, 247, 307-11, 332, 347 (*see also* Christianity)
Christianity, Christians, 29, 67, 70, 101, 228-29, 247, 255-58, 281-82, 307-28, 372-74
Christian State (*see* State, The)
Church and State, 102, 153-54
Church of England, 43, 49, 56, 314-19, 323-26
Cities, 57-58, 73, 115, 139, 242
Citizens, 334-35, 339-40
Citizens' Guard, 161-62 (*see also* Militia)
City Press (London), 8
City republics, 137
Civil society, 112-13, 228, 240, 306, 333-36, 340-45, 350-52, 377
Civil war, general, 50, 145 (*see also* Class Struggle)
Civil War in France, The (Marx), 12, 18, 35, 378-81
Civil War (U.S.), 82
Civilization, 139
Class, abolition, 74
Class rule, 56, 89
Class struggle, 3, 41-42, 57-58, 63-101, 135-36, 143-50, 159-61, 180, 183, 241-42, 245n, 316, 379
Class Struggles in France, The (Marx), 227
Classes, 29-62, 63-101, 134-36, 145-50, 159 (*see also* Class struggle)
Classless society, 64, 74
Clergy, 57, 154, 282, 296n, 323-61, 378
Clocks, 363 (*see also* Machines)
Coffee, 234
Cologne (Germany), 2, 7, 16, 91n, 279
Colonies, 49, 115, 136
Commerce, 44, 82, 85, 136, 140, 349
Commodities, 322-23, 326
Communes (*see* Cities)
Communications, 86, 136
Communism, Communists, 3-4, 6, 12, 72, 102-87, 247, 291-92, 298, 303-04, 311-12, 372, 378, 382, 388-89, 391-93 (*see also* Communist Manifesto)
Communist Correspondence Committee, 5, 16
Communist League, 3, 5-7, 154-68
Communist Manifesto, 6, 16-17, 33, 63-64, 81, 98, 102, 133-52, 155, 178-80, 211n, 313, 391
Communist membership, 166
Communist organizations, 165-68
Communist Party program, 152-54
Communist society, 175
Communist theory, 106-10
Compass, 363
Competence, 268-71
Competition, 54, 116-18, 120

Condition of the Working Class in England, The (Engels), 4 & n
Consciousness, 110-229, 232, 241, 249-50, 285, 288-96, 343
Conservatives, Conservatism, 42, 47, 52
Constitutionalism, 60
Consumption, 25, 174, 176, 178
Continental System, 234
Continent (*see* Europe)
Contribution to the Critique of Political Economy (*see Critique of Political Economy*)
Co-operatives, 88, 183-84
Corn, 24-25 (*see also* Bread)
Corn Laws, 43-46, 49
Corruption, 47
Cotton workers, 83 (*see also* Weaving)
Courtesans, 25
Craftsmen (*see* Artisans)
Crédit Mobilier, 23 & n, 61
Credit system, 116, 129, 153, 158, 326
Creditors, 90
Crime, 209, 303
Crimean War, 315, 317
Criticism, 108-10, 284, 286-88, 297, 330
Critique of Political Economy (Marx), 9, 10, 22, 122, 129, 239, 320
Culture, 171-72, 389 (*see also* Art)
Czarism, 94-95 (*see also* Russia)

Danzig, 91n
Debtors, 90
Declaration of the Rights of Man, 340 & n-343, 373
Deism, 302, 322 (*see also* Religion)

Democracy, Democratic, Democrats, 7, 49, 64, 103, 151, 155-64, 177-78, 183, 226, 262, 336, 338-39, 372, 377, 382-83
Denmark, 244
Despotism, 78, 279
Deutsch-Französische Jahrbücher, 2-3, 15, 66, 70, 107-09 & n, 240, 286, 326
Deutsche-Brüsseler-Zeitung, 75, 131, 282n, 311
Deutsche Jahrbücher, 232, 254
Deutsche Londoner Zeitung, 133
Development, historic, 228 (*see also* History)
Dialectical materialism (*see* Materialism)
Dialectics, 126, 130, 259, 291-92
Dictatorship of the proletariat, 63-64, 382
Difference Between the Democritean and Epicurean Philosophy of Nature, The (Marx), 2n, 15, 239n, 246-51, 283
Differential calculus (*see* Calculus)
Distribution (*see* Consumption)
Division of labor, 40, 42n, 114-17, 141, 205, 208, 213 & n, 231, 238, 296, 360, 378
Divorce, 385-88 (*see also* Family)
Doctors, 25, 27, 137 (*see also* Medicine)
Dogmatism, 107-10
Domestic industry, 215, 217n
Don Quixote, 31
Drama, 198-99 (*see also* Theatre)
Drunkenness, 400
Dualism, 121

Subject Index

Dutch (*see* Holland)
Duties, 90 (*see also* Rights)

Economic categories, 116-21, 126 (*see also* Economics; Political Economy)
Economic and Philosophic Manuscripts of 1844 (Marx), 246, 288-89, 388
Economic relationships, 127
Economics, 3, 18, 33, 182
Education, 61, 68, 103, 154, 184, 186-226, 273, 283, 302, 305, 333, 392, 394-96
Education, compulsory, 224-25
Education, industrial, 205
Education, national, 224-26
Education, technical, 226
Egypt, 23, 138, 231, 236, 245, 399
Eighteenth Brumaire of Louis Bonaparte, The (Marx), 17, 92, 227, 234
"Eisenachers," 169-70, 186 (*see also* Social Democratic Party)
Elections, British, 50-56
Electricity, 65, 354, 356-59
Emancipation, 69-71, 73-74, 80, 88-90, 99, 148, 165, 173-74, 178-80, 187, 327, 329, 331-32, 335, 339-40, 343-44, 346-50, 353 (*see also* Freedom; Labor)
Emigration, 86
Encyclopedias, 27
England, 8, 11, 17, 29-30, 39, 42-57, 64-65, 75-76, 79-89, 91, 94, 96-97, 114, 116, 129, 145, 151, 187, 206-24, 234, 313-20, 323-26, 356, 375-76, 381, 396-402 (*see also* British Empire)
English language, 30-31
Enlightenment, 243, 297

Entertainment places, 27
Environment, 204, 303
Equal rights, 173-76
Equality, 41, 90, 176-77, 181-82, 333, 341-43
Equilibrium, 121-22
Established Church (*see* Church of England)
Ethics (*see* Morality; Philosophy; Religion)
Ethnography (*see* Anthropology)
Europe, 8, 33, 64-65, 76, 85-86

Factories (*see* Industry)
Factory Act (British), 87, 206-24
Factory inspectors, 206-24
Family, 137, 149, 193, 214, 228, 344, 386, 390-93 (*see also* Women)
Farmers, 44, 50 (*see also* Peasants)
Feudalism, 47, 73, 77, 93, 136, 140-41, 146, 152, 158, 235, 344, 380-81 (*see also* Middle Ages)
First International, 9-10, 18-19, 65, 81-90, 99, 173, 178, 180, 378, 394, 401
Florence (Italy), 239
Food, 44, 82-83 & n (*see also* Corn Laws)
Forces of production (*see* Productive forces)
France, 10, 31-32, 35-37, 69, 75-77, 89, 94, 96-97, 100-01, 111, 130, 137, 145, 151, 155, 165, 233, 235-36, 330, 340, 378-80, 383, 399
Fraternal Democrats, 75
Free press (*see* Freedom of the press)
Free Trade, Traders, 42-43, 46, 48, 53, 75, 78, 84, 86, 137, 148, 180, 240

430 THE ESSENTIAL MARX

Freedom, 8, 41, 55, 118, 134, 243, 274-77, 283-84, 301, 340-41, 372, 374, 381
Freedom of assembly, 60, 186
Freedom of conscience (*see* Freedom of religion)
Freedom of the press, 60, 186, 261-80, 343
Freedom of religion, 103, 186, 226, 314, 330-31, 340, 345
Freedom of speech, 60
French language, 123 & n
French Revolution (1789), 3, 30 & n, 39, 46, 58, 76-77, 96, 101, 104-05, 151, 163-64, 233-35, 243, 258, 323, 341, 343, 373, 377, 379, 391
French Revolution (1848), 50, 64-65, 86-87, 128 & n, 235

Gallic rooster, 71
Gas, natural, 277
General Council, of First International, 89, 224
General German Workers Association, 169, 180-84, 381-83
Geology, 12
German Confederation, 58 & n
German Ideology, The (Marx and Engels), 5 & n, 16, 39, 71, 229, 252, 293, 390
German language, 126
German Workers' Party, 168-85
Germany, Germans, 29-31, 46-47, 59-62, 66-70, 75, 89, 91n, 92, 96-99, 102-07, 109, 122, 137, 145, 151-64, 180, 183-87, 225-26, 231-33, 242-44, 259, 281, 288, 327, 337, 381-83, 399 (*see also* Prussia)
"Glorious Revolution" (1688), 46

God, Gods, 189-90, 249, 251-52, 283-85, 293, 301, 307-11, 337, 366 (*see also* Religion)
Gotha Program, 12, 19, 103, 168-86, 188-89, 225-26, 372, 381-83
Gothic cathedrals, 138
Government (*see* The State)
Great Britain (*see* England)
Great Men, 229
Greece, Greeks (classical), 21-24, 244, 247-52, 258, 284, 365
Grundrisse (Marx), 320
Guilds, 61, 77, 113, 136, 238, 344, 348, 363
Gunpowder, 363

Hamburg, 62, 91
Hamburger Correspondenten, 254
Handicrafts, 208 & n, 213, 215, 216n, 219, 363, 396 (*see also* Artisans)
Handwork, 78
Health regulation, 185-86 (*See also* Child labor)
Hero, 30, 236, 252
Herr Vogt (Marx), 18
History, 3, 12, 40-41, 63-64, 112-14, 119-20, 135-36, 192-93, 227-45, 307, 356, 370
History, economic, 314
History, of ideas, 232
Holland, 65, 76, 91n, 399
Holy Alliance, 31n, 135 & n, 156, 257
Holy Family, The (Marx and Engels), 5, 15, 203-04, 297
Holy Roman Empire, 58, 67
House of Commons (*see* Parliament)
House of Lords, 49, 82, 94
Huguenots, 373

Subject Index

Human nature, 29, 273, 346 (*see also* Psychology)
Human race, 124n
Humanism, 292
Humanity, 192
Hyde Park (London), 314-19
Hypocrisy, 336, 391

Idealism, 3, 195, 199, 297, 304-05
Ideals, 107, 113, 119, 227-28, 241, 259, 274, 291, 293, 301 (*see also* Philosophy)
Ideology, 295
Iliad, 23, 26
Imperfection, 273
Imperialism, 380 (*see also* British Empire; Colonies)
Income tax, 186, 311 (*see also* Taxation)
India, 77-79, 234, 285
Industrial Revolution, The, 364
Industry, 80, 85, 87, 118-19, 136-42, 146, 164, 184, 206-23, 245n, 355-56, 363, 370, 392, 394-402
Inequality (*see* Equality)
Inheritance, 102, 154, 158
Insurance, 174
International class conflict, 75-76
International Courier, The, 394
International relations, 115
International Working Men's Association (*see* First International)
Ireland, Irish, 56, 78, 82-83, 220n, 373
Irish Tenants' Rights Bill, 88
"Iron law of wages," 181, 183
Italy, 77 & n, 78, 89, 96-97, 137, 239, 320-21, 399

Jahrbuch für Sozialwissenschaft und Sozialpolitik, 99n
Jansenists, 299
Japan, 399
Jena University, 2, 15
Jersey Islands, 12
Jesuits, 97, 351
Jesus (*see* Christ)
Jews, 281-82, 305, 320-22, 326-53, 372 (*see also* Judaism)
Journalism, 2, 9
Judaism, 3, 281, 326-53 (*see also* Jews)
Judiciary, 378
Juggernaut, 77
Junge Generation, Die, 103n
Jurisprudence, 246
Justice, 152, 225-26

Kapital, Das (*see* Capital)
Karlsbad, 12
Kölnische Zeitung, 252, 254, 258-59, 372
Königsberger Zeitung, 258
Kulturkampf, 226 & n

Labor, 24-28, 53-56, 72, 79-80, 90-91, 94, 136-46, 170-73, 213n, 323, 355, 362, 364, 389n (*see also* Proletariat; Workers)
Labor organizations, 81
Labor Parliament, 79-80
Labor, proceeds of, 173-78
Lancashire, 78, 82
Land tax, 33-34 (*see also* George, Henry: in Biographic Index)
Landed interests, 43
Landlords, 44, 55, 86-88, 153, 173, 334, 344, 379 (*see also* Aristocracy)
Land owners (*see* Landlords)
Law, 194, 201, 351

Lawyers, 137, 324
League of Peace and Freedom, 180, 382
Legal fees, 186
Leipzig Book Fair, 232
Leyden (Holland), 91n
Liability law (*see* Health regulation; Insurance)
Liberals, Liberalism, 52, 59, 226
Liberty (*see* Freedom)
Licensing, 267-68
Light, theory of, 365
Literature, 21, 29-31 (*see also* Authors; Novelists)
London, 8-9, 17
Louis Bonaparte (*see* Napoleon III)
Love, conjugal, 121-22 (*see also* Marriage)
Luddites, 92, (*see also* Machines)
Lutheranism (*see* Luther, Martin: in Biographic Index)

Machines, Machinery, 22, 54, 65, 72, 90-94, 115-17, 136, 141, 143, 208 & n, 215, 238, 354-55, 361-64, 370-71, 397, 401
Manchester, 4, 9, 17
Manchester School, 42, 48-49, 54 (*see also* Economics)
Manifesto of the Communist Party (*see* Communist Manifesto)
Manufacturers, 48-49, 55, 136-37 (*see also* Industry)
"Marginal Notes . . ." (*see* Gotha Program)
Markets, 115, 136-38, 180 (*see also* Colonies)
Marriage, 313, 385-388, 389 (*see also* Divorce; Family)
Marx-Engels-Lenin Institute (Moscow), 154, 289
Marxism, 19, 98, 154-65, 228-29 (*see also* Materialism)
Massachusetts, 224
Materialism, 3, 204, 227-34, 259, 295, 297-306, 354, 359, 370
Materialist interpretation of history, 112-14, 239-42 (*see also* History; Materialism)
Mathematics, 12, 195, 299, 301, 354, 363-65
Matter, 301 (*see also* Epicurus: in Biographic Index)
Mechanics (*see* Machines)
Mefistofeles (Leipzig), 104 & n
Mercenaries, 238 (*see also* Army)
Mesopotamia, 244
Metallurgy, 218
Metaphysics, 195, 294-95, 297-300, 302-03 (*see also* Philosophy)
Meteors (*see* Astronomy)
Middle Ages, 30, 46-47, 58n, 71, 90, 113, 135-37, 142, 144, 243, 320-21, 356, 365 (*see also* Feudalism)
Middle Class, 21-22, 45-47, 55, 60, 62, 69-70, 87-88, 105, 145, 179, 317, 319, 356, 378, 380-81, 395 (*see also* Bourgeois)
Militia, 103, 186 (*see also* Citizens' Guard)
Millionaires, 62, 80, 136 (*see also* Bankocracy)
Millocracy, 46 (*see also* Millionaires)
Mills, 363-64 (*see also* Industry)
Mining, 213n, 220-21
Mohammedanism, 228-29
Monarchy, Monarchist, 59-62, 69, 73, 76-77, 93, 137, 151
Monetary system, 320-21, 326 (*see also* Money)

Subject Index

Money, 72, 153, 320-21, 348-52 (*see also* Banks; Credit system)
Money lords, 87, 153 (*see also* Bankocracy; Banks)
Mongols, 239
Monopolies, Monopolists, 49, 80, 88-89, 93, 95, 117-18
Morality, 204, 282, 290, 294-96, 302-03, 307, 351, 386
Morning Post, 319
Mosel region (Germany), 277-78
Music, Musicians, 24, 26
Mysteries, 210 & n
Mystery, 276
Mysticism, 306
Mythology, 22 (*see also* Greece)

Nationalism, National character, 77, 145, 266, 361
Natural history, 359-60, 370
Nature, 171
Negro slaves, 93 (*see also* Slavery)
Neue Gesellschaft (Zurich), 98 & n
Neue Oder-Zeitung (Breslau), 9, 160, 314
Neue Rheinische Zeitung (Cologne), 7, 16, 205, 262, 278-79
Neue Rheinische Zeitung. Politisch-Oekonomische Revue, 17, 29
Neue Zeit, Die, 22
New American Encyclopaedia, 238n
New England, 349 (*see also* United States)
New-York Daily Tribune, 9, 17, 21, 42, 48, 59, 77, 79, 237
New York Herald, 11, 93 & n, 402

New York State, 224
Nobility (*see* Aristocracy)
Nominalism, 300
Novelists, 21-22 (*see also* Authors; Literature; Writers)

Occupation, 189-93
Oligarchy (English), 45-47
"On the Jewish Question," 3, 281, 326-53
Oppression (*see* Classes)
Orators, 27
Oulanem (Marx), 198

Painting, 27, 29n (*see also* Art)
Paleontology, 360-61, 370
Pandects, 195, 200 & n (*see also* Roman law)
Paradise Lost (Milton), 26
Parents, 219 (*see also* Family)
Paris, 2-4, 6-7, 15 (*see also* France)
Parliament, British, 51, 84, 87-88 (*see also* House of Lords)
Parliament, general, 58
Patriotism (*see* Nationalism)
Pauperism, 53-54, 82, 375-76 (*see also* Poverty)
Peasant War (German), 288
Peasants, 28, 58, 61, 80, 145, 153-54, 160, 163, 183, 239, 242 & n (*see also* Agriculture)
People's Paper, The, 64, 79, 355
Perfume, 24
Persia, Persians, 239, 244
Philosophy, Philosophers, 2 & n, 5, 71, 108, 11 & n, 194-96, 227, 229, 246-60, 290, 295-306

Philosophy of history, 228-34, 252-60 (*see also* History; Materialism)

Philosophy of Poverty (Proudhon), 11, 126-29, 147

Physics, 354 (*see also* Astronomy)

Poetry, Poets, 22, 137, 194, 198-99, 201 (*see also* Art; Literature)

Poland, 75-76, 130, 151, 282, 322

Police, 342, 378

Political Economy, 3, 8-9, 28-29, 34, 49, 87-88, 112, 124-29, 188, 213n, 239-42, 247, 323-24 (*see also* Economics)

Political movement, 95-96

Political parties, 42-48, 259

Political power, 74, 88-89, 95-96

Political state, 109-10, 112-13, 374-75 (*see also* The State)

Political theory, 69, 377-78

Political will, 378

Politicians, corrupt, 95

Politics, 109, 334-37, 339

Politische Wochenblatt, 59-60

Popes (*see* Catholics)

Popular Science Monthly, 34n

Population, 139, 296, 323-26, 376

Post offices, 153

Potatoes, 83n

Potteries, 218

Poverty, 55, 83 (*see also* Pauperism)

Poverty of Philosophy, The (Marx), 3, 5 & n, 16, 73, 126

Power (*see* Machines; Steam power)

Press, 252, 254-57, 261-80 (*see also* Freedom of the press; Newspapers)

Presse, Die (Vienna), 9

Priests, 27, 137 (*see also* Clergy)

Primogeniture, 77

Principle of Population (Malthus), 124 & n (*see also* Malthus, Thomas Robert: in Biographic Index)

Printing press, 23, 213n, 363

Prisons, 148, 185

Productive forces, 71-72, 74, 80, 86, 112-14, 116, 120, 125-26, 134, 138-41, 145, 178, 227, 229-30, 238, 240-41, 322-23 (*see also* Capitalism)

Profit, 43

Progress, 361

Progress and Poverty (George), 33-34 (*see also* George, Henry: in Biographic Index)

Proletariat, Proletarians, 3, 41, 47, 50, 57, 63-65, 69-71, 73-76, 86, 93, 95-99, 101, 118, 127, 132-33, 136, 141-52, 155-66, 178, 183, 232, 311-13, 355-56, 391-92 (*see also* Workers)

Propaganda, 165-66

Property, common, 173-74

Property, expropriation of, 74, 152-53, 164

Property, private, 71, 75, 80, 106, 108-09, 116, 123-25, 131-32, 134, 139-41, 145, 158, 164, 172-73, 196, 257, 291, 313, 332-33, 336, 341, 345, 350, 376, 388-90

Prostitution, 389 & n, 392 (*see also* Marriage; Women)

Protectionism, 43 (*see also* Free Trade)

Protestants, Protestantism, 255, 288, 322-26, 372-73 (*see also* Church of England)

Provence (France), 58 & n

Subject Index

Prussia, 7, 17, 36, 39, 59-62, 76-77, 103-06, 188, 205, 225, 261-72, 278-79, 282, 288, 311-12, 375-78, 380, 385-88 (*see also* Germany)
Psychology, 29, 204, 272, 393 (*see also* Children; Human nature)
Purchasing power, 55
Public opinion, 51
Publishers, 26
Puritans, 97

Railroads, 23, 139, 144, 153, 164, 183
Reason, 190, 204, 258, 301, 307, 374, 393
Red Republican, The, 17, 133
Reform, 147-48
Reform Bill (1831), 46
Reformation, German, 13n, 288 (*see also* Protestantism)
Reign of Terror, 77 (*see also* French Revolution (1789)
Relationships of production (*see* Productive forces)
Religion, 29, 78-79, 109-10, 129-30, 165-66, 189-90, 192, 200, 214, 227, 229-32, 247-48, 251-59, 281-353, 370, 372-74, (*see also* God)
Religious conceptions, 294-96
Religious illusion, 286-88
"Remarks on the Latest Censorship Instruction," 262-73
Rent, of land, 43-44
Republicanism, 326
Revelations about the Cologne Communist Trial (Marx), 170
Revolution, English (1648), 76-77, 114
Revolution, in England, 50, 94, 151, 315
Revolution, Die (New York), 17

Revolution, evolutionary, 65, 100, 288
Revolution, general, 8, 10, 30, 41-42, 63-101, 122, 145-46, 151, 154-64, 229-31, 234-35, 280, 288, 343, 354-56
Revolution, permanent, 154-65
Revolutionary ideas, 40-41
Revolutions of 1848-1849, 6-8, 35, 155, 280, 355, 379
Rheinischer Beobachter, 282n, 311
Rheinische Zeitung (Cologne), 2, 15, 103-04 & n, 106, 239-40 & n, 246, 252, 258, 261, 273-75, 277, 285, 372, 385, 386n, 393
Rights, 90, 340-43 (*see also* Duties)
Roberts & Co., 23
Roman Empire, 57-58, 85, 90, 92-93, 101, 135, 235, 237, 355, 363-65
Roman law, 195-98
Rome (*see* Roman Empire)
Royalty (*see* Monarchy)
Ruling class, 39-42, 51, 72, 95-98, 144-45, 180, 188, 312, 379, 392 (*see also* Classes)
Ruling ideas, 39-42 (*see also* Ideas)
Russia, 6, 10-12, 86, 94, 96, 130, 187, 282, 361, 381, 399
Russian language, 227

St. Martin's Hall, 89
Salaries, 153 (*see also* Wages)
Sawmills, 91-92 (*see also* Machines)
Saxony, 91n
Scandinavia, Scandinavians, 244
Sceptics, 252 (*see also* Philosophy)
Schools, 27 (*see also* Education)

Schools, technical, 212
Science, 12, 65, 109, 127-28, 186, 226, 241, 250, 257, 300-301, 328, 354-71
Scorpion und Felix (Marx), 198
Scotland, 82, 209n, 220n, 326
Second Empire, 379-80 (*see also* Napoleon III)
Security, 341-43
Self-consciousness (*see* Consciousness)
Senate, Roman, 58
Sensualism, 204, 301-06, 353
Separation of powers, 40
Serfdom, Serfs, 94 & n, 146, 282 (*see also* Slavery)
Sewing machine, 397-98
Sex, 296 (*see also* Marriage; Prostitution)
Sheffield (England), 92n
Shopkeepers, 54
Single Tax, 33-34 (*see also* George, Henry: in Biographic Index)
Slavery, Slaves, 79, 90, 92-93, 118-19, 182, 282, 377
Slavs, 361
Social contract, 252
Social Democrats, 151, 157
Social Democratic Party, German, 12, 19, 97, 103, 168-85
Social-Demokrat, Der (123, 186)
Social system, 75-76, 227
Social science, 206n
Socialism, Socialist, Socialistic, 50, 87-88, 96-100, 108-09, 121, 127, 147-51, 160, 164, 174, 177-79, 181-83, 185-87, 226, 298, 303, 313
Socialism, Christian, 313
Societal relations, 119-21
Spain, 31-32 & n, 76, 187, 237-38
Species being (*see* Species life)

Species life, 292, 333-34, 336, 338, 346, 390
Spinning, 91n, 361 (*see also* Weaving)
Starvation, 83, 86 (*see also* Pauperism; Poverty)
State, The, 72, 195, 226, 252, 256, 277, 290, 312-13, 327-53, 372-83, 387 (*see also* Government)
Statistics, 354
Steam power, 136, 208 & n, 213, 355, 362 (*see also* Machines)
Steamers, 153
Stock Exchange, 62 (*see also* Banks)
Stoics, 251, 310 (*see also* Greece)
Stone Age, 238
Suffrage, universal, 51, 53, 60, 103, 186, 382
Sugar, 234
Suicide, 377
Sunday closing, 314-18 (*see also* Church of England)
Sunday Trading Bill, 315
"Superstructure," 227, 241 (*see also* Ideas; Marxism)
Surplus labor, 54 (*see also* Labor)
Surplus value, 33 (*see also* *Theories of Surplus Value*)
Switzerland, Swiss, 7, 151, 225, 285, 321, 381-82

Talmud, 351-52
Taxation, Taxes, 33, 56, 60, 102-03, 116, 154, 164, 224, 287, 383
Teachers, 27 (*see also* Education)
Technology, 65, 212, 354-71 (*see also* Machines)
Telegraph, 22, 139, 206

Subject Index

Temperance, 45 (see also Drunkenness)
Ten Hours' Bill, 56, 87 & n, 144, 401
Tendency, 271-74 (see also Censorship)
Textiles, 218 (see also Weaving)
Theatre, 21, 27
Theft, 125 (see also Property)
Theology, 246-47 (see also God)
Theories of Surplus Value, 21, 24-27
"Theses on Feurbach," 5, 16, 304-06
Third Estate, 57, 74, 137 (see also Classes)
Thirty Years War, 13n
Tibet, 372
Tile making, 399
Times, The (London), 23n, 398n
Timur (Timurlane), 79 & n
Tools (see Machines)
Tories, 17, 42-48, 50, 53, 217-18 (see also Parliament)
Towns, 46-47, 58, 136 (see also Cities)
Trade unions, 143, 186 (see also Labor)
Transportation, 153
Trier (Germany), 243
Truth, 265-66
Turkey, Turks, 237, 239, 266, 399

United States, 33-34, 65, 95-97, 118-19, 187-88, 224-25, 330-31, 335, 340, 349, 381
Union Monarchique, 132-33 (see also France)
Urbanism (see Cities; Towns)
Use-value, 26-27, 171
Usury, Usurer, 28, 158, 320-21

Utilitarianism, 29 (see also Bentham, Jeremy: in Biographic Index)
Utopians, 102, 121-22, 126-27, 150

Value, 25-26, 127, 259, 321, 323, 350 (see also Use-value)
Vehmgericht, 356
Venice, 57
Verona, Congress of, 31 & n, 321
Vice, 304 (see also Crime)
Villages, 78 (see also Towns)
Violent revolution, 94-97
Virtue, 310
Vishna, 78 (see also India; Religion)
Volk, Das (London), 37
Vorwärts! (Paris), 3, 375
Voyage en Icarie, 109 (see also Cabet, Étienne: in Biographic Index)

Wages, Wage system, 54, 85-86, 181-82, 209, 238
Wales, 83, 85, 396-97
Wants, old and news, 138
War and Peace, 186
Wealth, 25-26, 171-72 (see also Capital)
Weaving, Weavers, 78, 83, 91 & n, 215-216 & n
What Is Property? (Proudhon), 123-24, 128
Whigs, American, 44
Whigs, British, 17, 42-48, 50, 52, 56 (see also Parliament)
Woman labor, 54, 184, 186
Women, 384-402
Workers, Working class, 3, 50, 63, 73, 75, 81-91, 94-97, 99, 205-24, 395-402 (see also Classes; Labor; Proletariat)

Workers education, 221-24
Workers organization, 95-96, 161-64
Working day, 184, 186
Working hours, 401
Workshops, national, 154, 183
Writers (*see* Authors)

Young Hegelians, 5, 201

Zoology, 285-86
Zukunft, Die (Berlin), 98 & n
Zurich (*see* Switzerland)